FROM THE LIBRARY OF
JEREMY D. PRUSKI

CORPORATOCRACY

CIARA TORRES-SPELLISCY

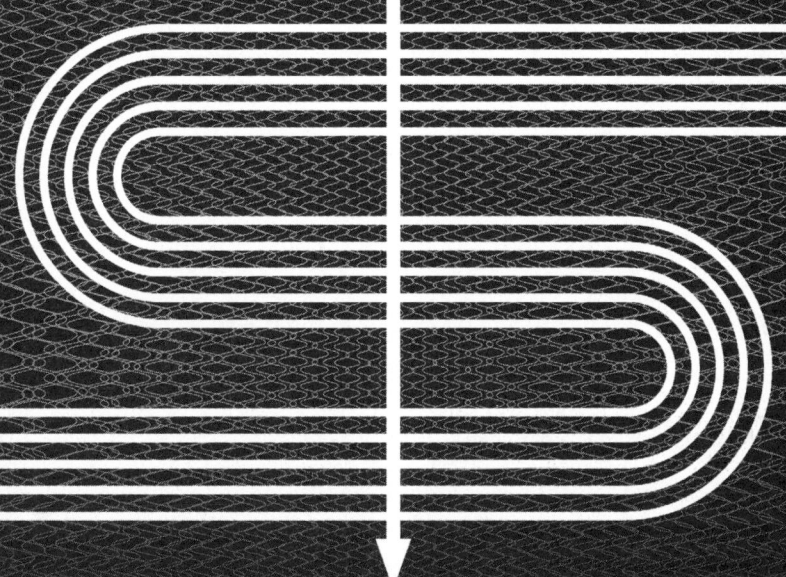

HOW TO PROTECT DEMOCRACY FROM DARK MONEY AND CORRUPT POLITICIANS

NEW YORK UNIVERSITY PRESS

NEW YORK UNIVERSITY PRESS
New York
www.nyupress.org

© 2024 by New York University
All rights reserved

Library of Congress Cataloging-in-Publication Data
Names: Torres-Spelliscy, Ciara, author.
Title: Corporatocracy : how to protect democracy from dark money
and corrupt politicians / Ciara Torres-Spelliscy.
Description: New York : New York University Press, 2025. |
Includes bibliographical references and index. |
Summary: "Corporatocracy looks at the January 6th, 2021 insurrection through the lens of
money in politics. It discusses past and present campaign finance scandals that illustrate
the risk of corporate political spending and dark money. It encourages average
Americans to use their vote and their pocketbooks to incentivize
pro-democracy behavior by politicians and corporations"—
Provided by publisher.
Identifiers: LCCN 2024019102 (print) | LCCN 2024019103 (ebook) |
ISBN 9781479828326 (hardback) | ISBN 9781479828371 (ebook) |
ISBN 9781479828395 (ebook other)
Subjects: LCSH: Corporations—Corrupt practices—United States. | Corporations—
Political activity—Law and legislation—United States. | Campaign funds—
Corrupt practices—United States. | Campaign funds—Law and legislation—
United States | Political corruption—United States. | Capitol Riot,
Washington, D.C., 2021. | Scandals—United States. |
Democracy—United States.
Classification: LCC KF9351 .T67 2025 (print) | LCC KF9351 (ebook) |
DDC 345.73/02324—dc23/eng/20240512
LC record available at https://lccn.loc.gov/2024019102
LC ebook record available at https://lccn.loc.gov/2024019103

This book is printed on acid-free paper, and its binding materials are chosen for strength
and durability. We strive to use environmentally responsible suppliers and
materials to the greatest extent possible in publishing our books.

Manufactured in the United States of America

10 8 6 4 2 1 3 5 7 9

Also available as an ebook

For my mom, who taught me to speak truth to power

CONTENTS

Preface: The Pathetic State of American Democracy   ix

PART 1. CORPORATIONS BEHAVING BADLY

1. Paying to Disrupt Democracy: The Companies You Love May Hate You   3
2. Backing the Antidemocratic: A History of Corporate Nazi Enablers   17
3. Democracy behind Bars: How Corporations Benefit from Civil Death   31
4. Corporate Bribery: Having Your Cake and Eating It, Too   52

PART 2. WHY DEMOCRACY IS ON A KNIFE'S EDGE

5. Scheming in the Shadows: Ghost Money, Ghost Candidates   71
6. Criminal Origins: Illegal Money in the 2012 Election   85
7. Creating a Monster: Donald Trump and the 2016 Election   96
8. The Big Lie: Bankrolling the Insurrection   112

PART 3. HOW TO FIX THE PROBLEM

9. Dusting off the Disqualification Clause: How to Hold Insurrectionists Accountable   131
10. Don't Be Fooled: Corporations Feigning Friendship   148
11. Go Directly to Jail, Do Not Pass Go: The Wheels of Justice   167
12. Democracy on the Ballot: Voting for Change   185

CONTENTS

Conclusion: Needed Reforms	197
Acknowledgments	201
Notes	203
Index	299
About the Author	307

PREFACE

THE PATHETIC STATE OF AMERICAN DEMOCRACY

On April 4, 2023, Donald J. Trump was booked in Manhattan for crimes related to his presidential election in 2016. A courtroom sketch artist captured the moment of his arraignment. Defendant Trump looked like the Dr. Seuss character "the Grinch," but with orange skin instead of green fur.[1]

Trump is the first ex-president ever to be charged with a crime.[2] The alleged crime was keeping fraudulent business records, in violation of New York State law, related to his then-lawyer Michael Cohen's use of the Trump Organization, an LLC called Essential Consultants, and American Media Inc. (the corporation that owns the *National Enquirer*) to make a hush-money payment on the eve of the 2016 election. The coconspirators' basic plan was to "catch and kill" negative stories so that they would not be revealed to the voting public in time to impact the 2016 election. Corporations facilitated these crimes during the 2016 election.[3] The opacity of corporations is often employed to further crimes that threaten the integrity of democracy in America as well as democracy abroad.

While pleading guilty, Cohen indicated that he committed these crimes at the instruction of the then-president of the United States, Donald Trump.[4] The DOJ could not prosecute President Trump for this crime in 2018 alongside Cohen because of their long-standing policy against prosecuting sitting presidents.[5] Upon assuming office, the Biden administration declined to prosecute Trump. After that, the normal five-year statute of limitations for campaign finance crimes expired without Trump facing federal prosecution for the hush-money scheme.[6] The Manhattan district attorney agreed with Trump that a mug shot would be unnecessary, given his fame, so police did not take one.[7] Nonetheless, Trump's campaign sold T-shirts with fake Trump mug shots to raise funds for his 2024 presidential run.[8] This was all a big scam.

Trump was able to fundraise off of his two impeachments and his loss of the 2020 election.[9] Why not fundraise off of criminal indictments, too?[10] He ran this gambit again in June 2023, when he was indicted for federal crimes related to hiding classified government documents, which were under subpoena, in Mar-a-Lago, his home in Florida.[11] He did it once more when he was booked in Washington, DC, on federal charges related to the events of January 6, 2021.[12]

When Trump was booked for his fourth indictment, in Georgia, his long streak of special treatment over other criminal defendants came to an end: he had his actual mug shot taken in the Fulton County Jail.[13] Chris LaCivita, a campaign manager for Trump 2024, warned the public to not to sell copies without permission.[14] This threat was absurd, as mug shots are in the public domain.[15] Presumably LaCivita issued this warning because the Trump campaign had been selling merchandise with Trump's mug shot for months.[16] The money went largely to Trump's defense attorneys, who were handling four simultaneous criminal cases, as well as a case for defamation of a sexual assault victim, and a civil fraud case against the Trump Organization.[17] The entire spectacle of a presidential candidate/criminal defendant selling bogus mug shots to raise money for a political campaign should serve as a confirmation of how far off the rails American democracy has careened.[18]

Americans should remember that, in the expanse of human history, democracies are young experiments. Corporations have existed far longer than democracies.[19] If voters, consumers, and investors are not careful, corporations may well outlive them.

Imagine a democracy as a precocious toddler. Spending corporate money in a democratic election is like handling that toddler a hand grenade. Under some circumstances, the toddler gets bored and puts the grenade down, and no one gets hurt. Under other circumstances, the toddler throws the grenade, and there is collateral damage done where the grenade lands, but the toddler survives. Then there is that horrible potential for the toddler to pull the pin on the grenade and be destroyed by their own naivete. Corporate political spending has this same potential to be democracy ending. This is particularly true in a post-January 6 world, where an audience and an appetite for antidemocratic propaganda exists in the United States, as do candidates who pander to this audience by spouting antidemocratic rhetoric. In this political milieu, corporations can function as arsenals for democracy or of despotism. Americans presently stand at that fork in the road.

This metaphor may seem extreme. However, the deaths and injuries that occurred on January 6, 2021, show the risk is all too real.[20] This book was written in the context of an attempt by a former American president, Donald Trump, to overthrow the last election who is currently the 2024 Republican presidential nominee. Part of what props Trump up is America's privately funded campaign finance system and his skillful exploitation of it.

History shows that corporate political spenders have the ability to completely topple a democracy if they back a party or politician with dictatorial tendencies. This is what actually happened in the 1930s, with the rise of the Nazi Party and Adolf Hitler. Corporate money poured into the party in 1933, when it was broke and poised to face a key election. German democracy was dead for the next decade under Hitler's rule.[21]

In the American context, corporations can erode faith in democratic institutions by trying to manipulate elected government to serve private ends. The voting public can easily lose trust in these institutions when scandal after scandal flood the news cycle.[22] The sheer volume of the influence of money in politics from corporate treasuries and wealthy CEOs can leave the impression for voters that politics is a rigged, unwinnable game.[23] As corporate governance guru Robert Monks worries, "The unrestrained [corporate] hunt for profits is taking a toll on the environment and society. . . . [These are] symptoms of a far greater threat to democratic society: corporate takeover of the political process."[24] As will be explored in this book, corporate crimes are often the precursors to violations of election laws.

On January 6, 2021, a crowd of angry Trump supporters stormed the U.S. Capitol and succeeded in halting the electoral college count for a few nail-biting hours through acts of violence and by sheer force of numbers in overwhelming the Capitol Police and the D.C. Metropolitan Police. After the mob was cleared from the building, 147 Republicans still objected to counting lawful electoral votes for Joe Biden.[25] The constitutionally required electoral count continued late into the evening and spilled over into the wee hours of January 7. In the end, Joseph R. Biden, who had won the most electoral college votes during the 2020 election, was declared the next president.[26] Just fourteen days later, he would assume power on the very spot where the riot had occurred—in front of the Capitol.[27]

For many Americans, January 6 was a scary, short-lived episode.[28] But it was more than that. Had the rioters succeeded, they would have ended hundreds of years of American democracy at the presidential level in one fell swoop. Only an admixture of luck on the part of Congress and law enforcement and poor planning on the part of the attackers made this American coup d'état fail. What is truly terrifying is the prospect that had the crowd been better armed or better financed, they could have easily held the Capitol for two weeks, through inauguration day on January 20, which would have likely caused enough chaos to allow President Trump to remain in power, however illegitimately.

In 2021, the wealthy and corporate sponsors of January 6 were relatively small. America may not be so lucky next time. Fortunately, many Americans recognize the peril that their democracy faces.[29] What is less widely known is that many of the legal structures that facilitated January 6 are still here, and, in some instances, they are getting worse—including the dark money problem. In the 2020 federal election, corporations spent over $100 million on the books, and they likely funded some of the $1 billion in dark money that was spent that year as well.[30] In 2021, the Supreme Court decided a case called *Americans for Prosperity Foundation v. Bonta* that bars California from asking for donor information from charities that raise money in their state.[31] This case was originally brought by the Koch brothers—Charles and David—who founded the Americans for Prosperity Foundation and wished to remain anonymous. The Court decided the case in their favor and, by extension, protected the ability of all wealthy donors, including corporate donors, to hide their identities. (David Koch died during the litigation in 2019.) The Kochs have long been a font of untraceable dark money in American elections.[32] The *Bonta* case is likely to make corporate dark money in elections increase markedly.[33]

This corporate political spending, both during the election and in the years preceding it, empowered the violent interruption of the electoral count as well as legal challenges in courts to the results of the 2020 election in multiple states.[34] Corporate funding of right-wing politicians, judges, and causes has placed Americans in a position where small-d democratic norms like free and fair elections are in peril. For one, corporate money has been pouring into 527s and political action committees (PACs) for years, providing campaign money for regressive politicians to build personal careers and long-term political power.[35] Corporate money that has poured into the Federalist Society under the leadership of Leonard Leo has tilted the Supreme Court to the far right and led to rulings that are hostile to voting rights and reasonable campaign finance reform.[36] Both historically and in the present day, corporations have also been known to attempt smaller-scale hijacking of the democratic process by bribing particular public officials to achieve short-term corporate goals at public expense.[37]

While corporations cannot give treasury funds to federal candidates because of the Tillman Act, in half of the states corporations can give directly to state candidates. In many states, offices from dog catcher to local prosecutors to Supreme Court Justices are elected posts.[38] Therefore, when the public thinks of corporations helping to elect regressive politicians, they should not forget the state prosecutors and judges who are on the ballot. If American democracy is going to survive in the long term, then the deep pockets of the largest corporations cannot be allowed to join forces with the antidemocratic fringe. What American democracy may not survive is the next January 6—the one with expansive corporate sponsorship. Stopping this synergy requires changing the incentives for corporations and other big spenders.

This book explores how America's privately-funded campaign finance system, combined with corporate avarice and the antidemocratic strains of the modern Republican Party, have placed American democracy on a knife's edge. In a defamation lawsuit about the lies that circulated around the 2020 election, lawyers suing Fox News argued that "President Trump had made the litmus test clear: either accept his narrative of election fraud, or lose his long-sought support."[39] If Trump had a litmus test that required loyalty to Trump, Americans need a new litmus test that requires loyalty to democracy, and they should deploy this Democracy Litmus Test in politics and the economy.

THE DEMOCRACY LITMUS TEST

The basic test that voters, consumers, and investors should put to corporations and politicians is this: Are corporations and politicians acting in ways that support American democracy or not? With January 6, 2021, still fresh in the American consciousness, four particular metrics are strikingly clear for the test: did an actor, whether a corporation or politician, (1) perpetuate election denialism; (2) try to overthrow the results of any election; (3) push legislation that makes voting more difficult; or (4) become a party to bribery or other corrupt actions that undermine democratic values? In the 2024 context, if they perpetuated the "big lie," tried to overthrow the 2020 election, passed legislation to stifle votes, or are guilty of bribery, then they fail. And, of course, they clearly fail if they have done all four. Corporations also fail they bankrolled the politicians who fail. Holding the financiers of politicians accountable is both fair and necessary. Without money in politics, many of these politicians would have no public offices to exploit. In the future, the Democracy Litmus Test will apply to new elections and another generation of bad actors. The test is nonpartisan. For example, if corruption charges against Democratic senator Bob Menendez that he was bribed by foreign nations while chair of the Senate Foreign Relations Committee are true, then he would fail the test, and he would not deserve to be reelected.[40] Republican Couy Griffin, a commissioner from Otero, New Mexico, would also fail due to his conviction related to his actions on January 6.[41]

Election denialism means denying the results of an election without any proof of wrongdoing. The Democracy Litmus Test would not be failed by litigants who have used the normal legal processes to question the results of an election. It is rare, but sometimes there is fraud. For instance, in 2018, in North Carolina's Ninth Congressional District, the election had to be rerun after massive fraud by a political consultant was discovered.[42] Thus, the litigation around that district in 2018 would not qualify as election denialism. By contrast, when courts find zero evidence of fraud, an individual fails the test if they continue to deny the result of that election.[43]

Unfortunately, both antidemocratic politicians and their corporate supporters are suffering few consequences post-January 6. Politicians—especially, let's be honest, Republicans—won primary and general elections in 2022 by embracing the falsehood that the 2020 election was stolen from President Trump.[44] This is a dangerous trend that evinces a tilt towards authoritarianism. Meanwhile, most of the 147 Republican members of Congress and the senators who objected to candidate Joe Biden's electors are still in office and still raking in corporate donations, either directly, through corporate PACs or indirectly, through corporate trade associations and leadership PACs.

What makes the money in politics hard to trace is the tendency of corporations to give to umbrella groups like the Senate Leadership Fund (run by Republican senator Mitch McConnell), the Congressional Leadership Fund (run by then-speaker Kevin McCarthy), or state-focused groups like the Republican Attorneys General Association (RAGA), Republican Governors Association (RGA), and Republican State Leadership Committee (RSLC). Many of these groups give to each other in a never-ending shell game. For example, in 2022, Leonard Leo's Judicial Crisis Network was RAGA's biggest donor.[45] Giving to Republican umbrella groups lends corporate donors a degree of plausible deniability when the politicians they support go rogue or get mired in a scandal.[46] These groups also act as financial pass-throughs for other more radical groups, like the Rule of Law Defense Fund (RLDF), which is an offshoot of RAGA.[47] If a corporation gives to RAGA, they can deny that they funded RLDF, which helped fund events on January 6.[48] When looking at the flow of money in politics, one thing to remember is that money is fungible. Once cash goes into an umbrella political group, it's hard to trace, but keep an eye on the big picture: corporate money is pouring into groups that support 2020 election deniers, electoral vote objectors, and lawmakers who are making it harder to vote in the United States in the future.

Another reason to take corporate political preferences seriously is the impact that the largest corporations often have on policy. As Delaware justice Leo Strine notes, "Not only do corporations have an advantage when it comes to getting their preferred candidates in office, but they have an advantage in steering the regulatory process as well. Regulators are deferential to industry input, and corporations use their huge financial advantage to dominate the regulatory and rule-making process, and to tie up agencies in litigation if they do not get their way."[49] Courts may lack the courage to hold politicians accountable for their worst acts.

This book gives citizens, consumers, investors, and corporations a different lens through which to consider decisions. If a decision or course of action would lead to failing the Democracy Litmus Test, that provides a strong reason not to do it. The more consumers care about democracy, the more they can use their buying power to incentivize corporate political spenders and politicians to take pro-democracy stances. Similarly, investors should steer their investment dollars to companies that are part of the democracy solution and not part of problem. As Allison Schrager argues, "Company leaders can't just consider profits anymore; business decisions carry a moral weight."[50] Consumer and investor pressure, along with electoral engagement, can push the election deniers to the margins by starving them of the money they need to amplify their lies.

But that is not the only path America could walk down. The more that the election deniers are elected or reelected, the more corporate lobbyists and corporate leaders will kowtow to please the election deniers' worldview. The more that election deniers are elected, the more normal their views will become. After all, of the 147 Republicans that voted to not recognize Biden's electoral college votes, Kevin McCarthy (followed by speaker Michael Johnson) and Steve Scalise had more power two years later than they did on January 6, 2021. They became the speaker of the House and the majority leader in 2023. Maddeningly, 128 of them still have their elected posts in Congress.[51] The longer they remain in power, the more rational it seems to a corporate donor to just "give to the incumbent," even if the incumbent is a raving lunatic.

PART 1

CORPORATIONS BEHAVING BADLY

PAYING TO DISRUPT DEMOCRACY

THE COMPANIES YOU LOVE MAY HATE YOU

Politically, American voters are divided roughly into thirds: "29 percent of Americans identify as Republicans, 31 percent as Democrats, and 38 percent as independents."[1] Yet the vast majority of corporate funding goes to the Right, and not just to reasonable fiscal conservatives. As reported by Popular Information, "over the last decade, public corporations have given Republicans at the state level a financial advantage that exceeds $200 million."[2] Specifically, "the three [biggest] Republican groups (RGA, RSLC, RAGA) have raised $1.05 billion over the last decade, considerably more than the $632 million that their Democratic counterparts (DGA, DLCC, DAGA) raised over the same time period."[3] Of course, the motivations for corporate political spending can vary corporation to corporation and CEO to CEO.[4]

Just because customers are left-leaning does not mean that the corporation that profits off of them are, too. Regularly, corporate leaders hold their typical customer in contempt, much like the former owner of the grocery store Whole Foods.[5] Before Amazon purchased Whole Foods, it had two seemingly contradictory reputations: it catered to left-leaning customers while it was owned by a man who fundamentally disagreed with the politics of his own customer base. As the *New York Post* once described him: "Whole Foods founder John Mackey is a well-known libertarian who is outspoken in defending free markets and capitalism."[6] Among CEOs, Mackey's spending is relatively modest, but he did have the ability to write big checks, such as the one for $225,000 that he gave the Concerned American Voters Super PAC during the 2016 election to support Rand Paul's short-lived presidential bid.[7]

COACHELLA'S OWNERS ARE NOT HIP

In the case of Coachella, when billionaire Philip Anschutz and his wife, Nancy, bought Golden Voice, the entity that originally put on the music festival, a similar mismatch arose between music lovers and those profiting from ticket sales.[8] In 2018, the Anschutz family had an estimated worth of $12.9 billion.[9] Philip Anschutz is the son of an oil tycoon.[10] While the Coachella music festival attracts free spirits both onstage and in the audience, the owners are very different.

The Anschutzes, who own the Anschutz Entertainment Group, or AEG, which owns Coachella, stadiums, and some of the LA Lakers,[11] have given money to right-wing politicians, the Republican Party, and conservative causes.[12] As the *Observer* reported, "Anschutz 'has contributed to the Institute for American Values, whose founder, David Blankenhorn, opposes same-sex marriage.'"[13] He has also given to the anti-gay groups the Alliance Defending Freedom, the National Christian Foundation, and the Family Research Council.[14] The *Observer* also noted Anschutz's financial support for the Americans for Prosperity, which is known for its climate-change-denial lobbying.[15] Other reporters found Anschutz supporting the Federalist Society, which has, with its leader Leonard Leo, spearheaded the effort to tilt the federal judiciary, including the Supreme Court, to the far right.[16]

OpenSecrets has documented that, starting in 2016, the Anschutz couple gave $3.7 million to Republican Party committees, Republican candidates, and conservative groups.[17] It found that "Anschutz and his wife gave $960,000 to the National Republican Senatorial Committee, over $632,000 to the National Republican Congressional Committee, and $660,000 to the RNC. Anschutz also gave $75,000 to the McCarthy Victory Fund, another joint fundraising committee that benefited the NRCC as well as (then-) House minority leader Kevin McCarthy and the Majority Committee PAC."[18] In 2020, he gave to Women for America First's PAC, which was involved in the events of January 6.[19]

Their pattern of political spending continued into the 2022 races. In 2022, *Rolling Stone* reported that the Anschutz Corporation also gave money to RAGA days after *Roe v. Wade* was overturned.[20] As *Rolling Stone* explained, "The money from Anschutz Corporation comes as RAGA gears up for election season with the aim of installing Attorneys

General who will enforce and champion anti-abortion laws in key states where abortion rights remain in limbo, such as Wisconsin, Michigan, Arizona, Ohio, and Florida."[21] The Anschutz Corporation gave $500,000 to senator Mitch McConnell's super PAC, the Senate Leadership Fund, in 2022.[22]

In addition to giving in their capacity as individuals and through for-profit corporations that they own, the Anschutz family also influences public policy through the Anschutz Foundation, which has donated to anti-gay groups.[23] As *Billboard* has reported, "According to The Anschutz Foundation's 2017 tax return, from December 2017 to November 2018, Anschutz donated $1,020,000 to two organizations that made public statements against LGBTQ people—Colorado Christian University and the Sky Ranch Christian camping organization."[24]

BEWARE OF THE BOX COMPANY

Have you ever considered who is getting rich from all your online shopping? Clearly there is a reason that Amazon's Jeff Bezos is one of the wealthiest men in the world: 60 percent of online shoppers start at Amazon.[25] Shipping all of those products to consumers has made a box company owner a billionaire, too. One of the biggest box companies, Uline, is owned by Richard "Dick" and Elizabeth Uihlein (whose name is pronounced like the company's). The *New York Times* once referred to them as "the most powerful conservative couple you've never heard of."[26] Dick Uihlein inherited money from his family, which founded Schlitz beer.[27]

The Uihleins are huge Republican donors. For example, "in the first 18 months of the 2022 election cycle, the Uihleins doled out $38 million to support federal GOP candidates, party committees, and Super PACs, ranking them 2nd among all individual contributors."[28] Over the years, the Uihleins have given to various far-right candidates, including Roy Moore of Alabama, after he was accused of sexual misconduct, and "a congressman from Georgia, Jody Hice, who divines significance in blood moons that fall on Jewish holidays. They supported Representative Louie Gohmert of Texas."[29] Uihlein gave $700,000 to elect Ron DeSantis governor of Florida in 2018 and the same amount to reelect him in 2022.[30]

Another parallel between Uihlein and Anschutz is the former's use of the Ed Uihlein Family Foundation to increase the reach of his influence. According to reporter Roger Sollenberger, this foundation also gave to several dark money groups involved in January 6.[31] As he reported, "Among the ranks of 'dark money' groups and anonymous megadonors who bankrolled the effort is a familiar name in GOP fundraising circles: Dick Uihlein, founder of the multinational Uline shipping company."[32] He found that, "according to the foundation's latest tax filing, the supply chain mogul contributed more than $4 million to groups affiliated with efforts to overturn the election and other acts of far-right extremism."[33] Specifically, the foundation has been a major funder of the Tea Party Patriots who helped bus participants to the January 6 events.[34] The foundation also gave $1 million to Turning Point, another January 6 participant.[35] Moreover, Dick Uihlein was the sole source of the foundation's $16.8 million in donations in 2020.[36]

Uihlein's foundation also gave $200,000 to the Federalist Society, and $750,000 to the Center for Security Policy, which the Southern Poverty Law Center calls an anti-Muslim hate group. Sollenberger further noted that

> Uihlein's largest gift of the year went to the Foundation for Government Accountability—a whopping $3,000,000 in January 2020 ... [who] launched a sprawling campaign ... to revise local and state election funding across the country. The group has framed Facebook CEO Mark Zuckerberg as the villain, trading on a popular right-wing conspiracy theory that Zuckerberg's $100 million in election integrity funding ahead of the vote unfairly helped swing the race for Biden. (It didn't.)[37]

In the 2022 midterm Uihlein was the second biggest political spender, shelling out over $90 million.[38] Some of this money went to attempts to elect election deniers.[39] Some of it went to help elect candidates who are hostile to reproductive freedoms for women.[40] In 2023, the Uilhleins gave $2,000,000 to Republican Florida governor Ron DeSantis's federal super PAC, Never Back Down.[41]

THE NEW MONEY USES AN OLD PLAYBOOK

If political spending in the late 1800s was led by business innovators such as the railroad robber barons, political spending today often comes from the nouveau riche, or "new money," such as the owners of ride-sharing firms, vaping companies and crypto firms.

What is "new money"? Companies make it from products that did not exist twenty years ago. The founders of multibillion-dollar companies were relatively young when they founded them. Juul was started by thirty-five-year-old James Monsees; Uber was started by thirty-three-year-old Travis Kalanick; Alameda/FTX was founded by twenty-five-year-old Sam Bankman-Fried; and Lyft was started by twenty-three-year-old Logan Green. Like gilded-age robber barons who shaped policy to magnify their opportunities for wealth (e.g., crushing unions, self-dealing, and creating trusts), these new players are doing the exact same thing—just with a modern twist. One way they attempt to mold the world in their own image is through corporate political spending to achieve policy outcomes that are good for them but not for the public.

RIDE-SHARING APPS TAKE VOTERS FOR A RIDE

Ride-sharing companies like Lyft and Uber, as well as apps that rely on drivers with their own cars, like DoorDash, Instacart, and Postmates, have been spending money in politics to protect their business model, which relies on categorizing drivers as independent contractors instead of employees. This allows the corporations to skip out on paying drivers benefits, like health care and a minimum wage.[42] This is just the new version of avoiding paying workers a living wage, which would have delighted a robber baron of old.

In 2021, Lyft spent $13 million to support a ballot initiative that would categorize drivers as independent contractors in Massachusetts.[43] This was the largest single political donation in the history of the state.[44] The measure was kept off of the ballot because of a lawsuit.[45] Lyft, Uber, and DoorDash have spent millions funding AstroTurf campaigns to have community groups tout their party line that drivers should not be considered employees.[46] Reporters found this astroturfing was happening in New York, Washington, and Illinois.[47] While AstroTurf campaigns appear to be organic community advocacy, they are really big-money operations. This approach has been used for years by the US Chamber of Commerce to trick lawmakers into thinking there is broader support for corporate positions than there actually is.[48]

The most expensive political battle for ride-sharing apps took place in California in 2020 over Proposition 22, which classified drivers as independent contractors. The price tag for the fight over the proposition was a quarter of a billion dollars (or $224,271,800, if you want to be exact).[49] Of that amount, Uber spent $58,361,469; DoorDash spent $51,905,814; Lyft spent $48,937,462; Instacart spent $31,584,393; and Postmates spent $13,319,307. After this record-breaking spending on the issue by the industry,[50] voters in California passed the measure and made it law. The industry won.[51]

VAPING COMPANIES BLOW POLITICAL SMOKESCREEN

The makers of electronic cigarettes known as "e-cigarettes," or vapes, have fought their own battle with regulators. Most of the conflict focuses on flavored vaping products that contain nicotine and are marketed and sold to minors, possibly hooking them for life, according to the Center for Disease Control.[52] In 2020, sixty-eight deaths were linked to vaping.[53] As a consequence, some states have banned the sale of flavored vapes.[54]

During the Obama administration, the FDA almost restricted the sale of flavored vapes, but, after concerted industry lobbying, this plan was dropped.[55] In 2020, during the Trump administration, the FDA went through with the flavor cartridge ban.[56] The FDA is also exploring more restrictions on e-cigarettes, especially after finding in 2022 that 16.5 percent of high school students and 4.5 percent of middle school students had used a tobacco product, and that vaping was the most common modality.[57]

Juul Labs, which is partially owned by Altria (formerly known as Philip Morris), who has a $12.8 billion stake and who sells e-cigarettes,[58] has spent gobs of money on lobbying and campaign contributions.[59] In 2019, Juul's PAC gave $100,000 to members of Congress in the face of threats to regulate sales.[60] Most of Juul's money in 2019 went to Democrats (two to one compared with the money they gave Republicans).[61] This could have been a strategy to give to incumbents, as Democrats had control of the House. They spent $4,340,000 lobbying Congress that year, too.[62] The company also "blanketed Washington with ads touting its efforts against underage vaping."[63] Juul/Altria have been accused of AstroTurf campaigns that aim to get vapers to tout their products to lawmakers.[64] The not-so-subtle message Juul was trying to get across was: DON'T REGULATE THIS ADDICTIVE PRODUCT.

Juul and Altria also spent in state elections, including $99,000 in California in 2019,[65] and $600,000 in Hawaii over several years.[66] In California, they beat back two efforts to ban flavored vapes.[67] In San Francisco, Juul spent $4.5 million trying to overturn a local ban on selling vaping products.[68] Juul's effort was rejected by San Francisco voters.[69] Juul has also targeted state attorneys general races.[70] This spending seemed to open doors to meetings between state AGs and Juul.[71] Juul hired a public relations firm, Locust Street, to push its agenda.[72] Altria is still interested in vaping: it bought another vaping company called Njoy for $2.75 billion in 2023.[73] The battle over whether they can sell their addictive products, and to whom, continues.

CRYPTIC POLITICAL SPENDING FROM CRYPTO COMPANIES

In 2021, supermodel Gisele Bündchen and her then-husband, quarterback Tom Brady, made television ads for a crypto exchange called FTX, owned by Sam Bankman-Fried (SBF).[74] Some of these ads aired during the 2022 Super Bowl.[75] A year later, FTX had imploded, and Bündchen and Brady, among other celebrity endorsers, were sued by individuals who lost money.[76] SBF hid in the Bahamas trying to avoid the consequences of what now looks like a massive multibillion dollar fraud.[77] As a *Vanity Fair* reporter wrote in a 2023 cover story, "Bündchen shot advertisements for—and invested millions in—Sam Bankman-Fried's recently collapsed cryptocurrency exchange, FTX, where Bündchen assumed the title of environmental and social initiatives head. 'I was blindsided,' Bündchen tells me. 'I'm no different than everyone else that trusted the hype.'"[78] Singer Taylor Swift was offered $100 million by FTX to sponsor one of her tours.[79] She turned it down after asking whether

FTX was dealing in unregistered securities and not receiving a satisfactory answer.[80] Others who took the money from FTX for celebrity endorsements like Gisele and Tom Brady could have avoided lawsuits if they had shown similar skepticism.

Allegedly "Bankman-Fried secretly moved $10 billion of customer funds from FTX [a crypto exchange] to trading company Alameda Research [a hedge fund] . . . with apparently $1 billion to $2 billion now missing."[81] As a result of this behavior, Bankman-Fried was convicted of securities fraud.[82] In the ensuing FTX bankruptcy, John Ray III, the lawyer who has been put in charge of FTX and previously worked on the massive Enron bankruptcy, said in court filings, "Never in my career have I seen such a complete failure of corporate controls. . . . From compromised systems integrity . . . , to the concentration of control in the hands of a very small group of inexperienced, unsophisticated and potentially compromised individuals, this situation is unprecedented."[83]

What does the FTX story have to do with corporate money in politics? Everything. Top executives who worked at FTX spent over $74 million in the 2022 election, making it the third biggest entity spending in that election.[84] They were also big players in the 2020 election.[85] The then-thirty-year-old leader, Sam Bankman-Fried, as well as two of his alleged coconspirators, who are FTX/Alameda executives, faced charges that they all violated campaign finance laws.[86] As FTX's bankruptcy overseer John Ray III also revealed, FTX "commingled customer deposits and corporate funds, and misused them with abandon. Bankman-Fried, . . . and . . . [FTX executives] . . . used . . . funds for . . . the purchase of luxury properties, as well as for political and other donations designed to enhance their own power and influence."[87]

Understanding why these executives of FTX and its sister firm Alameda with their smoke-and-mirrors business model would spend lavishly in politics shows how corporate political spending warps policy. Often the corporate motivation for campaign spending is to avoid reasonable governmental regulations that protect consumers and investors from snake oil salesmen. Too frequently, elected officials are all too obliging with their political donors, even if donors are peddling fool's gold to the unwitting public, so long as the campaign checks clear. According to the DOJ, the motive for SBF's campaign finance crime was "to improve his personal standing in Washington, D.C., increase FTX's profile, and curry favor with candidates that could help pass legislation favorable to FTX or Bankman-Fried's personal agenda."[88] Before he was arrested, SBF had been touting particular legislation around Capitol Hill called the "Digital Commodities Consumer Protection Act (DCCPA)" that would regulate cryptocurrencies in a way that would have benefited his firms.[89]

Before FTX imploded, CEO Ryan Salame wrote in a private text message that was used as evidence at Bankman-Fried's criminal trial: "Sam [Bankman-Fried] wants to donate to both [Democratic] and Republican candidates in the US but cause the worlds [sic] frankly lost its mind if you [donate] to a democrat no republicans will speak to you . . . We will be heavily putting money to weed out anti crypto dems for pro crypto dems and anti crypto repubs for pro crypto repubs."[90]

Salame pleaded guilty to participating in a conspiracy to make unlawful political contributions.[91] According to the DOJ, "Notwithstanding his awareness of the campaign finance laws, in order to conceal the true source of the funds, Salame agreed with others that funds for contributions would be transferred from Alameda's bank accounts, which also contained FTX customer funds, to bank accounts in the name of the political donors, and then quickly transferred from those individuals' bank accounts to political campaigns."[92]

In 2020, Alameda gave the single biggest corporate donation to a super PAC: a $5 million contribution.[93] Bankman-Fried gave an additional $5 million donation in 2020.[94] In 2022, Bankman-Fried, Ryan Salame, and Nishad Singh funneled money into elections on both the Left and the Right. As OpenSecrets has documented, "Bankman-Fried, co-CEO Ryan Salame and Director of Engineering Nishad Singh poured $70.1 million into the 2022 midterm election . . . That's ten times more than the $7 million FTX individuals contributed during the 2020 election cycle."[95] Salame gave $5.5 million to a conservative political group called One Nation that is associated with Republican senator Mitch McConnell, and Alameda CEO Caroline Ellison gave $6 million to a different conservative group, Defending America Together.[96] Meanwhile, playing the other side of the political aisle,

Bankman-Fried gave $8.5 million to a liberal group called Majority Forward that is associated with Democratic senator Chuck Schumer.[97] As the *Washington Post* once described Bankman-Fried and Salame: "[They] were essentially two giant piles of money oozing around Washington, asking who wanted to be friends. And all of Washington's instinctive suspicions about Silicon Valley, 'tech bros' and corporate greed withered away."[98]

The supermajority of the $111 million in corporate spending in the 2020 federal election flowed from corporations to the right side of the political spectrum (75 percent).[99] Is any corporate money flowing to the left side? The short answer is comparatively far less (20 percent).[100] The public-facing political spending by FTX and Alameda was out of step with most corporate political spending because theirs, like Juul's, supported Democratic candidates. Meanwhile, FTX's and Alameda's *dark money* supported Republicans. As the DOJ elaborated, "SALAME . . . and his co-conspirators made over 300 political contributions, totaling tens of millions of dollars, that were unlawful because they were made in the name of a straw donor or paid for with corporate funds."[101] In other words, the scheme was a straw-donor sham funded with illegal corporate money. FTX's dark spending fits the larger post-2020 trend of corporate money and money from wealthy CEOs boosting candidates on the far right, including members of the so-called Sedition Caucus in Congress, election deniers who ran for statewide offices, and legislators eager to strip reproductive freedoms from women and voting rights from all.[102]

FTX executive Nishad Singh also pleaded guilty to breaking federal campaign finance laws.[103] At Bankman-Fried's criminal trial, Singh testified: "I was a straw donor for campaign donations. . . . I knew that the money for those donations was coming from customer funds."[104] Singh also confessed to the jury: "I defrauded customers, investors, I participated in money laundering, and I violated campaign finance laws."[105]

Right around the time Bankman-Fried was indicted, he started talking to the press (which, if you are playing along at home and ever find yourself in a similar situation, is pure madness).[106] SBF told one reporter that not only had he supported Democratic candidates in 2022, but he had also supported Republican candidates, and with dark money. As *The Guardian* related, "'All my Republican donations were dark,' he said, referring to political donations that are not publicly disclosed. 'The reason was not for regulatory reasons, it's because reporters freak the fuck out if you donate to Republicans. They're all super liberal, and I didn't want to have that fight.'"[107] This confession inspired the watchdog group Citizens for Responsibility and Ethics in Washington (CREW) to file a complaint against Bankman-Fried with the FEC.[108]

After this media confession, federal prosecutors filed a new indictment that accused him of illegally spending $100 million in corporate money in federal elections. As the DOJ alleged in SBF's superseding indictment, "an internal Alameda spreadsheet noted over $100 million in political contributions, even though FEC records reflect no political contributions by Alameda for the 2022 midterm elections to candidates or PACs."[109]

If this is true, and the $100 million is in addition to the $38 million that the public already knew about, this would make Sam Bankman-Fried the single biggest spender in the 2022 midterm, catapulting him over George Soros.[110] The *Washington Post* called him "the disheveled 30-year-old MIT grad, [who was] manna from heaven for Democrats."[111] But the possibility that all of the $100 million went to Republicans prompted *The Atlantic* to ask whether "Bankman-Fried was in fact—and pun intended—a crypto-Republican."[112]

Sam Bankman-Fried was arrested in the Bahamas and extradited to the United States.[113] Shortly thereafter, Bankman-Fried's partner, Caroline Ellison, pleaded guilty.[114] SBF was on house arrest at his parent's home near Stanford,[115] until he leaked Ellison's diary to the *New York Times* and was thrown in pretrial detention for witness tampering.[116] Ellison testified at trial that Bankman-Fried "thought [political spending] was very effective, that you could get very high returns in terms of influence by spending relatively small amounts of money."[117] She added that "Sam [Bankman-Fried] gave $10 million to [Joe] Biden, he [SBF] thought it bought him access."[118] Bankman-Fried's lawyers tried to use recent Supreme Court cases *Ciminelli* and *Percoco* to get several of his federal charges dropped.[119] This did not work.[120] In his criminal trial Bankman-Fried was found guilty on all seven counts.[121] He was sentenced to 25 years.

Bankman-Fried even boasted that he planned to spend $1 billion on the 2024 presidential election to defeat Donald Trump.[122] But, as reporter Taylor Giorno wryly put it, "his pledge to spend up to $1 billion during the 2024 election cycle likely won't come to pass. Bankman-Fried's $16 billion fortune was wiped out almost overnight . . . , one of the largest ever single-day collapses among billionaires."[123]

Prosecutors are trying to get back FTX/Alameda money from politicians. As Semafor reported, "Federal prosecutors are demanding that lawmakers disgorge political donations from indicted FTX founder Sam Bankman-Fried and his employees. . . . The notice . . . states that the 'donations represent the proceeds of Bankman-Fried's crimes.' . . . It instructs recipients to return the cash to the U.S. Marshals."[124]

What is known so far is money from FTX and Bankman-Fried is being turned over to US Marshals from political sources.[125] Among the political contributions that have sent to the U.S. Marshals to date are:

Democratic Senatorial Campaign Committee: $36,500
Republican National Committee: $25,000
Former Republican senator Ben Sasse: $5,800
Rep. Mike Simpson (R-ID): $5,800
*Former rep. Lee Zeldin's (R-NY) Campaign Fund: $5,800
Sen. Maggie Hassan (D-NH): $5,800
Sen. John Boozman (R-AR): $5,800
Rep. Ruben Gallego (D-AZ): $5,800
Rep. Marc Molinaro (R-NY): $2,900
*Rep. Elise Stefanik (R-NY): $2,900
Rep. Bob Latta (R-OH): $2,900
Rep. Brian Fitzpatrick (R-PA): $2,900
Rep. Eli Crane (R-AZ): $2,900
Rep. Larry Bucshon (R-IN): $2,900
Rep. Chuck Edwards (R-NC): $2,900
*Rep. Alex Mooney (R-WV): $2,900
Rep. Julia Letlow (R-LA): $2,900
Rep. Greg Casar (D-TX): $2,900
Rep. Salud Carbajal (D-CA): $2,900
*Rep. Jeff Duncan (R-SC): $2,900
Rep. Dan Crenshaw (R-TX): $2,900

*Rep. Morgan Griffith (R-VA): $2,900
Rep. Maxwell Alejandro Frost (D-FL): $2,900
*Rep. Bill Johnson (R-OH): $2,900
Rep. John Moolenaar (R-MI): $2,900
Rep. Joyce Beatty (D-OH): $2,900
Rep. Kay Granger (R-TX): $2,900
Sen. Tim Scott's (R-SC) Presidential Exploratory Committee: $2,900
*Rep. Gary Palmer (R-AL): $2,900
*Rep. Buddy Carter (R-GA): $2,900
*Rep. Mario Diaz-Balart (R-FL): $2,900
Rep. Kathy Castor (D-FL): $2,900
Rep. Sean Casten (D-IL): $2,700
Athena PAC (Democratic Rep. Kathy Castor of Florida): $2,500
Axne PAC (Democratic Rep. Cynthia Axne of Iowa): $1,618
Rep. Lori Chavez-DeRemer (R-OR): $1,000.[126]

An additional $500,000 was sent to the US Marshals from politicians in Oregon.[127] According to FEC records, $500,000 was returned to the US Marshals from the liberal group Priorities USA Action,[128] $250,000 was returned by Democratic Congressional Campaign Committee (DCCC),[129] and $109,500 was returned by National Republican Senatorial Committee (NRSC).[130] Some of the returned funds even specified that they were originally from Ryan Salame, Sam Bankman Fried and/or Nishad Singh.[131] Thus, the FTX/SBF money reached at least nine members of the Sedition Caucus marked above with an asterisk. Most of the illegal $100 million from FTX has not been returned.

Puck News reported that SBF may have switched to giving to Republicans in 2022, when polling widely predicted a red wave that would flip both houses of Congress. As Puck surmised, "In the final days of the [2022] election season, FTX cut a newly-disclosed $1 million check to Senator Mitch McConnell's main super PAC. The donation was effectively another way of 'hedging the bet.'.... The S.B.F.-FTX team 'seemed pretty confident that [McConnell] would be the Majority Leader and there'd be a big margin in the House.'"[132] This red wave turned out to be a red trickle. The House flipped to the right, but only by a nine-seat margin. Meanwhile, the Senate gained an additional Democratic senator. Does the Republican majority that took over the House of Representatives in 2023 owe its existence to SBF's dark money? Would SBF have wanted a split Congress that would be incapable of passing any regulations of the crypto industry? I leave these mysteries to future political scientists and historians to unravel. But the nightmare scenario is that a future SBF with billions under their control doesn't just spend to benefit their own firm, but rather joins forces with antidemocratic politicians.

BACKING THE ANTIDEMOCRATIC

A HISTORY OF CORPORATE NAZI ENABLERS

What is the nightmare scenario for democracy when dealing with corporate political spending? It's when the biggest corporate political spenders back antidemocratic politicians who ultimately win and subvert democracy. This nightmare came true in Germany in 1933.

ADIDAS

For nearly a decade, rapper Kanye West worked with Adidas to sell incredibly strangely shaped shoes known as "Yeezys," some of which looked like a pair of plastic slippers that had been melted in a fire.[1] In 2022, Adidas was faced with a stark conundrum that illustrates the role played by corporations in democratic discourse. West had made a series of anti-Semitic statements that seemingly embraced White supremacy. The most virulent may have been a statement threatening that he would go "death con 3 on jewish people."[2] For weeks, public pressure mounted on Adidas to drop West as a business partner for his antisemitism. West poured fuel on this controversy by claiming publicly that Adidas could not afford to drop him because he had made the corporation so much money.[3] Finally, Adidas dropped West and his Yeezy shoe line in October 2022.[4] The breakup reportedly cost the company at least half a billion dollars.[5]

Adidas had a rather sordid history with anti-Semitism. In fact, Adidas had been founded by two German brothers who became members of the Nationalsozialistische Deutsche Arbeiterpartei (NSDAP), better known as the Nazi Party, in 1933.[6] "During this period, both men signed their letters "Heil Hitler," and German athletes wore the brothers' shoes during the infamous 1936 Nazi Olympics in Berlin."[7] As *Time* reported, "The

German shoe brand, launched in the 1920s, was one of many German companies to cooperate with the Nazi party."[8]

Adidas wasn't alone in collaborating. During the rise of Hitler and Nazism in Germany, the issue of whether corporations were funding an arsenal for democracy or an arsenal for dictatorship was a live debate. In retrospect, many German and American corporations were on the wrong side of history. Sometimes these corporations were merely complicit with Nazis, but, at other times, they were working hand in hand with them. The corporate backing of the Nazi Party is probably the most repugnant instance of corporate money being used to gut a democracy. If this book could offer any advice to corporate leaders today it would be this: don't be evil. Don't be like the corporations that funded the Nazis. Choose the right side of history. Choose democracy.

NAZI SABOTEURS ON AMERICAN SOIL

Few alive today can recall World War II or how close the battle came to spilling into the American mainland after Pearl Harbor. But, in June 1942, eight Nazi saboteurs landed in two U-boats on the eastern coast of the United States. Their plot was code-named Operation Pastorius.[9] One group of Nazis landed on Long Island, New York, and the other on the Florida coast, near Jacksonville.

The saboteurs, which included American and German citizens, brought with them two-years-worth of explosives for blowing up American bridges and factories. The operation's primary objective was to cripple American production of aluminum so that the United States could not build an air force to rival Hitler's Luftwaffe. The saboteurs carried with them hundreds of thousands of dollars that had been provided to them by the Reich.[10]

The New York Nazi crew was discovered by a member of the US Coast Guard. The Florida crew was betrayed by one of their own to the FBI.[11] The plot was quickly foiled: the eight Nazis were promptly arrested and tried by a military tribunal. Their case ended up before the Supreme Court in *Ex Parte Quirin*.[12] The saboteurs asked for their prosecutions to be conducted in a civilian court, but the Court refused this request.[13] After the military tribunal found them all guilty, six of the eight were executed, including the two Americans.[14] These Nazi saboteurs in Operation Pastorius had returned to the home country of one of Hitler's original inspirations: the anti-Semitic musing of one of America's most successful sons, the American industrialist Henry Ford.[15]

Hitler's rise to power wasn't just fueled with the money from German industrialists, though it surely was (keep reading); it was also bolstered by Ford intellectually, materially, and financially.[16] As Charles Higham writes, "Other precocious Hitler-admirers were press lord Randolph Hearst and Irénée Du Pont, . . . who . . . had already 'keenly followed the career of the future Führer in the 1920s' and supported him financially."[17] Multiple American firms were boosting Nazis as well—sometimes directly, at other times indirectly. "By the early 1930s," Higham notes, "an elite of about twenty of the largest American corporations had a German connection including Du Pont, Union Carbide, Westinghouse, General Electric, Gillette, Goodrich, Singer, Eastman Kodak, Coca-Cola, IBM, and ITT."[18]

General Motors (GM) was a key American corporate enabler of the Reich. GM's subsidiary in Germany converted its production to military uses.[19] According to Michael Dobbs, "American managers of . . . GM . . . went along with the conversion of their German plants to military production at a time when U.S. government documents show they were still resisting calls by the Roosevelt administration to step up military production in their plants at home."[20] The *Washington Post* reported that, "in 1935, GM agreed to build a new plant near Berlin to produce the aptly named 'Blitz' truck, which would later be used by the German army for its blitzkreig attacks on Poland, France and the Soviet Union."[21] Additionally, there was a "partial conversion of the principal GM automobile plant at Russelsheim to production of engines and other parts for the Junker 'Wunderbomber,' a key weapon in the German air force."[22] In 1941, GM's director of overseas operations, James Moody, said he would refuse to do anything that might "make Hitler mad."[23] Moody received an award from the Reich for "distinguished service."[24]

But the Ford Motor Company stood out among American firms, and Henry Ford stood out among American Hitler fans. Hitler had revealed himself to be an early menace to democracy by attempting a coup in Germany in 1923 in the Beer Hall Putsch, which led to his imprisonment, where he wrote *Mein Kampf*.[25] The only American mentioned in Hitler's book was car magnate Henry Ford.[26]

Perhaps there's nothing so dangerous as a millionaire who falls for conspiracy theories. Henry Ford fell for at least two. One was that the assassination of President Lincoln hadn't been plotted by John Wilkes Booth, and the other was his unhinged paranoia about Jewish people.[27] Ford didn't keep his anti-Semitism to himself. Rather, he used his wealth and his corporate network of car dealerships to spread his hatred worldwide. Not unlike Elon Musk buying Twitter in 2022, Ford bought his hometown paper, the *Dearborn Independent*, in 1918 and had it run ninety-one pieces in a row on anti-Jewish topics.[28] Next, he had these articles bound into four books: *The International Jew: The World's Foremost Problem* (November 1920), *Jewish Activities in the United States* (April 1921), *Jewish Influences in American Life* (November 1921), and *Aspects of Jewish Power in the United States* (May 1922). These books were translated into several languages, including German.[29] Ford purposefully did not copyright the material so that it could be more easily distributed worldwide.[30]

Not only did Ford sell subscriptions to the anti-Semitic *Dearborn Independent*; he also ordered his car dealerships to distribute the paper, too. As *American Experience* explained, "In some places, the dealership would actually put copies of the newspaper in the car, so that when you drove off with your Model T, there you had on the seat next to you a copy of *The Dearborn Independent*."[31] Even today, Ford's anti-Semitic screeds remain, as the Internet has given them a horrible second life.[32]

One of Ford's avid international readers was Adolph Hitler.[33] In 1931 Hitler told a reporter from Detroit, "'I regard Henry Ford as my inspiration,' . . . explaining why he kept a life-size portrait of the American automaker [Ford] next to [Hitler's] desk."[34] Ford was alleged to have supported a young Hitler. As the *New York Times* reported in 1922, "A rumor is current here that Henry Ford, the American automobile manufacturer, is financing Adolph Hitler's nationalist and antisemitic movement in Munich."[35]

The Nazi regime awarded Henry Ford the Grand Cross of the German Eagle in July 1938.[36] Two German consuls came to the United States to give him the award for his seventy-fifth birthday.[37] The mutual lovefest continued in 1939, when Ford's company gave Hitler thirty-five thousand Reichsmarks for his fiftieth birthday.[38] Meanwhile, Ford's German subsidiary was particularly active in supporting Nazi war efforts.[39] As

The Nation explained, "Following Hitler's 1939 invasion of Poland . . . , German Ford became one of the largest suppliers of vehicles to the Wehrmacht (the German Army)."[40] Moreover, "by 1941 Ford of Germany had stopped manufacturing passenger vehicles and was devoting its entire production capacity to military trucks."[41]

During World War II, for American audiences, Ford often touted his company "as 'the arsenal of democracy' by transforming [its] production lines in the United States to make airplanes, tanks and trucks for the armies that defeated Adolf Hitler."[42] But the truth was more complicatedand contradicted this P.R. In reality, "German Ford served as an 'arsenal of Nazism' with the consent of headquarters in Dearborn, [said] a US Army report prepared in 1945."[43] Even reporting from middle of World War II made clear "that while the American people were moving toward an alliance with the democracies, great sectors of American industry were strengthening their ties with Fascist Germany."[44]

Ford's German factories benefited from the slave labor authorized by Nazi policies. As the *Washington Post* noted, "When the U.S. Army liberated the Ford plants in Cologne and Berlin, they found destitute foreign workers confined behind barbed wire and company documents extolling the 'genius of the Fuehrer,' according to . . . soldiers at the scene."[45] The *Post* further explained that "[a] U.S. Army report . . . dated Sept. 5, 1945, accused the German branch of Ford of serving as 'an arsenal of Nazism, at least for military vehicles' with the 'consent' of the parent company in Dearborn."[46]

The Ford Motor Company was, arguably, acting treasonously during World War II by assisting the Nazis in Germany and either slow-walking or refusing to help the American government and her allies. As *The Nation* reported, "While Ford Motor enthusiastically worked for the Reich, the company initially resisted calls from President Roosevelt and British Prime Minister Churchill to increase war production for the Allies."[47] The *Washington Post* put the blame more squarely on Henry Ford, writing that, "in June 1940, after the fall of France, Henry Ford personally vetoed a U.S. government-approved plan to produce under license Rolls-Royce engines for British fighter planes."[48]

HITLER'S GERMAN CORPORATE CHEERLEADERS, ENABLERS AND COLLABORATORS

For years before gaining political power, Hitler courted industrial leaders in Germany. A Hitler speech from January 27, 1932, to a crowd of 650 people at the Industry Club in Duesseldorf included lines about democracy being objectionable because all races had an equal say. As Hitler told the businessmen, "[In a] democracy . . . there is no essential difference in value between Negroes, Arians, Mongolians, and Redskins. This view . . . is so far-reaching in its consequences that ultimately a Negro will be able to preside at the sessions of the League of Nations."[49] This troubling, racist speech inspired donations from businessmen to the Nazi Party in 1932, when Hitler was running to be president of Germany.[50]

During his presidential campaign, Hitler was not shy about expressing his contempt for multiparty democracy. He told an Eberswalde audience: "Our opponents accuse us National Socialists, and me in particular, of being intolerant. . . . The gentlemen are completely right, we are intolerant. I have set myself a goal, namely to sweep those 30 parties out of Germany."[51]

According to William Manchester's *The Arms of Krupp*, by the end of 1932 the Nazi Party was facing financial ruin.[52] They had also suffered electoral losses: "In the Reichstag election of [] November [6,] 1932, the Nazi Party lost two million votes and 34 seats. At this point, the Nazi Party was in a critical situation. Large bills were unpaid and the coffers were empty."[53] The press falsely believed in late 1932 that "the Nazi menace was receding—[and that] the republic had survived."[54]

Joseph Goebbels, who would later become the Nazi minister of propaganda, complained contemporaneously in his diary on December 8, 1932: "Deep depression is prevalent in the organization, financial worries prevent any constructive work. . . . The Fuehrer was at our house. We could not get into the right spirit. We are all very discouraged particularly in the face of the present danger that the entire [Nazi] party may collapse and all our work be in vain. The financial situation of the Berlin organization is hopeless. Nothing but debts and obligations."[55] Their fortunes were about to be reversed, figuratively and literally. How did the Nazis move from being broke to being in control of the German government just a year later? Here is that story.

Nuremberg prosecutor and US brigadier general Telford Taylor would note that the Nazi Party was in the red just as Hitler assumed the chancellorship in January 1933: "The [Nazi] Party was in a critical condition and badly in need of money. . . . Hitler's new seat of power [after January 30, 1933] was shaky enough. He was immediately confronted with an impending Reichstag election which could make or break him, and the Nazi Party lacked funds for this crucial test."[56] Moreover, "the Nazi Party's slender purse, which had worried Goebbels some weeks earlier, was a serious obstacle to success in the election which was scheduled for March 1933."[57] By one estimate, the Nazi Party was twelve million marks in debt.[58]

The industrialists who bailed out the Nazi Party were the heads of huge German firms I. G. Farben and Krupp. Leaders of both of companies were among the few civilians who were later charged with war crimes at the Nuremberg trials after World War II.[59] These legal proceedings put the story of their financial support of the Nazis—which had been a closely guarded secret—into the historical record. Krupp was a huge arms manufacturer, while I. G. Farben was a major chemical company that made everything from Bayer Aspirin to Zyklon B, the poison used in the gas chambers.[60] A third firm disciplined at Nuremberg, Flick, produced armaments for Hitler that were illegal under the Treaty of Versailles. As General Taylor said: "These are men who stopped at nothing. They were the magicians who made the fantasies of *Mein Kampf* come true."[61]

With less than two weeks left before the March 1933 vote, Herman Göering sent telegrams to Germany's twenty-five leading industrialists, inviting them to a secret meeting in Berlin on February 20, 1933, at his home.[62] Attending the gathering were four I. G. Farben directors; Krupp's chief executive, Gustav Krupp; and Friedrich Flick. The group also included "Günther Quandt, a textile producer turned arms-and-battery tycoon . . . ; Baron August von Finck, a Bavarian finance mogul; Kurt Schmitt, CEO of the insurance behemoth Allianz; [and] executives from . . . the potash giant Wintershall."[63]

Hitler addressed the group of businessmen assembled at Göering's house, saying that "*private enterprise cannot be maintained in a democracy.*"[64] He added, "We must not forget that all the benefits of culture must be introduced, more or less, with an iron fist," and the businessmen agreed to that as well.[65] According to Krupp's notes from the evening, Hitler said: "Now we stand before the *last* election. . . . If the election does not decide, the decision must be brought about even by other means."[66] In other words, "Hitler declared his treasonable purpose to seize power by violence if he failed to win it by votes."[67]

Hitler asked for the businessmen's financial support to back his vision for a democracy-less Germany, as did Göering, who "stressed the importance of the coming election [stating] '[w]ithout any doubt we must . . . penetrate with our SA men [Nazi Storm Troopers] into the darkest quarters of the cities . . . and fight for every single soul.' Goering then brought up the matter of financial contributions."[68] Göering asserted that the upcoming election might be the last election for the next one hundred years.[69] Prosecutor Taylor's opening statement in the *Flick* trial related that "the leaders of German industry were, in these words, promised that, if Hitler prevailed in the election, democracy would give way to dictatorship. They responded generously to this moving appeal by furnishing at least three million Reichsmarks . . . and in the March elections Hitler won 44 percent of the total vote. . . . Never has a political contribution had such far-reaching and devastating consequences."[70] After Hitler spoke, Mr. Krupp expressed to Hitler the industrialists' "gratitude for having given us such a clear picture of his ideas."[71]

As author David de Jong described the events at Göering's home:

> Right on the spot they allocated the sums. One million reichsmarks were to be paid by the black coal and iron industries from the Ruhr area, and 500,000 reichsmarks each by the potash mining and chemicals industries. The remaining million would be drawn from the brown coal industry, car-makers, and mechanical and electrical engineering firms. The men agreed that 75 percent of the money would go to the Nazi Party. . . . [Hjalmar] Schacht uttered the shortest and most expensive line of the evening: "And now, gentlemen, to the cash register!"[72]

Schacht, ex-president of the Reichsbank, would go on to organize a group of industrialists called the "Arbeitsstelle Schacht," or the "Schacht Circle." As Thomas Ferguson and Hans-Joachim Voth write in *Betting On Hitler*, "The businessmen who financed Schacht's [C]ircle included some of the biggest names in German business, including Albert Vogler of Vereinigte Stahl, Krupp . . . , Fritz Springorum [Head of German Ironmasters], Emil Georg von Stauss [ex-chairman of BMW] . . . , Rosterg of Winterhall, and Kurt von Schroder [president of the Rhineland Industrial Chamber]."[73]

On February 21, 1933, Goebbels was back to writing in his diary with more gusto: "Göering brings the joyful news that 3 million is available for the election. Great thing! I immediately alert the whole propaganda department. And one hour later, the machines rattle. Now we will turn on an election campaign. Today the work is fun. The money is there."[74] As Nuremburg prosecutors explained, what came next was the swift collapse of German democracy: "The Nazi Party received . . . 288 Reichstag seats out of a total of 647. Still lacking a majority, Hitler applied the 'other methods' which he had threatened to use. . . . Opposition members in the Reichstag were taken into 'protective custody' and in their enforced absence the Reichstag on 24 March 1933 passed the Enabling Act which gave Hitler . . . the power to deviate from the constitution."[75] As the Nuremberg prosecutors concluded: "Thus perished democracy and liberty in Germany."[76]

KRUPP

Gustav Krupp, the head of the Krupp corporation, was not passive as the Nazis rose to power. In June 1933, he organized the Adolf Hitler Spende, or Adolf Hitler Fund.[77] As Krupp's prosecutors explained, "This was a fund collected annually from every circle of German industry. . . . The proceeds were put at the disposal of Hitler and various Nazi Party organizations, including the SA, the SS, and the Hitler Youth."[78] I. G. Farben was "'naturally prepared' to contribute to the Adolf Hitler Fund."[79]

Academics later discovered that big business was spreading their money around the Nazi leaders. While Krupp and Farben were giving to the Adolf Hitler Fund, "industrialist Fritz] Thyssen . . . subsidiz[ed] . . . Hermann Goering . . . Hermann Bucher, head of . . . Allgemeine Elektrizitdts-Gesellschaft . . . [gave] financial aid to . . . storm troop leader Walter Stennes . . . the Bergbau-Verein [funded] . . . Gregor Strasser [a Nazi official who was murdered during the Night of the Long Knives in 1934]."[80] Much like political spending today in the United

States, business leaders hedge their bets by giving to multiple political leaders simultaneously instead of to a single party.

Krupp, the corporation, served as an arsenal of fascism. As the final report from Krupp's tribunal noted, "In a Germany pledged to rearmament, Krupp would again flourish as the 'weapons forge' of the Reich. . . . The Krupp board of directors were able to report for the business year following the Nazi seizure of power that, 'the business . . . yielded a profit.'"[81] Economists have looked at Nazi-affiliated firms and found they profited during Hitler's 1933 rise to power.[82] They report that "firms that had 'bet on Hitler' benefited substantially. They saw their stock price rise by 5% to 8% faster between January and March than comparable firms."[83] When Hitler was in power, he rewarded his corporate benefactors with political power.[84] Hitler granted Krupp the title of Fuhrer of Industry in 1933.[85]

FLICK

Friedrich Flick, the head of his eponymous company, Flick Konzern, was a financial booster of the Nazi regime.[86] At the fateful meeting between Hitler and the industrialists in 1933, Flick provided 240,000 Reichsmarks, which were contributed by one of Flick's companies, Mitteldeutsche Stahlwerke.[87]

In addition to funding the Nazi Party, Flick and thirty to forty industrialists belonged to a group known by various titles, including the "Freundeskreis der Wirtschaft," the "Circle of Friends," the "Keppler-Kreis," the "Keppler Circle," and, finally, the "Himmler Circle."[88] Wilhelm Keppler was a financial advisor to Hitler, and Heinrich Himmler was Reichsführer of the SS.[89] Farben's and Flick's stories overlap, as both firms supported the Himmler Circle. This group wasn't just a bunch of business chums; its "membership, in addition to leading German industrialists and bankers, included . . . Oswald Pohl, Chief of all concentration camps; Otto Ohlendorf, a leading official of the SS who testified before the [International Military Tribunal] that his SS Kommandos had killed 90,000 women, men, and children . . . ; and Wolfram Sievers, who directed the program of criminal medical experimentation on human beings."[90] There were also ties to Himmler's Circle to American firms like Standard Oil.[91]

Every year between 1933 and 1945, the Himmler Circle contributed about one million marks to Himmler to financially subsidize the activities of the SS.[92] The money went into a special account (lettered "R") at Dresdner Bank from which Karl Wolff, Himmler's personal assistant, wrote checks. Evidence at Flick's tribunal traced how the money was used to pay top SS brass, including Wolff himself: "Monthly payments out of special account R to the highest ranking SS officers ranged from 200 marks a month to 600 marks except in the case of Wolff who received 800 marks a month."[93]

Former SS lieutenant general Keppler testified that the genesis of the Himmler Circle was when "the Fuehrer [Hitler] said 'Try to get a few economic leaders—they need not be Party members—who will be at our disposal when we come into power.' . . . On 18 May 1932. . . . the Fuehrer made a short speech and in it disclosed among other things, as points of his program-[including] *abolition of parties other than the NSDAP.* No one raised any objection."[94]

Prosecutor Ervin in the *Flick* case argued that the Nazi SS was completely dependent on corporate sponsorship: "Adequate financing of the SS and its related organizations was vital to their success. It took a good deal of money to maintain many thousands of brown shirted SA Storm Troopers and black shirted SS men and permit them to devote their efforts, not to productive labor, but to intimidation, brutality, and murder. . . . The SS in its early days relied chiefly upon contributions from industrialists for its funds, since it had no budget of its own."[95]

In other words, without the corporate backing of the Himmler Circle, the SS would have been a far smaller force of oppression—or, at least, a less-well-financed one. As deputy chief prosecutor at the Nuremberg trials Charles Lyon explained, "By the end of the war, money from Flick and other members of the Himmler Circle went into the general funds of the SS and thus *became part of the financial life blood of the organization.* . . . The crimes of the Third Reich were not simple, common-law types of murder . . . The crimes of the Third Reich were the product of specialization and minute division of labor. Some people planned, some incited, some contributed money, and some were the 'trigger men.'"[96] If the SS were the trigger men, Flick, Farben, and their circle of industrialist "friends" were the money men.[97]

I. G. FARBEN

Among Krupp, Flick, and I. G. Farben, picking the worst of the worst is challenging; they were all awful. But I. G. Farben edges out the other two for its partial ownership of the Auschwitz concentration camp. I. G. Farben was Europe's largest corporation. Its full name was "Interessen Gemeinschaft Farbenindustrie Aktiengesellschaft," which translates to "Community of Interest of the Dyestuffs Industry, Incorporated"—or, as one of the Nuremburg prosecutors, Josiah DuBois Jr., put it in *The Devil's Chemists*, the name was "like the cross between a service club and Easter eggs."[98] But what I. G. Farben did with the Nazis was no laughing matter.

At the meeting on February 20, 1933, I. G. Farben executives pledged the Nazis 400,000 marks—the largest contribution from a single firm that night. The payment was made a week later on February 27, 1933, from a corporate account.[99] According to *The Crime and Punishment of I. G. Farben* by Joseph Borkin, Farben had given a total of 4.5 million marks by the end of 1933.[100]

As a report on the pro-Nazi industrialist trials written for the United Nations in 1949 explained, the use of slave labor was the primary violation of international law that these industrialists faced at Nuremberg.[101] In the *I. G. Farben* trial, General Taylor said that "the indictment accuses these men of major responsibility for visiting upon mankind the most searing and catastrophic war in modern history. It accuses them of wholesale enslavement, plunder and murder. . . . They were the warp and woof of the dark mantle of death that settled over Europe."[102] Other prosecutors noted that "they turned back the clock and revived slavery in Europe."[103]

I. G. Farben privately owned parts of Auschwitz known as "Monowitz" or "Auschwitz III." At Monowitz, "IG [Farben] took over responsibility for food and health care—a distinction of singular irrelevance to most prisoners because the provision of both was as criminally inadequate as anything supplied by the [Nazi] state."[104] General Taylor argued at Nuremberg that "the crimes with which these men are charged were not committed in rage, or under the stress of sudden temptation. . . . One does not build a stupendous war machine in a fit of passion, nor an

Auschwitz factory during a passing spasm of brutality. What these men did was done with the utmost deliberation."[105]

I. G. Farben also benefited from medical experiments conducted under the Nazi regime. According to the U.S. Holocaust Memorial Museum, "SS physician Helmut Vetter, who conducted drug trials for the Bayer subsidiary of IG Farben on prisoners at Dachau, Auschwitz, and Gusen concentration camps."[106] Moreover, "Bayer was particularly active in Auschwitz. A senior Bayer official oversaw . . . Monowitz. Most of the experiments were conducted in Birkenau in Block 20, the women's camp hospital. There, Vetter and Auschwitz physicians Eduard Wirths and Friedrich Entress tested Bayer pharmaceuticals on prisoners who suffered from and often had been deliberately infected with tuberculosis, diphtheria, and other diseases."[107] As General Taylor noted of the industrialists' activities, "Tolerance of such crimes will destroy man's capacity for self-respect; their repetition would destroy mankind itself."[108]

In the end, in the *Farben* tribunal at Nuremberg, "[Farben executive Carl] Krauch and four others of the accused were found guilty of the charges alleging the employment of prisoners of war, forced [labor] and concentration camp inmates in illegal work and under inhuman conditions."[109] Executives who were convicted got prison sentences ranging from eight years to eighteen months.[110] In a dissent, Nuremberg Judge Paul Hebert stated: "*Utilization of slave labor in Farben was approved as a matter of corporate policy*. To permit the corporate instrumentality to be used as a cloak to insulate the principal corporate officers who authorized this course of action is, in my opinion, without any sound precedent under the most elementary concepts of criminal law."[111]

Although Krupp, I. G. Farben, and Flick were prosecuted at Nuremberg, a much greater number of German firms benefited from slave labor during World War II, including BMW, Volkswagen, and the firm that became Daimler-Chrysler.[112] American firms also helped the Reich, either directly or indirectly. I. G. Farben was often the linchpin for American firms, bringing resources and knowhow to Germany for the Reich. For example, as the *New Republic* reported in 1942, "there was the wrong and unlawful conspiracy between Alcoa and I. G. Farben, by which the production of magnesium was suppressed in America while Germany developed the greatest magnesium industry in the world."[113] The magazine also reported on the synergy between Farben and Rockefeller's Standard Oil.[114]

As Diarmuid Jeffreys' book *Hell's Cartel* explains, the history of the German industrialists' support of Hitler shows "what can go wrong when political objectives and the pursuit of profit become dangerously entwined."[115] One can only surmise what might have happened if the businessmen had simply said "no" to Hitler in early 1933.

There is a small positive epilogue to all of this horror. The post–World War II German Constitution includes transparency of political party finance (making the secret funding of future-would-be Nazis illegal). It requires that "political parties . . . *must publicly account for their assets and for the sources and use of their funds.*"[116] This part of the Constitution goes on to outlaw antidemocratic parties by stating: "Parties that, by reason of their aims or the behaviour [sic] of their adherents, are oriented towards an undermining or abolition of the free democratic basic order or an endangerment of the existence of the Federal Republic of Germany shall be excluded from state financing."[117] As scholar Carl J. Schneider explains, "Behind the requirement that the financial backing of a party must be made public lay a conviction that German democracy may be endangered not only by authoritarian parties but also by democratic parties that cannot convince the people of their own integrity and independence. There is general agreement that the requirement is highly desirable as a means to prevent parties from becoming the tools of hidden or unrecognized special interests."[118]

The Nuremberg trials of *Flick*, *Krupp*, and *I. G. Farben* held certain executives at these firms accountable for war crimes that benefited their companies financially. To be sure, these are extreme examples. But, given the fragility of American democracy post-January 6, corporations are at a crossroads in the United States. They can help support candidates and policies that will strengthen democratic norms, practices, and laws, or they can do the opposite: support candidates who (arguably) cannot constitutionally run for office, erode the public's confidence in democratic norms, and endorse laws that make voting more difficult.

3

DEMOCRACY BEHIND BARS

HOW CORPORATIONS BENEFIT FROM CIVIL DEATH

On June 17, 2022, in a packed courtroom in Orange County, North Carolina, with the air conditioning struggling to keep up with the summer heat, with Superior Court Judge Allen Baddour presiding, four men—Andrew Johnson, James Felmet, Igal Roodenko, and Bayard Rustin—were exonerated posthumously for the crime of trying to racially integrate a bus seventy-five years ago. As the county reported, "[Judge] Baddour decided . . . to drop the charges because the men were convicted under state statutes that violated the Constitution."[1] The judge declared, choking back tears, "Today I am vacating these convictions and I am dismissing these charges."[2]

The now exonerated men were originally "charged with disorderly conduct for refusing to move from the front of the bus [they were trying to integrate]."[3] They were arrested in Chapel Hill, North Carolina.[4] Their convictions were ultimately upheld by the state Supreme Court.[5] These men, two Black, two White, were among the first Freedom Riders. Their ride in 1947 was called "the Journey of Reconciliation."[6] As punishment for trying to integrate a bus, African American Bayard Rustin was sentenced to hard labor on a chain gang, where he was literally chained to other prisoners and forced to work. Like many individuals on chain gangs, he faced involuntary labor building roads.[7]

Today, at sentencing in America, the convicted person suffers "civil death," comprising the loss of a number of different civil rights, including freedom of movement, the ability to hold public office, the right to possess firearms, and the right to vote.[8] Because civil death is essentially lifelong in certain states, returning citizens (i.e., ex-felons who have served their time and are living in their home communities) still cannot access the ballot.[9] As Michelle Alexander explains, "Once you're labeled a felon, the old forms of discrimination—employment discrimination, ... denial of the right to vote, denial of educational opportunity, ... and exclusion from jury service—are suddenly legal.[10]

Civil death dates as far back as ancient Greece.[11] Individuals who were convicted of "infamous crimes" were denied the right to vote, attend assemblies, or hold public office.[12] The Greeks also prohibited these individuals from appearing in court and from serving in the military.[13] The Greek concept of "civil death" eventually led to England's legal concept of "outlawry," which deemed that an outlaw must be stripped of all rights to legally protect his life or property.[14] The theory behind outlawry was that "he who breaks the law has gone to war with the community; the community goes to war with him. It is the right and duty of every man to pursue him, to ravage his land, to burn his house, to hunt him down like a wild beast and slay him; for a wild beast he is; not merely is he a 'friendless man,' he is a wolf."[15] As Sir William Blackstone states, "The criminal is no longer fit to live upon the earth, but is to be exterminated as a monster and a bane to human society."[16] American civil death took many awful forms, including chain gangs and convict leasing.

CHAIN GANGS

Bayard Rustin, a civil rights advocate who would go on to help Martin Luther King Jr. and A. Philip Randolph organize major marches on Washington in the 1960s, wasn't the typical prisoner. For one thing, he lived in New York City and was only in North Carolina in 1947 to help integrate interstate buses. For another, he was well educated: he had attended three different colleges.[17] Rustin eloquently wrote about his experiences in an exposé, "Twenty-Two Days on the Chain Gang at Roxboro, North Carolina." Rustin died in 1987 before he could be exonerated.[18] Walter Naegel, Rustin's surviving partner, would later explain, "The article, which was serialized in *The New York Post*, reported on a harrowing time working 12 hour days doing hard labor in brutal heat and being housed in inhumane conditions."[19] Rustin described a run-in with the White boss of the chain gang, to whom he gave the pseudonym "Captain Jones": "[Jones said to me], 'You're the one who thinks he's smart. Ain't got no respect. Tries to be uppity.... *You ain't in Yankeeland now....*' He was getting angrier by the moment, his face flushed.... 'You do what you're told. You respect us, or . . .' He raised his hand threateningly but, instead of striking me, brought the back of his hand down across the mouth of the man on my left."[20] Captain Jones followed up by "thrust[ing] a pick at me and ordered me to get to work."[21]

At the chain gang's next stop, Rustin tried to improve by performing his tasks quickly, but this, too, was met with threats. As Rustin related, "When the truck stopped . . . I made an effort to . . . begin[] work immediately. In my haste I came within twenty feet of the guard. 'Stop, you bastard!' he screamed, and pointed his revolver at my head. 'Git back, git back. Don't rush me or I'll shoot the goddamned life out of you.'"[22] Violence (both actual and threatened) was a constant risk.[23] As Rustin described working conditions:

> Captain Jones was displeased with the rate of our work. . . . In an attempt to obey, one of the chain-gangers struck another with his shovel. The victim complained, instantly and profanely. The words were hardly out of his mouth before the Captain . . . struck the cursing chain-ganger in the face with his fist again and again. Then Captain Jones informed the crew, using the most violent profanity, that cursing would not be tolerated. He . . . then yelled to the armed guard. 'Shoot hell out of the next one you find cursin'. Shoot straight for his feet. Cripple 'em up. That will learn 'em.' The guard lifted his rifle and aimed it at the chest of the man nearest him. 'Hell, no!' he drawled. 'I ain't aimin' fer no feet. I like hearts and livers. That's what really learns 'em.'[24]

These threats were not idle. Later studies would reveal that "the death rates on these chain gangs . . . were as high as forty-five percent."[25]

Rustin also described what amounts to physical torture of a prisoner too sick to work: "He was ordered 'hung on the bars' for 72 hours. . . . He stood facing his cell, with his arms chained to the vertical bars, and there he must stand."[26] The physical effects became excruciating: "His feet and often the glands in the groins begin to swell. If he attempts to sleep, his head falls back with a snap, or falls forward into the bars, cutting and bruising his face."[27]

Rustin warned that the impact of the brutality of the chain gang was to make prisoners either meek or vengeful men. As he put it, "One of the most stifling elements of life on the road gang is the authoritarianism. . . . [which] destroys the inner resourcefulness, creativity and responsibility of the prisoner and creates in the wardens and prisoners alike an attitude that life is cheap."[28] Elsewhere he asserted, "Nor could society be protected, for . . . these men and thousands like them return to society . . . with . . . a desire for revenge."[29] In the end, he found the experience dehumanizing. He wrote: "To me the most degrading condition . . . was the feeling, 'I am not a person; I am a thing to be used.'"[30] Rustin only had to endure this for twenty-two days. Many other prisoners had to suffer for the rest of their short lives.

CONVICT LEASING

In 1947, when Rustin was arrested, chain gangs were the tail end of a set of abusive practices known as "convict leasing."[31] In 1897, North Carolina amended its statutes to remove women from its chain gangs,[32] but it simultaneously passed a law to allow leasing of chain gangs: "The Board . . . is hereby empowered to hire out the Chain Gang."[33] For decades, Black prisoners were leased to companies, thereby providing cheap labor to corporations, revenue for southern states, and social control for African Americans, all in one fell swoop.

The Nazi German corporations were not the only ones using slave labor. American corporations have a long history of benefiting from the civil death of individuals sentenced for crimes. Convict leasing was empowered by the exploitation of a loophole in the Thirteenth Amendment, which says slavery that is allowed for "a punishment for crime."[34]

The post–Civil War South was so destitute that some states could not afford to run their prisons. Meanwhile, many Southern Whites wanted to reassert control over the freedmen.[35] According to Melvin Gutterman, the idea of convict leasing came from the following source: "Edmund Richardson . . . needed cheap laborers to work his land . . . , so he contracted with the state of Mississippi to feed, clothe, guard and treat well the criminals assigned to him provided he could keep all the profits. The state . . . agreed to pay him for the prisoners' maintenance. Richardson's proposal started the era of convict leasing in Mississippi."[36] Richardson's convicts were later "transferred to Nathan Bedford Forrest, . . . [who] founded the Ku Klux Klan."[37] Convict leasing was lucrative for states. As Stephen P. Garvey explains, "Having delegated to [the company] the costly duty of providing for the inmates' custody and care, the state likewise discovered that the lease could make punishment profitable."[38]

Post–Civil War Black Codes included laws that "required African Americans to maintain proof of employment, subjected them to harsh physical punishment for breaking labor contracts, subjected their families to work under their labor contracts, and subjected their children to 'apprenticeship' without any requirement of parental consent."[39] Many of these laws meted out heavy prison sentences (five years) for relatively minor offenses like stealing a pig.[40] There was also Arkansas's notorious two-dollar law, which made stealing things worth two dollars punishable by one to five years in penitentiary.[41] The purpose of the Black Codes was to exploit the Thirteenth Amendment's allowance of criminal peonage[42] and to "essentially . . . criminalize black life."[43]

Convict leasing was facially neutral (as, presumably, any convict could be leased), nonetheless, the practice was racialized, and nearly everyone caught up in this system was Black. Melvin Gutterman writes: "In the era of Jim Crow[] after emancipation, the jailhouse became a black preserve. Over ninety percent of the convicts were black."[44] As Teri A. McMurtry-Chubb explains, "The state's control over Black labor effectively created a system that replicated the master/slave relationship."[45] W. E. B. Du Bois came to a similar conclusion, while convict leasing was still happening, that "amid this chaos the courts sought to do by judicial decisions what the legislatures had formerly sought to do by specific law—namely, reduce the freedmen to serfdom."[46]

Under the convict leasing system, prisoners were at risk of physical violence, "[as] there was no financial or moral incentive to treat the convict well, or even keep him alive beyond his sentence."[47] Stephen Bright remarks that a "company that leased convicts had no interest in their nutrition, their health, the quality of their housing or any other aspect of their survival. They could literally be worked to death and then replaced by other leased convicts."[48] This led to enormous cruelty, such that "corporations . . . were empowered to chain, shoot, whip, starve, and brutalize prisoners to . . . maximize productivity."[49]

Under the systems of chain gangs and convict leasing, life was violent and cheap. As Edward Rubin writes: "As one Southerner explained: 'Before the war we [Whites] owned the negroes. If a man had a good negro, he could afford to take care of him: if he was sick, get a doctor. . . . But these convicts: we don't own 'em. One dies, get another.'"[50] Corporations often drove the demand for more convicts.[51] As James Gray Pope elucidates, "Arrest rates responded more to fluctuations in the demand for labor than in the crime rate."[52]

One survivor of convict leasing, Ezekiel Archey, reported "a daily struggle to survive. Convicts lived and worked in chains. Although the inadequate shored-up mines were constantly collapsing, the prisoners had little choice but to toil to their death. Guards whipped those who failed to submit and, if that didn't work, they tortured them with the 'water punishment.'"[53] Those in power knew of the violence.[54] George Washington Cable, a contemporary writer described an official report from Tennessee: "As the eye runs down the table of deaths, it finds opposite the names, among other moral causes, the following: Found dead. Killed. Drowned. Not given. Blank. Blank. Blank. Killed. Blank. Shot. Killed."[55] Cable also remarked that "in Louisiana . . . in 1881 . . . the year's death rate of the convict camps of Louisiana . . . exceed[ed] that of any pestilence that ever fell upon Europe in the Middle Ages."[56] And, "according to one report, many convicts simply 'disappeared as completely as if the earth had opened up and swallowed them.'"[57] Convict leasing victims who died were often buried in unmarked graves, including some only found a hundred years later.[58]

Once convicted of dubious crimes like vagrancy (a.k.a. not having a job), or, in Rustin's case, breaking the color line, this legal system produced a steady supply of convicts who could be fed into the chain gang or convict leasing systems at great profit to the state and corporate interests.[59] Labor from convict leasing was used across a broad range of industries. In Texas, convicts harvested sugarcane.[60] As Stephen P. Garvey notes, "Convicts made bricks for Atlanta's Chattahoochee Brick Company, built the railroads that ran across western North Carolina, . . . extracted iron ore from the mines surrounding Birmingham, drained the swamps of the Mississippi Delta, and made fertilizer out of phosphate taken from the mines of Florida. Other convicts waded in Florida's swamps, stripping trees . . . to make turpentine."[61] Those in Florida "caught up in this system and sent to work in the 'American Siberia' were said to have been 'turpentined.'"[62]

As reporter Richard Barry wrote contemporaneously, "The corruption begins in the convict [lease] system. Florida has no state prison. She has twelve hundred convicts and no place to put them. The state, therefore, is compelled to speculate in her criminals."[63] Barry added that "this might be all right if it were a business proposition. Instead it is politics, which means graft.... [Under a particular convict lease] ... contract the state receives $207.70 a year, or fifty-seven cents a day for each convict. But the operators who use those convicts pay from eighty-five to ninety-five cents a day a piece for them. The difference is the graft."[64]

African American children were particularly apt to get pushed into the convict leasing system. As Robin Walker Sterling described, "By 1880, at least 25 percent of Mississippi's convicts were under the age of eighteen. According to an 1890 census analysis ... more than 18 percent of all black prisoners were juveniles. No crime was too small to justify imprisonment.... In the 1880s, *six-year-old* Mary Gay ... was sentenced to thirty days incarceration at Parchman Farm plus court costs for stealing a hat."[65] Library of Congress photographs show that "juvenile offenders could be bought to serve as laborers for white planters in many Southern states from 1865 until the 1940s."[66] The results were often tragic—for instance, "[a] young girl at [a convict] camp in Hardmont, Georgia, in 1895, was repeatedly outraged [raped] by several of her guards, and finally died in childbirth while in camp."[67]

The convict leasing system became the revenue source for the judicial system, as "local Southern officials (e.g., sheriffs, deputies, judges, and other court officials) derived most of their compensation from 'conviction fees' charged to convicts for their arrest, conviction, and shipment to a private prison or non-prison company."[68] In fact, the revenue generated from convict leasing could be a sizable share of states' budgets. Ahmed White writes that "Alabama derived six to ten percent of its total state revenues from [convict] leasing."[69] One year, Ian F. Haney López notes, proceeds hit nearly 12 percent of Alabama's state budget.[70] Infrastructure produced by convict labor still exists, including streets and homes in Atlanta[71] and even the Capitol building in Texas.[72]

In America's privately funded elections, convict leasing fit right into the horrid gap between businesses willing to exploit cheap labor and politicians willing to take contributions to keep the gravy train rolling.

As Stephen P. Garvey observes, "Not surprisingly, a close relationship developed between lessees and state officials. Lawmakers supported the lessees with contracts and convicts, and lessees supported the lawmakers with contributions."[73] "As businessmen and officeholders jostled for and haggled over [convict] leas[ing]," Edward Ayers explains," widespread corruption grew up around the system."[74] A contemporary minister complained at the time: "While legislators are men, and money is money, the convict lease system will corrupt legislation."[75]

Beyond the campaign finance system, historian Ayers asserts, "first Republicans and then Democrats accepted bribes from prospective lessees to vote the right way or exercise their influence."[76] He added "the lease system simply offered too great an opportunity for corruption for many legislators to resist."[77] Often this political corruption related to convict leasing was shorthanded as being caused by so-called "penitentiary ring(s)." As contemporaneous writer Cable noted, "Legislatures and governors have, sometimes officially, sometimes unofficially allowed 'penitentiary rings' to become financial and political factors in the fortunes of their parties and their States."[78] W. E. B. Dubois summed it up: "The convict-lease system lowered the respect for courts, increased lawlessness, and put the states into the clutches of penitentiary 'rings.' The courts were brought into politics. . . . Finally, the state became a dealer in crime."[79]

Historian C. Vann Woodward found that "control over these Southern state 'slaves' was the foundation of several large fortunes, and in one case a great political dynasty. Robert McKee . . . wrote that the state warden of Alabama, John H. Bankhead 'grew rich in a few years on $2000 a year,' and manipulated the legislature at will. 'The penitentiary ring' is a power in the party,' [McKee] wrote privately, 'and it is a corrupt power.'"[80] Tennessee's legislature found that an anti-bribery law was needed because "corrupt practices have occurred in connection with what is known as the Penitentiary Ring, and other rings, whereby the interest of the State has suffered and public morality been outraged; and . . . it is openly charged that in order to influence legislation in the interest of said rings, 'lobbyists' have corruptly offered to bribe and influence the votes of members."[81] A contemporary observed that the demand for convicts in mining led "the Democratic politicians . . . to shoot and kill each other in order to get the spoils of their thieving legislation."[82] Michael Woodiwiss noted the problem of exploitation without accountability, writing that "prison officials, from the superintendents to the guards, took their share of the spoils in a system that paid everyone except those who did the work. . . . But no official was punished for taking bribes or for killing or maiming their [convict leasing] charges."[83]

Several White individuals who participated in the convict leasing system as politicians or businessmen became both rich and powerful.[84] In Florida convict leasing was described a "easy money."[85] In Louisiana, "according to the Louisiana Supreme Court in 1922, 'penal servitude' was 'customary.' . . . Servitude was . . . a way to make money: 'Louisiana officials always knew convicts were a valuable commodity.'"[86] As Garvey remarks, "It's probably no coincidence that in Georgia . . . , Joseph E. Brown, who had served as the state's governor and chief justice, became a millionaire as one of its biggest lessees."[87] Historian Edward Ayers further finds that "Jeremiah W. South, lessee of Kentucky convicts from 1869 to his death in 1880, supposedly exercised greater power over Kentucky's government than any other official, controlling a third of the legislators 'as absolutely as he controlled the convicts.'"[88] In Alabama, a governor went from leasing convicts to the Alabama and Chattanooga Railroad on one day to being the president of the railroad on another.[89] A retired Alabama official asked of the continuation of the convict leasing system in 1883, "Are we all thieves?"[90]

Convict leasing would last into the twentieth century. According to Jeffrey A. Drobney, the practice was phased out at different years in different states: "By the late 1890s . . . [u]nder pressure from their constituents, Louisiana officials ended the practice in 1901, Mississippi in 1906, Oklahoma in 1907, Georgia in 1907, and Texas in 1910."[91] But Ian F. Haney López and Douglas A. Blackmon have placed the end much later, during World War II.[92] As Gabriel J. Chin explains, "The Louisiana [convict] leas[ing] [system] proved problematic in that the prisoners were awarded based on patronage. . . . In 1901, Louisiana abolished the lease, and replaced it with a state agricultural plantation, Angola, now known as the Louisiana State Penitentiary. . . . Parolees were effectively leased out at least until 1944."[93] Thus, placing an official end date on convict leasing is difficult, as it varied from state to state and depends on how one defines the practice.

Most of the companies that leased convict labor no longer exist. But U.S. Steel, the first billion-dollar corporation, is still around.[94] As Haney López writes, "In 1907, U.S. Steel acquired ownership of a coal-mining interest [called Tennessee Coal and Iron or TCI] that was then largest customer of the Alabama convict slavery system. It quickly ramped up mining and the use of slave labor—paying one county $60,000 to acquire every prisoner arrested in 1908."[95] TCI was large, as evidenced by the fact that it "was one of the original 12 companies listed in the Dow Jones Industrial Index."[96] Matthew Mancini explains that "from 1888 to 1928. . . . the years of the TCI lease . . . virtually all convicts came under the almost complete control of the Tennessee Coal, Iron, and Railroad Company."[97] According to the Associated Press, "[U.S. Steel] has misrepresented its use of prison labor and has not acknowledge the men who died in its mines."[98]

COMPANIES STILL BENEFIT FROM PRISON LABOR

The problem of the corporate use of prison labor is still alive. While there is no more convict leasing in which a corporation takes over the control, housing, and feeding of an inmate (except in private prisons, in which case a corporation like CoreCivic or GEO Group owns the entire institution), corporations still benefit from work by inmates.[99]

Through a program overseen by the DOJ known as the Prison Industry Enhancement Certification Program (PIECP), private industry can use prison labor. As the DOJ explains, "PIECP programs place people who are incarcerated in realistic work environments . . . that will increase their potential for rehabilitation and meaningful employment on release."[100] Thus the DOJ frames this program as of benefit to inmates because they will get work experience.

However, this framing downplays the coercive nature of the work.[101] As of 2018, independent journalists found that the following corporations were using prison labor:

Abbott Laboratories, AT&T, AutoZone, Bank of America, Bayer, Berkshire Hathaway, Cargill, Caterpillar, Chevron, the former Chrysler Group, Costco Wholesale, John Deere, Eddie Bauer, Eli Lilly, ExxonMobil, Fruit of the Loom, GEICO, GlaxoSmithKline, Glaxo Wellcome, Hoffmann-

La Roche, International Paper, JanSport, Johnson & Johnson, Kmart, Koch Industries, Mary Kay, McDonald's, Merck, Microsoft, Motorola, Nintendo, Pfizer, Procter & Gamble, Quaker Oats, Sara Lee, Sears, Shell, Sprint, Starbucks, State Farm Insurance, United Airlines, UPS, Verizon, Victoria's Secret, Walmart and Wendy's."[102]

This is a veritable "who's who" of corporate actors.

In 2022, the American Civil Liberties Union (ACLU) issued a report, *Captive Labor*, which named names of corporations that were using U.S. prison labor in their supply chains.[103] For example, Walmart benefits from the prison labor used by one of its partners, the Jacobs Trading Company, which strips the branding off of returned items so that they can be resold.[104] Other companies using prison labor include Husky Hogs LLC in Kansas, Tyson Foods in North Carolina and, "in Mississippi[] . . . Arby's, Church's Chicken, McDonald's, and Popeyes."[105]

Tracking the use of prison labor is particularly difficult with food, as a consumer may have no idea where raw materials like milk originated. *Captive Labor* traced the prison labor from inmates in Colorado and South Carolina to milk sold to the Dairy Farmers of America, which in turn sells to customers under the brands Borden, Breakstone, Plugrá, and T. G. Lee Dairy.[106] T. G. Lee Dairy products are sold in supermarkets.[107] Meanwhile, Plugrá makes "European style" butter that shows up on the shelves of high-end shops.[108] The ACLU traced a similar milk trail from Colorado Correctional Industries to Leprino Foods, which supplies mozzarella to Domino's, Papa John's, and Pizza Hut.[109]

Just like convict leasing, the state benefits financially from letting private companies use inmate labor. As the ACLU documented, "Colorado Correctional Industries . . . sold goods and services to around 100 private companies, which generated more than $6.2 million in revenue for the state correctional industries program in 2020."[110] In Louisiana the state sold $2.4 million worth of corn and soybeans from 2017 to 2020 and sold $5 million in livestock over the same period. The ACLU noted that "Utah Correctional Industries sold goods and services to almost a thousand private companies, including such major corporation as 3M Company, Allstate Insurance Company, American Apparel, American Express, Apple Inc., FedEx, Frito Lay Inc., Fujifilm North America, . . . Hewlett-Packard, Hickory Farms, Infiniti Motor Company, Little

Caesars Enterprises, Lowe's, KFC, OfficeMax, Pepsi-Co, . . . Sara Lee Corporation, T-Mobile, . . . and Xerox Corporation."[111] In other words, many states and companies are benefiting from the undercompensated labor of prisoners.

In Arizona, the state allows for contracts with private business to employ inmates that are outside of the DOJ's PIECP program.[112] Hickman Family Farms paid Arizona $7 million in 2020 for inmates to process eggs and care for chickens.[113] Taylor Farms, which sells fresh produce, paid Arizona $2.2 million for prison labor; Taylor Farms then "supplies . . . Chipotle, Costco, Kroger, McDonald's, Pizza Hut, Ralphs, Safeway, Subway, Target, Walmart, and Whole Foods Market."[114]

Aramark, a $16.2-billion, multinational food services conglomerate, was sued in 2020 for making prisoners work without pay.[115] Hopefully this lawsuit will stop this behavior. For years, Starbucks used prison labor though one of its contractors, Signature Packaging Solutions.[116] After public pressure, Starbucks stopped the practice.

Depressingly, some states have reintroduced chain gangs.[117] But there is hope. Nebraska in 2020 voted to end the use of slave labor.[118] A nascent trend exists of states moving away from the slavery that is still permitted under the Thirteenth Amendment. This is one of many reasons why restoring voting rights to individuals who have experienced incarceration is so critical.

VOTING RIGHTS' IMPLICATIONS OF CIVIL DEATH

Supreme Court Justice Hugo Black once observed that "no right is more precious in a free country than that of having a voice in the election."[119] If the ability to vote is the measure of full citizenship, then America has long had first-class citizens who could vote and second-class citizens who could not. At the founding, only 6 percent of Americans could vote.[120] During the 2024 election, the difference between first-class and second-class citizenship was largely demarcated by whether an American had a felony conviction.[121]

In taking away a person's right to vote away upon conviction for a crime, America is an outlier.[122] In most Western democracies, prisoners still have the right while they are in prison.[123] For instance, the European Court of Human Rights in 2004 ruled that a UK law disenfranchising inmates was a human rights violation.[124] In America, Vermont and Maine act like the rest of the world's mature democracies.[125] In these states, prisoners retain voting rights while incarcerated.[126] In 2021, Washington, DC, followed suit.[127] But, for the remaining forty-eight states, individuals lose their right to vote while incarcerated.[128]

America is also an anomaly in withholding an individual's right to vote even after they have finished their prison sentences.[129] Whether a citizen returning from prison has their civil rights restored depends on the state.[130] New York restores voting rights. In Virginia, however, they can be lost for life.[131] According to the National Council of State Legislatures, which tracks these laws, "In 21 states, felons lose their voting rights only while incarcerated, and receive automatic restoration upon release. In 16 states, felons lose their voting rights during incarceration, and . . . while on parole and/or probation. . . . In 11 states felons lose their voting rights indefinitely for some crimes, or require a governor's pardon in order for voting rights to be restored."[132] In 2023, Michigan became the first state to register people to vote automatically when they left prison.[133] But, in most states, the right to vote remains out of reach for many who have served their time.

Between 1865 and 1880, while states were instituting convict leasing, at least thirteen states enacted felony disenfranchisement laws.[134] These laws were often racially motivated.[135] Future US senator Carter Glass in Virginia asserted that the purpose of the felon disenfranchisement law was to "eliminate the darkey as a political factor in this State . . . so that in no single county of the Commonwealth will there be the least concern felt for the complete supremacy of the white race in the affairs of government."[136] Courts have generally shown a complete lack of empathy for those impacted by felony disenfranchisement laws. As the Ninth Circuit wrote in 2010, "[O]nce a felon is properly disenfranchised a state is at liberty to keep him in that status indefinitely and never revisit that determination."[137] Felony disenfranchisement laws materialized as early as the 1600s, in what would later become the United States.[138]

Even though modern Americans are spatially and temporally separate from ancient Greece, these decrepit legal concepts of civil death still infect American laws. The highest state courts have upheld felony disenfranchisement, including in a case from the Alabama Supreme Court, which ruled—while invoking Greek imagery—that "it is quite common also to deny the right of suffrage . . . to . . . [those] convicted of infamous crimes. The manifest purpose is to preserve the purity of the ballot box. . . . The presumption is, that one rendered infamous by conviction of felony, . . . is unfit to exercise the privilege of suffrage . . . upon terms of equality with freemen who are clothed by the State with the toga of political citizenship."[139] This "purity of the ballot box" argument is based in the ancient notion that ex-felons will corrupt voting by "spreading their taint to the electoral process."[140]

Courts have upheld felony disenfranchisement in the twentieth century. Article 2 of California's Constitution said in 1972: "The Legislature shall . . . shall provide that no . . . person convicted of an infamous crime, nor person convicted of embezzlement or misappropriation of public money, shall exercise the privileges of an elector."[141] This was challenged in *Richardson v. Ramirez* as being unconstitutional.[142] The Supreme Court upheld California's felony disfranchisement pursuant to the U.S. Constitution's Penalty Clause, found in Section 2 of the Fourteenth Amendment,[143] which states: "Representatives shall be apportioned among the several States according to their respective numbers . . . *But when the right to vote . . . is . . . in any way abridged, except for participation in rebellion, or other crime*, the basis of representation therein shall be reduced."[144] The Penalty Clause was meant to incentivize Southern states after the Civil War to enfranchise their entire male adult population, both Black and White. If these states disenfranchised Black men, the "penalty" was that their states would lose seats in Congress. However, because of the wording of the clause, states would not lose congressional seats if the only people disenfranchised were ex-Confederates or criminals.[145]

The Supreme Court held that disenfranchisement did not violate equal protection.[146] This ruling irked Justice Thurgood Marshall, who wrote in dissent: "It is clear that [the Penalty Clause] was not intended and should not be construed to be a limitation on the other sections of the Fourteenth Amendment."[147] He also noted that "constitutional concepts of equal protection are not immutably frozen like insects trapped in Devonian amber."[148]

Reformers have tried to invalidate felony disenfranchisement, using a multitude of constitutional arguments. All have failed. The Supreme Court has rejected the argument that felony disenfranchisement violates that the Eighth Amendment's prohibition on cruel and unusual punishment.[149] Courts have found that felon disenfranchisement laws are not a bill of attainder, nor an ex post facto law.[150] Finally, they do not violate the First Amendment.[151]

The bigger picture is that the oppression of convict leasing and disenfranchisement historically worked hand in hand to harm Blacks. As the Alabama Voting Right Project explained to Congress: "Black Codes, the convict leasing system, and . . . criminal disenfranchisement provision all worked together to enforce white supremacy . . . The State convicted black citizens of . . . Black Code violations in the tens of thousands, leased them out to private entities for forced labor . . . and then excluded them permanently from the political franchise on the basis of those convictions."[152] Black Codes and convict leasing have, thankfully, been left in the dustbin of history, yet felony disenfranchisement—the fruit of the same poison tree—remains.

FLORIDA'S FELONY DISENFRANCHISEMENT

In Florida, despite recent attempts at reform by Florida voters, most individuals with a felony conviction will remain disenfranchised for the rest of their lives.[153] In the twenty-first century, felony disenfranchisement laws impacted 6.1 million American citizens, with a disproportionate impact on potential Black voters.[154] Of that 6.1. million, roughly 1.4 million lived in Florida.[155] In Florida, disenfranchisement is imposed on all persons convicted of a felony as a "collateral consequence" of a conviction.[156] To add to the Kafkaesque nature of felony disenfranchisement in the state, Florida has some very odd felonies. As voting rights advocate Desmond Meade told *60 Minutes*, "Releasing helium-filled balloons in the air is a third-degree felony in Florida. . . . Catching a lobster whose tail is too short, disturbing turtle nesting eggs, driving on a suspended license. Those are the types of crimes that if a person is convicted of, they would lose the right [to vote]."[157]

Prior to 2018, all felons in Florida were presumptively disenfranchised for life.[158] This policy dates back to before Florida was part of the United States.[159] It continued when Florida became a state in 1845.[160] Then the state kept disenfranchisement in the 1868 Florida Constitution after the Civil War.[161] In 1968, the Constitutional Revision Commission decided to leave this provision in the Florida Constitution, but with some differences.[162] The 1968 provision changed the class of individuals who could be disenfranchised from those who committed certain misdemeanors to only those with a felony.[163]

Voters tried to restore voting rights to most ex-felons in Florida in 2018 through a ballot initiative called "Amendment 4."[164] It said: "A person who has been disqualified from voting based on a felony conviction for an offense other than murder or a felony sexual offense must have such disqualification terminated and his or her voting rights restored pursuant to s. 4, Art. VI of the State Constitution upon the completion of all terms of his or her sentence, including parole or probation."[165] Amendment 4 passed by a supermajority in 2018,[166] and it became effective on January 8, 2019.[167] But then the Florida legislature swooped in to add language that was not in the ballot measure, which required felons to pay off fees and fines before their voting rights could be restored through legislation called S.B. 7066.[168] The fees and fines (a.k.a. legal financial obligations, or LFOs) that ex-felons owe can be dauntingly high. Pro Publica reported that, "on top of the fines and restitution, Florida layers on court fees that can run into the hundreds of dollars. Together, a voter's debt can run into the thousands, a financial hole that some may never climb out of."[169]

Plaintiffs challenged S.B. 7066, arguing that the requirement that felons must pay their fees and fines to get their right to vote back is unconstitutional.[170] According to political scientist Daniel Smith, 77.4 percent of individuals who have fulfilled the terms of their sentences and are thereby eligible to vote under Amendment 4 still have outstanding LFOs, which, under S.B. 7066, made them illegible to vote.[171] The trial judge referred to the system that Florida had constructed as a "pay-to-vote scheme,"[172] and he struck down S.B. 7066.[173]

In 2020 the Eleventh Circuit upheld the Florida's law, S.B. 7066, that undermined the restorative promise of Amendment 4.[174] The Supreme Court refused to take up the case.[175] Thus Florida's pay-to-vote scheme was blessed by the federal judiciary. The impact of the Eleventh Circuit's ruling was immediate, as the 2020 presidential election was just months away. It "disqualified nearly 900,000 individuals with previous felony convictions from voting in the November 2020 election."[176]

Years later, Florida still has not set up a system for felons to find out exactly how much money they owe to get their voting rights restored.[177] As the Brennan Center notes, "When a returning citizen requests a report from the Florida Department of Law Enforcement (FDLE) . . . [its] reports often mistakenly state that there are no fines, costs, or restitution ordered in relation to a conviction."[178] Then there is the added absurdity that Florida charges money to check how much a person owes.[179]

American states do not have to keep felony disenfranchisement. This is a policy choice. Drafters of the Model Penal Code, the American Law Institute (ALI), proposed that disenfranchisement coincide only with a felon's term of imprisonment.[180] Similarly, the American Bar Association (ABA) has argued that "failure to pay court fees and fines should never result in the deprivation of fundamental rights, including the right to vote."[181]

FLORIDA VOTING FRAUD SQUAD

Adding insult to injury, Florida decided that keeping most returning citizens off the voting rolls for their inability to pay fines was not enough. They also decided to prosecute individuals who guessed incorrectly about how Amendment 4 worked. In 2022, the Florida legislature created an Office of Election Crimes and Security to prosecute individuals who voted but were ineligible.[182]

Shortly before the 2022 election, when Governor DeSantis was on the ballot, the Voting Fraud Squad made twenty highly-publicized arrests of individuals who had voted in 2020.[183] The arrests took place directly preceding a press conference in which the governor highlighted them.[184] The arrests included overkill, such as using a helicopter to arrest only one person.[185]

As local newspapers reported, "Body-worn camera footage recorded by local police captured the confusion and outrage of . . . residents who found themselves in handcuffs for casting a ballot."[186] One fifty-five-year-old woman reacted to her arrest at 6:52 a.m. as she was planning to leave for work by exclaiming, "oh my God."[187] One reason for these individuals' bewilderment was that Florida had issued them voter registration cards.[188]

The first prosecution from the Voting Fraud Squad resulted in two years of probation.[189] The man involved maintained his innocence. He told the press: "I don't think that I willingly did . . . anything wrong. So I would like to fight to get it dismissed."[190] The prosecution of the remainder of the individuals fell apart quickly.[191] According to the Daily Beast, "Of the 20 cases, six have been dismissed, and five have resulted in plea deals carrying no jail time."[192]

The Voting Fraud Squad has drawn criticism for selective prosecutions, as their arrest sweep disproportionately involved Democratic and Black people. One reporter called it "a bumbling statewide crackdown."[193] One case the Florida government missed was that of a Republican who allegedly voted three times before she was a US citizen; she was caught by the FBI.[194] Four other Republican voters who voted twice in 2020 and lived in the heavily Republican enclave called "The Villages" also escaped their wrath.[195]

There is a partisan valence to the felony disenfranchisement debate. Modern-day Republicans typically champion stripping voting rights from returning citizens. Marty Conners of the Alabama Republican Party clarified the reason why: "As frank as I can be, we're opposed to [restoring voting rights] because felons don't tend to vote Republican."[196] Data from Florida after Amendment 4 showed that more returning citizens registered as Democrats (50 percent) than Republicans (24 percent).[197] If this motivated Florida's S.B. 7066 or the Voting Fraud Squad, then it constitutes the most rank partisan manipulation.

Data of national political spending shows that over the past three elections corporations preferred Republicans (70 percent) to Democrats (26 percent) in 2022; they preferred Republicans (76 percent) to Democrats (20 percent) in 2020; and they preferred Republicans (82 percent) to Democrats (15 percent) in 2018.[198] These patterns were even more extreme in Florida in its last two gubernatorial elections. In his 2022 reelection campaign, Ron DeSantis had nearly 6.5 times as much money ($210,869,792) as his challenger, Charlie Crist ($32,309,599).[199] In 2018, DeSantis had over three times as much money ($60,158,638) as his rival, Andrew Gillum ($18,877,471).[200] Some of the differential was attributable to corporate donors giving far more money to Ron DeSantis (to be discussed in more detail).

In 2022, Democrat Charlie Crist received donations from the following corporations: International Payout Systems Inc ($115,000);[201] GHH Inc. ($50,724);[202] P&T Construction Inc. ($50,000);[203] Retail Services & Systems ($35,000);[204] Golden Rule Financial Corp. ($27,087);[205] Legal Consultants Inc. ($25,000);[206] PrintConsultant Inc. ($20,000);[207] Integrated Data Technology Inc. ($20,000);[208] S/R Service & Support Corp. ($15,000);[209] City Wise Florida Inc. ($10,750);[210] and Abrikant International Corp. ($10,000).[211] Thus Crist got in total at least $373,561 from corporate sources for his failed run for governor in 2022 against DeSantis.

In 2018, Democrat Andrew Gillum received corporate support from the following: Liberty Mutual Co. ($3,000);[212] Brown & Brown of Louisiana ($3,000);[213] Universal Bond Inc. ($3,000);[214] American Income Life Insurance Co. ($3,000);[215] Frontier Communications ($3,000);[216] Desoto Beach Development Corp. ($3,000);[217] Halifax Injury Physicians ($3,000);[218] Johnson Armor Correctional Health Inc. ($3,000);[219] Servium Group Inc. ($3,000);[220] and Espmedia Corp. ($2,998).[221] Thus Gillum received in total at least $30,998 from corporate sources in 2018 in his run against DeSantis.

Meanwhile corporate donors to Ron DeSantis include Disruptor Inc. who gave $500,000 to his 2022 reelection.[222] Sun Labs USA gave DeSantis $509,200 for his 2022 reelection.[223] Hutson Companies gave DeSantis $405,000 for his 2022 reelection.[224] Florida Care Inc. gave DeSantis $400,000 for his 2022 reelection.[225] Phillips & Jordan Inc. gave DeSantis for his 2022 reelection.[226] JM Family Enterprises gave DeSantis $325,000 for his 2022 reelection.[227] Daytona Toyota gave DeSantis $325,000 for his 2022 reelection.[228] Fidelity National Financial gave DeSantis $325,000 for his 2022 reelection.[229] Hillcour Inc. gave DeSantis $312,409 for his 2022 reelection.[230] IGAS USA gave DeSantis $300,000 for his 2022 reelection.[231] Anderson Columbia Co. gave DeSantis $277,650 for his 2022 reelection.[232] Testing Matters gave DeSantis $258,308 for his 2022 reelection.[233] Dosal Tobacco gave $50,000 to DeSantis for his 2018 election and $200,000 for his 2022 reelection.[234] Eisenhower Management Inc. gave DeSantis $250,000 for his 2022 reelection.[235] United Automobile Insurance Co. gave $200,000 to DeSantis for his 2018 election.[236] Southern Wine & Spirits gave DeSantis $200,000 for his 2022 reelection.[237]

CFG Community Bank gave DeSantis $200,000 for his 2022 reelection.[238] JL Holding Corp. gave DeSantis $200,000 for his 2022 reelection.[239] South Development Corp. gave DeSantis $200,000 for his 2022 reelection.[240] Payward Inc. gave DeSantis $200,000 for his 2022 reelection.[241] Hudson Capital Group gave $25,000 to DeSantis for his 2018 election and $160,000 for his 2022 reelection.[242] JB Coxwell Contracting Inc. gave $100,000 to DeSantis for his 2018 election and $75,500 for his 2022 reelection.[243] ABC Fine Wine & Spirits gave DeSantis $175,000 for his 2022 reelection.[244] SPF Roofing Systems Inc. gave $23,000 to DeSantis for his 2018 election and $143,000 for his 2022 reelection.[245] Ring Power Corp. gave $35,000 to DeSantis for his 2018 election and $125,500 for his 2022 reelection.[246] Middlesex Corp. gave $115,000 to DeSantis for his 2018 election and $45,500 for his 2022 reelection.[247] Publix Super Markets gave DeSantis $165,000 for his 2022 reelection.[248] Nomi Health Inc. gave DeSantis $152,250 for his 2022 reelection.[249] Dentaquest gave DeSantis $150,000 for his 2022 reelection.[250] R & L Transfer Inc. gave DeSantis $150,000 for his 2022 reelection.[251] Lewis Bear Co. gave $50,000 to DeSantis for his 2018 election and $95,000 for his 2022 reelection.[252] St Joe Co. gave $28,000 to DeSantis for his 2018 election and $113,783 for his 2022 reelection.[253] ICI Homes gave DeSantis $136,071 for his 2022 reelection.[254] American Property & Casualty Insurance Associates gave $85,000 to DeSantis for his 2018 election and $50,000 for his 2022 reelection.[255] Sunshine Gasoline Distributors gave $78,000 to DeSantis for his 2018 election and $56,311 for his 2022 reelection.[256] Jacksonville Kennel Club gave $6,000 to DeSantis for his 2018 election and $128,000 for his 2022 reelection.[257] Managed Care of North America gave $125,605 to DeSantis for his 2018 election.[258] Palm Beach Kennel Club gave $75,000 to DeSantis for his 2018 election and $50,000 for his 2022 reelection.[259] Vecellio Group gave DeSantis $125,000 for his 2022 reelection.[260] Cheney Brothers Inc. gave $3,000 to DeSantis for his 2018 election and $112,500 for his 2022 reelection.[261] And Launched gave DeSantis $125,000 for his 2022 reelection.[262] This totals $13,455,005 from private corporations for his two gubernatorial election campaigns.

In addition to these privately held firms, DeSantis also received the following money from publicly traded corporations in his two runs for governor: TECO Energy gave DeSantis $367,750 for his 2022 reelection.[263] MasTec Inc. gave DeSantis $300,000 for his 2022 reelection.[264]

Charter Communications gave DeSantis $303,000 for his 2022 reelection.[265] Dream Finders Homes gave DeSantis $150,000 for his 2022 reelection.[266] United Health Group gave DeSantis $275,000 for his 2022 reelection.[267] Centene Corp gave DeSantis $120,000 for his 2022 reelection.[268] Walt Disney gave DeSantis $106,809 for his 2022 reelection.[269] Florida Power & Light (FPL) gave DeSantis $30,000 for his 2022 reelection;[270] FPL's parent company NextEra Energy gave $12,000 in the same election.[271] Reynolds American gave $50,000 to DeSantis for his 2018 election and $103,500 for his 2022 reelection.[272] Humana gave DeSantis $150,229 for his 2022 reelection.[273] International Game Technology gave DeSantis $103,000 for his 2022 reelection.[274] AT&T gave DeSantis $80,000 in his 2022 reelection.[275] Duke Energy gave DeSantis $25,000 in his 2022 reelection.[276] Finally, private prison company GEO Group have DeSantis $100,000 for his 2018 election.[277] This was an additional $2,116,288 from publicly traded corporations for DeSantis in his runs for governor.

If this corporate campaign support is what motivated Florida's S.B. 7066 or the Voting Fraud Squad, then it stands as an example of gross pandering to corporate campaign spenders, who in Florida can give directly to candidates in state elections. Right now there is no smoking gun, but there is plenty of corporate campaign cash and lobbying.[278]

4

CORPORATE BRIBERY

HAVING YOUR CAKE AND EATING IT, TOO

There is a strange monument to greed located in Albany County, Wyoming: a sixty-foot stone pyramid adorned with the faces of Oakes Ames and his brother Oliver Ames, built by the Union Pacific Railroad.[1]

Selling shovels may not seem like the route to riches, but Oakes Ames made his first fortune selling shovels, which were in high demand because of the 1849 gold rush in California. He earned the nickname the "King of Spades."[2] He was elected to Congress as a Republican from Massachusetts.[3] Near the end of the Civil War, in 1864, President Lincoln would set Ames on a task that would unravel his life: running the Union Pacific Railroad.[4]

The Union Pacific (UP) played a key role in completing the transcontinental railroad. Under Ames's leadership, with the help of UP vice president Thomas Durant and promoter George Train, the railroad outsourced the building of tracks to another company, Crédit Mobilier of America.[5] The scam was that many of the same shareholders in Union Pacific were also shareholders in Crédit Mobilier.[6] Moreover, they were also UP directors, which gave them the power to control Union Pacific.[7] Like the "penitentiary rings" described in chapter 3, according to Paul Kens, "the group soon became known as the Pacific Railroad Ring. Because they controlled the board of directors of the Union Pacific, the ring was able to award building contracts to Crédit Mobilier, giving wildly favorable terms and paying exorbitant prices for the work."[8] And "Credit Mobilier charged the [Union Pacific] tens of millions of dollars more than it spent on actual construction contracts."[9] When Crédit Mobilier overcharged UP for work, its shareholders got wildly rich. In fact, "Credit Mobilier stockholders were able to pay themselves dividends of 348 percent in a single year."[10]

One aspect of the scam's brazenness was that it wasn't a secret; the press reported how it worked as early as 1869.[11] What was secret was who was in on the scam, including members of Congress and the Grant administration.[12] That news broke in 1872 in the *New York Sun* after a tip from W. H. Holcomb, a disgruntled investor who wanted more Crédit Mobilier stock but was refused by Congressman Ames.[13] Ames told Holcomb that all of the stock needed to go congressmen and senators because "we want more friends in this Congress."[14] The stockholders of Crédit Mobilier read like a "who's who" of political power players in Washington, DC:

> Speaker of the house and future vice president Schuyler Colfax . . . signed on. So did Massachusetts senator and future vice president Henry Wilson, Ohio representative and future president James Garfield, . . . , [and] John Bingham of Ohio. . . . Like Ames, they were Republicans all, and all voted on railroad matters. . . . Ames dispensed securities in blocks of 10 or 20, often keeping them under his name to simplify matters. . . . Ames kept track of all offers and transactions in a little black ledger.[15]

Suddenly, the public knew that "to keep Congress quiet, Credit Mobilier directors sold stock at nominal prices to representatives and senators, and even to [the] Vice President."[16] Some have further accused Ames of distributing "cash bribes while selling shares at bargain rates to Senate and House members."[17] Ames's black ledger became a key piece of evidence in the congressional investigations into Crédit Mobilier, but, when "called before a Capitol Hill committee, Oakes Ames insisted that nothing illegal had conspired."[18]

Meanwhile, the risk of UP going belly up after being bilked by Crédit Mobilier really fell to US taxpayers who had provided subsidies in government bonds that a bankrupt UP would not be able to repay.[19] As Kens explains, the Crédit Mobilier scandal "brought to the surface an already growing public concern that, after making vast fortunes for promoters, financiers, and entrepreneurs, the Pacific railroads would not be able to repay the enormous sums of money the government had loaned to them to build their railroads."[20] In other words, while the profits from Crédit Mobilier would go into private hands, the danger of default would land on the public.[21]

This period is sometimes referred to as the "Gilded Age"—as Mark Twain called it—but others called it the "Great Barbeque" to capture the vast wealth that seeped from the US government into the hands of private profiteers.[22] Moreover, "many people also came to believe that railroad entrepreneurs were getting excessively wealthy by feeding at the public trough."[23]

After news broke that some of the Crédit Mobilier shareholders were politicians, Congress launched investigations. The investigative committee concluded that "only [Congressmen] James Brooks and Oakes Ames were influenced by corrupt motives, and they recommend[ed] the expulsion of these members."[24] Oakes Ames went from being known as the King of Spades to the King of Frauds.[25] In the end, "on Feb. 27, 1873, the House censured Ames and Brooks for enhancing their personal wealth by using their political influence."[26] The committee recommended that Ames be expelled from Congress because "[his] presence . . . tends to bring the body into contempt and disgrace."[27] After "extensive congressional hearings were held to appease an angry public . . . no one was convicted of a crime."[28] As a contemporaneous report put it: "The Committee [investigating Crédit Mobilier], after deliberately showing the denials of the implicated Congressmen to be false, declare that these gentlemen were innocent. . . . The people are at a loss . . . to comprehend the mental status of a Committee which can recommend the expulsion of Mr. Ames for bribing Members of Congress, and yet solemnly declare that they have no evidence that any one has been bribed."[29]

One of the acts revealed during the Senate's investigation of Crédit Mobilier was that its original founder, Thomas Durant, was also a huge contributor (to the tune of $10,000) to the campaign of senator James Harlan, who was initially implicated in the scandal.[30] Then-vice president Schuyler Colfax, when trying to explain away a $1,200 dividend from Crédit Mobilier, admitted that during the 1868 election he had received $4,000 from a stationary manufacturer, George F. Nesbitt, who went on to receive a contract with the U.S. Post Office.[31] But this was far worse than the typical modern campaign finance scandal, where money does not typically land in the bank account of a politician, because, by contrast, members of Congress, two future vice presidents, and a future president were all directly bribed with cheap

Crédit Mobilier stock. At the end of the day, these corrupt politicians got to keep the money.

After all he had done, Ames was not expelled from Congress, nor was anyone else involved in the scandal.[32] In other words, those who got rich through the Crédit Mobilier scam stayed rich. One of the only political impacts was that Vice President Colfax was dropped from Ulysses Grant's reelection ticket in 1872 only to be replaced by another Crédit Mobilier shareholder, Henry Wilson.[33]

When the United States sued UP for the Crédit Mobilier overcharges, the Supreme Court gave the government no relief.[34] The crooks, including those in Congress and the Old Executive Office Building, got away with it. As PBS once put it: "No criminal or civil charges were filed against any of the Crédit Mobilier's scoundrels."[35] With no consequences, this scandal did not inspire any reforms either. If anything, it encouraged businessmen and politicians in the Gilded Age to act more profligately and to scam the public.

THE OILY TEMPEST IN THE TEAPOT DOME SCANDAL

On April 28, 1924, at the Midland National Bank in Washington Courthouse, Ohio, a man named John McGrain asked for the president of the bank Mally Daugherty and arrested him.[36] McGrain was a long way from home. He worked for the sergeant at arms of the US Senate. McGrain had been sent by a congressional committee to arrest Mally because he had been ignoring congressional subpoenas to produce the bank's deposit ledger.[37]

Up until a month before his arrest, Mally's brother Harry Daugherty was the attorney general.[38] But on March 28, 1924, Harry resigned in disgrace as a result of the Teapot Dome scandal.[39] The Senate committee arresting Mally was investigating Teapot Dome and the reason why Attorney General Daugherty had failed to prosecute key players in the bribery scheme, including secretary of the interior Albert Fall and oilmen Harry Sinclair and Edward Doheny.[40]

Banker Mally Daugherty was taken into federal custody.[41] He submitted a writ of *habeas corpus* to a local federal judge, asking to be freed.[42] Judge Andrew Cochran agreed with Mally that the Senate did not have the power to arrest him and set him free.[43] The Senate ap-

[55]

pealed Mally's case to the Supreme Court in 1924. Then the Supreme Court did something rather unusual. It sat on the case for three years, only deciding it in 1927.[44]

What was going on? Attorney General Harry Daugherty and the president he served, Warren G. Harding, were part of a group derisively known as the "Ohio Gang."[45] A historian called Harry Daugherty "the Rasputin of the Harding administration."[46] One of Harry's lieutenants was a shady character by the name of Jess Smith who was also a member of the gang. Smith acted as a gatekeeper for Harry, sitting in anteroom outside of his office in the DOJ without being on the payroll. Smith allegedly told people that he could make DOJ investigations disappear for the right price.[47]

The Ohio Gang came to power one year into Prohibition, when the Constitution banned alcohol.[48] But that did not stop them from getting their hands on hooch. One biographer of First Lady Florence Harding wrote that, "through the Justice Department, [Jess] Smith had access to whiskey supplies confiscated by Prohibition agents, and some of the booze went directly to the White House."[49] The Ohio Gang had plenty at 1625 K. Street NW, known as the "Little Green House," where they essentially ran a speakeasy frequented by President Harding.[50]

Harding was known for cheating on his wife, drinking, and gambling. He once startled reporters at the National Press Club by stating, "'It's a good thing I am not a woman, I would always be pregnant. I can't say no.'"[51] Harding historians have had even more to chew on after the Library of Congress released love letters between Harding and his mistress Carrie Phillips. In one letter, Harding expresses his "mad, tender, devoted, ardent, eager, passion-wild, jealous, reverent, wistful, hungry, happy love" for her.[52] In steamier letters, Harding refers to his penis as "Jerry."[53] Harding would not live long enough for the Teapot Dome scandal to engulf him; he died in 1923.[54]

Albert Fall had been a senator from New Mexico and a gambling buddy of Harding when he was a senator from Ohio. Harding was an unlikely president, as he was most delegates' third choice at the Republican convention in 1920. When the supporters for the frontrunners deadlocked, Harding saw his opening.[55] Harry Daugherty was one of Harding's campaign managers. When Harding won the presidency, his poker buddy Fall became secretary of the interior. In this capacity Fall had control over oil fields that had been under naval dominion during World War I and strictly off limits for drilling, much to the chagrin of oilmen.[56]

In post–World War I peacetime, the oil fields were under Secretary Fall's purview, and oilmen eager to tap the reserves showed up, including Harry Sinclair of the Mammoth Oil Company and Edward Doheny of Pan American Petroleum. Fall gave Sinclair exclusive rights to drill in Teapot Dome, Wyoming, and Doheny the rights to drill in the Buena Vista Hills, California. In exchange for these lucrative drilling rights, Sinclair gave Fall a $269,000 bribe (worth roughly $2.5 million today) in cash and Liberty Bonds and Doheny gave Fall a $100,000 bribe (worth roughly $1 million today).[57] Sinclair apparently showed up at Fall's ranch personally dangling money.[58] Doheny was more indirect: "[His] son carried $100,000 in a little black bag to Fall in Washington."[59] The value of the Teapot Dome lease was $100 million at the time.[60]

Fall might have gotten away with taking the bribes, but for two things: nosy neighbors in Fall's hometown and around Teapot Dome. Neighbors in Wyoming saw Sinclair's Mammoth Oil trucks driving into the formerly off-limits oil reserve, and the neighbors in New Mexico reported remarkable improvements on Fall's previously ramshackle ranch.[61] Edward W. Knappman relates, "Soon Senator Robert M. LaFollette . . . [said] Fall's Interior Department was 'the sluice-way for ninety percent of the corruption in government.'"[62] The question for curious Senators was: "How did Albert Fall become so rich so fast?"[63]

Fall claimed that his wealth was really from a $100,000 loan from Ned McLean, the publisher of the *Washington Post* and a millionaire who bought his wife the Hope Diamond. McLean initially backed up Fall's version of events.[64] But this fell apart when Senate investigators started looking through McLean's bank accounts: there was no payment to Fall. They also discovered that McLean did not have $100,000 in his bank account to give to anyone. He might have been a millionaire, but apparently he wasn't liquid, or particularly honest. As Alice Roosevelt (daughter of President Teddy Roosevelt) quipped, McLean was a man with "no chin and no character."[65]

Investigators found that while Fall had a meager income from his time in government, he had miraculously spent $140,000 on improvements to his ranch, and, perhaps more damningly, Liberty Bonds in

Fall's account had the same serial numbers as those previously in Sinclair's account.[66] These bonds were the fruit of Crédit Mobilier–style scam. As described by Bruce Bliven, the separate scheme was hatched by oilmen who met in a hotel in New York on November 17, 1921:

> Besides Sinclair they included Colonel A. E. Humphreys; . . . Colonel Robert W. Stewart, chairman of the board of the Standard Oil Company of Indiana; James E. O'Neil of the Prairie Oil and Gas Company; and Henry M. Blackmer of the Midwest Refining Company. . . . A dummy corporation, the Continental Trading Company, Ltd., had been set up in Canada for the sole purpose of buying 33,333,333 1/3 barrels of oil from Colonel Humphreys at the going rate of $1.50 a barrel, and instantly reselling it at an unwarranted profit of twenty-five cents a barrel to the companies of Sinclair and O'Neil . . . [resulting in] fifty million dollars [for Humphreys].[67]

The profits from the dummy corporation, Continental Trading Company, ended up being $3 million before investigators started sniffing around, and Continental was quickly liquidated. The profits were converted into Liberty Bonds. As Bliven notes, "Turning [this money] into Liberty Bonds [was] an incredible blunder, since the bonds and their coupons were numbered, and the latter could be traced."[68] This is one reason why Fall was caught with Sinclair's bonds, which had come from Continental's liquidation because the bond numbers matched.

Congressional investigators also kept tripping over the lewd goings-on at the Little Green House, including the attorney general's various money-making rackets. One accusation was that Daugherty and Smith would sell liquor licenses to bootleggers. Then-bootlegger and later famous bourbon-maker George Remus claimed that he had paid Smith for such a license during Prohibition. The *New York Times* reported that after Remus paid $300,000 to Smith, Remus then processed 900,000 gallons of alcohol, and that Remus was told by Smith that he would not go to jail.[69] Another accusation was that Daugherty and Smith sold pardons.[70] As one author summed up: "The Ohio Gang eagerly solicited bribes from bootleggers seeking immunity, men in jail who wanted to be released, [and] men under indictment who wanted the proceedings dropped."[71] Under Daugherty leadership, "the facilities of the [DOJ] were for sale to the highest bidder."[72] This presented a huge rule-of-law problem.

As Teapot Dome investigations heated up, President Harding called Jess Smith to the White House to tell him that he was likely to be arrested.[73] Smith died the next day, on May 30, 1923, of an apparent suicide at the Wardman Park Hotel.[74] Jess's ex-wife, Roxy Stinson, testified before the Senate committee investigating Teapot Dome. Roxy and Jess had only been married for a year and half, but they remained friendly. Jess contacted her frequently when he was in Washington, as evidenced by letters and telegrams Roxy produced to the Senate. While Jess received more money from his various schemes running out the DOJ and the Little Green House, he sent Roxy a steady stream of cash, bonds, and stock tips. A reporter remarked that Roxy's appearances before the Senate committee "had all the atmosphere of a murder trial, combined with the bated breath excitement of opening King Tut's tomb."[75]

One of the remarkable things Roxy disclosed was that Jess and Harry were likely in a gay relationship, though she did not use that nomenclature. She said, "[Jess] was in constant touch with Harry Daugherty. They lived together. They were most intimate friends, and Jess adored him. He wanted to shield him in every possible way. He lived for him, he loved him."[76] One of the few times Roxy clammed up during her testimony was when she was asked about Jess and Harry's activities at the Little Green House. She responded: "It is purely personal and of absolutely no consequence to this committee."[77] Essentially, all she would reveal was:

> SENATOR ASHURST: Did Mr. Smith ever tell you for what purpose he met Mr. Daugherty [at the Little Green House]? . . .
> MISS STINSON: Because they could meet there privately. . . . So they would not be disturbed.[78]

The Teapot Dome scandal "was so monumental [that] a Senate Report called it a 'criminal conspiracy . . . unparalleled in the history of this or any other civilized nation.'"[79] One fact uncovered by the Senate's inquiries was that Sinclair gave the Republican Party $75,000 to help retire the party's debts from the 1920 campaign. One cost the party incurred was paying $25,000 to one of Harding's mistresses, Carrie Phillips. These payments were "funneled through a secret bank account kept, apparently, under Jess Smith's name."[80] As Will Hayes, the ex-chair of the Republican Party, testified:

> SENATOR WALSH: When [did] you personally solicit[] Mr. Sinclair to help make up the deficit [from the 1920 election]? . . .
> MR. HAYS: Well, I would say the summer of 1923. . . .
> SENATOR WALSH: And that was $75,000?
> MR. HAYS: I think that was the maximum amount was $75,000 . . .
> SENATOR WALSH: To whom was the payment made?
> MR. HAYS: Well, it was made to the committee [the RNC].[81]

Hays had also raised $50,000 for the RNC from Andrew Mellon, the secretary of the treasury.[82] Contemporaneously, Doheny had given $75,000 to the Democratic Party and $25,000 to the Republican Party in the 1920 election.[83] In other words, both alleged Teapot Dome bribers were also big political contributors. What Hays left out of his testimony was the fact that Sinclair had provided an additional $185,000 in Liberty Bonds to the RNC on top of the $75,000 cash.[84] These bonds were also from the Continental's liquidation, making them easy to trace between Sinclair and the RNC.

Mally Daugherty's bank in Ohio had all sorts of odd deposits in it. As Bruce Bliven details, "Senate investigators were able to discover that $75,000, its source unexplained, had been deposited to [Harry] Daugherty's account at a time when he swore on his income-tax return that he had no property. Also on deposit in the bank was $63,000 for Jess Smith, $50,000 for Mal[ly] Daugherty, and smaller sums for other members of the Ohio Gang. This bank had been for them what the cave was for Ali Baba's forty thieves."[85]

Accountability after Teapot Dome was a mixed bag. Secretary Fall became the first cabinet secretary to be convicted of a crime—namely, taking a $100,000 bribe from Doheny.[86] He was sentenced to a year in jail and given a $100,000 fine.[87] At his criminal trial for bribing Fall, Doheny was found not guilty.[88]

Teapot Dome briber Harry Sinclair stonewalled the Senate investigation so thoroughly that he was indicted for contempt of Congress.[89] At Sinclair's first criminal trial for bribery, he was acquitted, but there was evidence he had hired detectives to intimidate members of the jury and to bribe one jury member with "a car as long as this block."[90] This led to Sinclair's conviction for contempt of court, which was appealed to the Supreme Court, who affirmed his conviction, noting the seriousness of the charges against him: "Immediately after the jury [in Sinclair's Teapot Dome bribery case] was sworn Sinclair directed [his underling] to engage the William J. Burns International Detective Agency, . . . '[t]o spy upon said jurors . . . , to bribe, intimidate and influence said jurors . . . either by corruptly influencing said jurors to decide the issues . . . in favor of the defendants . . . , or . . . concocting false charges against one or more of the said jurors . . . with a view of bringing about a mistrial.'"[91] Sinclair got six months in jail for contempt of court in addition to three months for contempt of Congress.[92]

The ex-attorney general Harry Daugherty was found not guilty at both of his criminal trials.[93] The Supreme Court also got around to ruling that the Senate did have the right to arrest Mally Daugherty,[94] and that Congress had broad investigatory powers to gather information to craft future legislation.[95] Control of the Teapot Dome and Buena Vista Hills oil reserves were eventually restored to the US government by the Supreme Court's canceling the contracts that Secretary Fall brokered through bribes.[96]

Senator Walsh summed up the Teapot Dome scandal this way: "Trusted officers of great industrial houses, [were] pilfering from their own companies, robbing their own stockholders, the share of the boodle coming to one of the freebooters serving in part as the price of the perfidy of a member of the President's Cabinet."[97] Translating this into plain English: the oil executives first pulled off the phony oil sales through a dummy corporation, the Continental Trading Company, without informing their own investors, then oilman Sinclair took the profits from that scam, turned them into Liberty Bonds, and used those bonds to bribe Secretary Fall and to pay the RNC—or to put it even more succinctly, one corporate scam facilitated an even bigger crime.

One of the reasons why open questions exist about Teapot Dome is that many participants had a zest for destroying evidence.[98] After he was freed from detention, Mally Daugherty burned key documents that Congress wanted.[99] After President Harding died in 1923, his widow went to an estate owned by Ned McLean and destroyed several documents.[100] Records documenting that the RNC paid Harding's mistress

Carrie Phillips were burned by Harry Daugherty.[101] McLean told Congress that he destroyed his private checkbooks.[102] And Jess Smith destroyed nearly every financial record he had before his death. As Roxy Stinson testified to Congress: "[Jess Smith] had his business in order. . . . [After his death] I saw no bank books, no receipts, no checks; everything had been destroyed. . . . he asked me . . . , "Will you to-morrow afternoon destroy all these things?"[103] Before he killed himself, Smith told his ex-wife Roxy which of her documents to destroy. Unlike many in this tale, she didn't destroy evidence, which is why she had letters and telegrams to back up her version of events.[104]

The Teapot Dome scandal inspired two key reforms: the passage of the Corrupt Practices Act, which requires more transparency of money in politics, and the Revenue Act of 1924 (26 U.S.C. § 6103(f)) which allows the Ways and Means Committee to get copies of anyone's taxes.[105] This later act allowed Congress to get hold of Trump's taxes in 2022.[106]

THE NUCLEAR GRIFT OF THE FIRST ENERGY SCANDAL

On the Ides of March 2021, a bicyclist made a grim discovery near a pond in North Naples, Florida at 11:30 a.m.: the dead body of a sixty-seven-year-old man with a head wound from a gunshot.[107] The man was wearing a blue "DeWine for Governor" T-shirt—the first clue to who he was. DeWine was the governor of Ohio; the dead man turned out to be an Ohio lobbyist named Neil Clark. An autopsy determined he died by suicide.[108]

Clark had been charged with participating in a $60 million racketeering conspiracy that involved the then–Ohio speaker of the House, Larry Householder, and a company called FirstEnergy.[109] FirstEnergy changed its name to Energy Harbor after emerging from bankruptcy and was later bought by Vistra Corp.[110] The company wanted a bailout that would cost the taxpayers of Ohio $1.3 billion—and FirstEnergy got it, through legislation known as House Bill 6 (or H.B. 6). House Bill 6 was shepherded through the Ohio House by Householder, passed the Ohio Senate, and was signed into law by Governor DeWine in 2019. The bailout applied to two aging nuclear power plants in Ohio owned by FirstEnergy/Energy Harbor/Vistra. By October 2020, members of the conspiracy other than Clark had already pleaded guilty.[111] Clark pleaded not guilty.[112] As he colorfully recounted when the federal prosecutors asked him to cut a plea deal, his response was "that will never fucking happen."[113] And it didn't.

In the indictment against Householder, the DOJ made it clear that they had Clark on tape talking to undercover agents who pretended that they ran a sports betting firm, and that they wanted legislation moved in the Ohio legislature to help their business.[114] On the tapes, Clark referred to himself as Speaker Householder's "hitman," who "will go out there and do the dirty shit."[115] Clark advised the "businessmen" (who were really FBI agents) that they should set aside $50,000 to $100,000 to pay Householder and other lawmakers through a 501(c)(4).[116] The 501(c)(4) he referred to was Generation Now, and it was controlled by Householder.

On a wiretap on May 1, 2019, Clark explained the appeal of using a 501(c)(4): "[I]t's a secret, a (c)(4) is secret. Nobody knows the money goes to the Speaker's account, it is controlled by his people . . . and it's not recorded."[117] Clark also talked about the FirstEnergy scheme, referring to FirstEnergy as "the Bank."[118] In July 2019, he told undercover agents that "on HB 6, FirstEnergy got $1.3 billion in subsidies, free payments, . . . so what do they [FirstEnergy] care about putting $20 million a year for this thing, they don't give a shit."[119] Some of these tapes were played during Householder's and Ohio Republican Party chairman Matthew Borges's criminal trial. Clark said on tape that if lawmakers "like Householder 'go to the wall' too often, then 'everybody knows they're pay-to-play.'"[120]

In a wiretapped conversation between Clark and Householder on January 10, 2018, "Clark and Householder discussed their plan to 'orchestrate (c)(4) checks' to help Householder fund campaigns."[121] The prosecutors alleged that: "Clark estimated that Householder would 'need a hundred and twenty thousand [$120,000] per race,' to which Householder responded, 'I'd say one fifty [$150,000], but yeah, you're in the ballpark.' . . . Clark also mentioned that, 'some people decided to help [Householder's Republican opponent]' for Speaker, to which Householder responded, 'Yeah, we can fuck them over later.'"[122] Householder would go on to raise funds for Republican campaigns across Ohio, including $1 million for "Team Householder" candidates during the Republican primary in 2018.[123] The secretive 501(c)(4) Generation Now also spent $90,000 to elect Householder.[124]

In a posthumously published autobiography, *What Do I Know? I'm Just a Lobbyist*, Clark opened the book by claiming that famed political strategist "Machiavelli was a pussy."[125] Referencing H.B. 6, Clark wrote, "You call it a bailout. I did too. . . . It was 'Pay to Play.'"[126] He also claimed that *$69 million* was spent in the FirstEnergy scheme, not $60 million.[127] Clark also recounted discussions with federal investigators. As Clark told the story, he said to the FBI, "No company, no group, no individual has ever owned as many politicians as FirstEnergy, but you didn't charge them."[128] In October 2020, the CEO of FirstEnergy, Chuck Jones, who was also implicated in the Householder scandal, was fired along with vice president for external affairs Michael Dowling.[129] Shareholders sued FirstEnergy for breaching fiduciary duties.[130] The shareholders reached a settlement for $180 million.[131] As Clark said perplexedly to the FBI, it is true that Jones and Dowling have not yet been charged by federal prosecutors.[132] However, related state criminal cases were filed against Jones, Dowling, and former Public Utilities Commission of Ohio (PUCO) chairman Samuel Randazzo in 2024, and Randazzo was also charged in a federal case in 2023.[133] Like Clark, Randazzo killed himself in 2024.[134]

Clark told the undercover agents that the Supreme Court's 2010 decision in *Citizens United v. FEC* blessed Householder's behavior. As local press covering the trial summed up: "Pointing to the U.S. Supreme Court's disastrous *Citizens United* ruling, Clark described to undercover FBI agents how to make dark money contributions in a way calculated to get a public official's attention, saying those should come in chunks of $15,000, $20,000, $25,000 or more."[135] The jury in Householder's criminal trial heard Clark say on tape: "Based on a Supreme Court decision [*Citizens United*], businesses can do this and nobody can do anything about it. . . . Politicians can get a bunch of money and say, 'I didn't know.'"[136]

This reliance on *Citizens United* as a cover for crimes alarmed academics and reformers who watched the Householder trial. As Professor David Niven put it: "'They're arguing everybody does it,' and 'we didn't use the magic words [like vote for or vote against a candidate]. If that works, God help us all, because any entity operating with a detectable brain wave will be able to surmount public corruption law by being careful in their choice of words.'"[137] And, as reformer Catherine Turcer said, "'[*Citizens United*] doesn't mean that pay-to-play is legal or right.'"[138]

On July 30, 2020, the DOJ charged Larry Householder (alongside other defendants Jeffrey Longstreth, Neil Clark, Matthew Borges, Juan Cespedes, and Generation Now) with a RICO conspiracy. Householder remarkably won reelection after he was indicted. The race was, bizarrely, uncontested.[139] All of the lawmakers who had voted for H.B. 6 won their races in 2020 as well.[140] Householder is out of power after a unanimous vote to relieve him of his speakership, and another nearly unanimous vote kicked him out of the legislature for disorderly conduct.[141] A fellow Republican remarked that "if racketeering, bribery and money laundering do not constitute disorderly conduct, then frankly nothing ever could."[142]

One reason the criminal case against Householder was such a slam dunk was because FirstEnergy had already admitted its role. According to a deferred prosecution agreement signed by FirstEnergy, the company acknowledged that it gave millions of dollars to Householder's Generation Now.[143] To hide the money flow, FirstEnergy created 501(c)(4)s of its own, including one with the Orwellian name "Partners for Progress."[144] As FirstEnergy would later admit, "Although Partners for Progress appeared to be an independent 501(c)(4) on paper, in reality, it was controlled in part by certain former FirstEnergy Corp. executives, who funded it and directed its payments to entities associated with public officials."[145] FirstEnergy paid a penalty of $230 million.[146] This was the largest criminal fine paid in history in the Southern District of Ohio.[147]

Householder spread the $60 million (or, if Clark is correct, $69 million) from FirstEnergy around Ohio politics, helping to elect Republicans to the Ohio House who would elect him to be speaker. But he also kept hundreds of thousands of dollars for himself and used it to pay off $20,000 in credit card debt, to settle a lawsuit, and to make improvements to his second home in Florida.[148] At trial, federal prosecutors stated that "Householder personally received about $514,000 from the HB6 scheme, while [Matt] Borges got $366,000."[149] Testimony during the trial from one of Householder's codefendants who pleaded guilty included "[Juan] Cespedes [who] described how another FirstEnergy Solutions lobbyist, Bob Klaffky, slid a $400,000 check across a table to Householder."[150] Householder's codefendant Borges referred to funds from FirstEnergy as "monopoly money."[151] Borges also referred to the relationship among First Energy, Householder and other coconspirators as an "unholy alliance."[152] These quotes came back to bite him at his criminal trial and were impossible to explain away.

One of the details that sealed Householder's fate at trial was metadata. If nineteenth-century scandals were solved when secret leatherbound black ledgers finally saw the light of day, metadata is the modern investigator's best friend. This should have been apparent from the calamitous downfall of congressman Aaron Schock.[153] He made news for posting shirtless pictures of himself and redecorating his congressional office all in red in an homage to the TV show *Downton Abbey*.[154] In 2015, Associated Press reporters used metadata from Congressman Schock's profligate Instagram photos and matched them against official reports to show that he was either not where he said he was or was flying on campaign donors' private jets.[155] He ultimately resigned after reporters used metadata to show that he had asked the federal government for reimbursements for more miles than he had driven.[156] Schock was indicted.[157] He reached a plea deal with DOJ to avoid jail.[158]

Larry Householder did not learn from Schock's metadata trap. One of the things that undermined Householder's credibility at his corruption trial was the metadata in a colleague's cellphone photos. The FBI alleged that FirstEnergy conspired with Householder at two DC steakhouses, Charlie Palmer Steak and The Palm. But Householder claimed he wasn't there.[159]

Under oath, he lied. Householder testified:

Q During the entire time that you were in Washington, DC with your family, did you ever have dinner with Chuck Jones, Mike Dowling, and Jeff Longstreth?
A [from Householder] I did not.[160]

On cross examination, this claim fell apart. The Prosecutor showed him a photo and then said:

Q All right. Mr. Householder, so let's go over these photos again and next to the photos or below the photos is the metadata that is associated with this picture.[161] ...

Q All right. Now, let's go to the upper right hand. You see the picture of your son is right here in the limo, right?

A Yes.

Q Okay. And who is the person on the far left of that photo?

A That's a very bad picture of Mike Dowling.

Q Right. So Mike Dowling is in the limo with your son, and this is on January 18th, and let's look at the metadata, at 10:20 p.m.[162]

The metadata in a cellphone picture of Householder's son in a limo matched up with the location of Charlie Palmer Steak.[163] Householder and his son were in town for the Trump 2017 inaugural. They flew there on a FirstEnergy plane.[164] Two months later, Householder was getting quarterly $250,000 payments from FirstEnergy through his 501(c)(4) Generation Now.[165]

In 2023, Householder and his codefendant Matthew Borges were convicted on all charges.[166] Perhaps this outcome was inevitable, given the DOJ's belt-and-suspenders approach to the case: they were "armed with guilty pleas from accomplices, implicating texts, phone recordings, bank statements, and a 49-page mea culpa from ... FirstEnergy—which admitted to funding the scheme in exchange for a $1.3 billion energy bailout bill meant to support Ohio's two struggling nuclear power plants."[167] Their lawyers say that they will appeal the conviction. Borges is already trying to use two new Supreme Court cases, *Ciminelli v. U.S.* and *Percoco v. U.S.*, to get charges against him thrown out.[168] These new cases continue a long trend by the Roberts Court that makes prosecuting corruption difficult.[169]

The dark money group Generation Now was also charged as being a participant in the conspiracy.[170] This may be the first time a 501(c)(4) has been charged in a criminal case.[171] Another of Householder's codefendants, Jeffrey Longsteth (who was a Householder staffer), pleaded guilty and admitted that he set up Generation Now "for Householder, knowing the entity would be used to receive bribe money to further Householder's bid for Speaker of the House."[172] Generation Now eventually pleaded guilty, too.[173]

When Householder was using Generation Now, "in a mind-bending piece of dishonesty, Householder's dark money group even funded an ad against his primary opponent attacking him for accepting 'dirty' dark money."[174] Some of the ads it funded were particularly deceptive. As prosecutors described, "These advertisements intended to invoke fear by asserting that China was invading Ohio's energy grid."[175]

As FirstEnergy admitted, secrecy was key to the criminal scheme.[176] This is precisely the trouble with dark money in American elections: it can cover up all sorts of illegality, from bribes of Republican lawmakers in Ohio or illegal foreign money in American elections in the money from the 1MDB scandal (discussed in chapter 6), which went to reelecting Democrat Barack Obama.[177] Even when dark money simply hides a cowardly corporate donor, it still robs shareholders and voters of transparency and accountability.[178] The biggest losers here are Ohio taxpayers, who are still on hook for much of Householder's shenanigans. The Ohio saga demonstrates that the temptation to bribe politicians in power to get taxpayer money is an ever-present threat.[179] Especially when the payout is *a billion dollars* of taxpayer funds, multimillion-dollar bribes seem like an easy way to get a high return on an investment.[180] As a result of this scandal, the Ohio legislature repealed the nuclear bailout that had come from the Householder bribes by FirstEnergy.[181]

Householder's crimes, which were facilitated by dark money, are exactly the type of scheme that campaign finance advocates have been warning about for years. At the federal level, over $2 billion in dark money has been spent since 2008, and dark money has grown in state elections, as evidenced by the dark money behind the "ghost" candidate scandal in Florida. Dark money makes tracing what's going on in elections nearly impossible for voters. For good of our democracy, the loopholes allowing dark money should be ended at the federal level as well as in every state.

To the extent that the public knows about the actions in real time of the next Crédit Mobilier, Mammoth Oil, or FirstEnergy, these are precisely the type of firms who are worthy of boycotting under the Democracy Litmus Test, as each undermined the integrity of American democracy. Modern politicians who act like Oakes Ames, Albert Fall, and Larry Householder do not deserve support at the ballot under the Democracy Litmus Test either.

PART 2

WHY DEMOCRACY IS ON A KNIFE'S EDGE

5

SCHEMING IN THE SHADOWS

GHOST MONEY, GHOST CANDIDATES

On election night 2020, an ex–Florida senator, Frank Artiles, was drinking at the bar at an Irish pub called Liam Fitzpatrick in Lake Mary, Florida, and bragging that he was the mastermind behind Republicans' winning a certain legislative seat.[1] As election results flashed on the bar television from a state Senate race in south Florida, showing that a first-time Republican candidate was winning, he allegedly said to people nearby, "That is me, that was all me!"[2] Artiles likely felt comfortable speaking freely, as the crowd was full of Republicans celebrating the win of state senator-elect Jason Broduer.

Frank Artiles had a history of making bad decisions in bars. In 2015, while he was a representative in Florida's House, he was accused of punching a college student in a bar.[3] In 2017, he had to resign from his office as a Florida senator after calling fellow lawmakers the n-word in a bar.[4] And the barroom admission on election night 2020 may land Artiles in jail. Fast forward to March 18, 2021, when Artiles left the Turner Guilford Knight Correctional Center in Miami after posting $5,000 bail for charges that he violated Florida election laws for his role in bankrolling what the press in Florida called a "ghost" candidate.[5] Artiles is facing felony charges for allegedly bribing a man to run as a bogus candidate for a legislative seat. He will stand trial for his role in the scheme at a future date. He is, like all criminal defendants, innocent until proven guilty. Allegedly, the source of the money to run the ghost candidate scheme came from a large corporation called Florida Power & Light, or FPL.

As Thomas Paine wrote in *The Crisis*, "These are the times that try men's souls."[6] And Florida still takes the cake: it continues to distinguish itself with strange political scandals. The influence that sugar companies like US Sugar and Florida Crystals have on state politics has inspired both the novel and movie *Striptease*.[7] In real life, corporate sugar money has gone national after being poured into a super PAC that funded the failed 2020 Trump reelection campaign.[8] Florida is also home to one of the worst judicial political scandals in history, forcing justices of the Florida Supreme Court to resign over bribery involving dog racing.[9] A Miami mayoral race was once so tainted in 1997 that a judge threw out the election results.[10] The ghost candidate scandal fits the only-in-Florida mold of being outrageous.

A health insurance lobbyist named Stephanie Smith would later testify that she heard ex-senator Frank Artiles brag about his role in the scandal at the party for Brodeur, who was also elected with a different ghost candidate in his race named Jestine Iannotti.[11] Artiles was boasting about the race for Senate seat no. 37 in which Republican newcomer Ileana García won over incumbent Democratic state senator José Javier Rodríguez. The "ghost" non-party-affiliated candidate in District 37 was named Alex Rodriguez. The sound-alike candidate was placed there on purpose by Artiles to siphon votes from the Democrat.[12] The scheme worked. Incumbent Democratic senator José Javier Rodríguez lost the election by just 32 votes, and the shill candidate Rodriguez got 6,382 votes, arguably changing the outcome of the election.[13]

Democratic incumbent José Javier Rodríguez complained about the shenanigans in his 2020 election defeat in real time. As he told the press, "The Republicans ran . . . one unethical campaign, with two candidates."[14] In his concession speech, the Democrat Rodríguez asked for the election to be investigated by law enforcement.[15] Complaints from a losing candidate are easy to dismiss as sour grapes; usually that would have been the end of it, except for Artiles's self-incriminating bragging and local prosecutors who were willing to investigate a long and winding trail of political breadcrumbs to follow the money through a labyrinth of dark nonprofits, leading to the door of FPL.

Allegedly, the Rodriguez/Rodríguez plot was hatched at Artiles's house on May 15, 2020.[16] In forms filed with the state, Alex Rodriguez lied about where he resided so that it would seem like he lived in the district he sought to represent.[17] According to the *New York Times*, "Alex Rodriguez . . . did not disclose that he actually lived far from the district, in Boca Raton, or that the money for his candidacy came from Mr. Artiles."[18] The race was so close that it triggered a manual recount. When reporters came to interview Alex Rodriguez, he lied about who he was.[19]

According to the *Orlando Sentinel*, "On June 11 of [2020], authorities say Frank Artiles met Alex Rodriguez in the parking lot of a Miami bank, where Artiles gave Rodriguez $2,000 in cash so his friend could open a campaign account and run as a sham candidate... Then,... Artiles told Rodriguez he had to rush to the airport so he could fly to Tallahassee and hand-deliver [Alex] Rodriguez's elections paperwork."[20]

On March 18, 2021, Artiles was arrested in Miami for his alleged role in the in the ghost candidate scandal in the 2020 election.[21] A police affidavit in the case said that Artiles and Alex Rodriguez were in "a plot to 'confuse voters and siphon votes from the incumbent.'"[22] According to a warrant, Artiles allegedly paid candidate Alex Rodriguez to run as an independent because he had a confusingly similar name to the incumbent Democrat.[23]

Before 2020, Alex Rodriguez (the ghost) had been a registered Republican. He changed his registration to "no party" to run for the District 37 Senate seat. The *Orlando Sentinel* reported that "within days of submitting Rodriguez's paperwork, Artiles was being paid $15,000 a month plus expenses by [a Republican firm called] Data Targeting."[24] Data Targeting is owned by Republican Pat Bainter.[25] What this money was for is a bit opaque, but it could have included paying Artiles to spy on the Democratic candidate in Senate District 37.[26]

Prosecutors found that the bogus candidate Alex Rodriguez did no campaigning and yet pocketed around $45,000 from Artiles. Artiles and Rodriguez were each charged with three third-degree felony charges related to violating campaign finance law, including conspiracy to make campaign contributions in excess of legal limits, making those excess contributions, and false swearing in connection to an election. In other words, not only was there too much money changing hands, but Alex Rodriguez and Artiles also lied about it in their campaign finance filings.[27]

Artiles tried to make the money he provided to Rodriguez hard to trace by breaking it up: "Investigators found that... the payments came in various forms, including payments of $3,000 and then $5,000 that Mr. Artiles had stored in his home safe and recorded in a ledger on his desk as well as $2,400 that Mr. Artiles had wired to Mr. Rodriguez's landlord."[28] A few months after Alex Rodriguez and Artiles were arrested, Rodriguez decided to cut a deal, save himself, plead guilty, and turn against Artiles.[29] Rodriguez had been facing up to twenty years in prison. With the plea deal, he was given three years of probation.[30]

Some Democrats in Florida called for the Republican Iliana García, who won her seat through this Rodriguez/Rodríguez trickery, to resign so a special election could be held to fill the seat. Agricultural secretary Nikki Fried said, "They absolutely are ghosts and are just used as political tactics to really try and confuse the electorate."[31] Surprise, surprise: García has not resigned. Before running for office, García was the founder of Latinas for Trump.[32] As a state senator, she is part of a supermajority of Republicans in the Florida Senate. Those Republicans stood by Artiles, "who was arrested on election fraud charges . . . , rebuking Democratic calls to hold a special election in order to ensure a legitimate vote."[33]

All of the Republicans in the three ghost candidate races won.[34] One thing Alex Rodriguez's and Jestine Iannotti's races had in common is that both campaigns used the same stock photo in mailers to trick Florida Democratic voters. The photo in question was an attractive Black woman talking on the phone. As the *Orlando Sentinel* described it, "The mailers featured a stock photo of a Black woman, promised a candidate free from the influence of special interests who would change the politics in Tallahassee,' and emphasized [the candidate's] focus on social justice, climate change and campaign finance reform."[35] Just like in Alex Rodriguez's case, ghost candidate Iannotti did not campaign at all.[36] And Iannotti promptly moved to Europe after the 2020 election, belying her intent to ever serve as a state senator.[37]

Another thing Rodriguez and Iannotti have in common is that they were both arrested. Prosecutors took an extra year to get to Iannotti. She was the third-party candidate running against Republican Jason Brodeur.[38] Brodeur won by 7,644 votes; Iannotti got 5,787 votes.[39] Police also charged others allegedly involved in this ghost candidate scheme. According to one press report: "Charged alongside ghost candidate Jestine Iannotti are James 'Eric' Foglesong and Benjamin 'Ben' Paris. Foglesong is a political consultant involved in the launching of Iannotti's campaign, and Paris is Seminole County's Republican Party chairman."[40] Iannotti, Fogelsong and Paris have all pled not guilty.[41] When announcing the charges against them, Prosecutor Mark Glass said, "Lying about campaign donations is unacceptable because it provides an unfair advantage to the candidate. Protecting the integrity of our elections . . . includes making sure candidates follow the laws."[42]

In the *Paris* criminal trial, a key issue was whether a fake source was listed in the campaign finance reports that Iannotti's campaign filed with the state of Florida. The trial transcript contained this characterization from the prosecutor:

> We [the Florida prosecutors] submit that [the money] came from Foglesong's office in an envelope of $1,200 in cash, and that subsequent to that money being received, when they realized, hey, now we owe a report on the 19th and we have to figure out who we're going to say who this cash came from is when Mr. Paris . . . [said] . . . I'll call my cousin and we'll use his name and he got his permission and he did it.[43]

Paris's cousin Steven Smith's name ended up listed as a donor to Iannotti's campaign. The money did not come from him. As the prosecutor stated, "Steven Smith's name and address did not appear on that . . . treasurer's report by magic. Telepathy was not being used between Eric Foglesong and [Ben Paris]. . . . four hours and 18 minutes later, Steven Smith's name is on the . . . treasurer's report."[44] Paris was found guilty by a jury on September 1, 2022.[45] He asked for a new trial.[46]

WHO PAID FOR THE GHOST CANDIDATES?

The local *Orlando Sentinel* has been like white on rice with the ghost candidate scandal linking the money spent in the scandal to a local utility called Florida Power & Light (FPL). As the paper explained, it "has found that some of the architects of Florida's ghost candidate scheme have guided behind-the-scenes campaigns to tilt elections and influence public policy all across the state."[47] A whistleblower is apparently helping this paper and other Florida papers with documents to back up their reporting. As two of its reporters wrote, "Many details of the tactics—and the financial connections that link those using them—were exposed in late November, when the *Orlando Sentinel* was anonymously delivered a cache of checks, bank statements, emails, text messages, invoices, ledgers and more, covering the work of political consultants to FPL over a roughly four-year period between 2016 and 2020."[48]

In an editorial, the *Sun Sentinel*, another Florida paper, called out the problem of dark money in Florida's politics:

> Watergate taught us to follow the money in politics. No wonder so many of its practitioners take elaborate steps to cover their tracks. A horrific example is the laundering of $550,000 that promoted three "ghost" candidates. . . . Campaign filings and documents unearthed by Miami-Dade prosecutors . . . reveal footprints leading ominously to the doorsteps of several powerful entities:
> —Senate President Wilton Simpson, R-Trilby, and the Republican Party of Florida.
> —Florida Power & Light, one of the state's most politically influential companies.
> —Data Targeting, a Gainesville political firm that advised the GOP and employed a key figure in the sham candidate scandal.
> —Associated Industries of Florida, a statewide lobbying player supported by major utility companies.[49]

Ex-senator Artiles was not exactly hiding his role when he blabbed about participating in the ghost candidate scandal on election night in 2020. One of the reasons that Artiles might have been overconfident about getting away with this gambit is the roughly $45,000 he was paid through a dark money conduit called Proclivity Inc.[50] Money for Proclivity has been traced back to FPL, which is a subsidiary of publicly traded NextEra Energy.[51]

Once the scandal broke, NextEra conducted an internal review and promptly exonerated itself of any wrongdoing. On an earnings call with investors, "NextEra Energy CEO James Robo responded to a question from a Bank of America Securities analyst and said the company had FPL CEO Eric Silagy turn over emails and text messages and concluded there was 'no evidence . . . of illegality or wrongdoing on the part of FPL or any of its employees.'"[52] This is interesting, because the *Orlando Sentinel* discovered "that [FPL's CEO Eric] Silagy used a pseudonym email, 'Theodore Hayes,' to communicate with consultant Jeff Pitts, who controlled Grow United [formerly Proclivity], with the memos noting that one goal was to 'minimize all public reporting of entities and activities.'"[53] Also, Silagy appeared to have particular animus for the Democratic senator targeted by the Rodriguez/Rodríguez gambit; he once emailed his vice presidents and urged them that "I want you to make his life a living hell . . . seriously."[54] In 2023, Silagy abruptly retired.[55]

According to the *Orlando Sentinel*, FPL had donated more than $10 million in recent years to dark money nonprofits, using an intermediary called Matrix LLC, and that "Mr. Silagy, the CEO and president of Florida Power & Light, had personally coordinated with those consultants on campaign contributions made through their nonprofits."[56] The *Florida Times-Union* reported that, "beginning in 2016, the [Matrix]'s former employees created at least 19 different entities to use as vehicles for dark-money political contributions."[57]

Court documents show another secretive nonprofit in the ghost candidate mix called Let's Preserve the American Dream. These documents, "[from] the state attorney's investigation, have shown that as part of the ghost candidate scheme Let's Preserve the American Dream paid former state Sen. Frank Artiles $125,000 for 'research.'"[58] FPL and Grow United had the same political consultant, Matrix LLC.[59] According to tax records, Let's Preserve the American Dream provided $1.15 million to Grow United in 2020.[60]

The money—roughly $600,000—behind deceptive ghost candidate mailers was dark.[61] Some of it went through Proclivity.[62] The Proclivity money then went to two Florida super PACs, one called "Our Florida," and the other with the particularly Orwellian name "The Truth."[63] The mailers' printer also had Republican political connections.[64] Proclivity was itself a bit mysterious: "Its address is a UPS store in Atlanta, and is not a registered business in Georgia, nor is it registered as a political organization in Florida."[65] The plot thickens because, according to *Politico*, after the 2020 election Proclivity Inc. changed its name to Grow United Inc.[66]

According to the *Tampa Bay Times*, "Prosecutors have looked into a $600,000 transfer made on or around Sept. 30, 2020, from Foundation for a Safe Environment, a nonprofit organization controlled by prominent Republican operative Stafford Jones, to Let's Preserve the American Dream, a nonprofit organization run by Ryan Tyson, a top GOP pollster in Florida."[67] Foundation for a Safe Environment appeared to get its money from Secure Florida's Future, a nonprofit chaired by Florida Chamber of Commerce president and CEO Mark Wilson.[68] Testimony from Tyson, executive director of Let's Preserve the American Dream, show that $600,000 of the $1.15 million that Let's Preserve the American Dream gave to Grow United was earmarked to go to PACs to pay for the mailers that promoted the ghost candidates in Florida.[69]

Other players in this shell game included a group called TMP Interactive. Also, according to the *Tampa Bay Times*, "records show large sums of money changing hands between key figures in the ghost candidate scandal. For example, Let's Preserve the American Dream sent $30,000 to TMP Interactive, a firm run by Jeff Pitts, then the CEO of Matrix LLC. That Alabama-based political consulting firm in 2020 counted among its clients Florida Power & Light, among other major Florida businesses and Associated Industries contributors."[70] Confused yet? This daisy chain of political links and money transfers is meant to hide what is happening from the public. But the long and the short of it is that FPL gave to several dark money nonprofits, and that one of those nonprofits paid for the deceptive mailers promoting the ghost candidates in 2020.

Democratic lawmakers tried to get FPL's regulator, the Florida Public Service Commission, to investigate its alleged role in the ghost candidate scandal.[71] As reported by the *Tampa Bay Times*, "In a Jan. 5 [2022] letter, they asked the commission to determine whether the company was using ratepayer money for political purposes."[72] This was rejected by the regulator, who stated: "The commission 'has a long-standing prohibition on the inclusion of lobbying and other expenses, which have been determined to bring no benefit to ratepayers, among the expenses to be recovered through rates charged to the public for service.'" The regulator added that "when FPL filed its rate request, 'the appropriate auditing function was conducted during the commission's consideration of the most recent FPL rate case,' and the audit 'produced no evidence' that FPL 'used, or was intending to use, ratepayer funds for the private benefit of the company's lobbying, campaigning or marketing affairs.'"[73] The Democratic lawmakers responded that they had little faith in such audits, given the internal documents that the whistleblower had produced to local papers.[74] The Florida Public Service Commission members are confirmed by the Florida Senate, which might offer one explanation for why FPL was so interested in Senate elections.[75]

The ghost candidate investigations revealed a network of dark money trying to influence Florida politics. As the *Orlando Sentinel* explained in their exposé: "What has emerged from this flood of disclosures is something akin to a playbook: a collection of tactics and strategies deployed from the Panhandle to Miami to sway elections for everything from mayor to state senator, resist efforts to reshape Florida's Constitution—and advance the interests of some powerful corporations."[76] This Florida scandal has a link to broader national trend of the explosion of dark money in politics.[77] As OpenSecrets later reported, on closer inspection the 2020 election, which initially looked like it had a low level of dark money, only had a low level of *reported* dark money.[78] OpenSecrets now estimates that $1 billion in dark money was spent in the 2020 cycle.[79] This doubles the amount that was spent over the previous decade in a single election.

In addition to its role in the ghost candidate scandal, FPL appears to have indirectly purchased a Florida news outlet called *The Capitolist* just to attack its critics from behind a curtain. As the *Palm Beach Post* reported, *The Capitolist* "was secretly funded and controlled by consultants linked to Florida Power & Light to secure publication of positive stories about the state's most powerful public utility and get negative stories published about those FPL deemed as opponents."[80] According to the press, leaked "records obtained reveal that an operative for Matrix LLC, an Alabama-based political consulting firm, hired by FPL, had signed an agreement to purchase a controlling stake in *The Capitolist* before the 2020 election."[81] Matrix is the same political consultant that was mixed up in the ghost candidate scandal as well.

Some have argued that the ghost candidate gambit happened in Florida elections before 2020.[82] As Democratic gubernatorial candidate Gwen Graham tweeted, "FYI, the @FloridaGOP have been orchestrating these 'shill candidate' schemes for years. This time they got caught."[83] A report by Integrity Florida noted: "[In 2018] FPL used a Matrix-connected nonprofit called Broken Promises to secretly bankroll a spoiler in the Senate race. Leaked records from Matrix show FPL donated $200,000 to Broken Promises which then donated $20,000 to the spoiler candidate's political committee and spent another roughly $115,000 on mailers and advertising supporting him. As a nonprofit, Broken Promises did not have to disclose its donors so the money could not be traced back to Florida Power & Light."[84] Because of this devious behavior, the head of Integrity Florida called the use of ghost candidates "a political dirty trick."[85]

A story by the *Miami Herald* backs up this assertion, showing that Florida Power & Light ran the ghost candidate playbook in 2018 as well: "The documents show that FPL sent $200,000 to . . . Broken Promises, in the fall of 2018. Within five weeks, Broken Promises had donated $20,000 to [no-party-affiliated candidate Charles] Goston's political committee and spent roughly $115,000 on mailers and advertising supporting him. Best of all for FPL: . . . the cash was untraceable. No one would know that FPL had paid to secretly manipulate a state election in favor of Republicans."[86] Saurav Ghosh, director at the nonpartisan Campaign Legal Center told the *Miami Herald* of the Goston/FPL 2018 election revelations: "This is pretty much the nightmare scenario. You have a powerful corporate player in Florida politics using its financial resources to defeat a candidate without any disclosure to the public. . . . This is election rigging."[87]

A POSSIBLE SOLAR KILLING MOTIVE

Why was Florida Power & Light so involved in the 2018 and 2020 elections? As a *Miami Herald* editorial warned, "Florida Power & Light is used to getting what it wants from Tallahassee [Florida's capitol]. Friendly utility regulators. The approval of a rate hike last year. Cozy relationships with lawmakers from both parties thanks to generous political donations sometimes funneled through dark-money groups— more than $500,000 [in the 2022] election cycle alone."[88] One theory for its heavy involvement in Florida politics is that FPL is actively trying to stop net metering of roof top solar, which cuts into their business model. Ensuring a Republican supermajority in the state legislature is one way of achieving that goal.[89] As *The Guardian* revealed, Florida Power & Light was able to get draft bills introduced in the legislature to contain nearly the exact language the company requested on net metering.[90]

FPL, along with other power companies, have been fighting rooftop solar for years through electoral politics, including when the issue has been on the ballot in Florida. The nonprofit environmental group US PIRG reported that "Florida Power & Light (FPL), Duke Energy and

Tampa Electric Company—have engaged in aggressive anti-solar tactics that have kept solar power producing just 3% of all electricity in the Sunshine State. These tactics include donating to the campaigns of state political figures and parties, employing an army of lobbyists, funding a deceptive 2016 anti-solar ballot initiative (rejected by voters)."[91] Perhaps this activity in Florida is just following the Koch-funded American Legislative Exchange Council's (ALEC's) anti-solar script.[92]

The public got a peek into the energy industry's aggressive approach to solar power when, on October 18, 2016, leaked audio from the 2016 State Energy/Environment Leadership Summit captured comments made in a speech about Florida's Amendment 1, which was on the ballot that fall. The taped speech was made by Sal Nuzzo of the James Madison Institute (JMI) on October 2, 2016.[93] Nuzzo was then and is now JMI's vice president of policy and director of the Center for Economic Prosperity.[94] The *Miami Herald* reported: "According to federal tax documents, JMI has received more than $120,000 from the Charles Koch Institute and Charles Koch Foundation, and Stan Connally, the CEO of Gulf Power, sits on JMI's board of directors."[95] And Nuzzo himself described JMI—in a comment that he later said was made "in jest"—as "this right-wing think tank, the Koch Brothers-funded group, part of the vast right-wing conspiracy."[96]

Amendment 1 was on the Florida general election ballot in 2016. It said: "This amendment establishes a right under Florida's constitution for consumers to own or lease solar equipment installed on their property to generate electricity for their own use. State and local governments shall retain their abilities to protect consumer rights and public health, safety and welfare, and to *ensure that consumers who do not choose to install solar are not required to subsidize the costs of backup power and electric grid access to those who do.*"[97] The italicized portion has been interpreted as barring net metering.[98] But the language of Amendment 1 was deceptive, as the first part seemed to many lay readers to be pro-consumer. Also on the 2016 Florida ballot was Amendment 4, which made rooftop solar more attractive for homeowners in Florida because it would empower the legislature to exempt solar panels and other equipment from certain taxes.[99]

Nuzzo explained in his remarks that Consumers for Smart Solar, the pro-business sponsors of Amendment 1, had requested assistance from

James Madison Institute to combat the pro-solar Amendment 4 that had been proposed by Floridians for Solar Choice, an actual environmental group.[100] Nuzzo was particularly horrified that conservatives in the Tea Party were embracing rooftop solar. As Nuzzo said, "They [pro-solar groups] actually leveraged some of the less savvy, less informed, Tea Party groups and formed what is now called the Green Tea Movement. God help us. We're dead and destroyed."[101]

Nuzzo criticized supporters of solar energy in Florida. He stated: "The language of the ballot initiative [pro-solar Amendment 4] mandated, in the Florida Constitution, that solar would be [a] preferred energy source in the state of Florida. It directed . . . the legislature to create policy to advance solar interests in the state of Florida. We can all look at this and shake our heads and go, 'Are they nuts?'"[102] Nuzzo explained why the energy industry was supporting Amendment 1, which had been proposed by business group Consumers for Solar Choice: "That's why Amendment 1 . . . is so important for Florida for this election cycle. It would completely negate anything that they [pro-solar interests] would try to do, either legislatively or constitutionally, down the road."[103] As Nuzzo concluded:

> The point I would make . . . is as you guys look at policy in your state or constitutional ballot initiatives in your state, remember this: solar polls very well. To the degree that we can use a little bit of political *jiujitsu* and take what they're kind of pinning us on and use it to our [corporate] benefit either in policy, in legislation or in constitutional referendums if that's the direction you want to take, [and] use the language of promoting solar.[104]

After the leak of Nuzzo's remarks, many members of the press and the public accused Amendment 1's backers of trying to pull a bait-and-switch on Florida voters.[105] Some citizens even tried to get Amendment 1 taken off of the ballot, but the Supreme Court of Florida refused so close to the election.[106] In the aftermath of the release of Nuzzo's comments, both Consumers for Smart Solar and JMI distanced themselves from his statements. Sarah Bascom, a spokesperson for Consumers for Smart Solar, stated that "Consumers for Smart Solar did not engage or hire or ask JMI to do research regarding the effort."[107] And JMI's executive director said that Nuzzo "misspoke" at the conference.[108] But JMI could only have been so mad at Nuzzo, as he was still working there seven years later.

After Nuzzo's audio leaked, Florida voters did not fall for Amendment 1 and ultimately this effort at "political *jiujitsu*" was defeated by voters.[109] Thus the industry failed to get net metering curbed in the Florida constitution.[110] The industry was back in 2020 with a ballot measure to make future citizen-sponsored ballot measures harder to pass, but that failed, too.[111]

Returning to where this story started, with the ghost candidates spoiling at least one election in 2020, FPL—or, rather, its parent company, the publicly traded Next Era Energy—has felt some impact from the bad press generated by the scandal. One investment firm has downgraded its stock. "Seaport Global downgraded its stock recommendation for NextEra to 'neutral' from 'buy,' citing 'growing media scrutiny of FPL's lobbying practices against distributed solar and retail choice.'"[112]

The results in Senate District 37 were particularly tragic, as voters appeared to have been tricked into electing the candidate with the least support. As Brad Ashwell, the Florida state director of All Voting is Local, said of the Senate District 37 ruse: "'It's a complete and utter deception. . . . One of the existential threats to our democracy right now is misinformation and disinformation, and this is an example of that—probably one of the more nefarious ones because it led to a different candidate winning the race.'"[113]

Dismissing the ghost candidates as just another Florida backwater story would be wrong. For one, Florida is now the third biggest American state by population.[114] Moreover, these state races at issue in the Florida ghost candidate scandal matter for national politics, since who was in charge of the Florida legislature in 2021 redrew congressional maps used for a decade.[115] In other words, the fate of who controls the House of Representatives runs through Florida. As MSNBC political analyst Fernand Amandi put it, "This is the laboratory . . . for what Republican control would look like in the whole country."[116] Further, on the state legislative front, Florida has followed the regressive trend of rolling out restrictions on voting by two legislative houses that have supermajorities of Republicans, with Republican Ron DeSantis in the governor's mansion.[117] Also, in the future, disinformation is less likely to come in the form of old-school mailers; the next wave is more likely to come in the form of deceptive AI-generated digital ads, whether deepfakes or cheap fakes.

Here, a corporation used dark money to fund bogus candidates to trick Florida voters into voting for candidates that were friendly to this corporation. This scandal has led to criminal investigations and convictions. This example shows the lengths to which some corporate spenders will go to manipulate the democratic process.

THE FEDERAL FALLOUT

NextEra Energy's problems may have another phase that reaches far outside of Florida and has federal implications. According to a FEC complaint filed on October 27, 2022, by Citizens for Responsibility and Ethics in Washington (CREW), some of the same players in the Florida ghost candidate scandal were also spending dark money in the 2020 federal elections. More specifically, CREW alleged that nonprofits were used in the 2020 federal election to evade campaign finance reporting requirements, to wit:

> The nonprofits contributed a total of $1.27 million to super PACs through five channels: (1) Grow United contributed funds to Wingman PAC, (2) the Center for Advancement of Integrity & Justice contributed funds to American Valor PAC, (3) Florida Promise contributed funds to the Senate Leadership Fund, (4) Broken Promises contributed funds to Concerned Conservatives, Inc., and (5) Stand Up for Justice contributed funds to South Florida Residents First.[118]

CREW alleged that this behavior followed the suggestions by Matrix (who was involved in the ghost candidate scandal) that it laid out in two memoranda to Eric Silagy, the then-CEO of Florida Power & Light.[119] What CREW alleges is a massive straw donor scheme to evade federal election laws. Straw donor schemes are prosecuted.[120] If true, then FPL is using corporate political spending not only to allegedly trick voters in Florida with ghost candidates but also, potentially, to skirt around federal election laws as well.

6

CRIMINAL ORIGINS

ILLEGAL MONEY IN THE 2012 ELECTION

In November 2012 a chubby Malaysian businessman named Jho Low threw himself a lavish circus-themed birthday party in Las Vegas. He was turning thirty-one.[1] In attendance were actor Leonardo DiCaprio, rapper Kanye West, and South Korean singer Psy of "Gangnam Style" fame.[2] Britney Spears jumped out of Low's birthday cake.[3] Low allegedly paid Spears $1 million to sing him "Happy Birthday."[4] The *Hollywood Reporter* described it as the "party to end all parties."[5]

Two days after the party, the 2012 presidential election took place. Democrat Barack Obama was elected to a second term as president. Some of the money–around $2 million–supporting Obama's reelection came from the birthday boy, Jho Low. This was a problem because as a foreign national, Low was allowed spend exactly *zero dollars* in an American election.

Two months later, Low had a new idea: he wanted to do New Year's Eve twice in one day. To accomplish this, he would fly from Sydney to Los Angeles so that he could celebrate first in Australia and then fly over the international dateline and celebrate in the United States. Low wanted an audience for this stunt, so he invited fifty guests, including "DiCaprio, [Jamie] Foxx, Jonah Hill, [rapper Pras,] plus assorted friends and families, [who] flew to Sydney on a 500-passenger commercial airliner retrofitted with a lounge and nightclub."[6]

According to a DOJ indictment, "In his acceptance speech upon winning a Golden Globe for his role in [the film] *The Wolf of Wall Street*, [DiCaprio] thanked 'the entire production team,' singling out in particular 'Joey . . . and Jho,' whom he characterized as 'collaborators' on the film. . . . This reference was to Joey McFarland, a co-founder of Red

Granite Pictures, . . . and [Jho Low]."[7] During the height of their friendship, Low gave DiCaprio a Picasso entitled *Nature morte au crâne de taureau*[8] and Marlon Brando's Oscar for *On the Waterfront*.[9]

How did Jho Low have the money to throw this lavish Vegas fete, give DiCaprio a Picasso, pull off the double New Year's caper, and spend millions in the 2012 US presidential election? Because he is accused of being one of the biggest corporate thieves of all time. Jho Low allegedly stole between $4 billion and $5 billion from a Malaysian sovereign wealth fund that was primarily funded by the Malaysian government.[10] Then he allegedly absconded with the money.[11] If these accusations are true, Low was a scam artist—perhaps one of the most daring.

The investment fund's name was 1 Malaysia Development Berhad, or 1MDB; thus many reporters call Low's escapades the "1MDB scandal."[12] According to *Business Insider*, 1MDB "was originally set up to finance infrastructure and other economy-linked deals in Malaysia. But the fund veered into lavish spending, producing films such as *The Wolf of Wall Street* and buying casinos, champagne and *Dustheads*, a painting by US artist Jean-Michel Basquiat [of PCP addicts]."[13] Low bought the Basquiat painting at auction for $48 million and then had to sell it for $35 million years later when his legal woes piled up.[14] Low stands accused of paying corrupt officials in Malaysia.[15] The prime minister of Malaysia, Najib Razak, who was involved in the 1MDB scandal, was later jailed for corruption in 2020.[16] He lost his last appeal in 2023.[17] Obama's attorney general Loretta Lynch said of 1MDB that "a number of corrupt officials, treated this public trust as a personal bank account."[18]

Two reasons why Low got away with this scam for years was (1) he allegedly had coconspirators in high places such as the Malaysian prime minister;[19] and (2) he had the help of investment banks such as Goldman Sachs, which lent him the veneer of legitimacy.[20] As *The Guardian* explained, "[Prime Minister] Najib . . . used every ounce of his power to obstruct investigations into the scandal."[21] Goldman Sachs was likely in it for the lucrative banking fees for selling the fund's bonds.[22] The DOJ went after Goldman Sachs for alleged violations of the Foreign Corrupt Practices Act (FCPA), and the firm ended up settling with the US government for $2.9 billion.[23] This was the largest such fine in US history.[24] Executives at Goldman have been prosecuted for their roles,[25] including "Goldman's former Southeast Asia Chairman Tim Leissner [who] pleaded guilty to U.S. charges including conspiracy to launder money and has admitted to bribing officials in Malaysia and the United Arab Emirates to get bond deals for Goldman. He agreed to forfeit $43.7 million."[26] DiCaprio turned the Picasso over to the FBI.[27] He also returned Brando's Oscar which is apparently sitting somewhere in a government warehouse like the last scene of "Raiders of the Lost Ark."[28] DiCaprio has not been accused of a crime.

The fallout from the 1MDB scandal has taken years to clean up by Malaysian and U.S. authorities, who have gone globetrotting to at least ten different countries to repossess property, real estate, and artwork all bought with funds stolen from 1MDB. As the *Washington Post* recounted, "The U.S. Justice Department is seeking to seize (on Malaysia's behalf) about $1.7 billion in allegedly illegally acquired assets, including a private jet, artworks by Picasso and Monet, a $39 million Los Angeles mansion and a stake in the Park Lane Hotel in New York. . . . Malaysia sold Jho Low's super yacht, seized in Bali, for $126 million, and has been going after family properties."[29] In 2019 Low and the DOJ entered a civil forfeiture settlement and seized $700 million worth of assets from Low and his family.[30] This took the cooperation of the United States, Malaysia, Singapore, Switzerland, and Luxembourg. This was the largest recovery under the DOJ's Kleptocracy Asset Recovery Initiative.[31] In a particularly rich detail, the DOJ covered Low's lawyers' fees as part of this settlement, including those of ex-governor Chris Christie.[32] Red Granite, the film company that produced *The Wolf of Wall Street*, settled with the DOJ in 2017, and the DOJ thereby gained rights to the film's proceeds.[33]

The DOJ eventually charged Low in absentia with campaign finance crimes in 2019 related to his spending in the 2012 US election.[34] Fast forward eleven years after the banging birthday party in Vegas and the 2012 election to a somber Leonardo DiCaprio testifying in a federal courtroom in Washington, DC, in a criminal case about the $100 million that Low provided to finance *The Wolf of Wall Street*.[35] Jho Low was nowhere to be found in the criminal court in 2023. But his alleged codefendant, Grammy-winning Prakazrel Michel, better known by his rapper name "Pras," was there defending himself alone against charges that he, too, had taken Low's money, but, instead of pouring it into a film project (which is legal if the money hadn't been stolen), Pras allegedly poured it into American politics (which is illegal even if the money had been from a legitimate foreign source).[36]

Pras described the first night he met a twenty-four-year-old Jho Low in 2006 in a club in the meatpacking district of New York City. Low bought everyone in the club a drink and then bought everyone in the club across the street a drink. The estimated price tag for this largesse was upward of a million dollars.[37]

The DOJ alleges that Pras—who was one-third of the hip-hop group the Fugees with Lauryn Hill and Wyclef Jean—was part of two criminal conspiracies with Jho Low. In the DOJ's rendition of events, Low provided money (allegedly stolen from the 1MDB fund) to Pras, and then Pras used it to support Democratic president Barrack Obama's re-election in 2012 through straw donors.[38] This was illegal, because foreign money is not allowed in US elections.[39] It's also illegal to spend in an election through straw donors.[40] Then, later in 2017, Pras is alleged to have acted as an unregistered foreign agent working on China's and Low's behalf with the Trump administration to dissuade them from investigating Low and urging the United States to extradite a dissident billionaire named Guo Wengui (a.k.a. Ho Wan Kwok, "Miles Guo," "Miles Kwok," and "Brother Seven") back to China. During the Trump administration, Steve Bannon was arrested on Guo Wengui's yacht.[41] During the Biden administration, Guo Wengui was charged with his own billion-dollar fraud.[42]

In 2021, Pras was hit with a superseding indictment, which accused him of violating the Foreign Agents Registration Act (FARA) when he urged the extradition of Guo Wengui from the United States back to China as well as leniency for Low. In other words, Pras stands accused of violating campaign finance laws when Obama was president and violating foreign agent registration rules when Trump was president. Federal prosecutor Nicole Lockhart told the jury in his case, "The defendant [Pras] wanted money and was willing to break any laws necessary to get paid."[43]

Pras wasn't the only one prosecuted for this latter lobby-the-Trump-administration-for-China scheme. One of Pras's friends, Nickie Lum Davis, was also prosecuted for this 2017 scheme. She pleaded guilty and was sentenced to two years.[44] Another participant was Steve Wynn, the owner of the Wynn Casinos, and the then-finance chair of the RNC.[45] Wynn was only hit with a civil suit from the DOJ requiring him to register as a foreign agent of China, as required by FARA.[46] Wynn has not been charged with a crime. And Elliot Broidy, the deputy finance chair for the RNC, pleaded guilty in 2020 to his role in also advocating for Trump officials to drop the case against Low.[47] Both Wynn and Broidy had to step down from their posts at the RNC, not because of the 1MDB scandal, but because of unrelated sex scandals—Wynn was accused of sexual harassment,[48] and Broidy was accused of agreeing to pay a mistress who was a former Playboy playmate $1.6 million for her silence.[49] Broidy was pardoned by President Trump on his last day in office; thus Broidy did not see any jail time.[50] There was no pardon for Pras, which left him with extreme legal exposure.

As reporter Michael Ames wrote in *Rolling Stone* before Pras's criminal trial was set to begin in 2023, "After a four-hour interview [with Pras], weeks of follow-up conversations, and reading through piles of legal motions, I can confidently report that Pras has landed at the center of a remarkable legal clusterfuck."[51]

In federal court in 2023, as a criminal defendant, Pras opened his testimony by incongruously saying: "Mic check 1, 2. Mic check 1, 2," as if he were in a recording studio or concert hall instead of a courtroom.[52] Testifying in his own defense, Pras claimed that Low had given him $20 million in 2012 so that Pras would set up a photo op between Jho Low and President Obama. According to prosecutors, Pras gave roughly $800,000 of this money to twenty friends so that they could attend a $40,000-a-plate fundraiser to support Obama's reelection.[53] This fundraiser was at Frank White Jr.'s home.[54] Some of the Low-to-Pras-to-Pras's-friends money was given to the Obama Victory Fund.[55]

Low did eventually get a photo with both Obamas, in front a of Christmas tree, after the election.[56] Whether Pras had anything to do with the picture was not clear. One version of events is that it was the result of the legwork of Obama fundraiser Frank White Jr.[57] White did not face charges.

This isn't just a celebrity crime story—though, surely, that is part of why this string of events has already inspired a full book on the 1MDB scandal called *The Billion Dollar Whale*. This is also a story of how corporate structures are used in campaign finance crimes to try to evade accountability.[58] The evasion worked for over a decade, as justice was only served eleven years after the 2012 election.

As the DOJ laid out in Pras Michel's indictment: "[Pras] MICHEL, JHO LOW, and their intermediaries used shell entities and shell bank accounts to facilitate the transfer of millions of dollars from JHO LOW to MICHEL for the purpose of funneling significant sums of money into the United States presidential election as purportedly legitimate contributions, all while concealing the true source of the money."[59] The DOJ explained the daisy chain of entities that allowed Low's money to go to Pras and then into the American political system, thusly:

> JHO LOW directed the transfer of approximately $21,000,000 from Company A and Company B, both shell companies in the British Virgin Islands with bank accounts in Singapore, to Company C and Company D, companies in the United States with bank accounts under the control of MICHEL and/or his financial advisor. In addition, during the same period, JHO LOW directed the transfer of approximately $600,000 from Company B to one of MICHEL'S personal bank accounts in the United States.[60]

The DOJ alleged that a fifth company, Company E, which public records now show is SPM Holdings LLC, was also used in the conspiracy.[61] Reporters matched up the donations in the DOJ indictment to FEC files and stated, "The dates and numbers for those donations in the indictment match with federal fundraising disclosures made by Black Men Vote, a super PAC that was supportive of Obama's re-election efforts in battleground states."[62]

When Low's money first entered the 2012 election, it did so as dark money, obscuring its true source because of the secretive business entities that were used by Low and Pras. In 2015, money in politics watchdogs the Campaign Legal Center (CLC) and Democracy 21 filed a FEC complaint and a letter to the DOJ complaining about Pras's use of SPM Holdings LLC to spend money in the 2012 election.[63] At the time, the use of LLCs as political donors was nearly unheard of. But this was the first post–*Citizens United* presidential election. FEC records showed two big donations from SPM Holdings LLC to a super PAC called Black Men Vote in the 2012 election: one donation of $400,000 and another of $475,000.[64] CLC and Democracy 21 noted in their complaint that, by listing SPM Holdings LLC as the donor instead of his own name, Pras had likely spent through a straw donor in violation of federal election laws.[65] Whether this is how the DOJ first started looking at Pras for campaign finance crimes, or whether they already had him in their sights from the 1MDB investigation, is impossible to know from the outside.

According to reporting by NPR who covered the Pras's criminal trial, during cross examination by federal prosecutors, Pras was asked about "two of [Pras] Michel's friends, who later returned the money he gave them after consulting with their own attorneys about the legality of those payments, and about an Obama fundraiser telling Michel that any money he donated had to be 'legitimately your money.'"[66]

Pras testified at his criminal trial that he considered the $20 million from Low for the Obama photo to be "free money," that "I got some free money, I figured why not just pay it forward and also to help the cause . . . help President Obama get re-elected,"[67] and that "I could have bought 12 elephants with it."[68] In retrospect, buying twelve elephants would have been a wiser choice, as spending the foreign money in the 2012 election, which led him being faced with twenty-two years in prison after rejecting a plea deal.[69] Pras also received an additional $80 million for his illegal "lobbying efforts" with the Trump administration on China's and Low's behalf.[70]

One piece of context for Pras's political spending is 2012 was the most expensive presidential election in American history (it would later be surpassed by the cost of the 2020 election). The high price tag of the 2012 presidential election also explains why sophisticated political actors in the United States would gobble up campaign money without asking enough questions about its true—and illegal—source.

Moreover, the 2012 election was the first presidential election after the Supreme Court loosened campaign finance rules in *Citizens United v. FEC*. Pras might have mistakenly thought that campaign finance rules had been completely deregulated. But, in a 2012 case called *Bluman*, the Supreme Court left in place the ban on foreign spending in US elections. This proved fatal to his freedom. On April 26, 2023, a jury convicted Pras on all ten counts.[71] At the time of this writing, Jho Low was still at large and had yet to face justice anywhere.[72]

ILLEGAL MONEY IN THE 2018 AND 2020 ELECTIONS

With a privately funded campaign finance system, US elections are inherently vulnerable to criminal money flowing into the campaign finance system. This is a bipartisan problem. Above it was a Democratic president who benefited. Below it was Republicans. What both experiences have in common is the fact that dark money can operate as a cover for illegal foreign money. And in both cases corporations were used to hide the truth from the voting public.

In October 2019, Lev Parnas and Igor Fruman—both immigrants from the former Soviet Union who became naturalized Americans—were arrested at Washington Dulles International Airport with one-way tickets to Europe.[73] When he was arrested, Parnas apparently had on him five cell phones, Trump-campaign-branded plastic straws, cash, and the business card of a top Ukrainian anti-corruption prosecutor, whom Rudy Giuliani had met while trying to dig up dirt on Joe Biden during the 2020 election.[74] The DOJ charged Parnas and Fruman with campaign finance crimes including funneling illegal foreign money into US elections.[75]

Besides being a foreign-influence-in-US-elections story, the Trump-Giuliani-Parnas-Fruman story is also a corporate-money-in-politics story. Public records show that Parnas and Fruman incorporated an energy-trading company named Global Energy Producers (GEP) and used it to donate $325,000 to pro-Trump super PAC America First Action, which raised money for the 2020 election, and $15,000 to a super PAC that supported West Virginia attorney general Patrick Morrisey's 2018 bid for the Senate (both were defeated).[76] Some of the political donations were routed through another Parnas-Fruman company with the ridiculous name of Fraud Guarantee.[77] Trump's lawyer Giuliani did $500,000 worth of consulting work for Fraud Guarantee.[78]

The political watchdog the Campaign Legal Center (CLC) rang an early alarm on July 25, 2018, by filing a complaint against Parnas, Fruman, and their company, Global Energy Producers LLC (GEP).[79] CLC alleged in the complaint that GEP "may have violated 52 U.S.C. § 30122 by making contributions to [pro-Trump Super PAC] America First Action, Inc. (I.D.: C00637512) in the name of another person, namely GEP, and that GEP violated 52 U.S.C. § 30122 by knowingly permitting its name to be used for the making of such contribution."[80] In plain English, the CLC was accusing Parnas and Fruman of making illegal straw donations to a super PAC through the business entity Global Energy Producers.

CLC's researchers explained how they uncovered this mystery on a podcast. CLC lawyer Brendan Fischer noticed the six-figure donation to America First Action from GEP, an entity he had never seen before. He flagged it for CLC researcher Maggie Christ to investigate. "Can we figure anything out about this group?" he asked her. She looked for corporate filings for the LLC and discovered that GEP had been created in Delaware just five weeks before it started spending lavishly in politics. That raised red flags. While the entity was formed in Delaware, the filings from the pro-Trump super PAC listed a residential address as the LLC's location. That address was linked to Lev Parnas and Igor Fruman, who at the time were complete unknowns, at least in the English-speaking world. So, Christ switched from searching for them in English to searching for them in Russian. Suddenly Parnas and Fruman were no longer phantoms. They showed up in news items from Ukraine bragging about their connections to President Trump along with pictures of him at fundraising events.[81]

Spending money in politics through a corporation would have been perfectly legal post–*Citizens United v. FEC*, and its follow-on DC Circuit case *SpeechNow*, if the money had actually been from Parnas and Fruman, and they spent it under their real names.[82] However, prosecutors alleged that they acted as straw donors, and that the money came from a disallowed Russian donor named Andrey Muraviev.[83] To reiterate, under US campaign finance law, one is not allowed to give money in the name of another person. Giving through a straw donor is what got conservative pundit Dinesh D'Souza convicted of a campaign finance crime.[84] (President Trump later pardoned D'Souza for this crime.)[85] The Russian source of the $1 million Parnas-Fruman funds was charged in 2022 by the DOJ of breaking US campaign finance law with illegal foreign funding.[86] Parnas and Fruman were accused of illegally facilitating payments from foreign nationals into American elections. According to the DOJ, they helped arrange two $500,000 wire transfers in late 2018 to be sent "from overseas accounts to a U.S. corporate bank account controlled by Fruman and another individual."[87]

[93]

The Parnas-Fruman money got around American politics. According to the indictment, the money went to the pro-Trump group America First Action, as well as "state and federal candidates and politicians in Nevada, New York, and other states." According to the *Tampa Bay Times*, Parnas and Fruman—both Florida residents—contributed $50,000 to Governor DeSantis's political committee through a shell company.[88] Both appeared at DeSantis's inauguration in January 2019.[89] Parnas reportedly sought to join DeSantis's transition team.[90] The Second Circuit would later conclude that "evidence demonstrated that Fruman and Parnas made political donations that were funded or reimbursed by Muraviev, including donations to the Protect the House joint fundraising committee, Friends of Ron DeSantis, as well as to Adam Laxalt, then-Attorney General of Nevada, and Wes Duncan, who was running for Nevada Attorney General."[91]

The origin of the Parnas-Fruman-Muraviev plot was rooted in their desire to open a marijuana businesses in 2018.[92] According to Muraviev's indictment, Muraviev was going to fund this cannabis business.[93] Parnas and Fruman would get the licenses to operate them in Nevada, California, New York, and New Jersey.[94] The plan to procure these licenses allegedly involved spending $1 million to $2 million in state and federal elections funded by Muraviev, but under the names of Parnas and Fruman, who were American citizens.[95] The day after the 2018 election, the group congratulated themselves on supporting candidates that won, including in Florida.[96]

The actions of Parnas and Furman came up in President Trump's first impeachment, for various attempts to extort information out of Ukraine that could be useful to Trump's reelection. Consequently, Parnas and Furman appear in the House Intelligence Committee's Trump first impeachment inquiry report 103 and 41 times, respectively.[97] Parnas shows up an additional 85 times in the House Judiciary Committee's impeachment report with Fruman appearing 38 times.[98]

Once Parnas and Fruman were indicted, President Trump claimed that he did not know either man. Parnas responded to this by saying that every time Trump denied knowing him, Parnas would expose proof that they did know each other. True to his word, Parnas gave pictures of himself with President Trump, his daughter Ivanka, and his son Don Jr. as well as Giuliani to the House Judiciary Committee investigating Trump's first impeachment.[99] Parnas also produced audiotape of a donor dinner in 2018 where he and Fruman were close enough to President Trump to capture him talking on Fruman's cell phone. On the tape President Trump says of the respected US ambassador to the Ukraine, Marie Yovanovitch: "Get her out tomorrow. I don't care . . . Get her out tomorrow. Take her out. OK? Do it."[100]

Unfortunately for the American public's edification, Fruman's and Parnas's cases would not be resolved until long after the 2018 and 2020 elections were over. Fruman pleaded guilty in open court on September 10, 2021.[101] A month later, after a criminal trial, Parnas was found guilty on all charges.[102] But the fact remained that they used illegal foreign money to interfere in the 2018 and 2020 elections at both state and federal levels, using corporations as part of the scheme. Moreover, had Trump remained in power, or if he returns to power, he could pardon Fruman and Parnas, because they were convicted of federal crimes.

One common theme between the 1MDB scandal and the Parnas-Fruman affair is that dark money thwarted transparency of money in politics during American elections when the information would have been useful to voters. Prosecutors took years to unravel these schemes. By the time the perpetrators were arrested, tried, and convicted, the elections they meddled in were long since over.

These two tales raise the possibility of an ominous external threat. As long as US elections are privately funded, they run the risk of becoming playthings of unscrupulous foreign kleptocrats who know they can hide their identities behind corporate structures to spend millions in dark money in American elections. So far, the foreign sources in both cases have not faced legal consequences. Like alleged criminal Jho Low, alleged criminal Andrey Muraviev is still at large.[103]

7

CREATING A MONSTER

DONALD TRUMP AND THE 2016 ELECTION

On June 16, 2015, standing next to his former-model wife Melania, Donald Trump descended down his own golden-colored escalator in his own building, Trump Tower, to announce that he was running for president.[1] Was Donald Trump already an antidemocracy candidate when he rode that escalator? This is a very difficult question to answer, because, when he first threw his hat into the presidential race, he had never held any public office before. There was no record of how he would behave once he got political power.

The 2016 campaign revealed some troubling authoritarian tropes, including Trump's condoning violence by his supporters against political protestors at his rallies.[2] At a Trump rally in November 2015, "a black civil-rights activist who shouted 'Black lives matter!' as Trump called from the stage for the activist to be thrown out. Trump later said the activist was 'obnoxious' and deserved to be 'roughed up.'"[3]

He also seemed to threaten to use the DOJ to prosecute his political enemies, "'If I win,' Trump told Hillary Clinton during [their] debate, 'I am going to instruct my attorney general to get a special prosecutor to look into your situation.'"[4] He also added that, when he was president, Clinton "would be in jail."[5] Candidate Trump seemed hostile to the First Amendment when he said in 2016, "'we're going to open up libel laws, and we're going to have people sue you like you've never got sued before.'"[6]

Even before he was a candidate, Trump had a history of questioning election results. In 2012, on election night, when African American president Barack Obama was reelected, with an electoral college win of 302 votes to Mitt Romney's 206, Trump declared the election a "total sham" and a "travesty," while asserting that the United States is "not a democracy."[7]

During his candidacy in 2016, Trump said he would not necessarily support the Republican nominee for president if it wasn't him.[8] He made similarly alarming claims during a presidential debate with Hillary Clinton, claiming he'd keep the country in suspense about whether he would accept the results of the 2016 election, adding that he would only accept the results if he won.[9] These statements should have been flashing red warning lights that he did not accept the democratic process: where voters are the ultimate arbiter of who is in power, elected offices are for limited times, and those who lose elections don't get to hold office.

Strangely, after winning the 2016 election, Trump leveled accusations of voter fraud. He even appointed a commission to look into the nearly nonexistent problem. Trump's voter fraud commission imploded and disbanded.[10]

TRUMP'S CORPORATE FUNDERS IN 2016

In the 2016 election, candidate Trump made a big point of touting that he had a self-financed campaign. This claim was only partially true. Trump did fund roughly 20 percent of his first presidential run, but the supermajority of the funding (roughly 80 percent) was from other people's money.[11]

Candidate Trump has always been supported by corporate political spending. This money did not flow directly to him, which would be illegal; rather, it went to various super PACs that spent money boosting his candidacy. Tracking pro-Trump money requires kaleidoscopic vision and attention to detail: there is the Trump Make America Great Again PAC; the Make America Great Again Super PAC; the Make America Great Again, Again! Super PAC; the Rebuilding America Now Super PAC; America First Action Super PAC; and the Preserve America PAC, which is also a super PAC.[12]

In 2016, GEO Group, a private prison company, made news because it was the only publicly traded company to support Rebuilding America Now, one of the pro-Trump super PACs. GEO Group gave one donation of $100,000 and another of $125,000.[13] There were, however, many privately held companies that gave lavishly to pro-Trump PACs. One corporate donor to the Rebuilding America Now was Hamilton Co., a real estate firm, that gave $300,000 in 2016.[14] Anderson Columbia Co. Inc., a highway construction firm from Florida, gave $150,000.[15] Frank Calandra Inc., which owns Jennmar and produces coal mining products, gave $150,000.[16] Murray Energy Corporation, a coal company, gave $200,000.[17] Southeast QSR LLC, an entity that runs various Taco Bell franchises in the South, gave $150,000.[18] Bob Nardelli's investment and advisory company XLR-8 LLC gave $25,000, as did construction company Vecellio Group Inc.[19] Hubbard Construction Company of Florida gave $25,000.[20] GLC Farms, a sugar producer, gave $25,000. Americas Export Corporation of Miami, Florida, gave $25,000.[21] The sugar company Fanjul's affiliate Stofin Co. Inc. gave $25,000 in 2016 to the pro-Trump Super PAC Rebuilding America Now.[22] Another Fanjul affiliate, Okeelanta Corporation, gave $25,000. Yet another Fanjul affiliate, Agro-Industrial Management, gave $25,000.[23]

In addition to corporate treasury funds, corporate CEOs were big political spenders supporting Trump. In his first run for president in 2016, Linda McMahon ex-CEO of World Wrestling Entertainment (WWE) gave Rebuilding America Now $6 million.[24] Marcus Bernard, the cofounder of Home Depot, gave this super PAC $5 million in 2016.[25] Real estate developer Geoffrey Palmer gave it $4 million.[26] Ronald M. Cameron, the owner and chairman of Mountaire Farms, which produces poultry, gave it $2 million.[27] Stephen Feinberg of Cerberus Capital Management gave this super PAC $1,475,000.[28] All of these big spenders saw the antidemocracy warning signs that Trump had exhibited in 2016, and they spent money boosting his political career anyway.

DIRTY TRICKS AND FOREIGN INTERFERENCE IN THE 2020 ELECTION

Not since the reelection campaign of President Nixon in 1972 did an incumbent, President Trump, seem so hell bent on cheating in the election. In Nixon's case, his cheating arguably worked as a Nixon dirty trick knocked out a promising opponent, senator Ed Muskie. The dirty trick was known as the "Canuck letter." It was penned and planted in the *Manchester Union Leader* by the Nixon campaign. The bogus missive accused Senator Muskie of calling French Canadians the derogatory term "Canuck."[29] Muskie responded to the letter with anger and, as some witnesses claimed, tears. Others said what looked like tears were really melting snowflakes, as the Muskie press conference in question was outside, during a snowfall. The story picked up in the press was that Muskie had completely lost his cool over the Canuck letter, demonstrating that he wasn't fit to be president.[30] Muskie came in fourth in the primaries. If Nixon's point with the Canuck letter was to tank Muskie's candidacy, it worked.

The 2020 election also had its share of dirty tricks. During a call on July 25, 2019, with President Trump asked Ukrainian president Volodymyr Zelenskyy "to do us a favor, though" by finding compromising information about Joe Biden after Zelenskyy mentioned his country's urgent need for military aid to fight Russia.[31] Trump's lawyer Giuliani traveled to Ukraine to dig up opposition research that might help Trump's reelection.[32] Giuliani was working with Lev Parnas and Igor Fruman, who (as described above) were also up to no good.[33]

When the transcript of the Trump/Zelenskyy phone call came out, it led to President Trump's first impeachment on December 10, 2019, when the House of Representatives unveiled two articles of impeachment against him: one for abuse of power, and one for obstruction of Congress.[34]

Pursuant to the Constitution, removal of the president by the Senate requires a two thirds vote. Trump was acquitted by the Senate on both counts on February 5, 2020. The final vote was forty-eight yeas to fifty-two nays on abuse of power, and forty-seven yeas to fifty-three nays on obstruction of Congress.[35] Utah Republican senator Mitt Romney was the only one to cross party lines to vote yea for the first article of impeachment. With no other senator willing to break partisan ranks, Trump remained in power for the remainder of his term. President Trump was impeached by the House a second time with one week remaining in his term for trying to overthrow the results of 2020 election.

If Trump's efforts with Ukraine was an attempt to tank Biden's candidacy, it did not work. Biden rose in the polls as Trump's machinations against him became public. What's troubling is what might have happened if the Zelenskyy call never came to light, or if Ukraine had buckled and produced bogus dirt on Biden. Could Biden have gone the way of Muskie, a victim of political dirty trick?

For those who lived through the impeachment of President Bill Clinton in 1999 and the contested election between George W. Bush and Al Gore that followed in 2000, the impeachment of President Donald Trump in 2019 followed by another contested election in 2020 seemed hauntingly familiar.[36]

NAKED BALLOTS, CIVIC STRIPPERS, AND A RAPPER FOR PRESIDENT

The 2020 American presidential election was already one for the history books because it took place during a global pandemic.[37] The Spanish flu pandemic of 1918 did not stick round long enough to impact the 1920 election.[38] A century later, America was not so lucky. The 2020 presidential election took place smack dab in the middle of the COVID-19 pandemic, before there was a vaccine, and while doctors still had a steep learning curve for treating the virus.[39] For the immunocompromised or the unlucky, catching COVID-19 in 2020 could mean debilitating illness, hospitalization, or even death.[40] Days after the 2020 election, the United States reported its ten millionth case of COVID-19.[41]

Voters clamored for safe ways to vote in 2020, and many states responded by expanding ways to vote, including allowing voters to use collection boxes to drop off ballots (so called drop boxes) and expanding who was eligible to vote absentee.[42] With millions of American voters voting by mail for the first time, voter confusion surfaced.

NAKED BALLOTS

One 2020 Public Service Announcement (PSA) featured topless female Pennsylvania legislators reminding Pennsylvanians who were voting by mail to avoid the naked ballot problem.[43] (Viewers could not see their breasts, but they could see that the women were indeed topless. Sample ballots covered the upper half of their torsos.)

Inspired by these lawmakers, celebrities copying the trope also got naked for democracy. In a celebrity PSA, Chris Rock, Sarah Silverman, Mark Ruffalo, Amy Schumer, and other entertainers showed up in their birthday suits to remind Pennsylvania voters that they had to use a secrecy envelope when they returned their mail-in ballots—otherwise those ballots could be deemed "naked" and rejected by officials.[44] The celebrity ad was launched by the prodemocracy nonprofit RepresentUS.[45] Other PSAs were more staid, like one featuring African American Philadelphia Phillies outfielder Andrew McCutchen, who kept his clothes on while calmly explaining how to vote legally in Pennsylvania using the secrecy envelope.[46] (The ballot goes in the secrecy envelope, and the secrecy envelope goes into the larger mailing envelope.) Pennsylvania expanded the availability of mail-in ballots to all registered voters under Act 77 in 2019.[47] Partially because of this new law and partially because of the pandemic, the use of mail-in ballots in Pennsylvania jumped over tenfold from 2016 to 2020: from 266,208 to 2,704,147.[48]

The naked-ballot problem was the result of a ruling by the Pennsylvania Supreme Court that naked ballots could be rejected.[49] This was a reversal, as naked ballots counted during the 2020 primary.[50] The Republican-controlled legislature insisted upon the use of the envelopes in the general election.[51] Lisa Deeley, the top election official in Philadelphia, told *Politico*, "This [naked ballot problem] has the potential of disenfranchising tens of thousands of voters. [If] people . . . aren't using a 'secrecy' envelope, we're going to throw votes out based on a technicality. When you consider that the 2016 presidential election in Pennsylvania was decided by just over 44,000 votes, you can see why I'm concerned."[52] And, Deely argued, "one voter who is disenfranchised is one too many."[53]

In the end, the public doesn't know how many naked ballots were cast in Pennsylvania because there was no standard for tracking them. MIT researchers tried to gather this information, but only 32 of the 67 counties provided data. MIT found that in Philadelphia "only approximately 4,027 naked ballots [were] cast."[54] That's out of more than 749,000 ballots cast in Philadelphia, which isn't that bad.[55] On the positive side, far fewer naked ballots were reported in the general election than experts predicted, so perhaps all of the PSAs (clothed and naked) informed Pennsylvanians how to comply with the law.

CIVIC STRIPPERS

Get out the vote (GOTV) ads were particularly inventive in the swing state of Georgia. Folks who lived in Atlanta may have seen some unique PSAs featuring strippers urging voters to participate in the upcoming election. If amateur strippers showed up in the Pennsylvania ads, professional strippers appeared in the Georgia ads. As described by NPR, "[A] woman in knee high, lace up boots walks away from the camera, toward a stage decorated with patriotic bunting.... The beat drops, the woman and other dancers begin to perform, and the repeated message is a simple one: 'Get Your Booty To The Poll.'... As they perform a series of pole tricks, the dancers articulate why it is so important to engage in local elections and vote for down-ballot candidates."[56] The ad was shot on a shoestring budget funded by a GoFundMe page.[57]

As one of the dancers featured in the campaign, Coy Malone, told a reporter, "Yes, we were provocative, but we didn't do anything that sold our souls. We just sold a message."[58] To another member of the press, he stated: "A lot [of people] do not understand that when you're voting, you're also electing judges, you're selecting [district attorneys], you're voting on taxes you're voting on laws."[59] As a producer of the ads, Paul Fox, told the press, "We got your attention[,] and now we're talking about voting."[60] He continued to explain the genesis of the ad: "This video really started with the death of George Floyd in May [2020] [a Black man who was killed on video by Minneapolis police] and us feeling like there was a better way to voice a need for change ... We wanted to ... get people, especially men, to vote."[61] The film directors who crafted the ad worked with W. Mondale Robinson of the Black Male Voter Project (not to be confused with the Black Men Vote PAC to which Pras gave money) to pick issues that would resonate with Black men,[62] who often skip voting.[63] Thus, the Get Your Booty to the Poll PSAs mentioned police brutality, cash bail, and public schools.[64]

Get Your Booty to the Poll PSAs cleverly targeted a key demographic. As Pew noted, between 2000 and 2019 Georgia's eligible voter population grew by 1.9 million, and nearly half of those new eligible voters were Black.[65] By contrast, only one-quarter of the new eligible voters were White.[66] Simultaneously, there was a distinct gender gap in Black voting:

according to Pew, "in 2016, 64% of eligible Black women said they voted, compared with 54% of eligible Black men."[67]

Georgia in 2020 was a microcosm of a changing American electorate, and whoever cracked the code of GOTV efforts in Georgia would attain enormous political power. In postelection litigation in 2020, Trump's lawyers often focused on trying to throw out the votes from cities with large Black populations, like Atlanta, Detroit, and Philadelphia.[68] Because of social media, the Get Your Booty to the Poll ads had at least five million views.[69] In Georgia, more new voters were Black than any other racial group.[70] In the end, Georgia elected Biden for president, and, in a special election in January 2021, Georgia voters sent two Democrats to the Senate, which flipped from Republican to Democratic control.[71]

THE RAPPER RUNNING FOR PRESIDENT

On Independence Day 2020, long after the Democratic nomination had solidified around Biden and the Republican nomination around incumbent President Trump, a late entrant took the political stage: rapper Kanye West (also known as "Ye"). West, a longtime attention-seeker, was an unusual presidential candidate. This was an odd career move, as West had not been particularly political to this point. In contrast to rapper Sean "Puff Daddy" Combs, who once launched a pro-voting campaign called "Vote or Die," or any number of consciousness rappers like Chuck D., Talib Kweli, or Mos Def, who take political stances in their music, West had never seemed to pay much attention to democracy, elections, or politics, either in his lyrics or his life.

On August 30, 2015, Kanye West declared at the MTV Video Music Awards, "I have decided in 2020 to run for president."[72] Few took him seriously; most bona fide candidates do not declare they are running five years in advance. But then, on July 4, 2020, West made the announcement that he actually would be running for president.[73] This was also not taken particularly seriously; most candidates don't announce they are running mere months before an election, either. But, unlike 2015, in 2020 West filed the requisite paperwork with the Federal Election Commission (FEC).[74]

West tried to get on the general election ballot in 2020, but his late-breaking campaign missed filing deadlines and turned in petitions that were riddled with obviously fraudulent signatures.[75] In New Jersey, pages of them appeared to be in the same person's handwriting.[76] In Illinois, he only had half of the required signatures, and some of the signatures he turned in were questioned by election authorities.[77] In one key swing state, he was a just a few minutes late with his petition; as Politico reported, "West's effort to get on the Wisconsin ballot was challenged because his documents were filed one to two minutes after the 5 p.m. deadline."[78] West did not get on the Wisconsin ballot.[79]

In Virginia, West's campaign was accused of duping people into becoming electors for him.[80] As one person who submitted an affidavit, Matthan Wilson, told the *Washington Post*: "I am so embarrassed.... I don't want to be an elector for Kanye West. I don't want to vote for Kanye West. I only like one or two of his songs."[81] In the end, West was kept off of the Virginia ballot because a judge deemed his campaign to have committed fraud.[82]

In the end, West was on the ballot in twelve states and received 70,296 votes nationwide.[83] One of those votes was potentially his own, as West reportedly cast his first vote for president for himself in Wyoming.[84] Interestingly, though, in the official vote totals there are zero votes from Wyoming for West.[85] This is curious, as Wyoming typically counts write-in votes.[86] Perhaps West failed to follow the directions for how to vote for a write-in candidate? This is just one more mystery about his candidacy.

Reporting revealed that West's campaign was run entirely by Republican operatives.[87] As one political scientist told NPR, this Republican-backed effort was "bizarre and unusual."[88] The overlap between the strippers who urged Georgia voters to "Get Your Booty to the Poll" and the Republicans dangling West's candidacy was that both efforts focused on Black voters. Inspiring Black voters to vote Democratic or Independent could make a big difference in who won the presidency.[89]

Because of West's slapdash campaign and the bungling of his lawyers, he was not on the ballot in any of the swing states that ended up deciding the 2020 presidential election: Georgia, Arizona, Wisconsin, Pennsylvania, North Carolina, Michigan, Nevada, and New Hampshire.[90] West's highest vote totals were in Tennessee, where he got 10,256 votes, and Colorado, where he got 8,080 votes. Thus, West's paltry turnout did not swing the outcome in either state: one went deep red for Trump, and the other deep blue for Biden.

But had West been on the Arizona or Georgia ballots, he could have wreaked havoc. Arizona went 1,672,143 votes for Biden by a margin of 10,457 votes. In Georgia the vote was 2,473,633 for Biden by a margin of 11,779. A few thousand votes for Kanye West could have flipped these states and might have changed who won the White House. Given that his campaign was run by Republicans, West's entire campaign was likely an effort to have him play a spoiler role: splitting the Black vote in key states, thereby allowing Trump to remain in power.[91] It was sheer incompetence on the part of West's campaign that prevented him from becoming a bigger factor in the 2020 election.

TRUMP'S ASSAULTS ON HOW AMERICANS VOTE

The 2020 election was already off to a crazy start with a failed impeachment of the president in February and the COVID-19 pandemic catching fire in March. Meanwhile, President Trump was not behaving like a typical presidential candidate. For one thing, he would not say that he would agree to a peaceful transfer of power if he lost the election.[92] He laid the groundwork for claiming that the 2020 general election was stolen even as the election was ongoing.[93]

ATTACKS ON VOTE BY MAIL

Trump attacked the integrity of voting by mail, a method that millions of Americans utilized because of the pandemic.[94] He did this even as he had enjoyed the convenience of voting by mail in the past and as he voted by mail in 2020.[95] He spun many tall tales about the dangers of voting by mail; for example, "in a White House briefing in April, President Trump stated that if people vote by mail, 'You get thousands and thousands of people sitting in somebody's living room, signing ballots all over the place.'"[96] Trump fantasized that vote-by-mail ballots would be counterfeited by foreign nations.[97] To make matters even more convoluted, Trump often encouraged Republicans to vote by mail while simultaneously casting aspersions on voting by mail when done by Democrats.[98]

Harvard's Berkman Klein Center tracked media coverage of the vote-by-mail issue during the 2020 election and found that "most of the peaks in coverage of mail-in voter fraud, across all media and social media, were driven by Donald Trump using a combination of his Twitter account, his press briefings, and interviews on *Fox News*."[99] The center concluded that President Trump "uses the power of the office he holds and the horrified fascination with his norms-breaking expressions to force mainstream media to report on his agenda and reinforce the association of mail-in voting with fraud in the minds of distracted readers and viewers."[100]

Trump's anti-vote-by-mail rhetoric even alarmed some in the GOP.[101] Florida Republicans pushed back on his mischaracterizations.[102] He got similar reactions from Republicans in Wisconsin. As *USA Today* reported, "What the president is doing when he keeps saying that this mail-in balloting thing is fraudulent, he's scaring our own voters from using a legit way to cast your ballot."[103]

Making voting-by-mail a partisan issue had an negative impact on some voters, who eschewed this method.[104] As Sarah Niebler found, "Among Republican voters in Delaware, voters who did not support President Trump were more than twice as likely to vote by mail than supporters of the president."[105] Troublingly, as *Time* reported during the election, "the constant onslaught of misinformation about mail-in ballots led to a trend this summer where users who said they were Trump supporters posted videos of themselves throwing their absentee or mail-in ballot requests in the trash and encouraged others to do the same."[106] In retrospect, President Trump may have cost himself reelection by miscalculating the impact of denigrating a safe way of voting during a pandemic that his voters could have used but for his disinformation.[107]

Given the logistical challenges posed by COVID-19, the actual election went as smoothly as any other recent election.[108] Voters were aided in thirty states by new rules that made voting-by-mail easier than it had been before the pandemic.[109] Changes to state election laws included mailing ballots, paying postage for ballots, and easing rules about witnesses for absentee voting.[110]

TRUMP'S ATTACKS ON ELECTION ADMINISTRATION

In September 2020, President Trump complained without proof in a presidential debate that "bad things happen in Philadelphia."[111] He carped about his poll watchers being illegally kicked out of certain precincts during early voting when, in fact, the poll watchers had no legal right to be there, under state law.[112] Al Schmidt, the lone Republican on the Philadelphia Board of City Commissioners, expressed his exasperation with the Trump campaign's approach: "In a typical election, candidates attack each other. In this election, it is our electoral system that is under attack."[113]

Trump made threats about cutting funding to Nevada over its administration of elections.[114] At a political rally in September 2020, according to Polifact, "President Donald Trump made a series of false attacks on voting by mail at a Nevada rally, wrongly suggesting that Gov. Steve Sisolak, a Democrat, is in charge of millions of mail ballots and can 'rig' the election."[115] This was wrongheaded in a number of dimensions.[116] What money Trump was threatening to withhold was unclear, and it was also unlikely that he had any legal authority to withhold any federal money from any state.

In North Carolina, the Trump campaign got even more aggressive. In September 2020, the state board in charge of elections decided to relax the rules for spoiled ballots so that fewer voters would be disenfranchised for making simple mistakes.[117] Displeased with this turn of events, according to the Associated Press, "Donald Trump's campaign . . . wrote to some of the state's 100 local election offices with extraordinary guidance: Ignore that rule."[118] In other words, the Trump campaign was urging election administrators in North Carolina to break the law.[119]

Most remarkably, in September 2020, President Trump in an interview stunningly urged voters in North Carolina to vote *twice*: once in person, and once by mail. This is another instance of the sitting president encouraging breaking the law—this time by voters.[120] This prompted North Carolina's head of elections to clarify that voting twice would violate state law.[121] Double voting in a federal election violates federal law as well.[122]

THE MOST EXPENSIVE ELECTION EVER

2020 was the most expensive federal election in history, at $14.4 billion.[123] Democrats outspent Republicans $8.4 billion to $5.3 billion. Most of the money in the $5.7 billion presidential race was spent by Democratic candidates vying for the presidency. Two factors skewed this number: (1) there were twenty-nine Democrats who ran; and (2) Michael Bloomberg spent over $1 billion failing to capture the Democratic nomination.[124]

Trump started out with a fundraising advantage as he launched his reelection campaign the day of his inauguration in 2017, and until August 2020, Trump had raised more money than Biden. After that point, however, Biden outraised Trump.[125] It is possible that donors were already using their own Democracy Litmus Test in deciding who to support, since by late 2019 it was clear that Trump had committed antidemocratic actions in the 2020 election, as highlighted by his first impeachment. Biden was the first general election candidate in history to raise over $1 billion.[126] But, at the same time, many donors did not hold Trump to a Democracy Litmus Test: he raised $774 million, half of which was from small donors.[127]

In 2020, Trump spent nada, nothing, zilch—in other words, $0—supporting his own reelection.[128] Part of what kept Trump competitive throughout the 2020 election was a new fundraising platform called WinRed, which kept his campaign coffers flush with cash. In 2020, Trump was entirely (100 percent) reliant on other people's money.

Launched by Republicans in 2019, WinRed was a fundraising platform for capturing small donors. It was modeled after a left-leaning platform called ActBlue.[129] In contrast to the nonprofit ActBlue, WinRed is a for-profit corporation. In its first year, WinRed raised $510 million.[130]

The closer the election got, the more devious WinRed got. In March 2020, the WinRed page for Trump's campaign included prechecked boxes that made a donation a recurring donation on a monthly basis. Closer to the election, these boxes signed donors up for weekly donations. Consequently, a donor who thought they were giving a single donation of $250 could end up giving $1,000 in a month. The weekly donations were referred to by the Trump campaign as the "money bomb."[131] Using such prechecked boxes online to trick donors are sometimes referred to as "dark patterns," which are disfavored as unethical traps for the unwary.[132]

As the *New York Times* revealed in an exposé, many low-income donors had their bank accounts emptied or their credit cards maxed because of these unintentional recurring donations to the Trump campaign.[133] As Trump contested the results of the 2020 election, he returned to his donor base to beg for money with the same prechecked box gambit. Some unsuspecting donors complained to their banks or credit card companies, thinking they had been subjects of fraud. In a way, they had. The *Times* noted that "several bank representatives who fielded fraud claims directly from consumers estimated that WinRed cases, at their peak, represented as much as 1 to 3 percent of their workload."[134] The *Times* report also estimated that from June 15 to the end of 2020, 12 percent of Trump's online donors requested refunds. The Trump campaign had to refund millions of dollars to donors who complained.[135] Using these dark patterns was yet another Trump scam.

Even after he was impeached, Trump still had corporate and billionaire financial support. In his 2020 bid for reelection, he was primarily supported by two super PACs: America First Action, and Preserve America PAC.[136] America First Action had corporate contributions from Fanjul Corp ($725,000); Fanjul's affiliate Osceola Farms ($450,000); Fanjul's affiliate New Hope Sugar ($450,000); Fanjul's affiliate Agro-Industrial Management ($350,000); Fanjul's affiliate Americas Export Corp. ($350,000); West Side Avenue Holdings ($250,000); Fanjul's affiliate Sem-Chi Rice Products ($250,000); Vital Pharmaceuticals ($250,000), which sells the sports drink Bang; hedge fund JAT Capital Partners ($200,000); Fanjul's affiliate Vandegrift Williams Farms ($150,000); Fanjul's affiliate Closter Farms ($150,000); the now defunct Garatoni Holdings Investment Partnership ($150,000); Florida hedge fund Millennium Management ($145,000); Fanjul's affiliate Sun Corn ($125,000); and a $1 million donation from an LLC called Deuterium Electron, which is an investment adviser.[137] As this list indicates, while there were many different corporations listed, most were actually affiliates of the company that markets the Florida Crystal brand sugar. Meanwhile, Preserve America PAC was primarily funded by the late billionaire Sheldon Adelson and his wife's $90 million.[138] Home Depot's

Bernard Marcus contributed $10 million to the Preserve America PAC in 2020, doubling what he gave in 2016.[139]

CORPORATE MONEY FUNDS TRUMP 2024

Political scientists have sounded the alarm as Trump faces possible reelection in 2024. For example, Chris Edelson warned, "Trump has praised authoritarians including Hungary's Viktor Orban, Russia's Vladimir Putin and China's Xi Jinping. If he is given the chance, Trump will do all he can to rule in their image."[140]

As the data shows, corporate funding went to Trump during his first two runs for president in 2016 and 2020. Despite the insurrection in 2021, and the fact that Trump is the only president in American history to be impeached twice, corporate donors as well as wealthy businessmen are still funding his Make America Great Again Inc. Super PAC in the run-up to his 2024 presidential race. FEC filings show that businessman Timothy Mellon, a grandson of Andrew Mellon and an heir to the Mellon banking fortune, contributed $1.5 million.[141] These same FEC records show that evangelist author John Blanchard gave this Trump PAC $1 million.[142]

But it isn't just individuals giving to Trump's effort to regain the White House. Corporate entities are also giving to the Make America Great Again Inc. Super PAC, including BPH Properties Inc., which gave $500,000; Probity International Corporation, which gave $133,000; and Splitco Holdings, LLC gave $100,000. Probity International is a real estate firm according to Dun & Bradstreet.[143] According to CNBC, "BPH Properties [is] an Alabama-based business run by real estate titan Luther S. Pate,"[144] and "Splitco Holdings LLC . . . has a listed address that matches Houston-based Fertitta Entertainment, . . . run by businessman Tilman Fertitta [who] owns the . . . Houston Rockets and hospitality giant Landry's."[145] In 2023, Adam Kidan's Churchill Business Consultants Inc. gave Make American Great Again Inc. $250,000.[146]

Then there were donors to the Make American Great Again, Again! that is also supporting Trump's 2024 bid, which included repeat donors Jose Fanjul, the owner of Fanjul Corp. who gave $250,000 in 2021, and Fanjul-affiliated Florida Crystal gave $150,000.[147] Other business donors to Make American Great Again, Again! Super PAC included Tranquil Path Investments, Ltd, ($500,000); ML Organization LLC ($500,000);

45 SRL, Inc. ($250,000); North Point Mergers and Acquisitions, Inc. ($100,000); Sterling Medical Group ($100,000); MA Carr Enterprises LLC ($100,000); Aqua Waterfront LLC ($100,000); Don McGill Toyota of West Houston ($50,000) and Don McGill Toyota of Katy ($50,000); and Z & A Infotek Corp. ($5,000).

Then there were rich individuals who donated. Diana Pulte, the vice president of ML Organization LLC, gave an additional $500,000 out of her own pocket, and David Frecka, CEO of Next Generation Films, Inc. (which makes packaging and not feature films), gave $250,000. Kenny Troutt, an executive at Mt. Vernon Investments, gave $250,000, and D. Mayes Middleton II at Middleton Oil Co. gave $250,000.[148] Patricia "Trish" Duggan gave $5,000,000 to Make American Great Again Inc. in 2023,[149] while casino magnate Phil Ruffin gave the group $2,000,000,[150] and New York Jets Chairman Robert Wood "Woody" Johnson gave $1,000,000.[151] Charles Kushner, father of Jared Kushner, gave $1,000,000,[152] as did Trump's sister Elizabeth Grau.[153]

Across all of Trump's elections, money from Big Sugar stands out. Big Sugar has been shaping American policy through political spending for decades. The Fanjul family and its fellow sugar producers were involved in American politics long before Trump.[154] Reporter Amy Bracken notes, "The four Fanjul brothers have an outsize presence in . . . the United States. . . . In the U.S., the Fanjuls also grow cane and spend heavily in Washington, ranking among the sugar industry's top political donors and biggest spenders on lobbying."[155] They have been the beneficiary of "long-standing sugar quota policies meant to punish Cuba . . . , but which help domestic sugar producers like the Fanjuls. They even protected sugar from NAFTA."[156] As one report noted, "In the U.S., the Fanjuls sell their sugar at sometimes two to three times the global market price, thanks to import limits and price supports."[157] As the *Colorado Independent* reported, the industry as a whole benefits, and, "as a result, a handful of sugar producers pocket around $1 billion a year in excess profits. A portion of that revenue is eventually placed back into the political system, a win for both Big Sugar and lawmakers across the country."[158] The next time you rip open a packet of Domino sugar, think of Donald Trump and his unwavering support from the Fanjul family and their companies, who backed his runs for office through two impeachments and after the January 6 insurrection.[159]

8

THE BIG LIE

BANKROLLING THE INSURRECTION

On January 6, 2021, Carolyn Bourdeaux, a freshman member of the House of Representatives from Georgia, was hunkered down in her new House office with her sister, Dr. Margaret Bourdeaux. Carolyn had been sworn in as a member of Congress just days before. In her former life, she was a college professor who taught public policy. That morning she was preparing to speak in defense of her state's electoral college votes for Biden because Republicans had made clear that they would object to them. Suddenly, she had to lock herself, her staff, and her sister inside her office for hours as violent crowds overtook the Capitol complex.

The Bourdeaux sisters were expecting trouble that day given President Trump's tweet on December 19, 2020, encouraging his followers to gather for a "big protest in D.C. on January 6th" and to "be there, [because it] will be wild!"[1] That was why Margaret was with Carolyn. Margaret, who had worked with Doctors of the World during the war in Kosovo, worried that her sister could be targeted with violence.[2] YouTube videos shot from Congresswoman Bourdeaux's office on January 6 show both sisters. The Congresswoman is the blonde woman speaking and Margaret, the doctor, is the redhead standing stoically behind her.[3]

Why the FBI didn't see January 6 coming as clearly as the Bourdeaux sisters is an open question. Former FBI agent Michael German later told Congress, "The FBI's failure to prepare for the January 6th attack on the U.S. Capitol was a result of its long-standing de-prioritization of investigations regarding white supremacists and far-right militant violence and hate crimes."[4]

America has had close presidential elections before, including an election in 2000 that was decided by the Supreme Court, elections decided by the House of Representatives, and even one decided by a commission after the Civil War, but it has never seen anything quite like the 2020 election and its aftermath, which resulted in an insurrection at the Capitol by the losing side.[5] The events that occurred between the 2020 presidential election through January 6, 2021, now look like a failed coup d'état by the then-sitting-but-lame-duck-president Donald Trump.

THE BLUE SHIFT/RED MIRAGE

A phenomenon that is known as either the "blue shift" or the "red mirage" provided President Trump with an opening to falsely claim that there was fraud in the 2020 election.[6] Trump would repeat this claim ad nauseum, thereby branding the 2020 election as stolen.[7] There was no fraud, only the slow pace of states processing the tsunami of mailed-in ballots.[8] The term "blue shift" was coined by professor Ned Foley in 2013.[9] The "red mirage" was so called by Michael Bloomberg's data shop Hawkfish in 2020.[10] Both phrases refer to the phenomena of elections tilting to the right on election night when voting totals are incomplete and tilting left once all ballots are counted.

In the months before the 2020 election, election law experts predicted that, because of the pandemic, millions more American voters would vote by mail than usual.[11] These scholars (including the author) put out a white paper suggesting how to improve the administration of the 2020 election, entitled "Fair Elections during a Crisis."[12] The white paper predicted the blue shift/red mirage: if Republicans voted in person and Democrats voted by mail, then Republicans would appear to "win" on election day, but once all ballots were processed, it was possible for Democrats to actually win.[13] The blue shift/red mirage possibility was heavily covered by the press before election day in 2020.[14] As reporter Paul Blumenthal wrote, "Trump could easily go to bed with a lead in key states based on an incomplete tally on election night and wake up to see that lead eroding based on the totally normal counting of valid ballots—a 'red mirage.'"[15] The number-one suggestion in "Fair Elections during a Crisis" was for states to open mail-in votes as early as possible, so there would not be a delay in processing overall vote totals.[16] Unfortunately, many key swing states did not listen. This led to an entire week spent counting ballots.[17]

The red mirage indeed happened in the 2020 presidential election, which took place on November 3, 2020.[18] At approximately 2 a.m. EST on November 4 (in what was still election night in Hawaii), President Donald Trump prematurely and inaccurately declared victory.[19] While votes were still being counted in key swing states, he stated: "Frankly, we did win this election."[20] In another hypocritical claim that night, he said, "We want all voting to stop. We don't want them to find any ballots at four o'clock in the morning and add them to the list. Okay?"[21]

Trump's statements at 2 a.m. were hypocritical because, a month and half after this, Trump tried to force elections officials in Georgia to find him enough new votes so that he could win the swing state.[22] On January 2, 2021, Trump was caught on tape pressuring Georgia secretary of state Brad Raffensperger, stating: "All I want to do is this: I just want to find 11,780 votes, which is one more than we have. Because we won the state."[23] Raffensperger refused to manufacture votes and instead publicly released the audio of Trump's illegal request,[24] which took some guts, as he and his wife received death threats.[25] Two years later, a local prosecutor in Fulton County, Georgia, brought charges in a wide-ranging RICO conspiracy case against ex-president Donald Trump; his lawyers Kenneth Chesebro, John Eastman, Rudy Giuliani, and Sidney Powell; as well as fourteen other individuals for trying to overturn the results of the 2020 election in Georgia.[26]

Key swing states like Nevada, Georgia and Pennsylvania took days to process all of their mail-in votes. It was on Saturday, November 7, 2020, when Joe Biden's victory became clear, as slow-counting states finalized their vote totals. Many Biden supporters celebrated by dancing in the streets.[27]

THE ATTEMPTS TO OVERTURN THE 2020 PRESIDENTIAL ELECTION

THE BIG LIE

When President Donald Trump lost the election in November 2020, he aggregated his criticisms of the electoral process into one big lie (that I will refer to here as the "Big Lie") that he was the true victor of the 2020 election.[28] He was not.[29] Biden won the 2020 election with 306 electoral college votes to Trump's 232.[30] Biden also won the popular vote by 81,268,924 votes to Trump's 74,216,154.[31] Courts have roundly rejected the Big Lie, relying instead on the finding by the Cybersecurity and Infrastructure Security Agency (CISA) that the election was secure.[32]

The Big Lie was likely premeditated, as foreshadowed by Roger Stone, who said before the 2020 election, "I really do suspect it will still be up in the air. When that happens, the key thing to do is to claim victory. Possession is 9/10s of the law. No, we won. Fuck you. Sorry. Over. We won. You're wrong. Fuck you.'"[33]

THE TWO MEANINGS OF CONSPIRACY

As the US House Select Committee on the January 6 Attack revealed to the public through a series of gripping televised hearings during 2022, Americans have had to grapple with the two very different meanings of the word "conspiracy." Calling a bogus explanation for a series of events a "conspiracy" is shorthand way to signal to a listener that it is a fairy tale. Meanwhile, in criminal law, a "conspiracy" has a very different meaning: it is an agreement between two or more people to commit an illegal act. Being found guilty of an illegal conspiracy can lead to significant prison time.

The January 6 Committee hearings discussed "conspiracy" in both senses of the word. On the one hand, the committee demonstrated how President Trump pushed the bogus conspiracy theory that there was fraud in the 2020 election and that, therefore, he was the true victor. This conspiracy theory had many permutations, blaming voting machines, voters, election officials, and volunteer poll workers. As the committee showed, there was no credible evidence to back up the stolen-election fantasy that Trump sold to his followers.

Because Trump could not accept his electoral loss or his losses in court, Trump pushed forward with illegal ways of resisting peaceful transfer of power. As Rep. Liz Chaney summarized:

> President Trump ignored the rulings of our nation's courts . . . , his own campaign leadership, his White House staff, many Republican state officials . . . [,] the Department of Justice and the Department of Homeland

Security. President Trump invested millions of dollars of campaign funds purposely spreading false information, running ads he knew were false, and convincing millions of Americans that the election was corrupt and that he was the true President. . . . This misinformation campaign provoked the violence on January 6th.[34]

No lawful means could give Donald Trump the presidency for the 2021–25 term. As committee chair Bennie Thompson related, "Donald Trump was at the center of this conspiracy, and ultimately Donald Trump, the president of the United States, spurred a mob of domestic enemies of the Constitution to march down [to] the Capitol and subvert American democracy."[35] The last option to overturn the 2020 election was violence on January 6 to stop the lawful and constitutionally mandated counting of electoral college votes.

The January 6 Committee hearings also laid out a clear path for state and federal prosecutors to charge Trump and several of his inner circle with criminal conspiracies including wire fraud for misleading small donors, conspiring to illegally overturn the election results in Georgia, sending certificates of fake electors to Congress, and aiding and abetting obstruction of a congressional proceeding.[36]

WHO PAID FOR THE PRESSURE CAMPAIGN ON STATE LAWMAKERS?

Even before the physical insurrection at the Capitol, Trump and his supporters waged a campaign to pressure state elections officials into overturning the results of the 2020 election. President Trump had approved funding of ads that badgered state lawmakers—for example, in Arizona:

> President Trump personally approved a series of advertisements that the Campaign ran on cable television and social media in several important States. One advertisement in Arizona called for pressure on Governor Ducey . . . alleging, "The evidence is overwhelming. Call Governor Ducey and your legislators. Demand they inspect the machines and hear the evidence." . . . Stand up for President Trump. Call today. Paid for by Donald J. Trump for President, Inc."[37]

Top Trump advisors, including his son-in-law Jared Kushner, were involved in approving the ad campaign. As the January 6 Committee noted:

> Trump Campaign Senior Advisor Jason Miller . . . wrote that, "the President and Mayor Giuliani want to get back up on TV ASAP, and Jared [Kushner] has approved in budgetary concept, so here's the gameplan" in order to "motivate the GOP base to put pressure on the Republican Governors of Georgia and Arizona and the Republican-controlled State legislatures in Wisconsin and Michigan to hear evidence of voter fraud before January 6th." Miller anticipated a budget of $5 million . . . On December 22nd, Jason Miller texted Jared Kushner that "POTUS has approved the buy."[38]

This places President Trump, along with his key advisers, at the center of the effort to illegitimately overturn a democratic election at the state level.

After the 2020 election, President Trump and the Trump campaign encouraged its donors to give to a legal defense fund so that Trump could contest the 2020 election results. According to the January 6 Committee, this *legal defense fund did not exist*. Thus, the solicitations to give this money could well run afoul of federal wire fraud statutes. As of this writing, no federal prosecutions have been forthcoming on this front. As congresswoman Zoe Lofgren said, "The Big Lie was also a big rip-off."[39] In other words, this was one more big scam on hapless donors.[40]

INSURRECTION

President Trump continued repeating the Big Lie that he was the true victor of the 2020 election on January 6, 2021, at a "Stop the Steal" rally in front of the White House.[41] As CNN and *Rolling Stone* reported, other speakers included Trump's lawyer, Rudy Giuliani, who called for "trial by combat," and Congressman Mo Brooks of Alabama, who urged the crowd to "start taking down names and kicking ass" and to "do what it takes to fight for America" by "carry[ing] the message to Capitol Hill," since "the fight begins today."[42] At the rally, President Trump reiterated his claims that the election was "rigged" and "stolen" and urged then–vice president Mike Pence to "do the right thing" by rejecting various states' electoral votes and refusing to certify the election in Biden's favor.[43]

Trump, who has been called a cotton-candy-haired Mussolini,[44] exhorted the crowd in front of the White House on January 6 to "march to the Capitol to 'stop the steal,' which necessarily meant stopping Congress from counting the electoral votes."[45] He said during the speech that Republicans had been too "nice" and were "going to have to fight much harder." He continued: "You'll never take back our country with weakness. You have to show strength and you have to be strong." He said further that "if you don't fight like hell, you're not going to have a country anymore. . . . They need to take back our country."[46] At the end of his address, Trump said, "After this, we're going to walk down and I'll be there with you. We're going to walk down . . . to the Capitol.' The crowd applauded."[47]

As Congress assembled for the 2020 electoral count, thousands of the attendees from the Trump White House rally, as well as others who skipped it, surrounded the Capitol and fought with the Capitol police defending the building. The crowd overran the building, including the Senate chambers, which, under normal circumstances, would only be occupied by elected officials and a few staffers and pages. They also made it into the office of the Speaker of the House, where they rifled through desks and stole items. The public knows this because several of the participants took pictures and videos and even live-streamed the attack on social media.[48] Many participants in the riot talked to the press in the hours and days following the attack.[49] Others would be interviewed by law enforcement upon arrest.[50] Closed-circuit government video also documented the attacks, as did recordings of law enforcement radio communications.[51]

Senators and members of Congress were hidden in secured locations for their safety. As the DC Circuit described: "Rioters breached the Senate chamber. In the House chamber, Capitol Police officers 'barricaded the door with furniture and drew their weapons to hold off rioters.' Some members of the mob built a hangman's gallows on the lawn of the Capitol, amid calls from the crowd to hang Vice President Pence."[52] As the Capitol was under siege, Trump called in to Lou Dobb's show on Fox News.[53]

As DC District Chief Judge Beryl A. Howell described it: "The actions of this violent mob, particularly those members who breached police lines and gained entry to the Capitol, are reprehensible as offenses against morality, civic virtue, and the rule of law."[54] Finally, as the DC Circuit noted, "The Joint Session reconvened late that night. It was not until 3:42 a.m. on January 7th that Congress officially certified Joseph Biden as the winner of the 2020 presidential election."[55]

THE PROUD BOYS AND THE OATH KEEPERS

Another impact of the Insurrection at the Capitol was that it made far-right groups like the Oath Keepers and the Proud Boys household names. The DOJ charged the leaders of the Oath Keepers, including Stewart Rhodes, with seditious conspiracy for their role in the insurrection.[56] Seditious conspiracy is a federal crime defined as "two or more persons in any State or Territory . . . [who] conspire to overthrow, put down, or to destroy by force the Government of the United States, or to levy war against them."[57] This law was enacted during the Civil War in reaction to the Southern states seceding.[58]

As the *L.A. Times* explained, "Seditious conspiracy is an extremely rare and challenging crime to prosecute. . . . It is hard to prove, politically charged and requires federal prosecutors to show conspiracy . . . to use force to overthrow the government."[59] This charge was used before for a previous attack on the Capitol: "In 1954, four pro-independence Puerto Ricans entered the Capitol and started shooting from the House gallery onto the chamber floor, wounding a number of representatives. The four people, along with a number of their co-planners, were convicted of seditious conspiracy."[60]

The DOJ also charged members of the Proud Boys, including their leader Henry "Enrique" Tarrio, with seditious conspiracy.[61] It alleged that members of the Proud Boys "oppose[d] by force the authority of the Government of the United States and by force [tried] to prevent, hinder, and delay the execution of any law of the United States."[62] Further, "the purpose of the conspiracy was to oppose the lawful transfer of presidential power by force, by . . . delaying by force the execution of the laws governing the transfer of power, including the Twelfth Amendment to the Constitution and Title 3, Section 15 of the United States Code."[63] The

Twelfth Amendment explains how presidential elections work, and title 3, section 15, is the Electoral Count Act, which governs how electoral votes for president are handled.[64]

Charges of seditious conspiracy are rare. As Lawfare has noted, "The Justice Department had brought seditious conspiracy charges only three times in the previous 20 years: twice for small U.S. al-Qaeda cells and once for the Blind Sheikh . . . responsible for the 1993 World Trade Center bombing."[65] Proving seditious conspiracy is difficult, as demonstrated by the fact that the last time the DOJ leveled this charge, back in 2010, the case fell apart. It involved a militia group in Michigan that the DOJ alleged had plotted to overthrow the government; "however, a judge threw out those charges after ruling that the prosecution's case relied too heavily on speech protected by the 1st Amendment."[66]

Joshua James, the head of the Alabama chapter of the Oath Keepers, pleaded guilty to seditious conspiracy and agreed to cooperate.[67] According to the DOJ's account of James's actions on January 6 and the days leading up to it:

> On Jan. 4, 2021, James and others traveled to . . . D.C. . . . He brought a semi-automatic handgun and stored multiple firearms at a Virginia hotel. On Jan. 6, . . . He and others unlawfully entered the Capitol together through the East Rotunda doors. Inside the Rotunda, James assaulted a Metropolitan Police Department officer by grabbing the officer's vest and pulling him towards the mob . . . [and] yelled, "Get out of my Capitol! This is not yours! This is my Capitol!"

The members of the Oath Keepers were accused of marching in military stack to breach the Capitol on January 6.[68]

Oath Keepers leaders Stewart Rhodes and Kelly Meggs were convicted of seditious conspiracy.[69] In a separate trial, four additional Oath Keepers—Roberto Minuta, Joseph Hackett, David Moerschel, and Edward Vallejo—were found guilty of the same charge.[70] Moreover, Tarrio of the Proud Boys was convicted of seditious conspiracy.[71] On May 25, 2023, Rhodes was sentenced to eighteen years in prison, while Meggs received a sentence of twelve years.[72] Tarrio was sentenced to a twenty-two-year prison term.[73]

Besides the seditious conspiracy charges, many individuals face other serious federal criminal charges due to the fact that they were armed at the Capitol. For example, January 6 defendants Ronald Sandlin and Nathaniel DeGrave were accused by federal prosecutors of "[driving] to the D.C. area on January 5, bringing with them 'paramilitary gear, one Glock .43 pistol, an M&P bodyguard pocket pistol, two magazines of ammunition, knives, a handheld taser/stun gun, an expendable baton, walkie talkies, and bear mace.'"[74] Sandlin pleaded guilty and was sentenced to sixty-three months in prison.[75] DeGrave also pleaded guilty[76] and was sentenced to over three years in prison and a $25,000 fine.[77] At the time of writing, over 1,400 individuals had been charged with crimes related to January 6 insurrection,[78] including ex-president Donald Trump in two separate jurisdictions.[79]

WHO PAID FOR THIS INSURRECTION?

The question of who paid for the insurrection is a complicated one, as many groups and individuals, including the Stop the Steal Coalition, Women for America First, numerous social media influencers, and militia members converged on the Capitol. Not every person there was violent; some surely attended in the spirit of nonviolent political protest. Others, like the Proud Boys and the Oath Keepers, clearly arrived in DC with premeditated plans for violence.[80] There does not appear to be a single source that funded all of these disparate individuals for their participation in the resulting insurrection.

The planning for events on January 5–6 morphed over time, and different participating groups called the events in DC various names: "Million MAGA March," "March for Trump," "Stop the Steal Rally," and "Ellipse Rally." At one point, Ali Alexander was planning a Stop the Steal Rally at the Capitol that was distinct from the Stop the Steal Rally at the White House. The biggest gathering was supposed to be at Freedom Plaza and was moved to the Ellipse. Thus, one of the difficulties of unraveling the funding of the insurrection is that a group or an individual may have fundraised for one event, like the Alexander rally, and then the individuals who received that financial support may have shown up at a completely different event, such as the Ellipse Rally or the insurrection at the Capitol.

Many participants paid for their own travel to DC. Individuals who lived in Virginia or Maryland could take the DC Metro to the insurrection and pro-Trump rallies, as did Ginni Thomas, the wife of Supreme Court Justice Clarence Thomas.[81] Some drove themselves there. A few, like Katherine Schwab, Jason Hyland, and Jenna Ryan flew to the event in the same private jet.[82] Schwab would later plead guilty,[83] as did Hyland[84] and Ryan.[85] Ryan made headlines for claiming that she would not get jail time for her actions on January 6 because she was "blonde."[86] In the end she was sentenced to sixty days in prison, which was the longest sentence of the three private-jet passengers. Trump pardonee Roger Stone also arrived in DC for January 6 on a separate private jet.[87]

There were also coordinated efforts to get a huge crowd to the Capitol, using millions of dollars from Julie Fancelli, heiress to the Publix fortune.[88] She was inspired to donate to the January 6 effort because she watched an episode of Alex Jones's *InfoWars*.[89] The January 6 Committee noted that, "along with his *InfoWars* co-hosts, [Alex] Jones amplified President Trump's 'Big Lie' and relentlessly promoted President Trump's 'wild' protest. One of Jones' co-hosts floated the idea of 'storming right into the Capitol.' [Alex] Jones himself marched to the Capitol January 6th."[90]

According to sworn depositions, Julie Fancelli and a GOP fundraiser, Caroline Wren, coordinated funding bus rides to the Capitol.[91] According to Wren's deposition, "Fancelli said that 'she wanted to see a lot of people there in DC, so how much would that cost?'"[92] Then the two worked together to "create a multimillion-dollar budget to convene as many supporters of President Trump as possible."[93] The committee further discovered that "on December 29th, Wren told the Stop the Steal leader [Ali Alexander], 'I can pay for the buses . . . so let me know what cities you need them in!'"[94] The committee found that Fancelli "spent $3 million with the goal to 'get as many people there as possible.' It worked—Americans who believed [the Big Lie that] the election was stolen flocked to the Nation's capital."[95]

The January 6 Committee detailed how Fancelli's $3 million was spent: "The resulting budget allocated $500,000 to a busing program and a centralized ad campaign by the Tea Party Express to promote the event. Another $500,000 went to assisting WFAF [Women for America First] and [Alex] Jones in their organizational efforts."[96] Women for America

First was a 501(c)(4) group that held a permit from the National Park Service for a rally on January 6.[97] Alex Jones received $200,000 from Fancelli.[98] The committee obtained bank statements showing Fancelli made a payment of $750,000, as well as two additional payments of $250,000 (or $1.25 million total), to Charlie Kirk's Turning Point USA.[99]

The January 6 Committee reported that some of the funding streams that they had uncovered included thousands of dollars spent by Pennsylvania state senator Doug Mastriano to fund bus transportation from Pennsylvania.[100] Mastriano also attended events at the Capitol on January 6.[101] Michael "Mike" Lindell's company MyPillow was the sponsor of advertisements on red buses that drove around the country at "March for Trump" rallies organized by Women for America First between the 2020 election and January 6.[102] Some of those red buses rolled into DC on January 5 in a caravan.[103]

There was also fundraising by individuals who would later be charged with seditious conspiracy, including a Proud Boy named Zachary Rehl.[104] The government alleged that "on December 30, 2020, REHL posted a link to an online fundraiser campaign name of 'Travel Expenses for upcoming Patriot Events.' The campaign generated over $5,500 donations between December 30, 2020, and January 4, 2021."[105] The January 6 Committee also found that some of the rioters spent money on weapons and tactical gear right before the riot:

> [Stewart] Rhodes amassed an arsenal of military-grade assault weapons and equipment in the days leading up to January 6th. On December 30th, Rhodes spent approximately $7,000 on two night-vision devices and a weapon sight. . . . On January 1st and 2nd, Rhodes purchased additional weapons and accessories at a cost of approximately $5,000. The following day, . . . Rhodes and [lawyer] Kellye SoRelle departed . . . for . . . DC. While traveling, Rhodes spent an additional $6,000 on an AR-style rifle and firearms attachments. Making one final shopping trip in Mississippi, Rhodes purchased $4,500 of firearms equipment including more sights, magazines, and weapons parts on January 4th.[106]

Another source of funding for events on January 6 was the Trump campaign, which spent millions of dollars through an LLC called American Made Media Consultants throughout the 2020 reelection campaign.[107]

This LLC spent hundreds of thousands of dollars on messaging about January 6.[108]

During some of the planning for events for January 5–6, mainstream Republican sources also played a role in funding. According to reporting by Pro Publica, "Ahead of the Jan. 6 rally, [Caroline] Wren directed roughly $150,000 from Fancelli to the Rule of Law Defense Fund, the dark-money arm of the Republican Attorneys General Association, or RAGA. . . . The Rule of Law Defense Fund [RLDF] then paid for a robocall inviting people to the Capitol."[109] The "RLDF . . . robocall [said], 'At 1:00 p.m., we will march to the Capitol building and call on Congress to stop the steal. We are hoping patriots like you will join us to continue to fight to protect the integrity of our elections.'"[110]

This is where corporate funding enters the January 6 story. Wren/Fancelli were not the only sources of funds for RLDF/RAGA;[111] rather, "public companies and trade associations donated nearly $17 million to RAGA in the 2020 election cycle, or 51.6 percent of the money it took in during that cycle. They were the dominant funders of RAGA."[112] The Center for Political Accountability, which tracked the money flowing into RAGA, found that "top corporate donors giving directly to RAGA included Anthem, $336,025; Altria, $334,154; Comcast, $315,000; Walmart, $270,100; AT&T, $250,000; CVS, $213,407; Home Depot, $205,579; Anheuser-Busch InBev, $200,525; Fresnius Medical Care, $180,000; and Pfizer, $161,050."[113] In addition to individual corporations, trade associations played a large role in funding RAGA. As the Center for Political Accountability discovered, "Top trade association donors included the U.S. Chamber of Commerce, $750,375; American Fuel and Petrochemical Manufacturers, $220,725; Wine and Spirit Wholesalers of America, $136,305; PhRMA, $136,025; Entertainment Software Association, $105,000; Association of Dental Support Organizations, $100,550; and American Petroleum Institute, $100,000."[114]

According to OpenSecrets, "The Judicial Crisis Network [which is associated with Leonard Leo], a dark money group now renamed the Concord Fund, also contributed to multiple groups involved in the rally. The dark money group gave at least $4.7 million to the Tea Party Patriots, $50,000 to Turning Point Action and $1.9 million to the Rule of Law Defense Fund from 2013 to 2019. . . . And it gave millions more to the affiliated Republican Attorneys General Association a.k.a. RAGA."[115]

THE BIG LIE

Nick Fuentes, a White supremacist who rose to national prominence at the Charlottesville Unite the Right rally in 2017, was also a booster of not only the Capitol riot but also other violent events leading up to January 6.[116] He was "a key voice for 'Stop the Steal' conspiracy theories leading up to January 6th."[117] Fuentes raised $50,000 touting January 6.[118] Also benefiting were Kimberly Guilfoyle and Donald Trump Jr., who jointly earned $60,000 in speakers' fees for speaking at the Ellipse on January 6. Commissions totaling $198,000 were paid to Caroline Wren for raising the money from Fancelli for January 6 events.[119] Rally organizers were also well compensated: "Megan Powers . . . was paid around $300,000 as the Trump campaign's director of operations."[120] Some January 6 defendants have also tried to fundraise off of January 6. This has led to federal prosecutors to impose fines to prevent windfall profits generated by the federal crimes that occurred on January 6.[121]

CORPORATE MONEY KEPT FLOWING TO THE SEDITION CAUCUS

Even after the tear gas and dust had settled, and all the insurrectionists had been cleared from the Capitol building on the evening of January 6, 147 members of Congress still persisted in objecting to lawful electors for Joe Biden. Thus, some in the press have dubbed this group the "Sedition Caucus." Right after January 6, nearly 250 companies said that they would not support the Sedition Caucus.[122] This was a remarkable turn of events, given how reflexive corporate political spending through corporate PACs had become. The pause in corporate political spending was short lived.

While sixty-five corporate political spenders shunned the Sedition Caucus through 2023, a troubling number of corporations rapidly resumed their financial support for members of the Sedition Caucus, including "Goldman Sachs, Amazon, General Motors, Lockheed Martin and Boeing."[123] In 2021, reporter Andy Kroll found that "campaign records show that major corporations and trade groups donated nearly $2.5 million in the three months from July through September, nearly $640,000 of which went to members of the 'Sedition Caucus' in September [2021] alone."[124] The group Accountable US, which tracked corporate support of the Sedition Caucus, discovered that, in the year following January 6, "Lockheed Martin is one of the largest defense contractors in the world, counting the U.S. Department of Defense and U.S. federal agencies as its biggest customers. . . . However, the lawlessness displayed on January 6 was not enough to prevent the company from contributing to the campaign coffers of dozens of election objectors in 2021, for a total of $131,500."[125] Another defense contractor also reneged: "Northrop Grumman gave $81,000 to the Sedition Caucus."[126]

OpenSecrets found that by November 2022, $61 million from corporate PACs and trade associations went to the Sedition Caucus.[127] Some of the money came in the form of contributions to candidate committees as well as leadership PACs that funded members of the Sedition Caucus.[128] The largest trade association supporting the Sedition Caucus was the National Association of Realtors, which gave "$861,000 to 127 members of . . . the 'Sedition Caucus.'"[129] But other trade associations were big spenders, too, including the National Beer Wholesalers Association, which gave $744,500 to 121 members, and the American Bankers Association, which gave $668,500 to 110 members."[130] The largest individual corporate supporters of the Sedition Caucus were the Koch Industries' PAC, at $607,000; "Home Depot, Boeing Co. and United Parcel Service closely follow with more than $500,000 each in corporate PAC contributions."[131] AT&T's corporate PAC also gave over $500,000 in the two years following January 6.[132]

On the Senate side, senator John Kennedy of Louisiana was the Sedition Caucus member who received the most corporate PAC backing, at $720,000.[133] During the same two years, senator Tommy Tuberville of Alabama "received $133,500 from the corporate PACs of Southern Co, United Parcel Service, Maynard, Cooper & Gale, Drummond Co. and Torch Technologies."[134] Senator Rick Scott of Florida received money from the corporate PACs of "Koch Industries, Home Depot, Apollo Global Management and NextEra Energy, among others."[135] NextEra energy is the parent company of Florida Power & Light (FP&L), which featured prominently in the Ghost Candidate Scandal.

Money in politics often flows through several entities before reaching its final destination in a daisy chain of PAC-to-PAC and nonprofit-to-PAC transfers. Money went not only to individual members but also to umbrella party committees that shared funds with Sedition Caucus members.[136] As Citizens for Responsibility and Ethics in Washington

(CREW) found, "in total, 1,345 corporate and industry group PACs have given $50.5 million directly to the campaigns or leadership PACs of members of the Sedition Caucus, and $18.9 million to the National Republican Senatorial Committee (NRSC) and National Republican Congressional Committee (NRCC), two party committees that help elect Republicans to Congress."[137] These party committees also funneled money to election deniers who were running for office as challengers in 2022, like Blake Masters and Ted Budd.[138] Similar funding streams boosted election denying House candidates as well.[139] Corporate money even flowed to January 6 participant Derrick Van Orden.[140] The new senator from Ohio, J. D. Vance, was also a touter of the Big Lie who raked in corporate support in the 2022 midterm election.[141]

Two leaders of the Sedition Caucus, senators Ted Cruz and Josh Hawley, reacted to certain corporate boycotts of funding the Sedition Caucus by claiming that they would not take corporate PAC contributions. This was a fleeting commitment for Cruz. OpenSecrets found on closer inspection that, "despite his pledge, Cruz reported $31,500 in corporate PAC contributions since the Jan. 6 attack with most of that going to his leadership PACs. His funders include the corporate PACs of companies including Boeing Co, Community Bancshares of Mississippi, Brownstein Hyatt et al, Apache Corp and TC Energy."[142]

On the House side, OpenSecrets discovered that then–minority leader Kevin McCarthy was the biggest beneficiary of corporate PAC money in 2022.[143] As they found, "McCarthy has echoed Trump's false claims questioning 2020 election results and opposed the formation of the bipartisan commission for investigating the Jan. 6 attack. Nevertheless, McCarthy's campaign and leadership PAC received a total of $921,400 from the corporate PACs of 14 companies including Wells Fargo, Blue Cross/Blue Shield and Comcast."[144] McCarthy took in money from corporate trade associations as well: "Business PACs gave McCarthy's campaign committee and leadership PAC more than $2.1 million during the 2022 election cycle with $1.2 million of that going to his campaign committee and $868,000 going to McCarthy's leadership PAC, the Majority Committee PAC."[145] According to OpenSecrets, "Top 2022 cycle donors to McCarthy's leadership PAC included Fedex Corp, Exxon Mobil and Home Depot."[146] Meanwhile, then–House minority whip Steve Scalise received "about $1 million in [corporate] campaign contributions and about $941,000 more going to his leadership PAC."[147] By December 2023, over $90 million in corporate PAC contributions had gone to the members of the Sedition Caucus.[148]

In the years that followed January 6, the spigot of corporate political money kept flowing to most members of the Sedition Caucus in Congress and to Trump's 2024 presidential run. This raises a question: If the behavior of Trump and the Sedition Caucus was not appalling enough on January 6 to get corporations to permanently close their pocketbooks, what conduct would be antidemocratic enough to repulse them?

PART 3

HOW TO FIX THE PROBLEM

9

DUSTING OFF THE DISQUALIFICATION CLAUSE

HOW TO HOLD INSURRECTIONISTS ACCOUNTABLE

Does it matter whether courts consider the events from January 6 as a spontaneous "riot" or a planned "insurrection"?[1] It does. This is more than just a semantic difference. The choice of words has legal and constitutional consequences. Those who participate in an insurrection against the US government can be constitutionally barred from holding public office.[2]

One of the open questions after the January 6 insurrection is whether anyone will face constitutional consequences for their participating in an attempt to overturn an American election. One of the first test cases of whether there will be constitutional accountability involved a very young member of Congress named Madison Cawthorn.

Madison Cawthorn could have been a part-time model. He seemed to be on his way to do big things; at the age of twenty-five, he was one of the youngest people ever elected to House of Representatives and the first member of Congress to be born in the 1990s. But, much like his idol, President Trump, toe-headed Republican Cawthorn also seemed prone to lying about key parts of his autobiography, including about how he ended up in a wheelchair and whether he had been accepted into the US Naval Academy.[3]

Cawthorn spent much of his brief political career touting the Big Lie. In December 2020, after he had been elected but before he took office, he told his supporters, "If you don't support election integrity, I'm coming after you. Madison Cawthorn's coming after you."[4] There is nothing wrong with wanting elections to be secure; the issue here is that Cawthorn was echoing another aspect of the Big Lie—that somehow the 2020 election was fraught with fraud, when it wasn't. And the veiled threats of violence in his statement were problematic as well.

Like Buster Keaton making a series of painful pratfalls, as a member of Congress Cawthorn kept getting in trouble, from low-level offenses such as driving without a license and racking up speeding tickets to getting "busted, for the second time, for carrying a loaded pistol at an airport."[5] In a legally questionable move, he raised funds that he said would go to bailing out Republicans who were arrested for not wearing masks on the House floor and then parked the money in his own campaign account.[6]

In 2022, ex-president Trump backed Cawthorn's reelection campaign even while calling him a "handsome sucker."[7] During his Republican primary for reelection, Cawthorn's opponents dug up dirt on him. What his opponents—and the press—found out was that his short-lived college days at Christian Patrick Henry College (PHC), from which he did not graduate, seemed rife with allegations of predaceous sexual abuse of women.[8] Politico summed up the accusations against him: "In his short time at PHC Cawthorn 'established a reputation for predatory behavior' and 'gross misconduct towards our female peers,' taking them on 'joy rides' to secluded areas where he locked the doors and made 'unwanted sexual advances,' according to an open letter 148 former students . . . signed. 'He was a wolf in sheep's clothing who made our small, close-knit community his personal playground of debauchery.'"[9] Near the end of the primary season in 2022, he was accused of having an inappropriate relationship with a senior aide.[10] Adding fuel to the flames of what the opposition research had uncovered about him, Cawthorn stated that he had been invited to "cocaine-fueled orgies" in DC.[11]

By May 2022, a mere seventeen months after he became a congressman, Madison Cawthorn was defeated in his GOP primary, thus ending his meteoric rise to national prominence.[12] Shortly thereafter, the House Ethics Committee launched an investigation into him for insider trading about the cryptocurrency LGBCoin.[13] In December 2022, the committee fined Cawthorn over $14,000 for touting the cryptocurrency that he also owned.[14] Cawthorn could face liability from the SEC and the DOJ long after he leaves Congress.[15]

Cawthorn's ephemeral political career likely won't be remembered for his strange claims about the DC party scene. His most lasting legacy is likely to be the court cases surrounding the constitutional question of whether he was even eligible to be a member of Congress, given his actions on January 6.

Cawthorn was a congressional staffer for Mark Meadows's North Carolina district office.[16] After Meadows left Congress to become President Trump's chief of staff, Cawthorn ran for Meadows's old seat and won in 2020. He was sworn into federal office with the rest of his freshman class on January 3, 2021. Part of that ceremony required him to swear an oath to uphold the US Constitution, as required by article 6.[17] A day after becoming a member of Congress, on January 4, 2021, Cawthorn tweeted, alluding to upcoming events on January 6: "It's time to fight."[18]

Just three days after becoming a Congressman, Cawthorn spoke at the January 6 "Stop the Steal" rally in front of the White House. He was one of just thirteen people who spoke that day on that stage, including President Trump, his son Eric, his daughter-in-law Lara, his other adult son Don Jr., Don Jr.'s girlfriend Kimberly Guilfoyle, and two of Trump's lawyers, Rudy Giuliani and John Eastman.[19] The newly minted congressman must have felt like the golden boy sharing the stage with some of the most powerful people in the world, with his political star ascending.[20] His biography on his House of Representatives webpage started: "Congressman Cawthorn has rocked the status quo in Washington, D.C. following his election to Congress in 2020."[21]

Madison Cawthorn's first words to a group of armed Trump supporters assembled in DC on January 6 were, "Wow, this crowd has some fight in it. I am so thankful that each and every single one of you who've come."[22] He repeated the Big Lie: "My friends, the Democrats, with all the fraud they have done in this election . . . they are trying to silence your voice."[23] He rhetorically spoke of fighting, stating, "My friends, when I look out into this crowd, I can confidently say, this crowd has the voice of lions. There is a new Republican Party on the rise that will represent this country, that will go and fight in Washington D.C."[24]

In the ensuing hours, Cawthorn was one of 147 Republican House members who objected to counting electoral college votes for Joe Biden from key swing states.[25] Violent rioters overtook the Capitol building, attempting to stop the electoral college count. While the building was under siege, Cawthorn called into conservative commentator Charlie Kirk's radio show and, without any proof, accused the rioters of being

Democrats instead of Trump supporters.[26] In retrospect, this appears to be part of a purposeful disinformation campaign to blame "antifa" and thereby deflect responsibility away from Trump and Republicans.

Eight months later, Cawthorn was unrepentant for his behavior on January 6 and plainly supportive of the mob that attacked the Capitol that day (whom he no longer accused of being Democrats). On August 29, 2021, while addressing a local GOP group in North Carolina, Cawthorn grabbed headlines again by stating, "If our election systems continue to be rigged and continue to be stolen, it's gonna lead to one place and it's *bloodshed*. I will tell you, as much as I'm willing to defend our liberty at all costs, there's nothing that I would dread doing more than having to pick up arms against a fellow American. And the way that we can have recourse against that is that we all passionately demand that we have election security in all 50 states."[27] At the same event, Congressman Cawthorn called those arrested and held in pretrial detention for committing acts of violence at the Capitol on January 6 "political prisoners" who he wanted to break out of jail.[28] If reports alleging that Cawthorn helped plan events on January 6 are true, this sympathy for Capitol insurrectionists isn't surprising.[29]

When North Carolina voters sued to challenge Cawthorn's eligibility to run for office in 2022, the constitutional questions raised by Cawthorn's behavior on January 6 raised were whether he qualified as an "insurrectionist," and as such, if he was thereby barred from holding federal office under section 3 of the Fourteenth Amendment.

Understanding the *Cawthorn* litigation requires some basic understanding of the US Constitution and the impact of its amendments. The original unamended Constitution from 1787 not only embraced slavery; it also required the return of runaway slaves to their owners. It was silent on whether individuals who had tried to overthrow the government could serve as elected officials. These (and other) flaws were fixed by post–Civil War amendments. Barack Obama, America's first Black president, explained in a speech at Stanford that "if you think about the U.S. Constitution as software for running a society, [it was a] really innovative design. It, too, had some pretty big initial bugs. So, we came up with a bunch of patches, the 13th Amendment, the 14th Amendment, 15th Amendment.... We continued to perfect our union."[30]

In the aftermath of the Civil War, the Constitution was amended three times in five years. Famously, the Thirteenth Amendment ended slavery in the United States, and the Fifteenth Amendment granted Black men the right to vote. The Fourteenth Amendment is much longer and complicated; it does many things, including establishing birthright citizenship, requiring due process and equal protection of the laws from the fifty states, to declaring that the United States would not pay slaveholders for emancipated slaves. The Fourteenth Amendment also addressed issues specific to the Civil War and treasonous actions of individuals from the eleven states that rebelled against the US government and attempted to break up the Union.[31]

The pro-union antislavery Radical Republicans who held sway in the post–Civil War Congress did not want to share power with the very same Confederate politicians who had tried to break America asunder during the war. As the Supreme Court once explained, the House barred certain ex-Confederates from their elected seats in 1868: "[It] House voted for the first time . . . to exclude a member-elect. It refused to seat two duly elected representatives for giving aid and comfort to the Confederacy. 'This change was produced by the North's bitter enmity toward those who failed to support the Union cause during the war.'"[32] Many of the same men who voted to exclude these Confederates had a hand in drafting and adopting the Fourteenth Amendment.

An early draft of the Fourteenth Amendment would have temporarily stripped Confederate soldiers of the right to vote for members of Congress and the president.[33] It first read: "Until the 4th day of July, in the year 1870, all persons who voluntarily adhered to the late insurrection, giving it aid and comfort, shall be excluded from the right to vote for Representatives in Congress and for electors for the President and Vice President of the United States."[34] That provision was dropped. But what made the final cut was a bar on ex-Confederates serving in Congress and elsewhere in state and federal government that is now found in section 3 of the Fourteenth Amendment.[35] This part of the Constitution, added in 1868 and known as the "Disqualification Clause," bars members of Congress (and other elected and appointed offices) from returning to power if they participated in the Confederacy or "engaged in insurrection or rebellion against the same [United States], or given aid or comfort to the enemies thereof." As the Congressional Research Service explains, "Section 3 appears to apply to any covered person who has taken an oath to uphold the Constitution of the United States and thereafter either (1) engages in insurrection or rebellion against the United States, or (2) gives aid or comfort to the enemies of the United States, unless a supermajority of Congress 'removes such disability.'"[36]

Over the past one hundred years, Section 3 of the Fourteenth Amendment has not been used.[37] This is a good thing, because it indicates that most members of Congress and other elected officials haven't come anywhere close to meeting the definition of an "insurrectionist." But the events of January 6 inspired lawyers and voters in several states to dust off this part of the Constitution and attempt to enforce it by suing in an attempt to hold members of Congress who stand accused of helping the attack on January 6 accountable.[38]

One of these challenges was against the young and dashing Madison Cawthorn. As the complaint in North Carolina against him alleged, "Registered voters in the 13th Congressional District, have reasonable suspicion, pursuant to N.C. GEN. STAT. § 163–127, that Representative Madison Cawthorn, a candidate for North Carolina's 13th Congressional District, does not meet the federal constitutional requirements for a Member of the U.S. House of Representatives and is therefore ineligible to be a candidate for such office."[39] The complaint quoted the Constitution as the source of its authority: "Under Section Three of the Fourteenth Amendment to the U.S. Constitution, known as the Disqualification Clause, 'No Person shall be a . . . Representative in Congress . . . who, having previously taken an oath, as a member of Congress . . . to support the Constitution of the United States, shall have engaged in insurrection or rebellion against the same.'"[40] The voters in Cawthorn's case argued that "the idea behind Section Three was that politicians who took an oath to protect the Constitution and then disregarded the norms of peaceful and lawful political discourse could not be trusted to hold office—that was true then, and it remains true today."[41]

The complaint pointed to Cawthorn's actions on January 6 as qualifying as a constitutional "insurrection."[42] It also drew on statements of Neil Gorsuch, before he became a Supreme Court justice, that a state's "legitimate interest in protecting the integrity and practical functioning of the political process permits it to exclude from the ballot candidates who are constitutionally prohibited from assuming office."[43] Thus, the complaint argued, Cawthorn was constitutionally "disqualified from congressional office."[44]

Cawthorn's reaction to the voters' challenge to his constitutional eligibility to run for Congress before the North Carolina Board of Elections was essentially to countersue the board.[45] Cawthorn was represented in his case by the same arch-conversative lawyer who represented the conservative group Citizens United at the Supreme Court: James Bopp.[46]

Initially, Cawthorn's side won, when a lower federal court judge ruled that the Amnesty Act of 1872, which allowed most ex-Confederates to run for office, somehow also exonerated Cawthorn 149 years later. This legal conclusion was laughably bad. Section 3 of the Fourteenth Amendment provides a way to allow ex-confederates the ability to hold office again by votes of two-thirds of both houses of Congress.[47] The Amnesty Act of 1872 grew out of the inefficiency of Congress's having to restore the right to hold public office piecemeal to thousands of ex-Confederates who requested relief in a series of time-consuming private bills. As constitutional law professor Laurence Tribe and constitutional litigator Elizabeth Wydra explains, "In the years following the 14th Amendment's ratification, numerous Confederates petitioned Congress to have their disqualification [from holding office] removed in accord with the two-thirds clause of Section 3. Congress frequently granted amnesty, usually through private bills containing long lists of thousands of names. The final private bill Congress considered before passing the 1872 statute included some 17,000 names."[48] Four years after the Fourteenth Amendment became part of the Constitution, Congress exercised its constitutional authority to "remove such disabilit[ies]" by enacting the Amnesty Act of 1872, which reads:[49]

> Be it enacted by the Senate and House of Representatives of the United States of America in Congress assembled (two-thirds of each house concurring therein), That all political disabilities imposed by the third section of the fourteenth ... amendment[] of the Constitution of the United States are hereby removed from all persons whomsoever, except Senators and Representatives of the thirty-sixth and thirty-seventh Congresses, officers in the judicial, military, and naval service of the United States, heads of departments, and foreign ministers of the United States.[50]

The 1872 Act restored the right to hold office to most remaining confederates who had been constitutionally banned from office.[51] Between 1868, when Section 3 of the Fourteenth Amendment was first adopted, and 1872, when the Amnesty Act was enacted, courts had to decide which candidates were ineligible to run for office under the Constitution.[52] Simultaneously, during this period, for sitting members, each house could expel an ineligible member by a two-thirds vote; a simple majority vote would not suffice.[53]

In Cawthorn's case, the district judge ruled in his favor that he was eligible to run for reelection because "the North Carolina statute cannot grant such authority [to bar him], however, because Congress removed the disability stated in Section 3 for all members of Congress."[54] The judge reasoned that the Amnesty Act of 1872 provides that "*all political disabilities imposed* by the third section of the fourteenth . . . amendment[] of the Constitution of the United States are hereby removed *from all persons whomsoever*. . . . [except a short excluded list]."[55] The judge further reasoned that Congress had subsequently in 1898 restored the right to run for office to all of those who had been excluded from the 1872 Amnesty Act.[56] The judge then concluded that "the plain language of these statutes, first removing the disability from 'all persons whomsoever' *except* those listed in the statute and, second, removing the disability from the excepted persons, demonstrates that the disability set forth in Section 3 can apply to no current member of Congress."[57] This was a Looney-Tunes reading of these old laws. How a law about Civil War rebels would apply to current members of Congress was a real head scratcher.

Fortunately, this reading of the two Amnesty Acts was soon overturned by the Fourth Circuit Court of Appeals.[58] As the Fourth Circuit wrote, "The issue currently before us is whether that same 1872 legislation also prospectively lifted the constitutional disqualification for all future rebels or insurrectionists, no matter their conduct. To ask such a question is nearly to answer it. Consistent with the statutory text and context, we hold that the 1872 Amnesty Act removed the Fourteenth Amendment's eligibility bar only for those whose constitutionally wrongful acts occurred *before* its enactment."[59] The Fourth Circuit rejected Cawthorn's time-traveling reading of the applicable statutes and reasoned from the text: "The . . . problem . . . is that the Act's operative clause refers to those 'political disabilities *imposed*' in the past tense rather than new disabilities that might arise in the future. The past tense is 'backward-looking'; it refers to things that have already happened, not those yet to come."[60] The Fourth Circuit's majority opinion establishes the important precedent that Section 3 of the Fourteenth Amendment was not vitiated by the backward-looking Amnesty Acts. This means that present-day courts can apply the Disqualification Clause's constitutional bar to running for office to January 6 insurrectionists.

After Cawthorn lost his primary, he remained in Congress until January 2023 as a lame duck. Yet, disturbingly, after his defeat in court, he claimed on Instagram that it is "'time for Dark MAGA to truly take command,' referencing a growing far-right community that endorses former President Donald Trump punishing his political enemies."[61] Given this odd trajectory of speaking at the White House grounds to losing his first reelection bid, the *New Yorker* characterized Cawthorn as a modern-day Icarus: "A charismatic, home-schooled, college dropout with a tragic backstory, he flew into Washington and onto *Fox News*, only to fall just as fast."[62]

Other lawsuits trying to apply Section 3 of the Fourteenth Amendment to congresswoman Marjorie Taylor Greene and other members of Congress have thus far failed to stop their candidacies.[63] It is possible that these lawsuits were filed prematurely, given that the Select Committee on January 6 had yet to release conclusions about the insurrection.[64] Nonetheless, the framers of the Fourteenth Amendment clearly envisioned the problem of traitors trying to win seats in Congress and therefore specifically barred it. They knew after fighting a Civil War that having constitutional consequences such as the inability to run for certain offices is a fair punishment for treasonous, antidemocratic behavior.

Because Congressman Cawthorn lost his reelection bid in 2022, courts did not have an opportunity to rule on the merits of his eligibility under Section 3. However, should he run again from North Carolina, the Fourth Circuit's ruling forecloses him from arguing that the post–Civil War Amnesty Acts magically absolve him.

This context should be remembered about January 6, as the voters in Cawthorn's district argued to the North Carolina Board of Elections: "This was no mere riot; it was an attempt to disrupt an essential constitutional function and illegally prolong Trump's tenure in office."[65]

Courts should recognize this and bar January 6 insurrectionists from running for office, as the Constitution dictates.

APPLYING THE DISQUALIFICATION CLAUSE TO STATE OFFICIALS

After Cawthorn's case, attention on the disqualifying insurrectionists from office shifted to a local official in Otero, New Mexico, named Couy Griffin who participated in the January 6 insurrection. Griffin was a county commissioner in Otero with authority over elections. Commissioner Griffin had made national headlines when he refused to certify the outcome of the primary election in 2022. The New Mexico Supreme Court eventually ordered him to do his job and certify the election.[66]

Voters in New Mexico challenged Couy Griffin's constitutional eligibility to hold office. In this case, the voters won. As the trial court explained in granular detail, Griffin's actions on January 6 met the constitutional definition of "insurrection." Griffin was not documented as throwing punches or assaulting police, as many in the crowd did, but as cheerleading for the more violent members of the crowd. As the court explained, if one encouraged violence in others, that was enough to be an insurrectionist: "Knowledgeable nineteenth-century Americans understood that a person engaged in insurrection whenever they were leagued with insurrectionists—either by acting in concert with others knowing that the group intended to achieve its purpose in part by violence, force, or intimidation by numbers . . . Under nineteenth-century understanding, there [were] no accessories in an insurrection; rather everybody . . . involved was a principal actor."[67]

The court concluded that Griffin made many overt acts during his time around the Capitol on January 6, detailing "that Mr. Griffin's crossing of barricades to approach the Capitol were overt acts in support of the insurrection, as Griffin's presence closer to the Capitol building increased the insurrectionists' intimidation by numbers. Mr. Griffin's marching with the mob all the way to the inaugural stage, knowing the mob's insurrectionary purpose, likewise constitutes an overt act."[68] Thus, the court decided that a fair reading of Griffin's actions on January 6 would make him an insurrectionist: "Applying these principles, the Court concludes that Mr. Griffin 'engaged in' the January 6 insurrection."[69]

Given his actions on January 6, the court ruled that Griffin be constitutionally barred from office. It stated:

> The Court concludes that (1) Mr. Griffin took an "oath . . . to support the Constitution of the United States" as an "executive . . . officer of any State," (2) the January 6 Attack and surrounding planning, mobilization, and incitement were an "insurrection" against the Constitution of the United States, and (3) Mr. Griffin "engaged in" the insurrection. The Court therefore concludes that, effective January 6, 2021, Mr. Griffin became disqualified under Section Three of the Fourteenth Amendment from serving [in] . . . his current office as an Otero County Commissioner.[70]

Thus, the court ordered that Griffin be removed from office immediately, yet backdated the disqualification to January 6, 2021.[71] Griffin appealed his case but lost again in the New Mexico courts.[72] He launched a petition for certiorari at the Supreme Court that offered a range of arguments, including that the events on January 6 did not constitute an insurrection, and that his speech that day encouraging the violence of others was protected by the First Amendment.[73] In 2024, the Supreme Court denied cert. in Couy Griffin's case. Thus, he remains disqualified from holding any state office.

DISQUALIFICATION OF DONALD TRUMP?

What do the cases of Madison Cawthorn and Couy Griffin mean for Donald Trump? Legal accountability for the attempts to overturn the 2020 election is finally coming home to roost with an indictment for federal crimes brought by special counsel Jack Smith against ex-president Trump and an indictment for Georgia crimes against Trump and eighteen coconspirators brought by Fulton County district attorney Fani Willis.[74]

Meanwhile, as these criminal cases slowly unfold, nonprofit groups have been suing to get Trump off of the 2024 ballot using Section 3 of the Fourteenth Amendment. A suit was filed by Free Speech for People with the Minnesota Supreme Court seeking to disqualify Trump from Minnesota's ballot.[75] The court heard oral argument on November 2, 2023.[76] Less than a week later, it decided that Trump could be on the Minnesota ballot for the presidential primary, but left the door open that plaintiffs could renew its objections to Trump being on the 2024 general election ballot.[77] The basis of this opinion was rooted in Minnesota election law, which gave enormous control to the major political parties to decide who to field as candidates.

On September 6, 2023, Citizens for Responsibility and Ethics in Washington (CREW) filed a lawsuit on behalf of voters in Colorado seeking to invoke the Disqualification Clause against Trump.[78] This suit, *Anderson v. Griswold*, focused on both Trump's fake elector scheme as well as the violence on January 6 that interrupted the constitutionally mandated counting of electoral college votes.[79] While Judge Sarah Wallace decided that Trump had engaged in an insurrection, she allowed him to stay on the Colorado ballot, ruling that the Disqualification Clause does not apply to the president because that office is not explicitly listed in the clause.[80] Rather, it covers "offices under the United States," which the judge did not believe covered the presidency.[81] This case was appealed both by the Colorado voters, who didn't like the ruling that the president is excused from the Disqualification Clause,[82] and by ex-president Trump, who didn't like the conclusion that he had engaged in an insurrection.[83] The Colorado Supreme Court heard oral arguments in the case on December 6, 2023,[84] during which Trump's lawyers argued that Jefferson Davis, the president of the Confederacy during the Civil War, could have been constitutionally elected president despite the Disqualification Clause, and that Barack Obama could be elected to a third term in office despite the Twenty-Second Amendment.[85]

On December 19, 2023, the Colorado Supreme Court rendered its decision in *Anderson v. Griswold* and caused the equivalent of a constitutional earthquake. It concluded: "President Trump is disqualified from holding the office of President under Section Three; because he is disqualified, it would be a wrongful act under the Election Code for the Secretary to list him as a candidate on the presidential primary ballot."[86] Thus, this court ruled that Trump was constitutionally disqualified and, thus, that his name should not appear on the Colorado primary ballot for the Republican Party.

In an opinion sprawling over one hundred pages, the Colorado Supreme Court explained how they reached this legal conclusion. For one, it noted that it was appropriate for judges to police who can appear on a ballot: "As then-Judge Gorsuch recognized in *Hassan*, it is 'a state's legitimate interest in protecting the integrity and practical functioning of the political process' that 'permits it to exclude from the ballot candidates who are constitutionally prohibited from assuming office.'"[87] The court also noted the animating purpose of the Disqualification Clause, which was "to ensure that disloyal officers could never again play a role in governing the country.... The drafters of Section Three were motivated by a sense of betrayal; that is, by the existence of a broken oath, not by the type of officer who broke it."[88] The Court rejected the argument that Congress needed to pass implementing legislation to make the Disqualification Clause operative, concluding that "the Supreme Court has said that the Fourteenth Amendment 'is undoubtedly self-executing without any ancillary legislation, so far as its terms are applicable to any existing state of circumstances.'"[89]

The Colorado Supreme Court also had to judge whether Trump's speech on the Ellipse on January 6 was meant to provoke violence. They held that it did, detailing that "President Trump's calls . . . were likely to incite such imminent lawlessness and violence. When President Trump told his supporters that they were 'allowed to go by very different rules' and that if they did not 'fight like hell,' they would not 'have a country anymore,' it was likely that his supporters would heed his encouragement and act violently."[90] The court also considered Trump's actions in the lead up to January 6, noting that "far right extremists and militias such as the Proud Boys, the Oath Keepers, and the Three Percenters viewed President Trump's December 19, 2020 tweet as a 'call to arms,' and they began to plot activities to disrupt the January 6 joint session of Congress. In the meantime, President Trump repeated his invitation to come to Washington, D.C. on January 6 at least twelve times."[91]

Additionally, the Colorado high court affirmed the approach of the district court judge to consider Trump's speech in light of his personal history. As the Colorado Supreme Court explicated, "It was appropriate for the district court to consider President Trump's 'history of courting extremists and endorsing political violence as legitimate and proper, as well as his efforts to undermine the legitimacy of the 2020 election results and hinder the certification of the Electoral College results in Congress.'"[92]

While much of the *Anderson v. Griswold* opinion focused on constitutional law and post–Civil War history, the court explained how Colorado election law applied to the case as well, concluding that "certifying an unqualified candidate to the presidential primary ballot constitutes a 'wrongful act' that runs afoul of section [Colorado law] 1-4-1203(2)(a) and undermines the purposes of the Election Code.... And section 1-4-1203(2)(a) clearly limits participation in the presidential primary to political parties fielding 'qualified' candidates."[93]

The Colorado Supreme Court also specifically refuted some of the stranger arguments from Trump's lawyers: "Were we to adopt President Trump's view, Colorado could not exclude from the ballot even candidates who plainly do not satisfy the age, residency, and citizenship requirements of the Presidential Qualifications Clause of Article II. It would mean that the state would be powerless to exclude a twenty-eight-year-old, a non-resident of the United States, or even a foreign national from the presidential primary ballot in Colorado."[94]

The Colorado Supreme Court agreed with the trial court that "we have little difficulty concluding that substantial evidence in the record supported each of these elements and that, as the district court found, the events of January 6 constituted an insurrection."[95] In end, the Court determined that the former president was responsible, finding that "President Trump engaged in insurrection. President Trump's direct and express efforts, over several months, exhorting his supporters to march to the Capitol to prevent what he falsely characterized as an alleged fraud on the people of this country were indisputably overt and voluntary. Moreover, the evidence amply showed that President Trump undertook all these actions to ... prevent Congress from certifying the 2020 presidential election and stop the peaceful transfer of power."[96]

In the weeks after the Colorado Supreme Court's ruling, Michigan's Supreme Court decided to follow the approach of the Minnesota Supreme Court and allowed Trump to be on the Michigan GOP primary ballot.[97] Then the Maine secretary of state, Shenna Bellows, followed the Colorado approach and declared that Trump would not be on Maine's GOP primary ballot because he was disqualified under Section 3 of the

Fourteenth Amendment.[98] Bellows ruled, "I conclude that Mr. Trump's primary petition is invalid. Specifically, I find that the declaration on his candidate consent form is false because he is not qualified to hold the office of the President under Section Three of the Fourteenth Amendment."[99] She explained that "States have inherent authority over their ballots . . . The inevitable result of States managing their own elections is that each has different requirements and procedures for ballot access, even with respect to presidential candidates."[100] She also noted how Maine's election laws work: "Section 336 [of Maine's election law] requires all candidates, including presidential candidates, to submit a written consent . . . [including] a statement that the candidate 'meets the qualifications of the office the candidate seeks.' Section 336 also renders any primary petition void . . . where . . . 'any part of the declaration is . . . false.'"[101] And she added that "I am authorized, and indeed duty-bound under the terms of the oath of office to which I swore, see M. Const. Art. IX Section 1, to enforce Maine's election laws."[102] Thus, she was applying both the US Constitution and Maine law when she concluded that "the events of January 6, 2021 were unprecedented and tragic. They were an attack not only upon the Capitol and governmental officials, but also an attack on the rule of law. The evidence here demonstrates that they occurred at the behest of, and with the knowledge and support of, the outgoing President [Trump]. The U.S. Constitution does not tolerate an assault on the foundations of government and [Maine law] Section 336 requires me to act in response."[103]

Secretary Bellows laid out step by step how she made the decision that Trump was disqualified: "First, no Congressional action is necessary to render effective the qualification set forth in Section Three."[104] Then, "second, the presidency is covered by Section Three. It is an 'office, civil or military, under the United States,' and the President is an 'officer of the United States.'"[105] And, "[third,] the record demonstrates that the events of January 6, 2021 were an insurrection."[106] In conclusion, she said: "The weight of the evidence makes clear that Mr. Trump was aware of the tinder laid by his multi-month effort to delegitimize a democratic election and then chose to light a match. . . . Mr. Trump intended to incite lawless action, his speech is unprotected by the First Amendment. . . . Principles of free speech do not override the clear command of Section Three of the Fourteenth Amendment, namely that those who orchestrate violence against our government may not wield the levers of its power."[107]

In Maine, Trump's lawyers argued that he only had to swear he was qualified with reference to items listed on Maine's form. The Secretary of State rejected this argument by explaining that "the form . . . omits reference to the Twenty-Second Amendment prohibition of serving as President for more than two terms, but that qualification plainly still applies. Similarly . . . I would not . . . be required to place a teenager on the presidential primary ballot."[108] Bellows also added her acknowledgment of the solemnity and import of her decision: "I do not reach this conclusion lightly. . . . I am mindful that no Secretary of State has ever deprived a presidential candidate of ballot access based on Section Three of the Fourteenth Amendment. I am also mindful, however, that no presidential candidate has ever before engaged in insurrection."[109]

Reaction to the Colorado, Minnesota, Michigan, Maine, and other potential Section 3 decisions[110] ran the gamut from those cheering the application of constitutional accountability to Trump,[111] to those decrying it as a devious legal trick,[112] or just a wrongheaded decision.[113] I, for one, thought that Couy Griffin deserved to be constitutionally disqualified from office, and I likewise think that Donald Trump surely deserves a similar fate. Any suit trying to keep Trump off the ballot or out of office will inevitably end up at the doorstep of the Supreme Court. Many commentators predicted that the Roberts Court would rescue Trump from being removed from ballots because that would be antidemocratic. Conservative former judge Michael Luttig has argued forcefully and correctly that it would be antidemocratic to allow someone who tried to overthrow the last election the ability to run again as a candidate. As he explained, "It's the conduct that gives rise to disqualification that the Constitution tells us is antidemocratic. [And] it is the Constitution itself that provides for disqualification. So there's no possible way that the Constitution itself can be understood as antidemocratic."[114] As with many things about him, suits against Trump attempting to constitutionally disqualify him from office are all unprecedented.

On January 4, 2024, the Supreme Court agreed to hear Trump's appeal of the Colorado Supreme Court's decision throwing him off of the Colorado ballot pursuant to the Disqualification Clause.[115] The case name changed from *Anderson v. Griswold* to *Trump v. Anderson*.[116] On

March 4, 2024, a day before Super Tuesday, the Supreme Court ruled unanimously in a per curiam opinion that Trump could stay on the ballot because Colorado lacked the power to enforce the Disqualification Clause.[117] The Court ruled that only Congress had the power to enforce this part of the Constitution against federal candidates through federal legislation and explained that relief for Trump was appropriate, because, as a state, Colorado only had the power to enforce the Disqualification Clause against candidates for state office.[118] The concurrence in the judgment by Justices Sotomayor, Kagan, and Jackson countered that the Supreme Court's majority should not have opined on the way in which the clause should be enforced by Congressional legislation when the only question before the Court was the action of a state.[119] In *Trump v. Anderson*, the Supreme Court thereby gutted the ability of all states to keep insurrectionists off of the ballot for federal offices in the future. Thus, because of *Trump v. Anderson*, a state like Arizona cannot stop the so-called Q-Anon Shaman, who pled guilty to a January 6 felony, from running for a seat in the US House of Representatives unless and until Congress passes a new law barring people like him from office.[120]

The reality that American courts are failing to disqualify January 6 participants from office under the Constitution's Disqualification Clause is one more reason why voters, consumers, and investors should put politicians, and the corporations that fund their rise to power, to the Democracy Litmus Test. The courts lack the guts to keep the worst individuals out of power. This puts the ball in the hands of ordinary people to use their ballots and pocketbooks to incentivize politicians to do the right thing.

10

DON'T BE FOOLED

CORPORATIONS FEIGNING FRIENDSHIP

On September 27, 2021, attendees at a Cowboys vs. Eagles football game in the AT&T Stadium in Arlington, Texas, saw an odd sight: a plane flying above with a banner trailing behind it that read, in big bold caps: "AT&T: #1 ABORTION BAN NETWORK IN THE US."[1] In a Tweet containing a picture of the banner, sports reporter Michael Gehlken explained, "This plane is flying over AT&T Stadium before Cowboys host Eagles. Woman's advocacy group UltraViolet paid for banner, it says, because AT&T donations 'helped fuel and legitimize politicians pushing a radical anti-woman agenda that made Texas' newest abortion law possible.'"[2] The banner was accurate: AT&T is the largest corporate donor to anti-abortion politicians across the United States.[3]

This effort by UltraViolet was an attempt to encourage football patrons to follow the money and the way it is spent in political campaigns to impact policy outcomes. The stunt also highlighted Texas's 2021 abortion law, which was one of the most restrictive in the nation. At the time, abortions were banned after six weeks, and the state put out a bounty on individuals who aided or abetted women getting an abortion.[4] A year later, this would not be the most restrictive law in the nation after the Supreme Court overturned *Roe v. Wade* in *Dobbs v. Jackson Women's Health*. By 2023, fourteen states had completely banned abortion.[5] In 2024, Arizona became the fifteenth state to ban abortion when the Arizona Supreme Court upheld an abortion ban from 1864.[6] This plane also sent a message to shareholders of AT&T, encouraging them to consider the prudence of their political spending, bankrolling the politicians who enacted these abortion bans.

A PRESIDENTIAL VETO

On March 20, 2023, siting at the Resolute Desk in the Oval Office, President Joe Biden put pen to paper and used his veto power for the first time.[7]

Biden's first veto wasn't about abortion, COVID-19, infrastructure, Amtrak, or gay rights. It was about a rule from the Department of Labor (DOL) about ethical investment decisions. This veto is a small part of a much bigger fight about who can tell a corporation to be better. The rule at issue allowed the people who select investments for pension funds to consider ESG factors when making these decisions: environmental, social, or governance factors that are considered in comparing potential investments. So, for example, under the rule, a pension manager could consider whether a company was managing the risk of climate change effectively or poorly before investing.

The Congressional Review Act (CRA) allows Congress to repeal federal agency rules that it dislikes through a congressional resolution. On December 1, 2022, the DOL published its final rule, called the "Prudence and Loyalty in Selecting Plan Investments and Exercising Shareholder Rights."[8] This rule is colloquially known as the "DOL ESG Rule." Congress used its CRA power to roll it back.

Republicans in Congress referred to the DOL ESG Rule by their generically pejorative but nonspecific criticism that it was too "woke."[9] After the House flipped to Republican control in January 2023, the enemies of ESG in the House pushed for the rule to be scrapped. This resolution sailed through the Republican House and made through it the Senate with the help of Democratic senators Jon Tester and Joe Manchin. However, this effort by Congress to kill the DOL ESG Rule failed because President Biden vetoed it.

As Biden explained in his first veto message:

> There is extensive evidence showing that environmental, social, and governance [ESG] factors can have a material impact on markets, industries, and businesses.... This [Congressional] resolution would prevent retirement plan fiduciaries from taking into account factors, such as the physical risks of climate change and poor corporate governance, that could affect investment returns. Retirement plan fiduciaries should be able to

consider any factor that maximizes financial returns for retirees across the country.... Therefore, I am vetoing this resolution.[10]

The Republican House attempted to override this veto and failed. The DOL ESG Rule remains intact.[11]

This interbranch back and forth over the DOL ESG Rule is part of an epic struggle over how companies should be managed and how much input investors can have in shaping the trajectory of corporate governance. As Senate majority leader Chuck Schumer wrote in the *Wall Street Journal*, "Republicans talk about their love of the free market, small government and letting the private sector do its work. But their obsession with eliminating ESG would do the opposite, forcing their own views down the throats of every company and investor."[12]

Investors, including those running pension funds, have moved an enormous amount of money into investments that are strong on ESG metrics. US SIF, which tracks ESG and other sustainable investments, found that "$7.6 trillion in US-domiciled assets at the beginning of 2022 [were] held by 497 institutional investors, 349 money managers and 1,359 community investment institutions that . . . apply[] various ESG criteria in their investment decision-making and portfolio selection."[13] To put this number in context, US SIF estimates that in 2022, $66.6 trillion in total US assets were under professional management. In other words, over 1 in every 10 dollars is invested in an ESG asset. Following this trend, the Rockefeller Foundation, whose $6 billion endowment is traced back to Standard Oil, divested from fossil fuels in 2020.[14] The Ford Foundation ($10 billion) and the MacArthur Foundation ($8 billion) followed suit in 2021.[15] Harvard University divested its $50 billion endowment from fossil fuels in 2021.[16] By 2023, NYU ($5 billion) was the one-hundredth university to start divesting from these types of investments.[17]

Perhaps not surprisingly, given how much money has been invested in ESG, shareholder proposals on ESG topics have garnered strong shareholder support.[18] One study has showed that shareholder pressure to get corporations to disclose their climate risks actually changed the behavior of many firms by increasing transparency.[19] This same study demonstrated that stock prices rose with increased transparency about climate risk. As the authors concluded, "In the days following a shareholder-induced disclosure of climate-change risks, the disclosing firm's stock price increases by 1.21% on average. . . . Investors dislike uncertainty and are willing to pay a premium for less opaque companies."[20] As corporate scholars Quinn Curtis, Jill E. Fisch, and Adriana Robertson explain this trend: "The growing focus on ESG investing is reflected in the rapidly expanding number of mutual funds that purport to consider ESG factors. . . . Morningstar reports that the number of ESG-focused index funds and the total amount of assets held by such funds have each doubled in the past three years."[21]

Some of what has driven the growth in ESG investing is the fact that progressive investors, including those managing the massive pension funds of the biggest public sector unions from California and New York, have been flexing their muscles and pushing companies to be better stewards of the environment, as well as more transparent about their role as funders of political spending and more democratic in how the corporate structure is run. This has led to decades of shareholder proposals on environmental issues, and, more recently, to over a decade of shareholder proposals demanding more transparency around corporate money in politics.[22] As Si2, which tracks this data, found in 2020, "[with] corporate political activity[,] investor support for more oversight and disclosure continued its upward climb, with seven majority votes and 14 resolutions earning more than 40 percent. . . . Support [] this year reached all-time average highs of 44 percent on election spending and 34 percent on lobbying."[23]

Encouragingly, many more companies are more forthcoming about the corporate political spending than they were a decade ago. According to the Center for Political Accountability (CPA), which tracks this data, "The number of companies that fully or partially disclosed their political spending in 2022 . . . was 385."[24] The reason this is a big deal is because the Securities and Exchange Commission (SEC) has failed to require such disclosures through regulations; thus, "public companies are currently not required to, and most do not, report their political spending to shareholders."[25] However, in 2020, CPA found the following deficiencies:

- 48% of S&P 500 companies provide no disclosure of contributions to candidates, parties, and committees; . . .
- 57% provide no disclosure of ballot measure payments;

- 57% provide no disclosure of payments to trade associations; . . . ; and
- 69% provide no disclosure of payments to 501(c)(4) social welfare organizations.[26]

Thus, there is much room for improvement.

Like other ESG disclosures, disclosures on political spending are largely missing from most publicly traded companies, leaving investors in the dark. As Delaware Supreme Court justice Leo E. Strine Jr. complained, "Institutions . . . have no idea how much their portfolio companies spend on politics, and how that money is being spent."[27] Justice Strine noted that there is the further problem that political spending may indicate weakness in the overall business such that "if a business has to try to make money by influencing the political process, that suggests that its prospects for growth by developing improved products and services are not strong."[28] There are risks that those who have control over corporate resources will spend in their own self-interest. As Zicklin School of Business at Baruch College professor David Rosenberg argues, "[Corporate] directors might also make decisions to spend corporate funds on political speech that are based on self-interest and not the interests of the corporation."[29] Fordham University professor Miguel Alzola contends that shareholders should be able to consent to corporate political spending.[30]

Law professors Bebchuk and Jackson have further highlighted the problem that corporate political spending exposes corporations to reputational risks, arguing, "To the extent that spending on some controversial political causes favored by the company's management can generate risks to the company or provide a valuable window into the quality of the company's governance, investors solely focused on financial returns might still be interested in knowing about these payments even if the monetary amounts are not large."[31] This leads them to conclude that, "for a variety of reasons, . . . disclosure of corporate spending on politics should not be left to private ordering."[32] However, this is exactly the current state of play, as there is no SEC rule requiring disclosure of corporate money in politics (neither money spent elections nor money spent on lobbying is disclosed).

Mainstream investors like Blackrock endorsed ESG in 2020, stating, "We build investment products that can do more than grow your money. Align your investments to your values with funds that support ESG considerations."[33] Perhaps reacting to the success of ESG shareholder proposals, or because of statements like Blackrock's, in 2021 corporate managers and right-wing politicians started vocally pushing back against ESG. This included launching a bevy of op-eds and white papers criticizing ESG as being anti-business. Certain corporations have been hostile to having shareholder proposals on ESG topics like diversity. In 2021, "at its shareholder meeting . . . , Berkshire Hathaway rejected a shareholder proposal that would require the company to issue annual reports on diversity. Johnson & Johnson also asked the SEC to block shareholder votes on a similar diversity proposal."[34]

THE CONSERVATIVE BACKLASH

State attorneys general in red states have also been vocally anti-ESG. In 2022, the then–attorney general of Arizona Mark Brnovich argued in a *Wall St. Journal* op-ed that shareholder efforts to push ESG, especially the environmental aspect, could be an anti-trust violation. Brnovich wrote: "The biggest antitrust violation in history may be in plain sight. Wall Street banks and money managers are bragging about their coordinated efforts to choke off investment in energy."[35] This might be dismissed as hyperbole, except that, when he was writing this, Brnovich had the power to launch criminal investigations. And he did. As he added, "As attorney general of Arizona, . . . I've launched an investigation into this potentially unlawful market manipulation."[36] Attorneys General from 18 other states joined this investigation.[37] Later that year Brnovich lost his reelection.[38] His Democratic successor pulled Arizona out, but the investigation is ongoing.[39]

The fight over ESG is unfolding in many state legislatures, with the American Legislative Exchange Council (ALEC) at the forefront, pushing model anti-ESG legislation. ALEC is an organization that brings together Republicans state lawmakers and corporations.[40] The group hosts meetings where the lawmakers and corporate representatives can meet to discuss policy.[41] Corporations and state lawmakers also draft model bills together at ALEC.[42] As the Union of Concerned Scientists has warned, "The ALEC-drafted Energy Discrimination Elimination Act Texas passed [in 2021] is yet another example of the council deceiving state lawmakers. The bill targets the environmental, social and governance (ESG) standards that banks, investment firms and pension funds are increasingly applying to make it harder for fossil fuel companies to obtain insurance, financing and other support if they don't meet ESG criteria."[43] After Texas enacted this law, it banned 10 banks and 348 investment funds from doing business with it.[44] This law led five additional banks to stop underwriting 40 percent of municipal bonds in Texas, thereby making raising capital more expensive for Texas.[45]

The spate of anti-ESG bills in state legislatures is a growing trend. As Reuters reported, "So far 99 anti-ESG bills [were] filed in 2023 vs 39 in 2022."[46] In 2022 and 2023, many of these bills became law. Kentucky's S.B. 205 "ACT relating to state dealings with companies that engage in energy company boycotts" and North Dakota's bill on "Social Investment Prohibition" became law in 2022.[47] Montana's bill to "Generally revise public investment laws,"[48] Idaho's bill "To Require That Banks Holding State Funds Not Boycott Certain Industries,"[49] Indiana's "Pension Investment" bill,[50] Arkansas's bill "Concerning the Regulation of Environmental, Social Justice, or Governance Scores,"[51] and Alabama's anti-ESG bill all became law in 2023.[52]

Certain red-state governors also jumped on the anti-ESG bandwagon, particularly governor of Florida Ron DeSantis, who has made being "anti-woke" a key aspect of his 2024 presidential run.[53] DeSantis said: "I think this whole ESG movement is really trying to do through the financial sector what they could never achieve through the ballot box. . . . In Florida, I just signed anti-ESG legislation, which said things like no ESG criteria in our pension fund, we've got $180 billion state pension fund."[54] DeSantis's rant on ESG neglected to define his terms, so any voter listening in who hadn't been tracking this issue would be confused about what he was talking about; he just sounded like another politician spouting inscrutable acronyms.

Contrary to the rhyming slam that "woke investors go broke," many investors and studies have found that companies with an eye on sustainability have strong returns.[55] As the *Harvard Business Review* reported in 2019, "Sophisticated asset owners [are] aware that sustainable investing improves returns."[56] Meanwhile, since 2018, advocates for ESG have pushed the Securities and Exchange Commission (SEC) to put out a new rule on ESG.[57] In May 2022 the commission proposed rules to for certain investment advisers and investment companies about ESG investment practices.[58] This rule had yet to be finalized as of April 2024.[59]

However, the SEC did finalize a climate change disclosure rule for public companies that scheduled to go into effect in May 2024, so there has been some progress made by securities regulators.[60] However, the Fifth Circuit has enjoined this new rule, and there is a parallel effort in Congress to use the Congressional Review Act (CRA) to undo this climate change disclosure rule.[61] So only time will tell whether history will repeat itself and President Biden will veto this just as he vetoed the effort by Congress to kill the DOL ESG rule.

One of the reasons why having standardized disclosures on ESG from the SEC is necessary is because it mitigates the problem of "greenwashing" and "ethics washing" that can trick consumers into buying from or trick shareholders into investing in insincere companies. As corporate scholars have noted, "There is no settled notion of an environmentally responsible company. Is Tesla a green company because it makes electric vehicles, or is it not, because it harvests vast quantities of lithium for its batteries? . . . What is true of the 'E' in ESG is equally true of 'S' and 'G.' A company might be a leader in addressing workplace inequality but fail to oversee child labor practices in its supply chain."[62] The lack of this standardization has opened ESG to the apt criticism that "the great thing about sustainable investing is it can be whatever you want it to be."[63] Thus, another advantage of standardization is that it facilitates comparisons by investors apples to apples and oranges to oranges of corporate ESG disclosures.

Investors argue that, without standardization at the SEC level, "in the extreme, information asymmetries around ESG risk could cause markets to misprice risk or overvalue assets."[64] Moreover, investors that have focused on the environmental aspect of ESG are likely to be the ones most attuned to the stranded assets problem. As Boise State University professor Ruth Jebe explains, "Stranded assets are assets that have undergone unanticipated or premature devaluation, often as a results of environment-related risks. Fossil fuels provide an example of this risk as estimates suggest that a significant proportion of fossil fuel reserves, with a value in the trillions of dollars, would be considered 'unburnable' if the world is to avoid disastrous climate change."[65] As Sustainable investor Tim Smith told the press: "Investors globally are increasingly engaging companies and their trade associations on their climate-related lobbying, urging them to ensure all lobbying is in sync with the goals of the Paris Accord. . . . Unfortunately, a number of trade associations actively work against forward-looking legislation or regulation on climate change with a significant impact on government policy. This is a tragic misalignment."[66]

The greenwashing/ethics-washing problem is a real one.[67] Those in the PR departments of big corporations are no fools. Corporations are good at virtue signaling and paying lip service to social causes, including claiming to be a prodemocratic force. Many corporations make largely empty gestures to leave the impression that they are socially responsible, from tweeting support for events like International Women's Day, to sponsoring Pride parades in major urban centers. These actions cost firms very little and take little effort; mostly, they serve as a form of corporate branding to make a given firm appear generically progressive or tolerant.

PhMRA had a particularly poor record in the 2022 election when they gave over $1 million to election deniers. As Ed Silverman reported on election eve, "[PhMRA], the industry trade group, donated more than $1.2 million to organizations that then funneled money toward Republicans who are running for various state offices and have denied the 2020 election results. Pfizer spent $600,000, GSK contributed more than $280,000, Eli Lilly gave $265,000, and Novartis contributed $235,00[0], while Astellas Pharma spent $195,000, Johnson & Johnson provided $175,000 and Merck sent $125,000."[68]

ALEC is not just pushing anti-ESG legislation; when it comes to voter suppression at the state level, it continues to be a font of anti-voter ideas. For many years, it was the source of restrictive Voter ID bills. Then, after backlash and threats of consumer boycotts of corporate members of ALEC, it backed away temporarily in 2012. ALEC claimed that it does not work on election suppression bills. However, the CEO of ALEC, Lisa Nelson, was caught on video in 2021 saying just the opposite. She was recorded saying: "ALEC, which closely aligned itself with Trump and the GOP, is heavily invested in getting voter suppression bills passed in order to give Republicans an edge in coming elections."[69]

According to *The Nation*, ALEC got rid of its Public Safety and Elections Task Force and replaced it with the ALEC Political Process

Working Group.[70] Lawyer Cleta Mitchell is one of the group's leaders.[71] Mitchell became notorious for trying to overturn the 2020 election,[72] and for being on the phone call with President Trump where he pressured Georgia election officials to find him more votes.[73] In 2023, she was caught on tape saying pejoratively of college voters, "What are these college campus locations? . . . They basically put the polling place next to the student dorm so they just have to roll out of bed, vote, and go back to bed."[74] At another event, Mitchell "told a roomful of GOP donors . . . that conservatives must band together to limit voting on college campuses, same-day voter registration and automatic mailing of ballots to registered voters, according to a copy of her presentation reviewed by the *Washington Post*."[75] ALEC outsourced its anti-voter work to the Honest Election Project, whose funding is dark, but NPR has reported that it is linked to the Federalist Society's Leonard Leo.[76]

ALEC apparently also works with Heritage Action. According to an internal document, "ALEC would be a key policy and lobbying partner in their multi-year campaign to push anti-voter laws, many of which specifically target and limit voting access for people of color, young people, and the elderly."[77] As *Forbes* reported, "Heritage [Action] plans to work with ALEC to 'produce model legislation for state legislatures to adopt' as part of a $24 million push to enact tougher voting laws in swing states."[78] *Forbes* also noted that ALEC "gets most of its funding through its corporate partners, with revenue totaling more than $9 million in 2018 and over $10 million in 2017, according to IRS filings."[79]

ALEC worked hard on the 2020 redistricting cycle to advantage Republicans. It tried to keep this under wraps, but Slate revealed it to the public after crashing one of their conferences in 2019 (or, at least, was given audio recording by someone who did):

> Slate has obtained an exclusive audio recording of the closed-door panel called "How to Survive Redistricting," moderated by influential Republican lawyer Cleta Mitchell. The panel's four experts—Hans von Spakovsky of the Heritage Foundation, North Carolina election lawyer Thomas Farr, former Georgia Rep. Lynn Westmoreland, and Texas state Rep. Phil King—are among the architects and defenders of some of the most notorious gerrymanders and voter suppression plans of this decade.[80]

Troublingly, Slate reported that the discussion at this 2019 ALEC event included the following advice: "During the session, the legislators were advised to treat redistricting [in 2021] as 'political adult blood sport,' trash potential evidence before it can be discovered through litigation, avoid the word gerrymander, and make deals with black and Latino legislators that guarantee them easy reelections by packing as many minority voters as possible into their districts, thereby making the rest of the map whiter and more conservative."[81]

Cleta Mitchell also spoke at this event. She told the crowd: "You are going to be sued. Let's start with that."[82] Mitchell added, "*We're going to teach you how to gerrymander.*"[83] And, like the participants in the Teapot Dome scandal from one hundred years ago who burned evidence, she advised ALEC attendees to throw away documents from the meeting.[84] The legal advice also included adding language in bills that allows state legislatures to defend the law in court even if a state attorney general refuses.[85] Such language ended up in North Carolina law in 2017. This empowerment of state legislatures to defend laws was upheld as constitutional by the Supreme Court in *Berger v. North Carolina State Conference of the NAACP* in 2022.[86]

The term "Sedition Caucus" is the derisive name that has been given to the 147 Republicans who voted to not certify lawful electoral college votes for Joe Biden on January 6, 2021.[87] The caucus contains many ALEC alums who were state lawmakers before they were elected to Congress. The Union of Concerned Scientists found that "more than half of the 77 alumni listed on ALEC's website currently serving in Congress (40 in the House and one in the Senate) were among the 147 Republicans in Congress who voted to overturn the results of the 2020 presidential election."[88]

Because of ALEC's anti-voter history, in mid-2021 good-government groups tried to get corporations to leave ALEC. As *The Nation* reported, "More than 300 voting rights organizations and their allies, including Common Cause, Public Citizen, Fair Fight Action, Color of Change, the AFL-CIO, and the League of Women Voters, demanded that major corporations cut their financial ties with ALEC."[89] The League of Women Voters wrote to corporate funders of ALEC: "We are writing to urge you to cease your association with, and end your funding of, the American Legislative Exchange Council (ALEC) based on its active efforts to restrict the American people's freedom to vote and spread lies about the integrity of our elections to undermine American democracy."[90] These good-government groups wrote to corporate members of ALEC and told them: "Faced with public outrage over legislation that creates barriers to voting rights enacted or proposed in more than 47 states, and the bills' disproportionate impact on people of color, young people, and the elderly, hundreds of companies have publicly denounced any discriminatory legislation that makes it harder for people to vote. Perhaps your company is one of them.'"[91] This letter was sent to "Anheuser-Busch, Blue Cross Blue Shield Association, CenturyLink, Duke Energy, Eli Lilly, Fed-Ex, Koch Industries, Oracle, Raytheon, Salesforce, State Farm," and others.[92] After this effort, Pfizer cut ties with ALEC.[93] Dominion Energy said it was no longer a member of ALEC in 2021.[94] This good-government effort largely failed, but it was a worthy one that more investors and customers should support, as it is perfectly aligned with applying the Democracy Litmus Test. Customers can stop buying these antidemocratic brands. Meanwhile, investors can use their platforms under US securities laws to compel changes in corporate behavior from within the corporate structure or exercise their prerogative to exit these investments.

CONTRADICTIONS AFTER *DOBBS*

After *Dobbs v. Jackson Women's Health Organization* took away the constitutional right to abortion, corporate spenders were called out for their seeming contradictions. Post-*Dobbs*, corporate political spending flowed to anti-abortion law makers. Many states had so-called trigger bans that went into effect directly after the Supreme Court's ruling. As the Sustainable Investment Institute (Si2) documented, "Corporate donations to political campaigns from the 167 Fortune 250 companies shows striking support for state politicians who favor abortion bans, especially in the 26 states where abortion could soon be banned or restricted."[95] This group further found that "in five states where abortion bans are certain—Alabama, Kentucky, Louisiana, North Dakota and Utah—more than 95% of [corporate] contributions went to anti-abortion candidates."[96] They also discovered that a majority of Fortune 250 companies were giving exclusively to anti-abortion politicians.[97]

Other conservative states without trigger bans nonetheless amended their laws to implement either severe restrictions on abortion or outright bans. Blue states went in the entirely opposite direction: New York and states on the West Coast bolstered their access to reproductive care, including for women from out of state who might find themselves without local access to abortion.[98]

Single pharmaceutical companies have demonstrated enormous inconsistency between their public stances and their political spending.[99] Eli Lilly complained about abortion restrictions in Indiana, where it is headquartered, "saying that the measure would make it hard to attract talent and would force it to look outside the state for growth. But in the weeks and months that followed, Lilly continued to financially support Republican candidates and politicians who support bans on abortion across the country."[100] Pfizer in particular has unclean hands when it comes to supporting the politicians who support abortion bans: "An *Insider* analysis of campaign-finance data compiled by Followthemoney.org found that Pfizer gave about $341,000 to politicians in 13 states who drafted or signed [abortion trigger bans]."[101] This spending made Pfizer the biggest drug company that financially backed the politicians behind trigger bans. But Pfizer was not alone. *Business Insider* also discovered that "close to 1,000 healthcare companies, insurers, clinics, care facilities, pharmacies, drug companies, and medical associations (or their associated political-action committees) have collectively given more than $14 million to the 444 state legislators and 13 governors responsible for enacting trigger laws since 2005."[102] In addition, Pfizer gave $1 million to President Trump's inaugural committee.[103]

According to the feminist group Ultraviolet, which has been tracking political spending for anti-choice elected officials, "$323,916,394 was donated by corporations to anti-abortion lawmakers since 2020."[104] Nationally the top supporters of anti-choice politicians between 2020 and 2022 were Chevron ($21,505,283); Altria Group ($10,128,008); Anthem ($9,073,293); Comcast ($8,845,776); AT&T ($8,709,303); Valero Energy ($8,417,000); Centene ($8,182,756); Charter Communications ($8,128,219); Marathon Petroleum ($7,448,398); and Occidental Petroleum ($6,996,350).[105] In Florida, the top five corporate supporters of anti-choice politicians between 2020 and 2022 were Duke Energy ($3,225,174); Walt Disney ($1,991,067); NextEra Energy ($1,722,133); Centene ($1,456,000); and Comcast ($1,182,419).[106] NextEra Energy was also in the middle of the ghost candidate scandal.

One company that did not show up on Ultraviolet's list from 2020–22 is Coca-Cola, which shows up in Judd Legum's analysis of 2016–22. He found that "since 2016, Coca-Cola has donated $2,624,000 to anti-abortion political committees, including $105,000 to the NRSC, $2,325,000 to the RGA, and $194,000 to the RSLC."[107] Another company missing from Ultraviolet's Top 10 was Walmart: "Since 2016, Walmart has donated $1,140,000 to anti-abortion political committees, including $755,000 to the RGA, $195,000 to the NRSC, and $190,000 to the RSLC."[108] Legum also called out "other top contributors to anti-abortion political committees [which] include General Motors ($2,405,900), Comcast ($1,869,604), Walgreens ($496,700), Wells Fargo ($471,800), and T-Mobile ($343,400)."[109] The differences between the lists could be due to their distinct methodologies or different time frames.

As the *New York Times* reported in the wake of the *Dobbs* decision, "Apple, Amazon, ... and Yelp are among those offering to cover some costs for employees who need to travel out of state for an abortion."[110] CNN added Citigroup to this list,[111] and *Bloomberg* included AT&T and Disney as well.[112] As many as forty companies took this stance post-*Dobbs*.[113] While Amazon was on this list of the "good guy" corporations supporting the choices of their female employees, "since 2016, Amazon has donated $974,718 to anti-abortion political committees, including $75,000 to the NRSC, $789,718 to the RGA, and $110,000 to the RSLC."[114] Many companies touting the reproductive rights of their employees gave money to governors hostile to abortion rights.[115] For example, "in Florida, AT&T contributed $80,000 to Friends of Ron DeSantis, a political action committee aligned with the Republican governor ... in 2020 and 2021, according to state records."[116]

Meanwhile, some of the corporate political support for anti-abortion politicians makes them look like complete hypocrites, as the very same companies have policies or have made pronouncements supporting reproductive freedoms.[117] One of the ways corporate political spenders try to have it both ways is by giving to umbrella groups that provide a thin veneer of deniability. As Judd Legum and Tesnim Zekeria reported about Google (otherwise known as Alphabet): "Google, for example, presents itself as a champion of women. . . . Yet, after signing that letter and declaring its support for women's rights, Google donated $155,000 in corporate funds to the RSLC in 2021. The donations were made by three different Google entities: Google Corporate Services ($10,000), Google Inc ($95,000), and Waymo ($50,000)."[118] Google's support of these groups dates back before *Roe* was on the chopping block.[119] Legum and Zekeria also found contradictions in the stances of Citigroup, which claimed, on the one hand, "that it's working to advance women's rights as outlined by the UN's Sustainable Development Goals. . . . The company also asserted 'the right to vote is the foundation of American democracy' and said it 'strongly' opposes 'efforts to undermine the ability of Americans to avail themselves of this fundamental right.'" But on the other hand, it gave "$75,000 to the RSLC in 2021—money that was used to undermine both of these goals."[120] This support looks even more damning over a longer time span, as "since 2016, Citi has donated $685,000 to anti-abortion political committees, including $90,000 to the NRSC and $595,000 to the RSLC."[121]

THE SOON FORGOTTEN GEORGE FLOYD

There have been some progressive actions taken by corporations in recent years regarding race. For example, in the immediate wake of African American George Floyd's murder by police in Minneapolis, captured on video, in the summer of 2020, many corporate brands put out statements supporting Black Lives Matter and decrying racism. For example, "from Silicon Valley to Wall Street, companies proclaimed 'Black lives matter.' JPMorgan Chase CEO Jamie Dimon adopted the posture of former NFL quarterback Colin Kaepernick's protests against police brutality and took a knee with bank employees. McDonald's declared Floyd and other slain Black Americans 'one of us.'"[122] A few brands dropped arguably racists mascots such as Aunt Jemima and Uncle Ben.[123]

Cynical people understand that most brands know supporting racial justice is a selling point for most consumers.[124] As the *Harvard Business Review* found, "A majority of Americans of all generations—60% of the U.S. population—say that how a brand responds to racial justice protests will influence *whether they buy or boycott the brand* in the future. Additionally, 60% say brands should take steps to address the root causes of racial inequity and 57% say brands must educate the public."[125] These findings were backed up by similar surveys taken two years later: "62% of people said that their perception of the brand's service and products was influenced by their diversity, according to an Adobe survey. Lack of diversity will cost you sales: 53% of African-Americans, 40% of Hispanics and 58% of LGBTQ+ stopped using a brand because of representation issues."[126] Another study from Google found that "64% consumers are more likely to consider, or even purchase, a product after seeing an ad that they considered to be diverse or inclusive."[127] Advertisers know this as well. The Association of National Advertisers reported that "brands specifically embracing diversity and inclusion and making it a core part of their DNA and messaging are seeing increased business results across each stage of the purchase funnel—awareness, consideration, intent and sales." And they added, "brands that have launched inclusivity campaigns have seen double- and triple-digit increases in website traffic as well as sustained, and in some cases record-breaking, sales growth."[128]

Corporate spending that backs politicians who aim to make voting more difficult in many states post-2020 often appears to outside observers as hypocritical, given that some of the very same companies have publicly embraced diversity. As the Center for Political Accountability found, by funding umbrella groups like the RSLC (Republican State Legislative Committee), corporations were funding legislators who sponsored and voted for legislation that made voting more restrictive in Georgia and Texas in 2021. As they discovered, "after companies and trade groups that had endorsed racial diversity efforts made large donations in the 2020 election to the RSLC, more than $137,000 went from the RSLC to help elect 46 state legislators who voted for Georgia's SB 202 voting restrictions."[129] They found that "a similar political spending pattern in Texas . . . occurred on a larger scale. Companies and trade associations that had endorsed racial diversity efforts contributed in the 2020 election to partisan groups including the RSLC, and the groups spent $3.4 million helping to elect Texas legislators who introduced, or who voted for, legislation making it more difficult for Black, Latino and Asian citizens to vote."[130]

By participating in groups like ALEC that have a history of helping to undermine voters, corporations are often talking out of both sides of their mouths when it comes to racial justice. Scott Roberts, senior director at Color of Change, said, "Through the American Legislative Exchange Council (ALEC), dozens of corporations—many of whom pledged solidarity with Black workers and consumers just last year—are secretly funding efforts to silence Black voters."[131] The head of Color of Change Rashad Robinson wrote in *The Guardian*: "What goes unreported too often, however, is the role of corporations in sustaining, or worsening, the forces of racism in America. Media corporations—whether news, entertainment or social media—saturate our culture with stereotypes and racist misinformation. Corporations from every industry sponsor voter suppression by supporting politicians who need it to win, while funding policy groups like ALEC that propagate it. Because that's one way corporations make money: profitable returns on racism."[132]

Investor Julie N. W. Goodridge has argued that these types of contradictions present risks for shareholders. As she wrote with Christine Jantz, "Corporate contributions that contradict company values pose a direct and immediate risk to shareholder value."[133] Examples include "inconsistencies shown between corporations' publicly-stated values (e.g., environmental and health care policies, compensation and pension packages, and employee benefit issues) and their support of specific candidates whose public policy and government regulatory positions are in violation of company values can directly harm shareholder value."[134]

After George Floyd's murder, many brands promised to help support the Black community. In the years that followed, little money was actually given. As *Fortune* reported a year after the murder, "Corporations have increasingly pledged financial support for Black communities since the murder of George Floyd last summer, but a new study finds that much of the funding has yet to materialize."[135]

Not every corporation who promised Floyd-inspired funding reneged: "One of the largest donations came from Apple, which pledged $100 million to a Racial Equity and Justice Initiative last June."[136] Retailer Target "spread their investments out over a number of years. The Minneapolis-based retailer pledged in April to spend $2 billion with black-owned businesses by the end of 2025."[137] Even the typically conservative "Home Depot has contributed $1 million to the Lawyers' Committee for Civil Rights Under Law."[138]

Corporate concern for racism and racist laws proved to be short lived. The brief complaints from CEOs did not stop Georgia from enacting its harsh voting rights the law. Corporations also went from publicly denouncing restrictive voting laws in Georgia and Texas to staying nearly silent when seventeen other states also enacted harsher voting laws. Most money pledged to help fight racism after George Floyd's murder either didn't arrive or came in the form of interest-bearing loans that ultimately benefit the company who issued the loan. Troublingly, a year later, around 90 percent of the corporate money pledged could not be accounted for.[139] As one study showed, $50 billion was pledged. A year later only, $250 million could be accounted for.[140]

Further, many companies linked giving to anti-racist causes with sales. For example, "Aerosoles announced it would support racial justice and combat discrimination by donating 10% of sales proceeds to the NAACP. This is a proactive approach to supporting an important social issue, but it is still self-serving, since it will also bring in more revenue as consumers seek to support the cause through their purchases."[141] This approach ultimately benefits the company. But the most striking thing about the money pledged is that most of it was in the form of loans. As the *Washington Post* revealed, "Looking deeper, more than 90 percent of that amount—$45.2 billion—is allocated as loans or investments they could stand to profit from, more than half in the form of mortgages. Two banks—JPMorgan Chase and Bank of America—accounted for nearly all of those commitments."[142] A comparatively tiny amount $70 million went to grants to help organizations working on police violence or criminal justice.[143]

Customers, investors, and citizens all have the ability to decide which firms to patronize, which to criticize, which to shun, and which to boycott. The battle for the soul of corporate America is an ongoing one that takes place in multiple fora. One forum for this fight is the annual corporate proxy at publicly traded firms. For over a decade, investors have proposed ESG (environmental, social and governance) shareholder proposals, asking companies to do better and to be more transparent. Another battleground is the grocery aisle, the shopping mall, and, more and more frequently, on the pages of Amazon.com, where purchases are made.

There are thousands of metrics by which a customer might judge the worthiness of a brand, ranging from whether the firm tests on animals, has a diverse board of directors, or donates any profits to charity. A company's prodemocratic or antidemocratic behavior is worthy of customer and investor concern and should drive actions to support prodemocratic corporate actions and shun antidemocratic actions. The Democratic Litmus Test by which corporations should be judged is whether corporate political spending is supporting seditious politicians, politicians who spread the Big Lie, politicians who participated in the January 6 insurrection on the floor of Congress or outside the Capitol, politicians who are election deniers, or politicians who push voter suppression bills. Clearly corporations can either serve as arsenals of democracy or as arsenals of fascism. They can facilitate social progress or thwart it. They can support ethical governance or contribute to its demise. And, as the Center for Political Accountability argues, "with democracy in danger [post-January 6], these donor companies face a new imperative, out of both self-interest and the national interest: They must halt business as usual and act to strengthen democracy, not to undermine it."[144] To be clear, corporations also benefit from a healthy democracy. As Sarah Bonk, the founder and CEO of Business for America, explains, "The future of our republic relies upon effective election administration, public trust in the results, and the peaceful transfer of power—and so do our markets and businesses. Our country cannot afford a constitutional crisis."[145]

Corporate commitment to tolerance and a multiracial democracy is incredibly thin, as shown by the shallow corporate commitment to change after the murder of George Floyd, the Supreme Court's abortion decision, and calls for reform after January 6. Investors and consumers need to incentivize better behavior from corporations by holding those who support antidemocratic norms and antidemocratic candidates to a Democracy Litmus Test. If they fail, they should not get investor or consumer dollars.

11

GO DIRECTLY TO JAIL, DO NOT PASS GO

THE WHEELS OF JUSTICE

Will anyone who planned the events of January 6 and the attempted overthrow of the 2020 election ever face the music? Even the Colorado judge who ruled that Donald Trump had engaged in an insurrection allowed him to stay on the Republican primary ballot in Colorado.[1] And then the Supreme Court decision in *Trump v. Anderson* allowed him to be on the 2024 ballot in all fifty states and DC. One of the reasons corruption stories infuriate those who want better government and a better nation is that, too frequently, the corrupt parties not only get away with it, thereby avoiding jail time, but they also get to enjoy their ill-gotten wealth. As discussed earlier, this is what happened to the perpetrators of the Crédit Mobilier scandal, the Teapot Dome scandal, and even the modern 1MDB scandal.

This book was written over three years after January 6. During that time, one of the few moments of accountability came on June 20, 2023, as attorney John Eastman sat through a hearing initiated by the California Bar. The question at hand was whether Eastman should be disbarred for his efforts to overthrow the 2020 election on behalf of his client, Donald Trump. At the opening of the hearing, Eastman looked red-faced in a dour dark suit.[2]

The last time the public had seen John Eastman, he was exuberant, standing on the stage with President Trump at the Ellipse rally on January 6, 2021, wearing a brown cowboy hat, a beige overcoat, and a red-and-white patterned scarf that whipped in the wind as he told the rowdy, partially armed, and freezing crowd that the law was on their side. It was not. It would take until August 14, 2023, for a prosecutor in Fulton County, Georgia, to charge Eastman in the same RICO conspiracy case against ex-president Trump and seventeen other codefendants.[3] Eastman is also an unindicted coconspirator in special counsel Jack Smith's indictment of Trump.[4]

During his presidency, Trump showed contempt for the campaign finance law as well as other anti-corruption laws through his pardons. While president, he pardoned Dinesh D'Souza, John Frederick Tate, Jesse R. Benton, and congressman Duncan Hunter, who had been convicted of violating campaign finance laws. He also pardoned two campaign managers: Steve Bannon, who faced wire fraud charges, and Paul Manafort, who was convicted of conspiracy against the United States and conspiracy to obstruct justice, among other charges. He pardoned a lawyer and individuals who worked on his 2016 campaign after they were convicted of lying to Robert Mueller's investigators: Roger Stone Jr., George Papadopoulos, and Alex Van Der Zwaan.[5] He also commuted the sentence of Rod Blagojevich, who got in trouble for trying to sell Barack Obama's former seat in the US Senate.[6] These pardons gave the public the impression that if you were on "Team Trump," you were above the law, and thus you could break anti-corruption laws and face few, if any, consequences. As a candidate for the 2024 election, Trump has threatened that if he is elected that he will pardon those convicted of federal crimes related to January 6.[7] According to the DOJ, "since Jan. 6, 2021, more than 1,200 individuals have been charged in nearly all 50 states for crimes related to the breach of the U.S. Capitol, including more than 400 individuals charged with assaulting or impeding law enforcement, a felony."[8] As of 2024, this number rose to over 1,400.

ACCOUNTABILITY UNDER CRIMINAL LAW

Even if the wheels of justice were slow, they were moving. Finally a modicum of legal accountability arrived in April 2023, when Donald Trump was prosecuted in New York for falsifying business records related to hush-money payments made with the help of his then-lawyer Michael Cohen and the publisher of the *National Enquirer* to two women and a doorman on the eve of the 2016 presidential election.[9] *The People of the State of New York v. Trump* is interrelated with a federal campaign finance crime to which Cohen admitted when he pleaded guilty in 2018.[10] Cohen confessed that he had made a contribution to the Trump 2016 election that was excessive (i.e., too big to be legal), and that he facilitated a campaign payment through a corporation—an act that is also illegal. The corporation in question was American Media Inc. (AMI), the publisher of the *National Enquirer*. The point of this scheme was to "catch and kill" negative stories about Trump before voters could learn about them.[11] As was the case in other scandals explored in this book, the use of corporate structures such as AMI and the Trump Organization was key to hiding the truth from the public.

In *The People of the State of New York v. Trump*, the Manhattan district attorney (DA) Alvin Bragg charged Trump with thirty-four felony counts for allegedly falsifying business records. The action by DA Bragg to charge Trump was an important step in upholding the rule of law. As Bragg said in a press conference the day Trump was processed, "That is exactly what this case is about, 34 false statements made to cover up other crimes. These are felony crimes in New York State. No matter who you are, we cannot and will not normalize serious criminal conduct."[12] One of the remarkable things Bragg highlighted in his statement of facts was that President Trump met with his then-lawyer Michael Cohen in February 2017 in the Oval Office to discuss the reimbursements of the hush-money payments.[13] To put it another way: Bragg accused Trump of committing some of these crimes from the White House. On May 30, 2024, a Manhattan jury convicted Trump on all 34 felony charges.

On June 8, 2023, the public learned that Jack Smith had indicted the former president for his alleged illegal retention of classified documents that dealt with military and nuclear secrets. The thirty-seven charges in the indictment in *United States v. Trump* (Mar-a-Lago) included thirty-one counts of "willful retention of national defense information." Other counts included conspiring to obstruct justice, corruptly concealing a record or document, concealing a document in a federal investigation, scheming to conceal, and making false statements and representations.[14]

The details in the Mar-a-Lago federal indictment were eye-poppingly bad. Trump stands accused of taking boxes of classified documents, including secret, top-secret, and Five-Eyes-only documents from the White House to his home in Florida. After his presidency ended, he had no right to any of these documents.[15] He did not keep them in secure locations, either. At different times, the boxes were on a stage in a Mar-a-Lago ballroom, in a bathroom, and even in a shower.[16] Moreover, he is accused of sharing some of the contents of these sensitive documents with other individuals who, like him, did not have proper clearance to view them.[17] The National Archives and a federal grand jury asked for the documents back.[18] Trump even stands accused of tricking his lawyers by concealing the breadth of the number of documents in his possession.[19] The government retrieved classified documents from Mar-a-Lago when it searched the property pursuant to a warrant on August 8, 2022.[20]

This federal prosecution of ex-president Trump takes a strong step to uphold a core tenant of the rule of law: that no one is above the law, even an ex-president. When this book was written, Donald Trump had not been convicted of any of the charges brought by Prosecutor Smith. This federal case only dealt with Trump's alleged mishandling of government documents at Mar-a-Lago. This is an open-and-shut case, as there are clear statutes governing classified and national security documents, where possession is criminal, and the documents were found on his property. However, the judge in this case (a Trump appointee) seems to be slow-walking it. Thus, its resolution is unlikely to occur before the 2024 election.[21]

So far, over 1,200 lower-level participants have been arrested for their actions on January 6 on physical trespass, battery, and weapons charges.[22] In August 2023, Trump was hit with both an indictment from special counsel Jack Smith for his actions leading up to and on January 6 and an indictment by Fulton County district attorney Fani Willis for his attempts to overturn the results of the 2020 election in Georgia.[23] Four of Trump's codefendants in the Georgia case have pleaded guilty: attorneys Kenneth Chesebro, Sidney Powell and Jenna Ellis, as well as bail bondman Scott Hall.[24] Trump and the remaining codefendants in the Georgia case have pleaded not guilty. On the upside, a conviction in Georgia cannot be pardoned by any president.[25] And, under Georgia law, the governor does not control pardons; rather, a board handles them, and a convicted individual must serve their sentence before a pardon can be granted.[26] Despite Trump being convicted in his New York criminal case before the 2024 general election, bizarrely, he can run for president from jail. There is precedent for this: the first woman to run for president, Victoria Claflin Woodhull, ran from jail in 1872, as did Eugene Debs in 1920.[27]

Trump has asserted that presidential immunity should insulate him from prosecution in his federal January 6 criminal case. The district judge in his case rejected this argument, ruling that "Defendant's [Trump's] four-year service as Commander in Chief did not bestow on him the divine right of kings to evade the criminal accountability that governs his fellow citizens."[28] The Supreme Court, who heard oral arguments presidential immunity on April 25, 2024, will be the final arbiter of this claim of total immunity, which could destroy both the Georgia and federal prosecution of Trump for his role in the events of January 6.[29]

CIVIL ACCOUNTABILITY FOR THE BIG LIE

In the wake of the 2020 election, a veritable noise machine of disinformation spread the Big Lie that Donald Trump had really won the 2020 election. Trump didn't lie alone.[30] An entire cavalcade of lawyers, conservative media figures, and Republican elected officials repeated the Big Lie, thereby poisoning the perceptions of millions of their followers and viewers.[31] Some of this disinformation came from the president's lawyers in filings in over sixty failed litigations challenging the results of the 2020 election, but these lies were amplified and spread on conservative broadcast and cable networks owned by Newsmax, OAN (otherwise known as Herring Networks), and Fox.[32] One of the entities they blamed for Trump's loss was Dominion Voting Systems, a manufacturer of voting machines used in twenty-eight states during the 2020 election. This impacted how Republicans viewed the 2020 election years later.[33]

But this may change as a result of a group of eight libel lawsuits filed by Dominion Voting Systems Inc. ("Dominion").[34] This voting machine manufacturing company has civilly sued Trump lawyers Sidney Powell and Rudy Giuliani, among others, as well as media outlets Fox News, OAN, and Newsmax, for their role in falsely claiming that Dominion played a key role in flipping votes to Joe Biden's benefit.[35] If they get to trial, these lawsuits may change the actual malice standard from *New York Times v. Sullivan* that has long protected the press from libel judgments.[36] Holding these media outlets liable for libel could realign incentives for the press to tell the truth instead of creating an echo chamber for democracy-damaging falsehoods like the Big Lie.[37]

As *Bloomberg* reported, "Dominion is fighting to salvage its reputation even as millions of Americans continue to believe the conspiracy theory, which helped trigger the deadly Jan. 6 Capitol riot by a mob of Trump's supporters."[38] In a suit by Dominion against Fox, the voting machine company stated that "if this case does not rise to the level of defamation by a broadcaster, then nothing does."[39] In Dominion's suit against OAN, the complaint argued starkly that "OAN helped create and cultivate an alternate reality where up is down, pigs have wings, and Dominion engaged in a colossal fraud to steal the presidency from Donald Trump by rigging the vote."[40]

In a filing with the Delaware court overseeing its case against Fox, Dominion's lawyers put it colorfully: "Fox knew. From the top down, Fox knew 'the dominion stuff' was 'total bs.'"[41] In a ruling that allowed the case to go to trial, the Delaware court was more judicious in its word choice but nonetheless concluded: "The [false] Statements [about Dominion] are defamatory per se, which in turn creates a presumption of damages to Dominion, who may recover at least nominal damages."[42]

Dominion's defamation suit against Fox was on the eve of trial when Fox abruptly agreed to settle the case for $787.5 million—the largest defamation settlement ever in US legal history.[43] Why would Fox pay so much to make this suit go away? For one thing, filings in the case had already caused enormous embarrassment to Fox. As NPR reported, "Fox News has endured one humiliation after another from the rolling revelations in the case brought by Dominion Voting Systems. Private communications made public in legal filings demonstrate the network's producers, stars and executives—even controlling owner Rupert Murdoch—knew the claims they were broadcasting were false, and at times unhinged."[44] Discovery from the case revealed Fox's contempt for its own viewers. Privately, Fox hosts knew that Dominion had not changed any votes nor swung the election from Trump to Biden, but, publicly, Fox used its vast network of TV, radio, webpages, and social media to spread the Big Lie, naming Dominion as the culprit.

Another reason Fox likely settled is that rulings from the judge in the case were breaking in Dominion's favor. In particular, a ruling on cross motions for summary judgment from Judge Davis on March 31, 2023, showed how bad the facts were for Fox, and how little wiggle room this judge was going to give them at trial. Dominion's lawyers had clearly done their homework. During discovery, they unearthed that Fox's fact-checkers located in what was known internally as the "Brainroom" had concluded by November 13, 2020, ten days after the 2020 election that:

- There was "no evidence of widespread fraud."
- "Claims about Dominion switching or deleting votes are 100% false" and claims that votes for Former President Trump were deleted are "mathematically impossible."
- "Dominion has no company ownership relationships with any member of the Pelosi family, the Feinstein family, or the Clinton Global Initiative."
- "The U.S. Department of Homeland Security's Cybersecurity and Infrastructure Security Agency (CISA) has debunked viral claims about the existence of a secret CIA program for vote fraud called Hammer and Scorecard."
- "No credible reports or evidence of any software issues exist."
- "Claims about software updates being done the night before Election Day are 100% false."
- "There are no issues with the use of Sharpie pens related to hand-marked paper ballots."
- "All U.S. voting systems must provide assurance that they work accurately and reliably as intended under federal U.S. Election Assistance Commission and state certification and testing requirements."[45]

Despite this internal fact-checking by the Brainroom, Fox continued to perpetuate the Big Lie and their fanciful role that Dominion voting machines played in the made-up plot.

The Dominion litigation also uncovered text messages from Fox producers showing their frustration with on-air hosts like Laura Ingraham pushing the false narrative about Dominion. In one text message from November 12, 2020, Tommy Firth, the executive producer of *The Ingraham Angle*, said to Ron Mitchell, the vice president of prime-time programming and analytics for Fox News: "This dominion shit is going to give me a fucking aneurysm—as many times as I've told Laura [Ingraham] it's bs, she sees shit posters and trump tweeting about it—she wanted to invite an 8chan poster on about this."[46]

Fox's attorneys tried to argue that Fox wasn't being defamatory; they were merely reporting statements from the sitting president and his legal team. Judge Davis rejected this distinction, noting that Fox tried to effectuate this legal dodge in a footnote: "Fox invites the Court, in a footnote, to ignore the [false] Statements in determining falsity. Instead, Fox would have the Court look to see if it is true whether former President Trump made those allegations—purportedly through Ms. [Sidney] Powell and Mr. [Rudy] Giuliani—and that [Fox News Network] reported this accurately."[47]

Fox also tried to argue that its behavior after the 2020 election was covered by the neutral report privilege. The judge rejected this as well, in part because the judge was applying New York law to the case, and "[a New York case called] *Hogan* is binding on this Court. *Hogan* rejects the neutral report privilege and, therefore, the Court will not apply the privilege here."[48] Then the judge really brought down the hammer, stating that "even if the neutral report privilege did apply, the evidence does not support that [Fox News Network] conducted good-faith, disinterested reporting."[49]

One of the reasons *Dominion v. Fox* was an unlikely win for Dominion was that the actual malice standard for defamation is nearly impossible to meet for plaintiffs. But, here, Dominion convinced the judge of many of Dominion's views on actual malice. As the judge explained, "Actual malice can be proven 'through the defendant's own action or statements.' But actual malice can also be determined through the subjective determination of whether the defendant entertained serious doubts as to the truth of the statement, which can be proven by inference. A speaker cannot 'purposefully avoid[]' the truth and then claim ignorance."[50]

In the end, Judge Davis concluded in the *Dominion v. Fox* case that "*the evidence developed in this civil proceeding demonstrates that is CRYSTAL clear that none of the Statements relating to Dominion about the 2020 election are true.*"[51] Moreover, "the [Fox] Statements are defamatory *per se* because the Statements claimed [incorrectly] that Dominion committed election fraud; manipulated vote counts through its software and algorithms; is founded in Venezuela to rig elections for Dictator Hugo Chavez; and paid kickbacks to government officials who used the machines in the Election."[52]

As the AP reported, "Fox acknowledged in a statement 'the court's rulings finding certain claims about Dominion to be false,' but no apology was offered."[53] Fox conspicuously did not cover the settlement with Dominion on its own networks, while other networks led with the story. As *Reuters* noted, "[Fox] hosts Tucker Carlson and Sean Hannity, who had been expected to testify in the *Dominion* trial, did not reference the settlement, the largest struck by an American media company, during their primetime broadcasts."[54] Thus, anyone in Fox's news bubble would be none the wiser that they had paid so much for the network's foolish and vicious touting of the Big Lie.

The settlement also meant that this case could not serve as a test of the contours of defamation law, leaving less clarity for speakers as the 2024 race heats up. Still other cases may yet be such a vehicle to change constitutional law, including Dominion's defamation suits against OAN, Newsmax, Mike Lindell, Rudy Giuliani, and Sidney Powell, and another voting machine company Smartmatic's separate suit against Fox.[55] In 2024, Smartmatic settled a defamation suit with OAN.

On the positive side, the Fox/Dominion settlement showed that there were some legal consequences for spreading the Big Lie: paying hundreds of millions of dollars. If other news outlets wish to avoid being hit with similar suits, they will not emulate Fox's behavior in the post-2020 election period. Tucker Carlson was fired shortly after Fox settled the Dominion lawsuit. Whether these events were causally linked is unclear from the outside. But it did take one of the biggest purveyors of the Big Lie off the air.

CONSEQUENCES FOR BIG LIE LAWYERS

Depending on how the other Dominion defamation suits go, lawyers Rudy Giuliani or Sidney Powell could face financially crippling consequences for perpetuating aspects of the Big Lie with respect to Dominion.[56] But Dominion wasn't the only victim here. The legal system itself suffered as lawyers helped Trump and his campaign file scores of frivolous lawsuits after the 2020 election. Those lawyers may face sanctions or risk being disbarred. Courts have disciplined some of the lawyers involved in the attempts to overturn the 2020 election.

THE SUSPENSION OF GIULIANI'S NEW YORK LAW LICENSE

As vice chair of the January 6 Select Committee, congresswoman Liz Cheney said at a public hearing: "The President had every right to litigate his campaign claims, but he ultimately lost more than 60 cases in state and federal courts. The President's claims in the election cases were so frivolous and unsupported that the President's lead lawyer, Rudy Giuliani, not only lost the lawsuits, his license to practice law was suspended."[57] As she said, President Trump's former lawyer Rudy Giuliani has lost his ability to practice law in New York State after spreading the Big Lie inside and outside of courtrooms.

The New York court reviewing Giuliani's law license concluded that he deserved to lose the ability to practice law for his role in spreading the Big Lie in and out of court: "There is uncontroverted evidence that [Giuliani] communicated demonstrably false and misleading statements to courts, lawmakers and the public at large in his capacity as lawyer for former President Donald J. Trump and the Trump campaign in connection with Trump's failed effort at reelection in 2020. These false statements were made to improperly bolster respondent's narrative that due to widespread voter fraud, victory in the 2020 United States presidential election was stolen from his client."[58]

Giuliani argued that the First Amendment allowed him to lie. He may well have thought Supreme Court precedents such as *United States v. Alvarez* supported his prevarication.[59] The court did not buy this, concluding that

> we reject [Giuliani]'s argument [that the investigation into his conduct violates his First Amendment right of free speech]. This disciplinary proceeding concerns the professional restrictions imposed on respondent as an attorney to not knowingly misrepresent facts. . . . It is long recognized that "speech by an attorney is subject to greater regulation than speech by others." . . . As officers of the court, attorneys are . . . perceived by the public to be in a position of knowledge, and therefore, "a crucial source of information and opinion."[60]

The court was particularly galled by a particular lie Giuliani made when he was President Trump's attorney: that there were more absentee votes than absentee ballots in Pennsylvania, a key swing state in the election.[61] The court held Giuliani responsible for lying about the dead voting in Philadelphia.[62] The court also noted that he had made similarly misleading statements about the elections in Georgia and Arizona litigations, including an false allegation that underage voting had happened.[63]

The New York court also lambasted Giuliani for his role in undermining the faith of Americans in elections while he was the lawyer for the president. As the court stated: "The seriousness of respondent's uncontroverted misconduct cannot be overstated. This country is being torn apart by continued attacks on the legitimacy of the 2020 election and of our current president, Joseph R. Biden. The hallmark of our democracy is predicated on free and fair elections. False statements intended to foment a loss of confidence in our elections . . . damage the proper functioning of a free society."[64] The court even pointed to the insurrection at the Capitol as evidence of the harm that Giuliani had wrought as the president's lawyer: "Where . . . the false statements are being made . . . using his large megaphone, the harm is magnified. . . . [His] misconduct directly inflamed tensions that bubbled over into the events of January 6, 2021 in this nation's Capitol."[65] In a separate proceeding, Giuliani also lost his ability to practice law in Washington, DC.[66]

SANCTIONS FOR THE "KRAKEN" LAWYERS

Federal Judge Linda Parker in the *King v. Whitmer* (a.k.a. "Kraken") case sanctioned the lawyers who brought the case and litigated it without evidence to back up their outrageous claims. *King v. Whitmer* was one of the several suits in Michigan that challenged the state's vote for Biden in the electoral college. All nine lawyers on the pro-Trump side were sanctioned for their behavior during this postelection litigation. As the federal judge in the *King* case noted, the lawyers lied to the American people and the court about the 2020 election: "It is one thing to take on the charge of vindicating the rights associated with an allegedly fraudulent election. It is another to take on the charge of deceiving a federal court and the American people into believing that rights were infringed."[67] The court concluded that the lawyers had abused their role and undercut faith in America's democracy[68] by relying on debunked myths as facts.[69]

Judge Parker also pointed to the lawyers' litigation position being linked to the events on January 6, 2021 at the U.S. Capitol, noting: "[These nine] lawyers brazenly assert that they 'would file the same complaints again.' They make this assertion even after witnessing the events of January 6 and the dangers posed by narratives like the one counsel crafted here. An attorney who willingly continues to assert claims doomed to fail, and which have incited violence before, must be deemed to be acting with an improper motive."[70]

The *King* court shut down the defense that the First Amendment somehow licensed what they had done in court: "Plaintiffs' counsel's politically motivated accusations, allegations, and gamesmanship may be protected by the First Amendment when posted on Twitter, shared on Telegram, or repeated on television. The nation's courts, however, are reserved for hearing legitimate causes of action."[71] The *King* court may have even obliquely referenced the Big Lie when it wrote, "As officers of the court, Plaintiffs' counsel had an obligation to do more than repeat opinions and beliefs, even if shared by millions. Something does not become plausible simply because it is repeated many times by many people."[72] Judge Parker hit the lawyers with sanctions of $175,000, the amount that the state and the City of Detroit wasted in legal fees fighting the case.[73] Judge Parker referred all nine lawyers to their respective state bars for possible disciplinary actions for their actions in the "Kraken" case.[74]

THE REPRIMAND OF JENNA ELLIS

In a Colorado proceeding that considered whether Trump lawyer Jenna Ellis should be sanctioned or disbarred for her actions after the 2020 election, she was allowed to keep practicing law after she admitted that she had lied ten times about the election.[75] As the court in the case wrote: "Respondent [Ellis] and the People agree that [Ellis] made ten misrepresentations on Twitter and to nationally televised audiences in her capacity as personal counsel to the then-President of the United States and as counsel for his reelection campaign. . . . The parties agree that [Ellis], through her conduct, undermined the American public's confidence in the presidential election, violating her duty of candor to the public."[76] The court publicly censured Ellis for this behavior.[77] Ellis would go on to be charged in the Georgia RICO case. She pled guilty.[78]

POSSIBLE DISBARMENT OF JEFFEREY CLARK, L. LIN WOOD, AND SIDNEY POWELL

Trump DOJ official Jefferey Clark also faces possible disbarment in DC. As Reuters described, "Legal licensing authorities in Washington announced . . . they have filed disciplinary charges against Jeffrey Bossert Clark, a former Trump administration Justice Department official who tried to get himself appointed as attorney general to help promote Donald Trump's false election fraud claims."[79] Clark was identified by the January 6 Select Committee as a participant in Trump's attempt to overthrow the 2020 election by gutting the leadership at DOJ that might otherwise stand in his way. This effort ultimately failed.[80] Clark has been charged in the Georgia RICO case.[81] Clark has tried and failed to get this case moved into federal court.[82] The DC Bar made a primarily finding that Clark likely violated ethics rules in 2024.[83] This is a first step toward his disbarment.

Meanwhile, on February 5, 2021, the Bar of Georgia wrote a 1667-page grievance letter against L. Lin Wood, one of Trump's lawyers in the "Kraken" case in Michigan.[84] The Georgia Bar asked Wood to undergo a mental health evaluation. Wood then sued the Georgia Bar, trying to stop this request in federal court.[85] The trial court in his case refused to stop the Georgia Bar, and the Eleventh Circuit Court of appeals affirmed this decision.[86] Wood later retired as a lawyer instead of facing disbarment.[87]

The State Bars had particular power over the Trump lawyers because they are members of a profession with ethical standards. But not every court will discipline a lawyer for this type of behavior. Sidney Powell kept her law license in Texas after a judge threw out the complaint against her by the Texas Bar because their exhibits were mislabeled.[88] The Texas Bar is appealing this ruling.[89] Like Ellis, Powell was charged in the Georgia RICO case, and, like Ellis, she pled guilty.[90] Powell's guilty plea in Georgia inspired another bar complaint against her by Texas lawyers.[91]

LEGAL CONSEQUENCES FOR EASTMAN AND TRUMP FOR JANUARY 6

While President Trump faced a historic second impeachment over his incitement of violence on January 6, he was not removed from office by the Senate for his deeds that day. For two and half years, federal prosecutors were hesitant to go after Trump.[92]

The first time a court had to opine on the actions of ex-president Trump undermining the 2020 election was in litigation by the January 6 Select Committee over documents in possession of his one-time lawyer John Eastman. Eastman had been a respected lawyer and a dean of Chapman Law School before he crossed paths with Trump. But, when examining Eastman's and Trump's actions leading up to January 6, Federal District Judge David Carter had to consider the question of whether attorney-client privilege would shield these documents from the congressional committee investigating January 6. He concluded that many of the documents fell under the crime/fraud exception to attorney-client privilege and thus must be disclosed to Congress.[93]

Eastman was one of the few speakers to share the stage with President Trump on January 6 at the Ellipse.[94] At that event, "Eastman began lying immediately. He claimed 'dead people voted' and 'machines contributed to that fraud' by 'unloading the ballots from the secret folder,' a reference to the debunked conspiracy theory that Dominion voting machines were rigged against Trump."[95]

After the 2020 election, Eastman, working as then-president Trump's lawyer, wrote two legal memoranda that urged Vice President Pence to disregard lawful electoral college votes for Biden.[96] As George Thomas portrayed one of the memos: "Eastman argued for Pence's constitutional authority to act in a six-page memo. Indeed, Eastman's memo practically screams at Pence to act. You can almost see the spittle coming from Eastman's mouth as he works himself into a frenzy and channels Trump: 'this election was Stolen.'"[97] Legal commentator Elie Honig issued withering critiques about the memo—for instance: "The memo is a perfect encapsulation of Trump's overarching strategy to steal the 2020 election. Eastman casually adopts as true a bold legal fiction that '[t]here is very solid legal authority, and historical precedent, for the view that the President of the Senate does the counting, including the resolution of disputed electoral votes . . . and all the Members of Congress can do is watch.'"[98] President of the Brennan Center viewed the Eastman memoranda as a guide to a coup d'état.[99] While he was Trump's attorney, Eastman also wrote a Supreme Court brief on the president's behalf urging the high court to overthrow the election results.[100]

In his opinion about the applicability of the crime/fraud exception to attorney-client privilege, Judge Carter wrote at great length about what he perceived as a possible criminal conspiracy between then-president Donald Trump and lawyer John Eastman:

> On January 4, President Trump and Dr. Eastman hosted a meeting in the Oval Office with Vice President Pence. . . . Dr. Eastman presented his plan to Vice President Pence, focusing on either rejecting electors or delaying the count. . . . On the morning of January 6, President Trump made several last-minute "revised appeal[s] to the Vice President" to pressure him into carrying out the plan. At 1:00 am, President Trump tweeted: "If . . . @Mike_Pence comes through for us, we will win the Presidency . . ." At 8:17 am, President Trump tweeted: "All Mike Pence has to do is send them back to the States, AND WE WIN. Do it Mike, this is a time for extreme courage!" Shortly after, President Trump rang Vice President Pence and once again urged him "to make the call" and enact the plan.[101]

After laying out these details of the conspiracy, Judge Carter concluded: "*Together, these actions more likely than not constitute attempts to obstruct an official proceeding.*"[102] As he further explained, "The entire plan was unlawful."[103] Moreover, "based on the evidence, the Court finds it more likely than not that President Trump corruptly attempted to obstruct the Joint Session of Congress on January 6, 2021."[104]

Judge Carter summed up with the stark declaration that:

> Dr. Eastman and President Trump launched a campaign to overturn a democratic election, an action unprecedented in American history. . . . *it was a coup in search of a legal theory.* The plan spurred violent attacks on the seat of our nation's government, led to the deaths of several law enforcement officers, and deepened public distrust in our political process. . . . *If Dr. Eastman and President Trump's plan had worked, it would*

have permanently ended the peaceful transition of power, undermining American democracy and the Constitution.[105]

Then he warned ominously, "If the country does not commit to investigating and pursuing accountability for those responsible, the Court fears January 6 will repeat itself."[106]

One of the most damning details is that even after violence erupted at the Capitol and peace was restored several hours later, Eastman was still urging the vice president, whose life had been repeatedly threatened by the crowd who chanted "Hang Mike Pence," to participate in his plan to overthrow the 2020 election.[107]

When the January 6 Committee decided that criminal referrals were the appropriate result of their nearly two-year investigation, they voted unanimously to refer "Donald Trump, John Eastman and others" to the DOJ.[108] That Eastman was the only other individual that the committee called out besides Donald Trump was remarkable. Not surprisingly, many lawyers, including some of his fellow law school deans, have called for Eastman to be disbarred, which is why his law license was on the line in California.[109] The special counsel has asked for materials from Eastman's disbarment proceedings in California.[110] Eastman was charged in the Georgia RICO case as a codefendant, and he has asked for his case to be severed from Trump's.[111] In 2024, a California judge finally recommended that Eastman be disbarred.[112]

LACK OF LEGAL CONSEQUENCES BREEDS MINI-TRUMPS

Trump's lawlessness, especially with respect to election law, seemed to embolden a new band of Trump wannabes like Republican George Santos, who was elected to Congress representing the Third District of New York. Almost as soon as he won his election in 2022, the press realized that he had told lie after lie about his biography to voters, including the college he graduated from, the sports he played, and whether or not he had been a drag queen or the producer of the Broadway play *Spider-Man: Turn Off the Dark*. The local press "revealed that parts of his resume and biography—including claims that he was Jewish, his grandparents fled the Holocaust and that he worked at Goldman Sachs—were false."[113]

Congressman Santos's full name is George Anthony Devolder Santos. Another thing he appears to have done is give people misleading versions of his name, referring to himself alternatively as "Anthony Devolder" or "George Santos."[114] For instance, he is accused of stealing dogs using the name "George Santos."[115] And he was accused of running a bogus fundraiser for dogs using the name "Anthony Devolder."[116]

Two Democratic congressmen asked the House Ethics Committee to investigate Santos.[117] A former aide accused him of sexual harassment.[118] *Reuters* reported in 2023 that he is being investigated by a New York prosecutor,[119] and the *New York Times* reported that he is also being investigated by the House Ethics Committee.[120] This latter investigation covered "whether Mr. Santos had failed to properly fill out his House financial disclosure forms, violated federal conflict of interest laws or engaged in other unlawful activity during his 2022 congressional campaign."[121]

Congressman Santos had a number of strange campaign finance issues as well. For example, the money for his campaign seemed to come out of nowhere. According to an investigation by the *New York Times*, there were "numerous irregularities in the way his campaign raised and spent money, including rental payments to a house Mr. Santos was known to have stayed at, and the existence of a fund called RedStone Strategies that hit up donors for tens of thousands of dollars and shared an address with his campaign and business."[122] Money going out of the campaign seemed, implausibly, to often cost $199.99.[123] The reason for this odd "$199.99" phenomenon is likely because political committees must keep receipts for any expenditure that costs $200 or more.[124]

Then, many of his expenditures seemed to oddly fall under the receipt threshold, thwarting normal audits. Soon after he took office, watchdog group the Campaign Legal Center filed a complaint with the FEC.[125] They alleged that Santos "'appears to have spent $13,500 on rent payments for Santos's personal residence in blatant violation of the law.'"[126] They also asserted that "the overall circumstances instead indicate that unknown individuals or corporations may have illegally funneled money to Santos's campaign,' according to the complaint."[127]

On May 9, 2023, Congressman Santos was indicted by the DOJ on seven counts of wire fraud, three counts of money laundering, one count of theft of public funds, and two counts of making materially false statements to the House of Representatives.[128] Santos is accused of asking campaign donors to give money to a company he controlled instead of a lawful campaign committee,[129] allegedly transferring this money to his own bank accounts,[130] and allegedly using the money for his own personal use, which is not allowed under federal law.[131] According to the DOJ, he "allegedly used the funds to make personal purchases (including of designer clothing), to withdraw cash, to discharge personal debts, and to transfer money to his associates."[132]

Donors allegedly gave more to this company than they would have legally been able to give to Santos's federal congressional campaign committee, thus violating campaign finance limits. Corporate structures have allegedly been used to thwart required transparency of money in politics as well as the contribution limits that are normally required in federal election campaigns.

Santos is also accused by DOJ of lying in his disclosures to the House of Representatives about his assets. If a member of Congress gets hit for poor disclosures, it is because they have underreported what they own, trying to seem salt-of-the-earth, middle-class, and humble (e.g., that they don't own multiple houses). But the accusations by the DOJ against Santos are striking because they accuse him of inflating his assets by pretending that he is a richer man than he actually is. The House Ethics Committee found that Santos had spent campaign funds on Botox and on an OnlyFans account.[133] This seemed to be the last straw. Santos was expelled from Congress on December 1, 2023.[134]

One campaign treasurer said he shouldn't have been listed on Santos's campaign fillings at all.[135] When a watchdog accused Santos of having a nonexistent person as his campaign treasurer, he abruptly named himself as campaign treasurer and then switched to another name.[136] A campaign treasurer for Santos, Nancy Marks, pled guilty to conspiracy to commit offenses against the United States, involving wire fraud, the falsifying of records, and identity theft.[137] A Santos fundraiser, Samuel Miele also pled guilty to wire fraud.[138] Santos has been hit with a superseding indictment from DOJ.[139] Santos maintains his innocence.

The fate of this legal story for Trump, those in his inner circle, or would-be mini-Trumps lies in the hands of prosecutors, judges, and jurors. If the ringleaders of January 6 get away with their crimes, they will only inspire new generation of corrupt individuals to get into politics who think, "If Trump can get away with it, then so can I."

12

DEMOCRACY ON THE BALLOT

VOTING FOR CHANGE

Tragically, the 2022 election was marred by violence. On election day, November 8, 2022, two Black churches in Jackson, Mississippi, were burned down by an arsonist.[1] Fortunately, these were isolated local incidents. The widespread violence that many feared would impact the 2022 election thankfully did not happen.

As this book has shown in granular detail, corporations can spend millions in elections, but, fortuitously, they cannot vote. In the first federal election after January 6, democracy prevailed, despite the hurdles placed in the way of voters by legislatures, courts, and a pessimistic president. In 2022, American voters had to navigate a spate of new voting laws in most states, violent rhetoric in political speech, actual threats of violence at the polls, a large number of election deniers seeking power, as well as the sitting president warning them that their democracy was in peril.

President Biden's speeches on democracy were criticized as divisive.[2] In real time, no one knew whether the warnings about democracy being at risk would inspire or depress voters.[3] While the turnout in the 2022 midterm elections was high for an American election (47 percent), it did not break the record set in 2018 (49 percent).[4]

In 2020, many states had relaxed their voting rules to allow more safe voting options for Americans during the covid pandemic.[5] This led to a record number of Americans voting in 2020.[6] One reason that turnout may have dipped in the 2022 election is that many states passed laws in 2021 and 2022 to make registering to vote and voting harder than it had been in 2020.[7] By one count, 250 bills were introduced in state legislatures in 2021 to make voting more difficult.[8] Another count in 2022 placed the number of regressive voting bills at 440.[9] At least 19 states enacted voting restrictions in 2021.[10] In 2022, 8 states enacted 11 new restrictive voting laws and 12 election interference laws.[11] The excuse that was given for all of this legislation was "voting integrity."[12] But these legal developments drew criticism as the International IDEA added the United States to their annual list of "backsliding" democracies for the first time in 2021,[13] because of recent voting laws that disproportionately restricted the voting rights of racial minorities.[14]

One of the justifications often given by Republican lawmakers for enacting stricter voting laws was their embrace of the Big Lie that Trump had really won the 2020 election.[15] The myth of voter fraud has been quite resilient, nearly impervious to mountains of facts to the contrary.[16] As professor of law Penny M. Venetis plainly states: "Any claims that efforts to stop vote-by-mail are attempts to root out fraud are completely unsubstantiated. They are not backed up by data or the experiences of thousands of elections administration officials across the nation."[17] The *Atlanta Journal Constitution* noted this about a recount of the 2020 election: "[The] results bring to a close an arduous process that included a hand audit of every ballot.... But they likely will not end the unproven cries of 'voter fraud' from Trump and his supporters."[18] Or, as political science professor Julia Anzari explains, "Well before Trump took office, Americans had shown that their views on voter fraud mostly reflected party cues."[19]

Some Republicans were so cynical they would tell journalists that it didn't matter that voter fraud hadn't been proven in their states when passing voter suppression bills. For example, House member John Kavanaugh of Arizona told CNN, "We're moving forward to do bills to correct problems that came up during the election that need to be solved, regardless of whether there was actual fraud or nonexistent fraud."[20] Rep. Kavanaugh has a flair for grabbing headlines on voting law changes; he once claimed that expanding the franchise was a bad thing: "There's a fundamental difference between Democrats and Republicans.... Democrats value as many people as possible voting, and they're willing to risk fraud. Republicans are more concerned about fraud, so we don't mind putting security measures in that won't let everybody vote—but everybody shouldn't be voting."[21]

The push to tighten voting rules was well funded. According to a report in the *L.A. Times*, Heritage Action, an arm of the Heritage Foundation, was one of the sources bankrolling the effort. As the *Times* noted: "Conservative advocacy groups such as Heritage Action have rallied around the state-level efforts. 'After a year when voters' trust in our elections plummeted, restoring that trust should be the top priority of legislators and governors nationwide,' Jessica Anderson, executive director of the nonprofit, said in announcing the group's $10-million push to support the GOP-led proposals."[22]

Republicans in state legislatures may have played on Americans' pessimism about democracy, as polling before and during the Trump presidency showed a loss of faith in American democracy. Polling in 2015 revealed that "Americans aren't just souring on particular institutions or particular politicians. To a surprising degree, they have begun to sour on liberal democracy itself."[23] As early as 2016, election law experts Nathaniel Persily and Jon Cohen argued that "the values that support American democracy are deteriorating. Large numbers of Americans across party lines have lost faith in their democracy."[24]

Not only were pollsters picking up evidence that Americans were losing faith in democracy as an abstract concept; they also discovered increasing distrust of their fellow Americans. For example, Monmouth found in 2019 "that just 16% of voters have a great deal of trust and confidence in the American people as a whole when it comes to making judgments under our democratic system about the issues facing our country."[25] Meanwhile, as confidence in democratic institutions was dipping, the pall from the violence on January 6 hung over the midterm election in 2022.

VIOLENCE IN THE 2022 MIDTERM

During the 2022 election, candidate for governor of Arizona Katie Hobbs was criticized for not debating her opponent, election denier Kari Lake. But a peek into Hobbs's life as Arizona's secretary of state during the election might explain why she did not feel physically safe, and why she did not want to provide a bigger stage for her opponent's unhinged ideas. As reported by Time, Hobbs regularly received death threats via voicemail that menaced: "I am a hunter—and I think you should be hunted. You will never be safe in Arizona again." And "you're a traitor to this country," another voicemail on Aug. 2 warned. "You better put your f——g affairs in order, cause your days are extremely numbered. America's coming for you, and you will pay with your life."[26]

Just days before the midterm election, political violence reared its ugly head at the home of speaker of the House Nancy Pelosi. As he later confessed, David Depape broke into Pelosi's home seeking to either harm or kidnap her. As stated in DOJ's criminal complaint against Depape: "DEPAPE stated that he was going to hold Nancy hostage and talk to her. If Nancy were to tell DEPAPE the 'truth,' he would let her go, and if she 'lied,' he was going to break 'her kneecaps.' . . . DEPAPE also later explained that by breaking Nancy's kneecaps, she would then have to be wheeled into Congress, which would show other Members of Congress there were consequences to actions."[27] Speaker Pelosi wasn't home, so Depape allegedly hit her elderly husband, Paul, on the head with a hammer, fracturing his skull.[28]

President Biden linked the attack on Speaker Pelosi's home to the attack on her office on January 6: "The assailant entered the [Pelosi] home asking, 'Where's Nancy? Where's Nancy?' Those were the very same words used by the mob when they stormed the United States Capitol on January the 6th when they broke windows, kicked in the doors, brutally attacked law enforcement, roamed the corridors hunting for officials, and erected gallows to hang the former Vice President, Mike Pence."[29] Biden added, "[Depape] carried in his backpack zip ties, duct tape, rope, and a hammer. As he told the police, he had come looking for Nancy Pelosi to take her hostage, to interrogate her, to threaten to break her kneecaps."[30] Depape was convicted in November 2023.[31]

A month earlier, an armed man named Ricky W. Shiffer attacked an FBI field office in Cincinnati, Ohio. After fleeing the office, he then got into an armed standoff with police and was killed. No one knows for sure what he was up to in attacking the FBI. His social media was rife with right-wing conspiracy theories, and Shiffer at been at the Capitol on January 6.[32]

Election workers (individuals who sit at the polls and check voters in or help with election administration by counting votes) faced threats of violence starting in the 2020 election, continuing through January 6, and lasting through the 2022 midterm.[33] Reuters tracked at least one thousand such threats between 2020 and 2022.[34] In 2021, the DOJ launched a task force on threats to election workers.[35] By August 2022, this DOJ task force had reviewed one thousand complaints from election workers and found that 11 percent met the threshold for criminal investigation.[36] But, as of election day 2022, only one person had been successfully prosecuted for making threats against an election worker.[37] A survey of election officials by the Brennan Center found one in six had experienced threats.[38] By August 2023, DOJ had only achieved nine convictions for threats against election workers.[39] This sorry state of affairs led many election workers to quit out of fear.[40] Unsurprisingly, a month before the midterm election, many states experienced shortages of election workers.[41] This problem of intimidation of election workers could become even worse in future elections with the advent of AI, which could automate threats.

Congressman John Lewis, the late civil rights movement icon and voting rights advocate, once wrote, "In democracy, one act of voter discrimination should be too much."[42] In 2022, some voters faced harassment and intimidation. In Arizona, armed vigilantes from groups called Clean Elections USA and Lions of Liberty intimidated voters who were using lawful ballot drop boxes to vote. As the head of elections for Maricopa County, Arizona, stated in a press release before the 2022 midterm election:

> Two armed individuals dressed in tactical gear were onsite at a ballot drop box in Mesa. . . . The Maricopa County Sheriff's Office responded. The individuals left the drop box area. Below is a joint statement from Maricopa County Board of Supervisors Chairman Bill Gates and Recorder Stephen Richer[:] "We are deeply concerned about the safety of individuals who are exercising their constitutional right to vote and who are lawfully taking their early ballot to a drop box. Uninformed vigilantes outside Maricopa County's drop boxes are not increasing election integrity. Instead they are leading to voter intimidation complaints."[43]

The League of Women Voters of Arizona filed suit to stop this heinous behavior,[44] as did the Arizona Alliance for Retired Americans and Voto Latino.[45] In a consolidated case, a federal judge granted a temporary restraining order against the vigilantes, stating that they could not (1) get within 75 feet of the drop boxes; (2) follow voters after they voted; (3) yell at voters; or (4) openly carry fire arms within 250 feet of ballot drop boxes.[46] The court also ordered the leader of the Clean Elections

USA, Melody Jennings (whose social media handle was @TrumperMel), to post the following statements on the organization's webpage and on Truth Social through election day: "It is legal to deposit the ballot of a family member, household member, or person for whom you are the caregiver."[47] This case was civil, but voters should know that there are federal and state criminal laws that protect voters from intimidation, and that people found guilty of intimidating voters can face up to ten years in jail (five years for state crimes and five years for federal crimes).[48]

These threats of harassment and violence might explain in part why over forty-two million Americans voted early in the 2022 election.[49] Typically, when voters vote early, there is a shorter line than on election day. Thus, by voting early, voters could avoid any potential trouble at the polls that might be invited by congregated groups of voters waiting in an hour-long line on election day. Additionally, voting early by mail was one way to avoid any drop-box vigilantes altogether.

As President Joe Biden said in speeches during the midterm, "Democracy [was] on the ballot."[50] On September 1, 2022, Biden addressed the nation from Philadelphia, standing outside of Constitution Hall. He warned: "Equality and democracy are under assault. We do ourselves no favor to pretend otherwise."[51] He stated bluntly: "MAGA Republicans do not respect the Constitution. . . . They refuse to accept the results of a free election. And they're working right now, as I speak, in state after state to give power to decide elections in America to partisans and cronies, empowering election deniers to undermine democracy itself."[52] Moreover, Biden tried to rhetorically separate MAGA Republicans from mainstream Republicans by saying: "Democrats, independents, mainstream Republicans: We must be stronger, more determined, and more committed to saving American democracy than MAGA Republicans are . . . to destroying American democracy."[53]

Biden repeated these themes at White House event on the International Day of Democracy: "We pause to reflect on the power that we hold in our in our hands and our sacred charge to preserve the soul of our Nation. To preserve that idea of America. To . . . defend free and fair elections."[54] At a speech at the United Nations in September 2022, Biden acknowledged: "It's no secret that [there is a] contest between democracy and autocracy [in] the United States. . . . The United States is determined to defend and strengthen democracy at home and around the world."[55]

Just days before the election on November 2, 2022, Biden urged his fellow citizens to stand up and vote: "Nothing has been guaranteed about democracy in America. Every generation has had to defend it, protect it, preserve it, choose it, for that's what democracy is: It's a choice—a decision of the people, by the people, and for the people. . . . We, the people, must decide whether we will have fair and free elections and every vote counts."[56] He continued, "With democracy on the ballot, we have to remember these first principles. Democracy means the rule of the people—not the rule of monarchs or the monied, but the rule of the people."[57]

President Biden wasn't exaggerating in these speeches, as election deniers ran for office all over the nation. As NPR reported during the midterm: "At least 20 Republican candidates [for Secretary of State are] running who question the legitimacy of President Biden's 2020 win, even though no evidence of widespread fraud has been uncovered about the race over the last 14 months."[58] Election deniers were also running for state attorneys general in 2022.[59] For instance, "Attorney Matthew DePerno . . . [the Republican] nominee in the attorney general race to take on Democratic incumbent Dana Nessel . . . has repeatedly espoused debunked conspiracy theories surrounding the 2020 election results in Michigan, winning him the endorsement of former President Donald Trump in his primary race."[60]

Besides the actual harassment facing certain voters, many political ads in 2022 election glorified violent imagery. The most violent ad was run by disgraced former governor of Missouri Eric Greitens, who was seeking a Senate seat. The ad in question ran during the Republican primary and looked like the trailer for a low-budget—and low-imagination—action film.[61] As NPR described it: "'Today, we're going RINO hunting,' Greitens, a Republican, said with a smile as he slid the action on his shotgun in the 38-second ad. RINO stands for 'Republican in name only.' Greitens and a team of men outfitted in military gear are then shown bursting into a home, guns raised."[62] After this troubling RINO-hunting ad generated both attention and alarm, Greitens did not win his primary.[63] Greitens was an election denier—but, sadly for Republican Missouri primary voters, so was his primary opponent, Eric Schmitt.[64] Election denier Schmitt would go on to win the Senate seat in 2022.[65]

During the 2022 general election, Blake Masters, who was running for the Senate from Arizona, aired a campaign ad of himself shooting a gun with a silencer in a quarry outside of Tucson after saying that "shooting with a silencer makes it a whole lot pleasanter."[66] As one commenter described the images in the ad: "[Masters's] demeanor suggests calm yet fathomless obsession. His reed-thin arms make him look like a teenage psychopath training to annihilate his junior high."[67] Masters lost his race to Democratic incumbent senator Mark Kelly.[68]

Masters was one of many election deniers running for office in 2022.[69] In the midterm, around three hundred candidates who were election deniers ran for federal or state office, including twelve for secretary of state and twenty-two for governor.[70] In fact, an election denier was on the ballot in forty-eight of fifty states.[71] An analysis by FiveThirtyEight estimated that 60 percent of Americans had an election denier on their ballot in 2022.[72] The bad news is that most of these election deniers made it through a Republican primary—demonstrating the hold that the Big Lie still has among Republican primary voters.[73] If anything, election denialism by Republicans candidates is a cruel scam on Republican voters.

With everything going on in the 2022 election, the explanation of why certain Republicans won certain primaries may be complex, as it appears that some Democratic voters and donors backed the most extreme Republican candidates in certain primaries in the hopes that they would be easier to beat in the general.[74] (This was the same tactic that some Republicans utilized during the 2020 Democratic presidential primary called Operation Chaos 2020.)[75] In one extreme case, a candidate for governor funded his opponent: "Illinois Gov. J.B. Pritzker, a billionaire, spent $9.5 million of his own money, combined with about $25 million from the Democratic Governors Association, to push Darren Bailey, a far-right, Trump-endorsed state senator, during the primary season."[76] Pritzker then went on to defeat Bailey in the general election. All of this was playing with fire, as election-denying candidates could have been elected. This awful strategy should not be replicated.

THE PEOPLE VOTE

Several election deniers were endorsed by ex-president Trump.[77] A few of these candidates had been active in challenging the 2020 election by attending the January 6 insurrection, including the Republican candidate for Pennsylvania governor Doug Mastriano,[78] "Ohio 9th Congressional District nominee J. R. Majewski, Oregon senatorial nominee Jo Rae Perkins and North Carolina 1st Congressional District nominee Sandy Smith."[79] Outdoing all the other election denier candidates, Jeremy Brown ran for the Florida House from jail because he was in pretrial detention for his actions on January 6.[80] All five of these January 6 participants/election deniers lost their elections.

In the general election, American voters were mostly repelled by the election deniers. The especially good news is that every election denier running for secretary of state or governor in a swing state lost.[81] As Paul Smith of the Campaign Legal Center said, "The truth is, in the swing states, [election deniers] haven't won very much."[82]

This may go to show that Americans' faith in democracy is stronger than the more pessimistic polls quoted earlier would suggest. Most Americans still conceptualize democracy as the ideal government.[83] As Larry Diamond reports, "The American public still backs democracy overwhelmingly as the best form of government. 86 percent say it's a good or very good system. 82 percent say it's very important to live in a democracy.... And 78 percent say democracy is always 'preferable to any other kind of government.'"[84]

Election deniers didn't lose *every* election in 2022. One election denier in Wyoming won as secretary of state because he ran unopposed.[85] Others won in races in deep red Alabama,[86] Indiana,[87] and South Dakota.[88] But where voters were given a choice in swing states, they voted for the more small d-democratic candidate for secretary of state.[89]

Thanks to American voters, on the whole democracy won more than it lost. According to one count by the BBC, of the approximately 300 election deniers running, only 125 won their elections[90] Most of those were members of Congress who had been in power in 2021 and voted against certification of Biden votes on January 6. The reelection of most of what critics call the "Sedition Caucus" is testament to the power of partisan gerrymandering, since many were running from uncompetitive red districts that favored Republicans.[91] In the House, this was partially a legacy of a little-noticed decision called *Rucho v. Common Cause*, in which the Supreme Court ruled that federal courts would no longer hear partisan gerrymandering cases.[92]

One member of the Sedition Caucus, Ted Budd, was elevated from the House to the Senate.[93] Thus, the Congressional election denier problem is an ongoing one.[94] Another contributing factor to the Sedition Caucus's reelection, both literally and figuratively, was $61 million in corporate PAC money and funds from trade associations.[95] However, the members of Congress elected in 2022 will not be in charge of opening electoral college votes in 2025 after the 2024 presidential election. Rather, it will be the Congress newly elected in 2024 and seated on January 3, 2025, that will have those honors and duties. Thus, American voters have one last chance to rid itself of election deniers before the pivotal date of January 6, 2025. Another key outcome of the 2022 election was that more state legislative houses ended up in Democratic hands. In Michigan, Democrats flipped the House and Senate, and in Minnesota, Democrats flipped the Senate.[96] Democrats also flipped control of the Pennsylvania House.[97]

The majority of likely voters in the 2022 midterm were concerned about democracy itself. As the Leadership Conference for Civil Rights publicized, "The Leadership Conference poll [from September 2022] found that 67 percent of likely voters were worried that democracy was under threat."[98] This was reflected in later voting patterns. Many voters in 2022, especially from Generation Z (Gen Z), born between 1997 and 2012, appeared to have been placing candidates to a Democracy Litmus Test.[99] As ABC News reported, "Youth voting organizers emphasized that in their view, this cycle was remarkable because of its number of young leaders . . . who mobilized peers to cast ballots for 'pro-democracy' candidates."[100] Gen Z turned out in 2022 and largely voted against election deniers.[101] As William Bunch describes it, "Shocked into action by the loss of their reproductive rights and repulsed by candidates who threatened not to count their votes going forward, Millennials and Gen Z put down their books (or their beers) to make sure any 'red wave' was subsumed by the deep blue sea."[102]

Many candidates who failed the Democracy Litmus Test with voters young and old lost their elections.[103] For these voters, Trump's endorsement was the kiss of death. As *Vox* noted, "When the election came, the most high profile of those election-denier nominees, many of whom were favored to win, actually lost. And the story of why many of them lost is actually the story of thousands of ordinary citizens using the tools of democracy to protect democracy."[104] This was the third election in row (2018, 2020, and 2022) when the youth vote showed up and mattered.[105] But the reason it was so significant that all of the election denying candidates for secretaries of state and governors in swing states lost was that individuals in these offices run elections at the state level. Had election deniers been elected in 2022 in swing states, they would have been in charge of running the 2024 presidential election.[106] Who knows what type of foolishness this could have wrought. But, as reporter Ryan Teague Beckwith put it, "the 'Big Lie' lost where it mattered the most."[107]

This book went to press after Trump was convicted of 34 felony counts in his first criminal trial in Manhattan.[108] The future of American democracy is ultimately in the hands of Americans voters, and this will be true long after anyone named Trump is on the ballot. Voters should put candidates to the basic Democracy Litmus Test by asking: Did they (1) perpetuate election denialism; (2) try to overthrow the results of any election; (3) push legislation that makes voting more difficult; or (4) are party to bribery or other corrupt actions that undermine democratic values? If the answer to any of those questions is yes, then voters should either not vote for that candidate or vote for the opponent who passes the Democracy Litmus Test. Fortunately for Americans, the youngest voters who belong to Generation Z seem to get this imperative instinctively. But these youngsters cannot save American democracy alone.

CONCLUSION

NEEDED REFORMS

EXPAND THE BAN ON CORPORATE CONTRIBUTIONS

Each level of government should keep as much money out of American elections as possible. Congress should keep the Tillman Act on the books, which currently bans contributions from corporate treasury funds to federal candidates. Each state that lacks such a ban should enact state analogs, and large metropolitan centers that have home rule should enact corporate contribution bans that apply to local elections.[1]

ENACT PUBLIC FINANCING

The Presidential Public Financing system should be refreshed so that major party candidates have an incentive to participate in the program again. Congressional public financing should finally be enacted. Several cities and states already have public financing, like Maine, Arizona and Connecticut, as well as New York City and Seattle, Washington. These programs should be expanded across the nation so that candidates are not solely dependent on private money to run for office.[2]

DISCLOSURE ACROSS ALL MEDIA

Require disclosure of money spent in politics regardless of the media. The same rules should apply to print, broadcast, and online political advertisements. This reform is needed at the federal level and in most states. New disclaimers should inform the public if AI-generated images have been used in a given political ad.[3]

CONCLUSION

CORPORATE LAW REFORMS

SEC DISCLOSURE FOR SPENDING IN ELECTIONS

The Securities and Exchange Commission should promulgate a new rule requiring disclosure of where publicly traded companies and other regulated entities spend money in politics. Look at the disclosures that FirstEnergy agreed to in order to get a deferred prosecution agreement. Those types of disclosures should be required across the board.[4]

SEC DISCLOSURE FOR LOBBYING

The Securities and Exchange Commission should promulgate a new rule requiring disclosure of corporate lobbying at the state and federal level. Lobbying at the state level is particularly opaque. A disclosure rule would allow transparency for customers, investors, and voters. [5]

VOTES FOR SHAREHOLDERS

The UK Companies Act allows shareholders to vote on corporate political budgets. The United States should adopt that approach. This could be achieved through congressional action. Similar impacts could also be achieved if Delaware, California, and New York mandated shareholder votes in each of their respective state corporate laws.[6]

ELECTION LAW REFORMS

ALLOW EARLY VOTING NATIONWIDE

Voters, especially in national elections, should have the same amount of time to vote. Whether a voter has the ability to vote early is a matter of state and local law. The ability to vote early should not be determined by zip code. Congress should use its power over federal elections to mandate a full week of early voting nationwide.[7]

CLARIFY DISQUALIFICATION

Congress should pass a law that clarifies how to assert that a federal candidate is disqualified under the Disqualification Clause of the Fourteenth Amendment and what process must be followed. Courts have struggled with applying the clause during an election year. Providing such clarity before the next federal election would be better for all future elections.[8]

EXPAND AUTOMATIC VOTER REGISTRATION

In many states, citizens who are eligible to vote cannot vote because they did not register on time. Voters should be presumed to be registered to vote. Many states have already embraced automatic voter registration. This reform should be expanded to every state.[9]

RESTORE VOTING RIGHTS

Mass incarceration impacts who can vote because of the ancient legal concept of civil death. For best practices, states should look at Maine, Vermont, and DC, which never take the right to vote away from an individual for a criminal conviction. For those states that take away the right to vote, that right should be restored as soon as possible, and certainly when the returning citizen has been released from incarceration.[10]

CONSTITUTIONAL REFORMS

REVERSE *CITIZENS UNITED V. FEC*

Citizens United allows corporations to spend an unlimited amount of money on advertisements in American elections. This should be reversed either through a new ruling by the Supreme Court or via constitutional amendment.[11]

REVERSE *BUCKLEY V. VALEO*

Buckley ruled that expenditure limits were unconstitutional. This gave the wealthy more influence over American elections. This decision has hampered the ability of Congress and states to limit the role of money in politics. This should be reversed either by a new ruling by the Supreme Court or via constitutional amendment.[12]

REVERSE *RUCHO V. COMMON CAUSE*

Rucho decided that partisan gerrymandering claims could not be litigated in federal court. This leaves this matter to state courts. Federal courts should remain an open forum for voters hurt by partisan gerrymandering to seek judicial relief. This should be reversed either by a new ruling by the Supreme Court or via constitutional amendment.[13]

SUPREME COURT REFORMS

ETHICS

Because so many of the issues raised in this book often end up as legal questions before the highest Court, the Supreme Court needs binding ethical rules and clear consequences for violating those ethical rules.[14]

TERM LIMITS

When the Constitution gave Supreme Court justices lifetime appointments, lifetimes were far shorter. Having justices in their eighties and nineties presents all sorts of problems, including the problem of mental acuity. Having term limits may also lower the stakes of confirmation battles.[15]

RECUSAL RULES

The Supreme Court Justices should not sit on cases where their benefactors' interests are at stake.[16]

NO GIFTS OR MONEY FOR JUSTICES

Even better yet, Supreme Court justices should not have benefactors. They are civil servants. If they cannot get by on a salary of a justice, then they can resign and work in private practice.[17]

ACKNOWLEDGMENTS

The author thanks Stetson University College of Law for its generous support of this work. The author is also eternally grateful to her Stetson Law research assistants Rebecca Doloski, Hanley Gibbons, Jeremy Haas, Hannah Klonowski, Sierra Luther, Colin Sullivan, Alexis Thomas, and Mia Tolliver, as well as Stetson Law librarians Kristen Moore and Sally Waters for their help doing years of legal and historical research. She also thanks the Brennan Center for Justice at NYU School of Law for her ongoing fellowship. She thanks the many people who were willing to be interviewed for this book and helped her think through this strange moment in American history that we are experiencing. She is also grateful to her son, her husband, and her labradoodle, who put up with the late nights and travel.

NOTES

PREFACE

1 Françoise Mouly, *Jane Rosenberg's "Courtroom Sketch, Manhattan Criminal Courthouse,"* NEW YORKER (Apr. 5, 2023), https://www.newyorker.com/culture/cover-story/cover-story-2023-04-17.
2 Gregory Korte, *Donald Trump's Criminal Charges Present Constitutional Questions*, BLOOMBERG (Nov. 7, 2023), https://www.bloomberg.com/news/articles/2023-11-07/trump-on-trial-criminal-charges-present-constitutional-questions.
3 Statement of Facts, *New York v. Trump*, IND-71543–23 (N.Y. App. Div. Apr. 5, 2023).
4 Devlin Barrett, Matt Zapotosky & Rosalind S. Helderman, *Cohen Says He Lied About Deal; Admits Trying to Minimize Links Between Moscow Project and Trump*, BOSTON GLOBE A1 (Nov. 30, 2018).
5 Office of Legal Counsel, *A Sitting President's Amenability to Indictment and Criminal Prosecution*, DOJ (Oct. 16, 2000), https://www.justice.gov/olc/opinion/sitting-president%E2%80%99s-amenability-indictment-and-criminal-prosecution; *but see* Danielle Brian & Sarah Turberville, *Not the Final Word*, JUST SECURITY (June 15, 2018), https://www.justsecurity.org/57871/final-word/ (arguing a sitting president could be indicted).
6 Jose Pagliery, *Time Is Running Out to Indict Trump for His Sex Hush Money Payment to Stormy Daniels*, DAILY BEAST (Oct. 13, 2021), https://www.thedailybeast.com/time-is-running-out-to-indict-donald-trump-for-his-sex-hush-money-payment-to-stormy-daniels.
7 Michelle L. Price & Jill Colvin, *Trump Raised $34M So Far in 2023, Including Indictment Bump*, AP (Apr. 15, 2023), https://apnews.com/article/trump-campaign-presidential-fundraising-indictment-e679f7c8a6a4981cd721371c29fa9e2c.
8 Alex Woodward, *Trump's Campaign Is Selling $47 T-Shirts Commemorating His Latest Indictment*, INDEPENDENT (Aug. 2023), https://www.independent.co.uk/news/world/americas/us-politics/trump-indictment-shirts-campaign-donations-b2386497.html.
9 Brian Bennett & Chris Wilson, *The Trump Campaign Has Raised Millions Off Impeachment*, TIME (Dec. 5, 2019), https://time.com/magazine/us/5744386/december-16th-2019-vol-194-no-26-u-s/.
10 Jennifer Tucker, *Trump May Spin His Mug Shot into Gold, but for Others It's an Unnecessary Humiliation*, MSNBC (Aug. 24, 2023), https://www.msnbc.com/opinion/msnbc-opinion/trump-mug-shot-arrest-georgia-humiliation-rcna101646.
11 Sareen Habeshian, *Trump Campaign Fundraises with Fake Mug Shot Merch*, AXIOS (Apr. 4, 2023), https://www.axios.com/2023/04/04/trump-fake-mugshot-campaign-merch-donations.

NOTES

12 Mary Yang, *Donald Trump Uses His Legal Woes to Plead for Money from Supporters— Again*, GUARDIAN (June 10, 2023), https://www.theguardian.com/us-news/2023/jun/10/trump-indictment-supporter-fundraising-strategy-donation-money.

13 Kate Brumback, Jill Colvin & Eric Tucker, *Mug Shot of Donald Trump Shows Scowling Former President During Speedy Booking at Atlanta Jail*, AP (Aug. 24, 2023), https://apnews.com/article/trump-atlanta-indictment-republican-primary-7f4e9860859fbb-71221b6a5163aaa42f.

14 Chris LaCivita, (@LaCivitaC), TWITTER (Aug. 24, 2023, 9:25 p.m.), https://twitter.com/LaCivitaC/status/1694883551664115860 ("If you are a campaign, PAC, scammer and you try raising money off the mugshot of @realDonaldTrump and you have not received prior permission . . . WE ARE COMING AFTER YOU").

15 Sam Gringlas, *Trump's Campaign Is Making Millions off His Fulton County Mugshot, but Who Owns the Rights to the Image?*, WABE (Nov. 21, 2023), https://www.wabe.org/trumps-campaign-is-making-millions-off-his-fulton-county-mugshot-but-who-owns-the-rights-to-the-image/.

16 Sharon Knolle, *Trump's Mug Shot an Instant Phenomenon as Merch Hits Online Stores and Memes Overrun X*, YAHOO (Aug. 24, 2023), https://www.yahoo.com/entertainment/trump-mug-shot-t-shirts-010014815.html.

17 Anna Massoglia, *Trump Political Operation Steers $130 Million in Donor Money to Cover Legal Fees*, OPENSECRETS (Aug. 4, 2023), https://www.opensecrets.org/news/2023/08/trump-political-operation-steers-130-million-in-donor-money-to-cover-legal-fees/; Dan Mangan, *Trump suffers big loss in E. Jean Carroll Defamation Case, Judge Says He's Liable*, CNBC (Sept. 6, 2023), https://www.cnbc.com/2023/09/06/trump-suffers-big-loss-in-e-jean-carroll-defamation-case-judge-says-hes-liable.html; Sareen Habeshian, *Where Trump's Civil Fraud Trial Stands*, AXIOS (Dec. 4, 2023), https://www.axios.com/2023/12/04/trump-civil-fraud-trial-where-it-stands.

18 Domenico Montanaro, *Most Republicans Would Vote for Trump Even if He's Convicted of a Crime*, NPR (Apr. 25, 2023), https://www.npr.org/2023/04/25/1171660997/poll-republicans-trump-president-convicted-crime.

19 *See generally* CIARA TORRES-SPELLISCY, CORPORATE CITIZEN? AN ARGUMENT FOR THE SEPARATION OF CORPORATION AND STATE (2016).

20 Jack Healy, *These Are the 5 People Who Died in the Capitol Riot*, N.Y. TIMES (Jan. 11, 2021), https://www.nytimes.com/2021/01/11/us/who-died-in-capitol-building-attack.html; Olafimihan Oshin, *GAO Says 114 Capitol Police Officers Reported Injuries on Jan. 6*, THE HILL (Mar. 7, 2022), https://thehill.com/homenews/state-watch/597258-gao-says-114-capitol-police-officers-reported-injuries-far-more-than/.

21 Ciara Torres-Spelliscy, *How Big Business Bailed Out the Nazis*, BRENNAN CENTER (May 20, 2016), https://www.brennancenter.org/our-work/analysis-opinion/how-big-business-bailed-out-nazis.

22 Joshua Goodman & Eric Tucker, *"Fat Leonard," Contractor in Navy Bribery Case, May Face More Charges*, AP (Dec. 21, 2023), https://www.navytimes.com/news/your-navy/2023/12/21/fat-leonard-contractor-in-navy-bribery-case-may-face-more-charges/; Annie Vainshtein, *S.F. Environment Director Quits Amid Corruption Probe*, SAN FRAN. CHRONICLE C1 (Apr. 8, 2023); Kara Scannell & Lauren del Valle, *Trump Organization Found Guilty on All Counts of Criminal Tax Fraud*, CNN (Dec. 7, 2022), https://www.cnn.com/2022/12/06/politics/trump-organization-fraud-trial-verdict/

index.html; Karl Vick, *"I'll sell my soul to the devil,"* NBC NEWS (Nov. 12, 2007), https://www.nbcnews.com/id/wbna21744055 (referencing Alaska's Corrupt Bastards Club).

23 *Americans' Dismal Views of the Nation's Politics*, PEW (Sept. 19, 2023), https://www.pewresearch.org/politics/2023/09/19/money-power-and-the-influence-of-ordinary-people-in-american-politics/.

24 ROBERT A. G. MONKS, CORPOCRACY: HOW CEOS AND THE BUSINESS ROUNDTABLE HIJACKED THE WORLD'S GREATEST WEALTH MACHINE— AND HOW TO GET IT BACK, 1 (2007).

25 Li Zhou, *147 Republican Lawmakers Still Objected to the Election Results After the Capitol Attack*, VOX (Jan. 7, 2021), https://www.vox.com/2021/1/6/22218058/republicans-objections-election-results.

26 *Final Report, Select Committee to Investigate the January 6th Attack on the United States Capitol December 00, 2022*, 117th Congress Second Session House Report 117–000 (2022), https://january6th.house.gov/sites/democrats.january6th.house.gov/files/Report_FinalReport_Jan6SelectCommittee.pdf (Hereinafter *Final January 6 Report*).

27 *Examining the U.S. Capitol Attack: A Review of the Security, Planning, and Response Failures on January 6*, SENATE COMMITTEE ON HOMELAND SECURITY & GOVERNMENTAL AFFAIRS & SENATE COMMITTEE ON RULES & ADMINISTRATION (2021), https://www.rules.senate.gov/imo/media/doc/Jan%206%20HSGAC%20 Rules%20Report.pdf.

28 P. Michael McKinley, *January 6th and America's Ambivalence About Political Accountability*, JUST SECURITY (July 12, 2022), https://www.justsecurity.org/82276/january-6th-and-americas-ambivalence-about-political-accountability/.

29 *6 in 10 Americans Say U.S. Democracy Is in Crisis as the "Big Lie" Takes Root*, NPR (Jan. 3, 2022), https://www.npr.org/2022/01/03/1069764164/american-democracy-poll-jan-6.

30 Ciara Torres-Spelliscy, *Dark Money in the 2020 Election $100 Million May Just Be the Tip of an Iceberg*, BRENNAN CENTER (Nov. 20, 2020), https://www.brennancenter.org/our-work/analysis-opinion/dark-money-2020-election.

31 Ciara Torres-Spelliscy, *The Supreme Court Moves the Goalposts on Donor Transparency*, BRENNAN CENTER (July 13, 2021), https://www.brennancenter.org/our-work/analysis-opinion/supreme-court-moves-goalposts-donor-transparency.

32 JANE MAYER, DARK MONEY: THE HIDDEN HISTORY OF THE BILLIONAIRES BEHIND THE RISE OF THE RADICAL RIGHT (2016).

33 Lloyd Mayer, *Justices Open the Door Wider for Donor Info Law Challenges*, LAW360 (July 2, 2021), https://www.law360.com/articles/1400104/justices-open-the-door-wider-for-donor-info-law-challenges.

34 *Practical Stake: Corporations, Political Spending, and Democracy*, CENTER FOR POLITICAL ACCOUNTABILITY (2022), https://www.politicalaccountability.net/wp-content/uploads/2022/04/Practical-Stake.pdf.

35 Ian Vandewalker, *Since Citizens United, a Decade of Super PACs*, BRENNAN CENTER (Jan. 14, 2020), https://www.brennancenter.org/our-work/analysis-opinion/citizens-united-decade-super-pacs.

36 Heidi Przybyla, *Dark Money and Special Deals: How Leonard Leo and His Friends Benefited from His Judicial Activism*, POLITICO (Mar. 1, 2023), https://www.politico.com/news/2023/03/01/dark-money-leonard-leo-judicial-activism-00084864; Robert Maguire, *Leonard Leo's Mysterious $200 Million Dark Money War Chest*, CREW (Dec.

7, 2022), https://www.citizensforethics.org/reports-investigations/crew-investigations/leonard-leos-mysterious-200-million-dark-money-war-chest/.

37 Ty Haqqi, *15 Biggest Bribery Cases in Business History*, YAHOO (Feb. 9, 2021), https://www.yahoo.com/now/15-biggest-bribery-cases-business-091849714.html.

38 *See generally* Carissa Byrne Hessick & Michael Morse, *Picking Prosecutors*, 105 IOWA L. REV. 1537 (2020).

39 Complaint and Demand for Jury Trial at 39, *US Dominion Inc. v. Herring Networks Inc.*, Doc. 1, No. 1:21-cv-02130 (D.D.C. Aug. 10, 2021), https://www.documentcloud.org/documents/21039565-dominion-oan-complaint.

40 Superseding Indictment, *United States v. Menendez*, No. S223Cr.490SHS (Jan. 2, 2024), https://static01.nyt.com/newsgraphics/documenttools/f1859c2d74793a36/f2b0fdc7-full.pdf.

41 Kyle Cheney & Zach Montellaro, *Supreme Court Lets "Insurrectionist" Ban Against New Mexico Official Stand*, POLITICO (Mar. 18, 2024), https://www.politico.com/news/2024/03/18/supreme-court-new-mexico-griffin-00147547. (Griffin was removed from office under the Constitution's Disqualification Clause. The Supreme Court allowed his removal to stand by not granting cert. in his case).

42 Andrew Hay & Gabriella Borter, *North Carolina Orders New U.S. House Election after "Tainted" Vote*, REUTERS (Feb. 21, 2019), https://www.reuters.com/article/idUSKC-N1QA1QF/.

43 Lauren Irwin, *Kari Lake's Lawyers Could Face Discipline over Election Cases*, THE HILL (Dec. 13, 2023), https://thehill.com/regulation/court-battles/4359147-kari-lakes-lawyers-could-face-discipline-over-election-cases/.

44 Alice Herman et al., *The Election-Denying Republicans Who Aided Trump's "Big Lie" and Got Promoted in 2022*, GUARDIAN (Mar. 9, 2023), https://www.theguardian.com/us-news/ng-interactive/2023/mar/09/trump-big-lie-2020-election-republican-supporters-congress.

45 *Top Contributors Republican Attorneys General Assn.*, OPENSECRETS (June 13, 2022), https://www.opensecrets.org/527s/527cmtedetail_contribs.php?cycle=2022&ein=464501717.

46 Anna Massoglia, *Details of the Money Behind Jan. 6 Protests Continue to Emerge*, OPENSECRETS (Oct. 25, 2021), www.opensecrets.org https://www.opensecrets.org/news/2021/10/details-of-the-money-behind-jan-6-protests-continue-to-emerge/ ("Two of the other organizations . . . store[d] funds for the rally, Rule of Law Trust and Turning Point, are dark money groups that were listed as organizers of the rally.").

47 *Id.*

48 *Id.* ("Other Rule of Law Defense Fund donors included opaque nonprofits such as the Koch network's Freedom Partners Chamber of Commerce, the Edison Electric Institute, Empowering Ohio's Economy and the Alliance Defending Freedom.").

49 Leo E. Strine Jr., *Fiduciary Blind Spot: The Failure of Institutional Investors to Prevent the Illegitimate Use of Working Americans' Savings for Corporate Political Spending*, 97 WASH. U. L. REV. 1007 (2020).

50 Allison Schrager, *ESG Means No More Buying the World a Coke*, BLOOMBERG (Mar. 24, 2022), https://www.bloomberg.com/opinion/articles/2022-03-24/esg-means-no-more-buying-the-world-a-coke.

51 *Election Denial in U.S. Congress*, STATES UNITED ACTION (Jan. 8, 2024), https://electiondeniers.org/congressional.

NOTES

1. PAYING TO DISRUPT DEMOCRACY

1 Leo E. Strine Jr., *Fiduciary Blind Spot: The Failure of Institutional Investors to Prevent the Illegitimate Use of Working Americans' Savings for Corporate Political Spending*, 97 WASH. U. L. REV. 1007, 1038 (2020).
2 Judd Legum, *How Corporations Give Republicans a Massive Financial Advantage in State Politics*, POPULAR INFORMATION (July 15, 2021), https://popular.info/p/how-corporations-give-republicans.
3 *Id.*
4 ROBERT HEALY, CORPORATE POLITICAL BEHAVIOR: WHY CORPORATIONS DO WHAT THEY DO IN POLITICS 1 (2014).
5 Virginia Chamlee, *The Most Politically Minded Restaurants and Food Brands*, EATER (Aug. 23, 2016), https://www.eater.com/2016/8/23/12480824/starbucks-shake-shack-chipotle-political-restaurants-food-brands.
6 Carrie Sheffield, *Whole Foods Founder John Mackey: Liberals Are Forcing Companies to Back Their Political Agenda*, N.Y. POST (Aug. 11, 2022), https://nypost.com/2022/08/11/whole-foods-john-mackey-liberals-force-companies-to-back-their-agenda/.
7 *Contributor John Mackey*, OPENSECRETS, https://www.opensecrets.org/search?order=desc&q=john+mackey&sort=A&type=donors (last visited Jan. 1, 2024).
8 Spencer Kornhaber, *Waking Up to Coachella's Conservative Tinge*, ATLANTIC (Jan. 13, 2017), https://www.theatlantic.com/entertainment/archive/2017/01/coachella-conservatism-philip-anschutz-aeg-live/513092/.
9 Amy Zimmerman, *Your Coachella Money Is Going to a Right-Wing Billionaire Who Funded Anti-LGBT and Anti-Marijuana Causes*, DAILY BEAST (Apr. 13, 2018), https://www.thedailybeast.com/your-coachella-money-is-going-to-a-right-wing-billionaire-who-funded-anti-lgbt-and-anti-marijuana-causes.
10 Ben Ryder Howe, *Why Philip Anschutz, Known as the "Anti-Trump," Is Spending a Fortune on Old Hotels*, TOWN & COUNTRY (Mar. 21, 2017), https://www.townandcountrymag.com/society/money-and-power/a9156879/philip-anschutz-interview/.
11 Justin Joffe, *Coachella Owner Funds Anti-Gay, Climate-Change-Denying Hate Groups*, OBSERVER (Jan. 6, 2017), https://observer.com/2017/01/coachella-owner-homophobic-climate-change-denier/.
12 *Id.*
13 *Id.*
14 Zimmerman, *supra* note 9.
15 Joffe, *supra* note 11.
16 Zimmerman, *supra* note 9.
17 Anna Massoglia, *Billionaire Coachella-Owner Pours Money into Political Contributions Boosting Republicans*, OPENSECRETS (Apr. 26, 2022), https://www.opensecrets.org/news/2022/04/billionaire-coachella-owner-pours-money-into-political-contributions-boosting-republicans/.
18 *Id.*
19 Anna Massoglia, *Details of the Money Behind Jan. 6 Protests Continue to Emerge*, OPENSECRETS (Oct. 25, 2021), https://www.opensecrets.org/news/2021/10/details-of-the-money-behind-jan-6-protests-continue-to-emerge/ ("Uihlein was also a major donor to other groups affiliated with [January 6] rally organizers.").

20 Judd Legum & Jon Blistein, *Coachella's Parent Company Is Donating Major Cash to a Political Organization Pushing Anti-Abortion Agenda*, ROLLING STONE (July 25, 2022), https://www.rollingstone.com/music/music-news/coachella-aeg-republican-donation-1385947/.
21 *Id.*
22 Judd Legum, *Who Is Really Financing Herschel Walker's Campaign?*, POPULAR INFO. (Oct. 10, 2022), https://popular.info/p/who-is-really-financing-herschel.
23 Kornhaber, *supra* note 8.
24 Stephen Daw, *AEG Owner Phil Anschutz Is Still Donating to Causes Promoting Anti-LGBTQ Beliefs*, BILLBOARD (Feb. 11, 2020), https://www.billboard.com/pro/aeg-owner-phil-anschutz-anti-lgbtq-conservative-donations/.
25 Clark Schultz, *Amazon the First Stop for 60% of All Online Shoppers*, SEEKING ALPHA (Sept. 28, 2020), https://seekingalpha.com/news/3617671-amazon-first-stop-for-60-percent-of-all-online-shoppers.
26 Stephanie Saul & Danny Hakim, *The Most Powerful Conservative Couple You've Never Heard Of*, N.Y. TIMES (June 7, 2018), https://www.nytimes.com/2018/06/07/us/politics/liz-dick-uihlein-republican-donors.html.
27 *Id.*
28 *Influence Peddler for August 2022—Richard and Elizabeth Uihlein*, WISCONSIN DEMOCRACY CAMPAIGN (Aug. 1, 2022), https://www.wisdc.org/news/press-releases/136-press-release-2022/7161-influence-peddler-for-august-2022-richard-and-elizabeth-uihlein.
29 Saul & Hakim, *supra* note 26.
30 *Uihlein, Richard Ellis (Dick)*, FOLLOW THE MONEY, https://www.followthemoney.org/entity-details?eid=2691126&default=contributor (last visited Dec. 6, 2023).
31 Roger Sollenberger, *New Filings Reveal Another Billionaire Behind the Big Lie*, DAILY BEAST (Jan. 20, 2022), https://www.thedailybeast.com/new-filings-reveal-another-billionaire-dick-uihlein-behind-the-big-lie.
32 *Id.*
33 *Id.*
34 *Id.* ("Uihlein also provided a pillar of financial support for the Tea Party Patriots, a far-right activist group which helped organize rally events on Jan. 6. Since 2016.").
35 Massoglia, *Details of the Money Behind Jan. 6*, *supra* note 19.
36 Sollenberger, *Another Billionaire Behind the Big Lie*, *supra* note 31.
37 *Id.*
38 *Donor Profile: Elizabeth and Richard Uihlein*, OPENSECRETS (Feb. 13, 2023), https://www.opensecrets.org/featured-datasets/51.
39 *Influence Peddler for August 2022—Richard and Elizabeth Uihlein*, WISCONSIN DEMOCRACY CAMPAIGN (Aug. 1, 2022), https://www.wisdc.org/news/press-releases/136-press-release-2022/7161-influence-peddler-for-august-2022-richard-and-elizabeth-uihlein.
40 David Armiak, *uline ceo Pours Another $7.1 Million Into His Restoration PAC to Boost Anti-Abortion and Right-Wing Candidates and Causes*, CENTER FOR MEDIA & DEMOCRACY (Oct. 18, 2022), https://www.exposedbycmd.org/2022/10/18/uline-ceo-pours-another-7-1-million-into-his-restoration-pac-to-boost-anti-abortion-and-right-wing-candidates-and-causes/.

NOTES

41 *Never Back Down, Receipts*, FEC (last visited Dec. 6, 2023), https://www.fec.gov/data/receipts/?cycle=2024&data_type=processed&committee_id=C00834077&contributor_name=uihlein&two_year_transaction_period=2024&line_number=F3X-11AI (last visited Dec. 6, 2023) (listing Uihlein).

42 Kai Ryssdal & Livi Burdette, *How Ride-Hail Companies Use Data to Pay Drivers Less*, MARKETPLACE (Apr. 10, 2023), https://www.marketplace.org/2023/04/10/how-ride-hail-companies-use-data-to-pay-drivers-less/.

43 Laney Ruckstuhl, *Lyft Gives Record $13 Million to Back Ballot Question*, WBUR (Jan. 20, 2022), https://www.wbur.orgnews/2022/01/20/lyft-campaign-donation-ballot-question-massachusetts-financial-report.

44 *Id.*

45 *Massachusetts App-Based Drivers as Contractors and Labor Policies Initiative*, BALLOTPEDIA (2022), https://ballotpedia.org/Massachusetts_App-Based_Drivers_as_Contractors_and_Labor_Policies_Initiative_(2022)#cite_note-Text1-2.

46 Dara Kerr & Maddy Varner, *Uber and Lyft Donated to Community Groups Who Then Pushed the Companies' Agenda*, MARKUP (June 17, 2021), https://themarkup.orgnews/2021/06/17/uber-and-lyft-donated-to-community-groups-who-then-pushed-the-companies-agenda.

47 *Id.*

48 ALYSSA KATZ, THE INFLUENCE MACHINE: THE U.S. CHAMBER OF COMMERCE AND THE CORPORATE CAPTURE OF AMERICAN LIFE 1 (2015) ("The Chamber . . . can take credit for . . . the most disturbing trends in American life: the reversal of environmental protections, the destruction of unions and worker protections, the rise of virulent antigovernment ideology, the enlarged role of money in campaigns, and the creation of "astroturf" movements as cover for a corporate agenda.").

49 Ryan Menezes, Maloy Moore & Phi Do, *Billions Have Been Spent on California's Ballot Measure Battles*, L.A. TIMES (Nov. 13, 2020), https://www.latimes.com/projects/props-california-2020-election-money/.

50 *Id.*

51 Aarian Marshall, *With $200 Million, Uber and Lyft Write Their Own Labor Law*, WIRED (Nov. 4, 2020), https://www.wired.com/story/200-million-uber-lyft-write-own-labor-law/.

52 *Quick Facts on the Risks of E-cigarettes for Kids, Teens, and Young Adults*, CDC (Nov. 10, 2022), https://www.cdc.gov/tobacco/basic_information/e-cigarettes/Quick-Facts-on-the-Risks-of-E-cigarettes-for-Kids-Teens-and-Young-Adults.html.

53 *Outbreak of Lung Injury Associated with the Use of E-Cigarette, or Vaping, Products*, CDC (Feb. 25, 2020), https://www.cdc.gov/tobacco/basic_information/e-cigarettes/severe-lung-disease.html.

54 *States & Localities That Have Restricted the Sale of Flavored Tobacco Products*, TOBACCO FREE KIDS (2022), https://www.tobaccofreekids.org/assets/factsheets/0398.pdf.

55 *How E-Cigarette Companies Manipulated the Government and Burned America's Youth*, UNION OF CONCERNED SCIENTISTS (May 25, 2021), https://www.ucsusa.org/resources/how-e-cigarette-companies-manipulated-government.

56 *Enforcement Priorities for Electronic Nicotine Delivery System (ENDS) and Other Deemed Products on the Market Without Premarket Authorization*, FDA (Apr. 2020), https://www.fda.gov/regulatory-information/search-fda-guidance-documents/

enforcement-priorities-electronic-nicotine-delivery-system-ends-and-other-deemed-products-market.
57 *Results from the Annual National Youth Tobacco Survey*, FDA (Nov. 2022), www.fda.govhttps://www.fda.gov/tobacco-products/youth-and-tobacco/results-annual-youth-tobacco-survey.
58 *Spinning a New Tobacco Industry: How Big Tobacco Is Trying to Sell a Do-Gooder Image and What Americans Think About It*, TRUTH INITIATIVE (Dec. 20 2019), https://truthinitiative.org/research-resources/tobacco-industry-marketing/spinning-new-tobacco-industry-how-big-tobacco-trying.
59 Sheila Kaplan, *Juul is Fighting to Keep Its E-Cigarettes on the U.S. Market*, N.Y. TIMES (July 5, 2021), https://www.nytimes.com/2021/07/05/health/juul-vaping-fda.html; *Massive "Influence Campaign" Includes Hefty Campaign Donations*, TRIAL LAWYER (Dec. 2020), https://thetriallawyermagazine.com/2020/12/juuls-influence-campaign/.
60 Richard Lardner & Matthew Perrone, *Juul's Political Contributions on the Rise, Favor Democrats*, KQED (Aug. 2, 2019), https://www.kqed.org/news/11765172/juuls-political-contributions-on-the-rise-favor-democrats.
61 *Id.*
62 *JUUL Labs, Lobbying*, OPENSECRETS (2019), https://www.opensecrets.org/orgs/juul-labs/summary?toprecipcycle=2022&contribcycle=2022&lobcycle=2022&outspendcycle=2022&id=D000070920&topnumcycle=2020.
63 Theodoric Meyer, *Juul Threw Millions of Dollars at Washington*, POLITICO (Sept. 11, 2019), https://www.politico.com/story/2019/09/11/juul-vaping-lobbying-washington-1491029.
64 Angelica LaVito, *Juul Hires "Political Dark Arts" Firm Led by Ex-Clinton Campaign Director in Its Fight for Survival*, CNBC (Oct. 1, 2019), https://www.cnbc.com/2019/10/01/vaping-company-juul-recruits-customers-for-shadow-grassroots-lobbying-campaign.html.
65 Richard Lardner & Matthew Perrone, *Juul's Political Contributions on the Rise, Favor Democrats*, KQED (Aug. 2, 2019), https://www.kqed.org/news/11765172/juuls-political-contributions-on-the-rise-favor-democrats.
66 Joel Lau, *Hawaii Seemed Poised to Adopt a Vape Flavor Ban. Then Came the Amendments*, CIVIL BEAT (Mar. 2022), https://www.civilbeat.org/2022/03/hawaii-seemed-poised-to-adopt-a-vape-flavor-ban-then-came-the-amendments/.
67 Meyer, *supra* note 63.
68 *Id.*
69 Laura Klivans, *San Francisco Voters Uphold Ban on E-Cigarette Sales, Rejecting Juul-Funded Proposition C*, KQED (Nov 5, 2019), https://www.kqed.org/news/11784856/san-francisco-voters-uphold-ban-on-e-cigarette-sales-rejecting-juul-funded-proposition-.
70 *Juul's Massive "Influence Campaign" Includes Hefty Campaign Donations*, TRIAL LAWYER (Dec. 2020), https://thetriallawyermagazine.com/2020/12/juuls-influence-campaign/.
71 *Id.*
72 LaVito, *supra* note 64.
73 Breanna Bradham, *Altria Buys Njoy, Abandons Juul as It Shifts Vaping Strategy*, BLOOMBERG (Mar. 6, 2023), https://www.bloomberg.com/news/articles/2023-03-05/altria-swaps-juul-stake-once-worth-12-8-billion-for-some-vaping-ip#xj4y7vzkg.

NOTES

74 *Tom Brady and Gisele Bündchen to Star in $20 Million Campaign for Crypto Exchange*, WALL ST. J. (Sept. 8, 2021), https://www.wsj.com/articles/the-celebrities-including-tom-brady-tied-to-ftx-see-the-list-11668109684#:~:text=Tom%20Brady%20and%20Gisele%20Bündchen&text=FTX%20Trading%20Ltd.-,Mr.,to%20join%20the%20FTX%20platform.

75 Eli Tan, *FTX Scores Another Sports Sponsorship With Super Bowl Ad*, COIN DESK (Oct. 27, 2021), https://www.coindesk.com/business/2021/10/26/ftx-to-run-ad-during-super-bowl-as-it-delves-further-into-sports-sponsorships/.

76 Allison Morrow, *FTX Investor Sues Tom Brady, Gisele Bundchen and Others as Crypto Contagion Spreads*, CNN (Nov. 16, 2022), https://www.cnn.com/2022/11/16/business/crypto-contagion-genesis-ftx-ctrp/index.html.

77 Joshua Oliver, *"Sam? Are you there?!,"* FINANCIAL TIMES (Feb. 9, 2023), https://www.ft.com/content/6e912f25-f1b7-4b19-b370-007fbc867246.

78 Michelle Ruiz, *"It's Not So Black and White": Gisele Bündchen*, VANITY FAIR (Mar. 22, 2023), https://www.vanityfair.com/style/2023/03/gisele-bundchen-cover-story.

79 Derek Saul, *Taylor Swift Asked FTX About Its Legality Before Balking on $100 Million Sponsorship Deal, Lawyer Claims*, FORBES (Apr. 19, 2023), https://www.forbes.com/sites/dereksaul/2023/04/19/taylor-swift-asked-ftx-about-its-legality-before-balking-on-100-million-sponsorship-deal-lawyer-claims/.

80 *Id.*

81 Jim Geraghty, *The Crypto Dollars in Politics Flowed to Republicans, Too*, WASH. POST (Dec. 1, 2022), https://www.washingtonpost.com/opinions/2022/12/01/crypto-politics-ryan-salame-sbf-sam-bankman-fried/.

82 Press Release, *SEC Charges Samuel Bankman-Fried with Defrauding Investors in Crypto Asset Trading Platform FTX*, SEC (Dec. 13, 2022), https://www.sec.gov/news/press-release/2022-219.

83 In re: FTX Trading Ltd. at 2 (D. Del. Bankr. Nov. 17, 2022), https://pacer-documents.s3.amazonaws.com/33/188450/042020648197.pdf.

84 *FTX.US in 2022 Cycle*, OPENSECRETS, https://www.opensecrets.org/orgs/ftx-us/summary?id=D000073694&topnumcycle=2022 (last visited Mar. 25, 2023).

85 *Id.*

86 Press Release, *United States Attorney Announces Charges Against FTX Founder Samuel Bankman-Fried*, DOJ (Dec. 3, 2022), https://www.justice.gov/usao-sdny/pr/united-states-attorney-announces-charges-against-ftx-founder-samuel-bankman-fried.

87 In re: FTX Trading Ltd. at 5.

88 *United States v. Sam Bankman-Fried*, S322CR.673LAK at 14 (Feb. 22, 2023) https://s3.documentcloud.org/documents/23688593/sdnys-superseding-indictment-of-sam-bankman-fried-feb-22-2023.pdf (superseding indictment).

89 Cheyenne Ligon, *The "SBF Bill": What's in the Crypto Legislation Backed by FTX's Founder*, COIN DESK (Nov. 15, 2022), https://www.coindesk.com/policy/2022/11/15/the-sbf-bill-whats-in-the-crypto-legislation-backed-by-ftx-founder/.

90 Andrew R. Chow, *The Bombshell Evidence That Led to Sam Bankman-Fried's Conviction*, TIME (Nov. 2, 2023), https://time.com/6330323/sbf-trial-biggest-bombshells/.

91 Press Release, *Statement of U.S. Attorney Damian Williams on the Guilty Plea of Ryan Salame, Former CEO of FTX*, DOJ (Sept. 7, 2023), https://www.justice.gov/usao-sdny/pr/statement-us-attorney-damian-williams-guilty-plea-ryan-salame-former-ceo-ftx.

NOTES

92 Superseding Information, *United States v. Salame*, S722CR.673LAK at 6 (Sept. 2023), https://www.justice.gov/d9/2023-09/u.s._v._salame_information_0.pdf.
93 *Future Forward USA PAC Donors in 2020*, OPENSECRETS, https://www.opensecrets.org/political-action-committees-pacs/future-forward-usa/C00669259/donors/2020 (last visited Mar. 25, 2023).
94 *Id.*
95 Taylor Giorno, *Megadonor No More: Sam Bankman-Fried Spent His Way into the Good Graces of Washington*, OPENSECRETS (Nov. 15, 2022), https://www.opensecrets.org/news/2022/11/megadonor-no-more-sam-bankman-fried-spent-his-way-into-the-good-graces-of-washington-then-lost-it-all/.
96 Brian Schwartz, *Sam Bankman-Fried, FTX Allies Secretly Poured $50 Million into "Dark Money" Groups, Evidence Shows*, CNBC (Oct. 20 2023), https://www.cnbc.com/2023/10/20/sam-bankman-fried-ftx-allies-donated-millions-in-dark-money.html.
97 *Id.*
98 Geraghty, *supra* note 81.
99 *Corporate Contributions to Outside Groups 2020*, OPENSECRETS, https://www.opensecrets.org/outside-spending/corporate-contributions (last visited June 27, 2023) (showing $111,153,076 spent in 2020 election).
100 *Id.*
101 *Id.*
102 *Total Corporate and Industry Spending on Sedition Caucus Members*, CITIZENS FOR RESPONSIBILITY & ETHICS IN WASHINGTON, https://www.citizensforethics.org/reports-investigations/crew-reports/this-sedition-is-brought-to-you-by/ (last visited Dec. 11, 2023) (listing $91 million from corporate PACs to members of the Sedition Caucus).
103 Jody Godoy & Luc Cohen, *FTX's Singh Pleads Guilty as Pressure Mounts on Bankman-Fried*, REUTERS (Feb. 28, 2023), https://www.reuters.com/legal/ftxs-singh-agrees-plead-guilty-us-criminal-charges-lawyer-says-2023-02-28/.
104 Corinne Ramey, *FTX's Political Donations Came From Stolen Customer Funds, Testifies Company Insider Nishad Singh*, WALL ST. J. (Oct. 16, 2023), https://www.wsj.com/finance/currencies/ftxs-political-donations-came-from-stolen-customer-funds-testifies-company-insider-nishad-singh-a4d7dd84.
105 David Gura, *They Were Sam Bankman-Fried's Friends*, NPR (Oct. 21, 2023), https://www.npr.org/2023/10/21/1207143248/sam-bankman-fried-trial-ftx-crypto-fraud-alameda.
106 Theodore Schleifer, *The Confessions of S.B.F.*, PUCK (Dec. 6, 2022), https://puck.news/sam-bankman-fried-sbf-interview/.
107 Dominic Rushe, *FTX Billionaire Sam Bankman-Fried Funneled Dark Money to Republicans*, GUARDIAN (Nov. 30, 2022), https://www.theguardian.com/technology/2022/nov/30/ftx-billionaire-sam-bankman-fried-dark-money-republicans.
108 Dan Managan, *Former FTX CEO Sam Bankman-Fried Hit with Campaign Finance Complaint over GOP "Dark" Money*, CNBC (Dec. 8, 2022), https://www.cnbc.com/2022/12/08/ftx-ceo-sam-bankman-fried-hit-with-campaign-finance-complaint.html.
109 Superseding Indictment, *United States v. Sam Bankman-Fried*, S322CR.673LAK at 17 (Feb. 22, 2023), https://s3.documentcloud.org/documents/23688593/sdnys-superseding-indictment-of-sam-bankman-fried-feb-22-2023.pdf.

NOTES

110 Pete Syme, *Sam Bankman-Fried Says He's the Republicans' Third-Biggest Donor, but Used "Dark Money" to Avoid Media Criticism*, BUSINESS INSIDER (Nov. 30, 2022), https://www.businessinsider.com/sam-bankman-fried-says-hes-the-republicans-third-biggest-donor-2022-11.

111 Geraghty, *supra* note 81.

112 David A. Graham, *Sam Bankman-Fried, Crypto-Republican?*, ATLANTIC (Dec. 6, 2022), https://www.theatlantic.com/ideas/archive/2022/12/sam-bankman-fried-donations-democrat-republican/672368/.

113 Allison Morrow, *Sam Bankman-Fried, FTX's founder, Is Arrested in the Bahamas*, CNN (Dec. 13, 2022), https://www.cnn.com/2022/12/12/business/sam-bankman-fried-arrested/index.html.

114 Press Release, *United States Attorney Announces Extradition of FTX Founder Samuel Bankman-Fried to the United States and Guilty Pleas of Former CEO of Alameda Research and Former Chief Technology Officer of FTX*, DOJ (Dec. 22, 2022), https://www.justice.gov/usao-sdny/pr/united-states-attorney-announces-extradition-ftx-founder-samuel-bankman-fried-united.

115 Theodore Schleifer, *The Only Living Boy in Palo Alto*, PUCK (Jan. 10, 2023), https://puck.news/the-only-living-boy-in-palo-alto/.

116 Ben Weiss, *Sam Bankman-Fried Is Headed to Jail: Judge Revokes Bail After DOJ Alleges He Tampered with Witnesses, Including Ex-Girlfriend Caroline Ellison*, FORTUNE (Aug. 11, 2023), https://fortune.com/crypto/2023/08/11/sam-bankman-fried-bail-revoked-going-to-jail-witness-tampering/#.

117 Luc Cohen & Jody Godoy, *Sam Bankman-Fried Directed Fraud on FTX Customers, Caroline Ellison Tells Jury*, REUTERS (Oct. 11, 2023), https://www.reuters.com/legal/sam-bankman-frieds-ex-girlfriend-set-take-stand-fraud-trials-star-witness-2023-10-10/.

118 Jamie Redman, *Inside Caroline Ellison's Explosive Testimony—Former Alameda CEO Accuses SBF of Directing Fraud at FTX*, BITCOIN (Oct. 10, 2023), https://news.bitcoin.com/inside-caroline-ellisons-explosive-testimony-former-alameda-ceo-accuses-sbf-of-directing-fraud-at-ftx/.

119 Josh Russell, *New Crypto Bribe Charges Against Bankman-Fried Spun Off for Separate Trial*, COURTHOUSE NEWS (June 15, 2023), https://www.courthousenews.com/bankman-fried-says-new-charges-on-crypto-bribe-go-too-far ("[Bankman-Fried's lawyer Christian] Everdell . . . argued . . . that several charges should be thrown out . . . [because of] Percoco.").

120 *United States v. Bankman-Fried*, 2023 WL 4194773 at *1 (S.D.N.Y. June 27, 2023) (refusing to dismiss campaign finance charges against Bankman-Fried).

121 Press Release, *Statement of U.S. Attorney Damian Williams on the Conviction of Samuel Bankman-Fried*, DOJ (Nov. 2, 2023), https://www.justice.gov/usao-sdny/pr/statement-us-attorney-damian-williams-conviction-samuel-bankman-fried (his convictions were not on campaign finance grounds).

122 Graham, *supra* note 112.

123 Giorno, *supra* note 95.

124 Kadia Goba, *Prosecutors to Lawmakers: Hand over Sam Bankman-Fried's Political Donations*, SEMAFOR (Mar. 21, 2023), https://www.semafor.com/article/03/21/2023/doj-ftx-contributions-letter.

NOTES

125 Alexandria Jacobson, *Five More Republican Lawmakers Surrender FTX Money to U.S. Marshals Service*, Raw Story (May 18, 2023), https://www.alternet.org/five-republican-lawmakers-surrender-money/.
126 *Id.* (the people with * are members of the Sedition Caucus).
127 Andrew Selsky, *Oregon Democratic Party to Send Federal Officials a $500,000 Donation from Former FTX Executive*, AP (June 9, 2023), https://apnews.com/article/oregon-democratic-party-ftx-donation-b29f4dd2efc8c449096a474a5c096fef.
128 *Disbursements to the U.S. Marshals*, Federal Election Commission (2023–24), https://www.fec.gov/data/disbursements/?data_type=processed&recipient_name=US+Marshals&two_year_transaction_period=2024&min_date=01%2F01%2F2023&max_date=12%2F31%2F2024 (from Priorities USA Action).
129 *Disbursements to the United States Marshals*, Federal Election Commission (2023–24), https://www.fec.gov/data/disbursements/?data_type=processed&recipient_name=United+states+marshals&two_year_transaction_period=2024&min_date=01%2F01%2F2023&max_date=12%2F31%2F2024 (from DCCC).
130 *Disbursements to the United States Marshals*, Federal Election Commission (2023–24), https://www.fec.gov/data/disbursements/?data_type=processed&recipient_name=United+states+marshals&two_year_transaction_period=2024&min_date=01%2F01%2F2023&max_date=12%2F31%2F2024 (from NRSC).
131 *Disbursements to Marshal Service*, Federal Election Commission (2023–24), https://www.fec.gov/data/disbursements/?data_type=processed&recipient_name=Marshal+Service&two_year_transaction_period=2024&min_date=01%2F01%2F2023&max_date=12%2F31%2F2024 (noting, for example, Joni for Iowa returned $8,700 as a disgorgement from Sam Bankman Fried and Ryan Salame; and Nevadans for Steven Horsford returned $5,800.00 as disgorgement of Contributions from Sam Bankman-Fried and Nishad Singh).
132 Theodore Schleifer, *S.B.F.'s McConnell Money Tickle*, Puck (Dec. 2, 2022) https://puck.news/s-b-f-s-mcconnell-money-tickle/.

2. BACKING THE ANTI-DEMOCRATIC

1 Matthew Kish & Danni Santana, *Here's the Nine-Year Timeline of Adidas and Yeezy's Turbulent Partnership*, Business Insider (Nov. 29, 2022), https://www.businessinsider.com/kanye-wests-turbulent-9-year-history-with-adidas-2022-11.
2 Bobby Allyn, *Adidas Cuts Ties with Ye over Antisemitic Remarks That Caused an Uproar*, NPR (Oct. 25, 2022), https://www.npr.org/2022/10/25/1131285970/adidas-ye-kanye-west-antisemitic.
3 @StopAntisemites, Twitter (Oct. 20, 2022), https://twitter.com/StopAntisemites/status/1583151910932336641 (showing video clip of West saying, "The thing about it being Adidas I can say antisemitic things and Adidas can't drop me . . . now what . . . now what?").
4 Press release, *Adidas Terminates Partnership with Ye Immediately*, Adidas (Oct. 25, 2022), https://www.adidas-group.com/en/media/news-archive/press-releases/2022/adidas-terminates-partnership-ye-immediately/ ("Ye's recent comments and actions have been unacceptable, hateful and dangerous.").
5 *Adidas Reports a $540M Loss as It Struggles with Unsold Yeezy Products*, AP (Mar. 8, 2023), https://www.npr.org/2023/03/08/1161905306/adidas-ye-kanye-west-yeezy-loss.

NOTES

6 Josh Marcus, *Kanye West Antisemitism: Was Adidas Really Founded by a Nazi?*, INDEPENDENT (Oct. 27, 2022), https://www.independent.co.uk/news/world/americas/kanye-west-antisemitism-adidas-nazi-b2211571.html.
7 *Id.*
8 Olivia B. Waxman, *Adidas' Dark History Is in the Spotlight as It Ends Deal with Kanye West Over His Antisemitic Comments*, TIME (Oct. 26, 2022), https://time.com/6224899/adidas-kanye-west-antisemitism-nazis/.
9 Paul Andrews, *Operation Pastorius: The Forgotten Nazi Terror Plot on U.S. Soil*, LOST IN HISTORY (July 16, 2022), https://paulwandrews.wordpress.com/2022/07/16/operation-pastorius-the-forgotten-nazi-terror-plot-on-u-s-soil/.
10 *Nazi Saboteurs and George Dasch*, FBI, https://www.fbi.gov/history/famous-cases/nazi-saboteurs-and-george-dasch (last visited Mar. 13, 2023).
11 David A. Taylor, *The Inside Story of How a Nazi Plot to Sabotage the U.S. War Effort Was Foiled*, SMITHSONIAN (June 26, 2017), https://www.smithsonianmag.com/history/inside-story-how-nazi-plot-sabotage-us-war-effort-was-foiled-180959594/.
12 Ex parte Quirin, 317 U.S. 1 (1942).
13 *Id.*
14 Christopher Klein, *When the Nazis Invaded the Hamptons*, HISTORY (Nov. 28, 2018), https://www.history.com/news/when-the-nazis-invaded-the-hamptons.
15 Paul A. Eisenstein, *Mayor's Attempt to Censor Local Article About Henry Ford's Anti-Semitism Draws National Attention*, CNBC (Feb. 4, 2019), https://www.cnbc.com/2019/02/04/mayors-bid-to-censor-article-on-henry-fords-anti-semitism-goes-viral.html.
16 Ken Silverstein, *Ford and the Führer*, NATION (Jan. 6, 2000), https://www.thenation.com/article/archive/ford-and-fuhrer/ ("Up until Pearl Harbor, Dearborn made huge revenues by producing war matériel for the Reich.").
17 Jacques R. Pauwels, *Profits über Alles! American Corporations and Hitler*, 51 LABOUR/LE TRAVAIL 223, 224 (2003), quoting CHARLES HIGHAM, TRADING WITH THE ENEMY: AN EXPOSÉ OF THE NAZI-AMERICAN MONEY PLOT, 1933–1949 162 (1983).
18 *Id.* at 225.
19 Silverstein, *supra* note 16.
20 Michael Dobbs, *Ford and GM Scrutinized for Alleged Nazi Collaboration*, WASH. POST A1 (Nov. 30, 1998).
21 *Id.*
22 *Id.*
23 *Id.*
24 *Id.*
25 *Germany 1933: From Democracy to Dictatorship*, ANNE FRANK HOUSE (2022), https://www.annefrank.org/en/anne-frank/go-in-depth/germany-1933-democracy-dictatorship/.
26 Bill McGraw, *Henry Ford and the Jews, the Story Dearborn Didn't Want Told*, BRIDGE MICHIGAN (Feb. 4, 2019), https://www.bridgemi.com/michigan-government/henry-ford-and-jews-story-dearborn-didnt-want-told ("Hitler wrote, 'One great man, Ford, to their exasperation, still holds out independently.'").
27 Richard Snow, *The Wonderful, Horrible Life of Henry Ford*, DAILY BEAST (July 11, 2017), https://www.thedailybeast.com/the-wonderful-horrible-life-of-henry-ford.

[215]

NOTES

28 *Ford's Anti-Semitism*, PBS (Jan. 29, 2013), https://www.pbs.org/wgbh/americanexperience/features/henryford-antisemitism/.
29 *The International Jew: 1920's Antisemitism Revived Online*, ANTI-DEFAMATION LEAGUE (Jan. 30, 2017), https://www.adl.org/resources/backgrounder/international-jew-1920s-antisemitism-revived-online.
30 McGraw, *supra* note 26.
31 *Ford's Anti-Semitism*, *supra* note 28.
32 McGraw, *supra* note 26.
33 Dobbs, *supra* note 20.
34 *Id.* (quoting Hitler).
35 *Berlin Hears Ford Is Backing Hitler*, N.Y. TIMES (Dec. 20, 1922), https://timesmachine.nytimes.com/timesmachine/1922/12/20/98799625.pdf?pdf_redirect=true&ip=0.
36 ANTI-DEFAMATION LEAGUE, *supra* note 29.
37 *Henry Ford Receiving the Grand Cross of the German Eagle from Nazi Officials*, RARE HISTORICAL PHOTOS (1938), https://rarehistoricalphotos.com/henry-ford-grand-cross-1938/.
38 Silverstein, *supra* note 16.
39 *Id.*
40 *Id.*
41 *Id.*
42 Dobbs, *supra* note 33 ("They deny that their huge business interests in Nazi Germany led them, wittingly or unwittingly, to also become 'the arsenal of fascism.'").
43 Silverstein, *supra* note 16.
44 Michael Straight, *Standard Oil: Axis Ally*, NEW REPUBLIC (Apr. 6, 1942), https://newrepublic.com/article/104346/standard-oil-axis-ally (referencing Thurman Arnold's testimony before the Truman Committee).
45 Dobbs, *supra* note 20.
46 *Id.*
47 Silverstein, *supra* note 16.
48 Dobbs, *supra* note 20.
49 *Adolf Hitler: "We have a number of nations which have created for themselves an outlook on life based upon their inborn superior value": Dusseldorf Industry Club—1932*, SPEAKOLA (Jan. 27, 1932), https://speakola.com/political/adolf-hitler-dusseldorf-industry-club-1932.
50 FRITZ THYSSEN, I PAID HITLER 101 (1941).
51 *Adolf Hitler Election Speech in Eberswalde*, NATIONAL HOLOCAUST MUSEUM (July 27, 1932), https://collections.ushmm.org/search/catalog/irn1004183.
52 WILLIAM MANCHESTER, THE ARMS OF KRUPP: THE RISE AND FALL OF THE INDUSTRIAL DYNASTY THAT ARMED GERMANY AT WAR 364 (2003).
53 RICHARD A. OLBETER ET AL., EDS., TRIALS OF WAR CRIMINALS BEFORE THE NUERNBERG MILITARY TRIBUNALS UNDER CONTROL COUNCIL LAW NO. 10 VOL. VII "THE I. G. FARBEN CASE" at 16 (Oct. 1946–Apr. 1949) (Hereinafter "THE I. G. FARBEN CASE").
54 Thomas Ferguson & Hans-Joachim Voth, *Betting on Hitler: The Value of Political Connections In Nazi Germany*, 123 (1) Q. J. OF ECON. 101, 110 (Feb. 2008), http://www.stat.columbia.edu/~gelman/stuff_for_blog/Ferg%20QJE%20Vol.%20123,%20No.%201%202008-1.pdf.

NOTES

55 RICHARD A. OLBETER ET AL. EDS., TRIALS OF WAR CRIMINALS BEFORE THE NUERNBERG MILITARY TRIBUNALS UNDER CONTROL COUNCIL LAW NO. 10 VOL. IX "THE KRUPP CASE" at 79 (Oct. 1946–Apr. 1949) (quoting Goebbels's diary) (Hereinafter "THE KRUPP CASE").

56 RICHARD A. OLBETER ET AL. EDS., TRIALS OF WAR CRIMINALS BEFORE THE NUERNBERG MILITARY TRIBUNALS UNDER CONTROL COUNCIL LAW NO. 10 VOL. VI "THE FLICK CASE" at 43 (Oct. 1946–Apr. 1949) (Hereinafter "THE FLICK CASE").

57 "THE I.G. FARBEN CASE," *supra* note 53, at 122.

58 David de Jong, *In the Room Where German Tycoons Agreed to Fund Hitler's Rise to Power*, LIT HUB (Apr. 22, 2022), https://lithub.com/in-the-room-where-german-tycoons-agreed-to-fund-hitlers-rise-to-power/.

59 Ciara Torres-Spelliscy, *How Big Business Bailed Out the Nazis*, BRENNAN CENTER (May 20, 2016), https://www.brennancenter.org/blog/how-big-business-bailed-out-nazis.

60 Straight, *supra* note 44.

61 "THE I. G. FARBEN CASE," *supra* note 53, at 16.

62 *Translation of Document D-201 Prosecution Exhibit 1995: Telegram of 16 February 1933 from Goering to Krupp Inviting Krupp to Election Fund Conference with Hitler and Goering* (Feb. 16, 1933), https://web.archive.org/web/20120213004038/http://www.mazal.org/archive/nmt/07/NMT07-T0557.htm.

63 De Jong, *supra* note 58.

64 "THE FLICK CASE," *supra* note 56, at 33.

65 *Id.*

66 "THE KRUPP CASE," *supra* note 55, at 80 (emphasis added).

67 "THE I. G. FARBEN CASE," *supra* note 53, at 17.

68 "THE KRUPP CASE," *supra* note 55, at 81.

69 *Id.* (quoting Goering) ("Election of 5 March will surely be the last one for the next 10 years, probably even for the next hundred years.").

70 "THE FLICK CASE," *supra* note 56, at 44.

71 "THE I. G. FARBEN CASE," *supra* note 53, at 17.

72 De Jong, *supra* note 58.

73 Ferguson & Voth, *supra* note 54, at 110. http://www.stat.columbia.edu/~gelman/stuff_for_blog/Ferg%20QJE%20Vol.%20123,%20No.%201%202008-1.pdf.

74 De Jong, *supra* note 58.

75 "THE KRUPP CASE," *supra* note 55, at 82.

76 *Id.*

77 Companies/Institutions folders Reichsstand der Deutschen Industrie Wikidata item Hamburgisches Welt-Wirtschafts-Archiv (HWWA)—(1933–1935), https://pm20.zbw.eu/mirador/?manifestId=https://pm20.zbw.eu/iiif/folder/co/045372/manifest.json (including documents showing the Adolf Hitler Spende).

78 "THE KRUPP CASE," *supra* note 55, at 83.

79 "THE I. G. FARBEN CASE," *supra* note 53, at 309.

80 Henry Ashby Turner Jr., *Big Business and the Rise of Hitler*, 75 (1) AM. HISTORICAL REV. 56 64–65 (Oct. 1969).

81 "THE KRUPP CASE," *supra* note 55, at 83.

82 Ferguson & Voth, *supra* note 54, at 115 ("From mid-January to mid-March [1933] Nazi affiliated firms saw their prices increase by almost 7% more than the rest.").

83 *Id.* at 131.
84 "The Krupp Case," *supra* note 55, at 15.
85 Cyprian P. Blamires, World Fascism: A Historical Encyclopedia, vol. 1, at 366 (2006) (the original German term for Krupp's title is "Wehrwistschaftsführer").
86 "The Flick Case," *supra* note 56, at 43–44.
87 *Id.* at 44–45.
88 Fritz Thyssen, I Paid Hitler at 163 (1941) ("Himmler has his own personal circle of industrialists.").
89 "The Flick Case," *supra* note 56, at 1012.
90 "The I. G. Farben Case," *supra* note 53, at 56.
91 Anthony C. Sutton, *Wall Street and the Rise of Hitler*, Voltaire Net 1, 118 (July 1976), https://www.voltairenet.org/IMG/pdf/Sutton_Wall_Street_and_Hitler.pdf ("Standard Oil of New Jersey not only aided Hitler's war machine, but had knowledge of this assistance. Emil Helfferich, the board chairman of a Standard of New Jersey subsidiary, was a member of the Keppler Circle before Hitler came to power; he continued to give financial contributions to Himmler's Circle as late as 1944.").
92 "The Flick Case," *supra* note 56, at 108.
93 *Id.* at 1016–17.
94 *Id.* at 285–86 (Keppler affidavit) (emphasis added).
95 *Id.* at 103.
96 *Id.* at 1016–17.
97 *Id.* at 44 (emphasis added).
98 Josiah E. DuBois Jr., The Devil's Chemists (1952).
99 "The I. G. Farben Case," *supra* note 53, at 124.
100 De Jong, *supra* note 58.
101 United Nations War Crimes Commission, *Law Reports of Trials of War Criminals*, Vol. 10, 84 (1949).
102 Doug Linder, *The Subsequent Nuremberg Trials: An Overview*, UMKC, http://law2.umkc.edu/faculty/projects/ftrials/nuremberg/subsequenttrials.html.
103 "The Flick Case," *supra* note 56, at 43–44.
104 Diarmuid Jeffreys, Hell's Cartel: IG Farben and the Making of Hitler's War Machine 310 (2008).
105 "The I. G. Farben Case," *supra* note 53, at 100.
106 *Joseph Mengele*, U.S. Holocaust Memorial Museum, https://encyclopedia.ushmm.org/content/en/article/josef-mengele (last visited Mar. 1, 2023).
107 *Bayer*, U.S. Holocaust Memorial Museum, https://encyclopedia.ushmm.org/content/en/article/bayer (last visited Mar. 1, 2023).
108 "The Flick Case," *supra* note 56, at 33.
109 United Nations War Crimes Commission, *supra* note 101.
110 Jeffreys, *supra* note 104, at 398–99.
111 DuBois, *supra* note 98, at 348 (quoting Judge Hebert) (emphasis added).
112 Silverstein, *supra* note 16.
113 Straight, *supra* note 44.
114 *Id.*
115 Jeffreys, *supra* note 104.

NOTES

116 Grundgesetz Für Die Bundesrepublik Deutschland [Gg] [Constitution], May 24, 1949, art. 21 (Ger.) (emphasis added).
117 *Id.* (emphasis added).
118 Carl J. Schneider, *Political Parties and the German Basic Law of 1949*, 10 W. POLITICAL Q. 527, 534 (Sept. 1957).

3. DEMOCRACY BEHIND BARS

1 *Journey of Reconciliation*, ORANGE COUNTY, N.C. (June 17, 2022), https://www.orangecountync.gov/2937/Journey-of-Reconciliation.
2 *75 Years Later: Sentences Vacated for Four Original Freedom Riders*, WRAL (June 17, 2022), https://www.wral.com/75-years-later-sentences-vacated-for-four-original-freedom-riders/20336108/.
3 Tom Foreman Jr., *Freedom Riders' 1947 Convictions Vacated in North Carolina*, AP (June 17, 2022), https://apnews.com/article/north-carolina-race-and-ethnicity-racial-injustice-government-politics-eb1a6308edb82eb271ed92c32dbe432d.
4 *Id.*
5 *Id.*
6 *Journey of Reconciliation*, *supra* note 1.
7 Scott W. Howe, *Slavery as Punishment: Original Public Meaning, Cruel and Unusual Punishment, and the Neglected Clause in the Thirteenth Amendment*, 51 ARIZ. L. REV. 983, 1014–15 (2009).
8 Alec C. Ewald, *"Civil Death": The Ideological Paradox of Criminal Disenfranchisement Law in the United States*, WIS. L. REV. 1045, 1060 (2002).
9 *Id.*
10 MICHELLE ALEXANDER, THE NEW JIM CROW 2 (2010).
11 KATHERINE IRENE PETTUS, FELONY DISENFRANCHISEMENT IN AMERICA 28–29 (2013).
12 Mark Haase, *Civil Death in Modern Times: Reconsidering Felony Disenfranchisement in Minnesota*, 99 MINN. L. REV. 1913, 1918 (2015).
13 Ann Cammett, *Shadow Citizens: Felony Disenfranchisement and the Criminalization of Debt*, 117 PENN. ST. L. REV. 349, 358 (2012).
14 *The Disenfranchisement of Ex-Felons: Citizenship, Criminality, and "The Purity of the Ballot Box,"* 102 HARV. L. REV. 1300, 1301 (1989); quoting Special Project, *The Collateral Consequences of a Criminal Conviction*, 23 VAND. L. REV. 929, 941 (1970).
15 Carlos M. Portugal, *Democracy Frozen in Devonian Amber: The Racial Impact of Permanent Felon Disenfranchisement in Florida*, 57 U. MIAMI L. REV. 1317, 1318–19 (2003) (quoting SIR FREDERICK POLLOCK & FREDERIC WILLIAM MAITLAND, THE HISTORY OF ENGLISH LAW BEFORE THE TIME OF EDWARD 1:448 [reprint 1923; 2nd ed. 1898]).
16 Jason Schall, *The Consistency of Felon Disenfranchisement with Citizenship Theory*, 22 HARV. BLACKLETTER L.J. 53, 80 (2006); Heather Lardy, *Prisoner Disenfranchisement: Constitutional Rights and Wrongs*, 2002 Pub. L. 524, 530 (2002); citing 4 WILLIAM BLACKSTONE, COMMENTARIES ON THE LAW OF ENGLAND 373–74 (1769).
17 *Rustin, Bayard Biography March 17, 1912 to August 24, 1987*, MARTIN LUTHER KING JR. RESEARCH & EDUCATION INSTITUTE AT STANFORD, https://kinginstitute.stanford.edu/encyclopedia/rustin-bayard (last visited May 12, 2023).

18 David Smith, *"He never hid himself": The Incredible Life of Gay Civil Rights Leader Bayard Rustin*, GUARDIAN (Nov. 21, 2023), https://www.theguardian.com/film/2023/nov/21/bayard-rustin-movie-lgbt-civil-rights-netflix.
19 Carrie Maxwell, *Walter Naegle Keynotes Bayard Rustin Event*, WINDY CITY TIMES (Apr. 29, 2015), https://www.windycitytimes.com/lgbt/Walter-Naegle-keynotes-Bayard-Rustin-event/51329.html.
20 BAYARD RUSTIN, TWENTY-TWO DAYS ON THE CHAIN GANG AT ROXBORO, NORTH CAROLINA 5 (1947) (emphasis added).
21 *Id.*
22 *Id.* at 6.
23 *Id.* at 23.
24 *Id.* at 7.
25 Jennifer Roback, *Southern Labor Law in the Jim Crow Era: Exploitative or Competitive?*, 51 U. CHI. L. REV. 1161, 1170 (1984).
26 RUSTIN, *supra* note 20, at 8; *see also id.* at 23.
27 *Id.* at 8.
28 *Id.* at 20–21.
29 *Id.* at 14.
30 *Id.* at 27.
31 Howe, *supra* note 7, at 1016; Josephine Ross, *From Slavery to Prison in Rinkitink in Oz*, 20 S. CAL. INTERDISC. L.J. 107, 116 (2010).
32 North Carolina Statutes 1897, Chapter 270 at (1897), https://digital.ncdcr.gov/digital/collection/p249901coll22/id/228088.
33 North Carolina Statutes 1897, Chapter 54 at (1897), https://digital.ncdcr.gov/digital/collection/p249901coll22/id/227742.
34 13th Amendment, U.S. CONSTITUTION CENTER, https://constitutioncenter.org/interactive-constitution/amendment/amendment-xiii.
35 Sharon Dolovich, *State Punishment and Private Prisons*, 55 DUKE L.J. 437, 451 (2005).
36 Melvin Gutterman, *"Failure to Communicate" the Reel Prison Experience*, 55 SMU L. REV. 1515, 1528 (2002).
37 DOUGLAS A. BLACKMON, SLAVERY BY ANOTHER NAME: THE RE-ENSLAVEMENT OF BLACK AMERICANS FROM THE CIVIL WAR TO WORLD WAR II 55 (2012).
38 Stephen P. Garvey, *Freeing Prisoners' Labor*, 50 STAN. L. REV. 339, 356 (1998).
39 Christopher N. Lasch, *Rendition Resistance*, 92 N.C. L. REV. 149, 184 (2013).
40 Sharon Dolovich, *State Punishment and Private Prisons*, 55 DUKE L.J. 437, 452 (2005).
41 Garland E. Bayliss, *The Arkansas State Penitentiary Under Democratic Control, 1874–1896*, 34 ARK. HIST. Q. 195, 198 (1975).
42 David M. Oshinsky, *Convict Labor in the Post–Civil War South: Involuntary Servitude After the Thirteenth Amendment*, in THE PROMISES OF LIBERTY: THE HISTORY AND CONTEMPORARY RELEVANCE OF THE THIRTEENTH AMENDMENT 100, 101 (Tsesis Alexander ed., 2010).
43 BLACKMON, *supra* note 37, at 53.
44 Gutterman, *supra* note 36, at 1528–29.
45 Teri A. McMurtry-Chubb, *The Codification of Racism: Blacks, Criminal Sentencing, and the Legacy of Slavery in Georgia*, 31 T. MARSHALL L. REV. 139, 141 (2005).

NOTES

46 W. E. B. Du Bois, Notes on Negro Crime Particularly in Georgia 4 (1904), https://babel.hathitrust.org/cgi/pt?id=inu.32000001728924&seq=14&q1=%22penitentiary+rings%22.
47 Gutterman, *supra* note 7, at 1529.
48 Stephen B. Bright, *The Role of Race, Poverty, Intellectual Disability, and Mental Illness in the Decline of the Death Penalty*, 49 U. Rich. L. Rev. 671, 677 (2015).
49 Shaytonna V. Bullock, *Fee Simple Subject to Executory Interest: An Analysis of the Preemption and Revocation of Black Property Rights*, 12 S.J. Pol'y & Just. 205, 214 (2018).
50 Edward L. Rubin, *The Inevitability of Rehabilitation*, 19 Law & Ineq. 343, 357 (2001).
51 Alfreda Robinson, *Corporate Social Responsibility and African American Reparations: Jubilee*, 55 Rutgers L. Rev. 309, 354 (2003).
52 James Gray Pope, *Mass Incarceration, Convict Leasing, and the Thirteenth Amendment: A Revisionist Account*, 94 NYU L. Rev. 1465, 1514 (2019).
53 Howe, *supra* note 31, at 1012.
54 William Todd, *Convict Lease System*, New Georgia Encyclopedia (Dec. 12, 2005), https://www.georgiaencyclopedia.org/articles/history-archaeology/convict-lease-system/ ("Reports to then-governor Rufus Bullock indicated that leased convicts were being overworked, brutally whipped, and kill[ed] while under the care of Grant, Alexander, and Company.").
55 Edward L. Ayers, Vengeance & Justice: Crime and Punishment in 19th-Century American South 329 n. 23 (1984) (quoting Cable).
56 George Washington Cable, *The Convict Lease System* in The Silent South at 173 (1899).
57 Michael Woodiwiss, Organized Crime and American Power: A History 84 (2003).
58 Matt Clarke, *Texas Convict-Leasing Burial Ground Uncovered*, Prison Legal News (Jan. 8, 2020), https://www.prisonlegalnews.org/news/2020/jan/8/texas-convict-leasing-burial-ground-uncovered/.
59 *Prison Labor and the Private Sector, the Corporate Exploitation of Prison Labor Reaches Deep into the Supply Chain*, Worth Rises (Dec. 9, 2021), https://worthrises.org/blogpost/the-corporate-exploitation-of-prison-labor-reaches-deep-into-the-supply-chain.
60 Clarke, *supra* note 58.
61 Garvey, *supra* note 38, at 355–56.
62 *Id.* at 356–57; Howe, *supra* note 7, at 1010 ("In 1869, . . . Florida convicts soon found themselves working in railroad construction and in swampy turpentine forests infested with alligators and serpents.").
63 Richard Barry, *Slavery in the South To-Day*, The Cosmopolitan at 484 (Mar. 1907).
64 *Id.*
65 Robin Walker Sterling, *"Children Are Different": Implicit Bias, Rehabilitation, and the "New" Juvenile Jurisprudence*, 46 Loy. L.A. L. Rev. 1019, 1049–50 (2013) (internal citations omitted) (emphasis added).
66 *Convict Leasing*, Equal Justice Initiative (Nov. 1, 2013), https://eji.org/news/history-racial-injustice-convict-leasing/ (Library of Congress, Prints & Photographs Division) (showing photo of black boys in prison garb).

NOTES

67 Du Bois, *supra* note 46, at 4–5.
68 Robinson, *supra* note 51, at 346.
69 Ahmed A. White, *Rule of Law and the Limits of Sovereignty: The Private Prison in Jurisprudential Perspective*, 38 AM. CRIM. L. REV. 111, 128 (2001).
70 Ian F. Haney López, *Post-Racial Racism: Racial Stratification and Mass Incarceration in the Age of Obama*, 98 CALIF. L. REV. 1023, 1042 (2010).
71 Thomas Wheatley, *Chattahoochee Brick Site to Memorialize Convict Leasing Victim*, AXIOS (Dec. 1, 2021), https://www.axios.com/local/atlanta/2021/12/01/chattahoochee-brick-company-memorialize-convict-leasing-victims.
72 Kate Groetzinger, *Civil Rights Activists Push Lawmakers to Confront Texas' Dark History of Convict Leasing*, TEXAS OBSERVER (Mar. 26, 2019), https://www.texasobserver.org/civil-rights-activists-push-lawmakers-to-confront-texas-dark-history-of-convict-leasing/.
73 Garvey, *supra* note 38, at 356.
74 AYERS, *supra* note 55, at 195.
75 *Id.* (quoting minister Atticus Haygood).
76 *Id.*
77 *Id.* at 196.
78 GEORGE WASHINGTON CABLE, THE NEGRO QUESTION 150 (1890).
79 DU BOIS, *supra* note 46, at 5.
80 C. VANN WOODWARD, ORIGINS OF THE NEW SOUTH, 1877–1913 at 215 (1971); *see also* WILLIAM B. HESSELTINE & DAVID L. SMILEY, THE SOUTH IN AMERICAN HISTORY 460 (1960) ("The 'penitentiary ring;' was as unscrupulous and as corrupt . . . and [they] manipulated state legislatures [ ] cynically.").
81 *Acts of the State of Tennessee Passed at the Forty First Session of the General Assembly* at 350 (1879), https://babel.hathitrust.org/cgi/pt?id=uc1.b3693031&seq=356&q1=%22penitentiary+ring%22.
82 AYERS, *supra* note 55, at 123 (quoting a man named Dawson).
83 WOODIWISS, *supra* note 57, at 85 (internal citations omitted).
84 AYERS, *supra* note 55; *see also* ALEX S. VITALE, THE END OF POLICING 47 (2017) ("Local police were the essential front door of the twin evils of convict leasing and prison farms. . . . Sheriffs and judges also received kickbacks and in some cases generated list of fit and hardworking blacks to be incarcerated on behalf of employers, who would then lease them out to perform forced labor for profit.").
85 Bullock, *supra* note 49, at 214 (quoting reporter for *The Literary Digest*) (1914).
86 Gabriel J. Chin, *The Jena Six and the History of Racially Compromised Justice in Louisiana*, 44 HARV. C.R.-C.L. L. REV. 361, 372 (2009).
87 Garvey, *supra* note 38, at 356.
88 White, *supra* note 69, at 129–30 (quoting Ayers).
89 Howe, *supra* note 7, at 1009.
90 AYERS, *supra* note 55, at 195 (quoting former secretary of state Rufus Boyd).
91 Jeffrey A. Drobney, *Where Palm and Pine Are Blowing: Convict Labor in the North Florida Turpentine Industry, 1877–1923*, 72 (4) FL. HIST. Q. 431 (1994).
92 Haney López, *supra* note 70, at 1045 (quoting DOUGLAS A. BLACKMON, SLAVERY BY ANOTHER NAME: THE RE-ENSLAVEMENT OF BLACK PEOPLE IN AMERICA FROM THE CIVIL WAR TO WORLD WAR II 380) (2008).
93 Chin, *supra* note 86, at 374.

NOTES

94 Margie Mason & Robin McDowell, *Locked Up: The Prison Labor That Built Business Empires*, AP (Sept. 22, 2022), https://apnews.com/article/ap-investigation-convict-leasing-reveal-podcast-71bcdbeff840ff4bfbbea48ea50a1cb5.
95 Haney López, *supra* note 70, at 1042–43.
96 Ellen Terrell, *The Convict Leasing System: Slavery in its Worst Aspects*, LIBRARY OF CONGRESS (June 17, 2021), https://blogs.loc.gov/inside_adams/2021/06/convict-leasing-system/.
97 MATTHEW J. MANCINI, ONE DIES, GET ANOTHER: CONVICT LEASING IN THE AMERICAN SOUTH, 1866–1928 105 (2006).
98 Mason & McDowell, *supra* note 94.
99 CAPTIVE LABOR: EXPLOITATION OF INCARCERATED WORKERS, ACLU 41 (2022).
100 *Prison Industry Enhancement Certification Program (PIECP)*, DOJ (Mar. 14, 2023), https://bja.ojp.gov/program/piecp/overview.
101 CAPTIVE LABOR, *supra* note 99, at 71.
102 Chris Hedges, *The Slaves Rebel Hundreds of Prisoners Across 17 States Are Striking over Pay and Horrific Living Conditions*, TRUTH DIG (Sept. 3, 2018), https://www.truthdig.com/articles/the-slaves-rebel/
103 CAPTIVE LABOR, *supra* note 99, at 9.
104 *Id.* at 44.
105 *Id.* at 46.
106 *Id.* at 41–42.
107 *Where to Buy, Zip Code Search for Tampa Bay*, T. G. LEE, https://tgleedairy.com/where-to-buy/ (last visited May 25, 2023).
108 *Plugra European Style Unsalted Butter*, CHEESE SHOP SANTA BARBARA, https://www.cheeseshopsb.com/products/baguette-yrhxe-jxzgf-ss8lg-pnc7k-ydplt-ppy92-dxhr7-5aag4-ckd82-5r639-6a8rc-dfjzr-fch6f-ebpsl-tsbe6 (last visited May 25, 2023); *European Style Butter Plugra*, IGOURMET, https://igourmet.com/products/butter (last visited May 25, 2023).
109 CAPTIVE LABOR, *supra* note 99, at 42.
110 *Id.* at 41 and 42.
111 *Id.* at 41.
112 *Id.* at 42.
113 *Id.*
114 *Id.* at 43.
115 Madison Pauly, *Jail Inmates Worked for a $16 Billion Company Without Pay*, MOTHER JONES (Jan. 6, 2020), https://www.motherjones.com/crime-justice/2020/01/alameda-santa-rita-jail-aramark-unpaid-wages-lawsuit/.
116 Erica C. Barnett, *Prison Coffee Starbucks Admits Its Contractor Uses Prison Labor*, SEATTLE WEEKLY (Oct. 9, 2006), https://www.seattleweekly.com/news/prison-coffee/.
117 Rick Bragg, *Chain Gangs to Return to Roads of Alabama*, N.Y. TIMES (Mar. 26, 1995) at 9.
118 *Nebraska Amendment 1, Remove Slavery as Punishment for Crime from Constitution Amendment (2020)*, BALLOTPEDIA (2020), https://ballotpedia.org/Nebraska_Amendment_1,_Remove_Slavery_as_Punishment_for_Crime_from_Constitution_Amendment_(2020).
119 *Wesberry v. Sanders*, 376 U.S. 1, 17 (1964).

[223]

120 Pamela S. Karlan, *Ballots and Bullets: The Exceptional History of the Right to Vote*, 71 U. CIN. L. REV. 1345 (2003).
121 Richard Briffault, *The Contested Right to Vote*, 100 MICH. L. REV. 1506, 1522 (2002).
122 Brandon Rottinghaus, *Incarceration and Enfranchisement: International Practices, Impact, and Recommendations for Reform*, PRISON POLICY 22 (June–July 2003), https://www.prisonpolicy.org/scans/08_18_03_Manatt_Brandon_Rottinghaus.pdf.
123 *Out of Step with the World: An Analysis of Felony Disenfranchisement in the U.S. and Other Democracies*, AMERICAN CIVIL LIBERTIES UNION 4 (2006), https://www.aclu.org/sites/default/files/pdfs/votingrights/outofstep_20060525.pdf.
124 *Hirst v. United Kingdom* (no. 2), 74025/01, ECHR 681 (2005).
125 Nicole Lewis, *In Just Two States, All Prisoners Can Vote. Here's Why Few Do*, MARSHALL PROJECT (June 11, 2019) https://www.themarshallproject.org/2019/06/11/in-just-two-states-all-prisoners-can-vote-here-s-why-few-do.
126 ME. Rev. Stat. Ann. tit. 21, § 115 (2001); VT. Stat. Ann. tit. 17, § 2121 (2002).
127 Restore the Vote Amendment Act of 2020, D.C. Law 23–277 (Apr. 27, 2021); DC Board of Elections, *Incarcerated Voters & Returning Citizens*, https://www.dcboe.org/Voters/How-to-Vote/FAQ%E2%80%99s-for-Incarcerated-Voters-Returning-Citizens (last visited May 4, 2023).
128 *See* Ala. Const. Art. VIII, § 177; Alaska Const. Art. V, § 2; Ariz. Const. Art. VII, § 2; Ark. Const. Art. III, §§ 1, 2 and Ark. Const. Amend. LI, § 11; Cal. Const. Art. II, § 4; Colo. Const. Art. VII, § 10; Conn. Const. Art. VI, § 3; Del. Const. Art. V, § 2; Fla. Const. Art. VI, § 4; Ga. Const. Art. II, § 1, para. III; Haw. Const. Art. II, § 2; Idaho Const. Art. VI, § 3; Ill. Const. Art. III, § 2; Ind. Const. Art. II, § 8; Iowa Const. Art. II, § 5; Kan. Const. Art. V, § 2; Ky. Const. § 145; La. Const. Art. I, §§ 10, 20; Md. Const. Art. I, § 4; Mass. Const. Amend. Art. III; Mich. Const. Art. II, § 2; Minn. Const. Art. VII, § 1; Miss. Const. Art. XII, § 241; Mo. Const. Art. VIII, § 2; Mont. Const. Art. IV, § 2; Neb. Const. Art. VI, § 2; Nev. Const. Art. II, § 1; N.H. Const. Pt. 1, Art. XI; N.J. Const. Art. II, §§ 1, 7; N.M. Const. Art. VII, § 1; N.Y. Const. Art. II, § 3; N.C. Const. Art. VI, § 2; N.D. Const. Art. II, § 2; Ohio Const. Art. V, § 4; Or. Const. Art. II, § 3; R.I. Const. Art. II, § 1; S.C. Const. Art. II, § 7; S.D. Const. Art. VII, § 2; Tenn. Const. Art. I, § 5 and Tenn. Const. Art. IV, § 2; Tex. Const. Art. VI, § 1; Utah Const. Art. IV, § 6; Va. Const. Art. II, § 1; Wash. Const. Art. VI, § 3; W. Va. Const. Art. IV, § 1; Wis. Const. Art. III, § 2; and Wyo. Const. Art. VI, § 6.
129 *Davis v. Beason*, 133 U. S. 333, 345–347 (1890).
130 *Simmons v. Galvin*, 575 F.2d 24, 31 (1st Cir. 2009).
131 *Felony Disenfranchisement Laws (Map)*, ACLU (2023), https://www.aclu.org/issues/voting-rights/voter-restoration/felony-disenfranchisement-laws-map.
132 *Felon Voting Rights*, NATIONAL CONFERENCE OF STATE LEGISLATURES (June 28, 2021), https://www.ncsl.org/research/elections-and-campaigns/felon-voting-rights.aspx.
133 Press Release, *Groups Applaud Governor Whitmer for Signing Legislation Automatically Registering People to Vote as They Leave Prison*, SENTENCING PROJECT (Nov. 30, 2023), https://www.sentencingproject.org/press-releases/groups-applaud-governor-whitmer-for-signing-legislation-automatically-registering-people-to-vote-as-they-leave-prison/.
134 Jeff Manza & Christopher Uggen, *Locked Out: Felon Disenfranchisement and American Democracy* 37–39, 235 (2006).

NOTES

135 Neel U. Sukhatme, Alexander Billy & Gaurav Bagwe, *Felony Financial Disenfranchisement*, 75 VAN. L. REV. 1, 7 (2023).
136 REPORT OF THE PROCEEDINGS AND DEBATES OF THE CONSTITUTIONAL CONVENTION OF VIRGINIA HELD IN THE CITY OF RICHMOND JUNE 12, 1901 TO JUNE 26, 1902, VOLUME 2, 3076 (1906) (quoting Glass).
137 *Harvey v. Brewer*, 605 F.3d 1067, 1079 (9th Cir. 2010) (citing *Richardson*, 418 U.S. at 26–27).
138 George Brooks, *Felon Disenfranchisement: Law, History, Policy, and Politics*, 32 FORDHAM URB. L.J. 851, 852–853 (2005).
139 75 Ala. 582, 585 (1884).
140 George P. Fletcher, *Disenfranchisement as Punishment: Reflections on the Racial Uses of Infamia*, 46 UCLA L. REV. 1895, 1899 (1999).
141 Art. II Sec. 1 Cal. Const. (1972).
142 *Richardson v. Ramirez*, 418 U.S. 24, 43 (1974).
143 Richard W. Bourne, Richardson v. Ramirez: *A Motion To Reconsider*, 42 VAL. U. L. REV. 1, 4 (2007).
144 U.S. CONST. amend. 14, §2 (emphasis added).
145 Ethan Herenstein & Yurij Rudensky, *The Penalty Clause and the Fourteenth Amendment's Consistency on Universal Representation*, 96 NYU L. REV. 1021 (2021).
146 Fletcher, *supra* note 140, at 1900–02 (criticizing *Richardson* as a contrary reading of the Fourteenth Amendment, which was designed to prevent disenfranchisement).
147 *Richardson v. Ramirez*, 418 U.S. 24, 74 (1974) (Marshall, J., dissenting).
148 *Id.* at 76.
149 *Trop v. Dulles*, 356 U.S. 86, 96 (1958) (Holding that permanent felon disenfranchisement does not constitute cruel and unusual punishment under the Eighth Amendment); *Thiess v. State Administrative Bd. of Election Laws, State of Md.*, 387 F. Supp. 1038 (D. Md. 1974), Otsuka v. Hite, 44 Cal. Rptr. 251 (App. 2d Dist. 1965).
150 *Green v. Board of Elections of City of New York*, 380 F.2d 445 (2d Cir. 1967); *King v. City of Boston*, 2004 WL 1070573 (D. Mass. 2004).
151 *Hayden v. Pataki*, 2004 WL 1335921 (S.D. N.Y. 2004); *Howard v. Gilmore*, 205 F.3d 1333 (4th Cir. 2000); *Texas Supporters of Workers World Party Presidential Candidates v. Strake*, 511 F. Supp. 149 (S.D. Tex. 1981).
152 *Written Testimony of the Alabama Voting Rights Project Before the U.S. House of Representatives Committee on Administration Subcommittee on Elections*, CAMPAIGN LEGAL CENTER (May 13, 2019), https://campaignlegal.org/sites/default/files/2019-10/AVRP%20Testimony%20Subcommittee%20on%20Elections.pdf.
153 *Felony Disenfranchisement Laws (Map)*, ACLU (2023), https://www.aclu.org/issues/voting-rights/voter-restoration/felony-disenfranchisement-laws-map.
154 Christopher Uggen, Ryan Larson & Sarah Shannon, *6 Million Lost Voters: State-Level Estimates of Felony Disenfranchisement, 2016*, SENTENCING PROJECT (Oct. 6, 2016), https://www.sentencingproject.org/app/uploads/2022/08/6-Million-Lost-Voters.pdf.
155 Frances Robles, *1.4 Million Floridians With Felonies Win Long-Denied Right to Vote*, N.Y. TIMES (Nov. 7, 2018), https://www.nytimes.com/2018/11/07/us/florida-felon-voting-rights.html.
156 Gabriel J. Chin & Richard W. Holmes Jr, *Effective Assistance of Counsel and the Consequences of Guilty Pleas*, 87 CORNELL L. REV. 697 (2002).

157 *Florida's Amendment 4*, 60 MINUTES (Sept. 20, 2020), https://www.cbs.com/shows/60_minutes/video/82FxqM_9J_ZbXpQb1PmxLFZ9BykZXlGg/florida-s-amendment-4-the-wall-sir-david/.
158 *See* FLA. CONST. art. VI, § 4(a) (1968).
159 Bianca Fortes, *A Government Official Helped Them Register. Now They've Been Charged with Voter Fraud*, PRO PUBLICA (July 21, 2022), https://www.propublica.org/article/florida-felonies-voter-fraud.
160 1845 Fla. Laws. Ch. 38, art. 2 § 3.
161 David Schultz & Sarah Clark, *Wealth v. Democracy: The Unfulfilled Promise of The Twenty-Fourth Amendment*, 29 QUINNIPIAC L. REV. 375 (2011).
162 FLA. CONST. art. VI § 4 (1968).
163 FLA. CONST. art. VI, § 4 (1885); Fla. Const. art. VI, § 4 (1968); this was changed by Amendment 4 in 2019.
164 Samantha J. Gross, *Florida Voters Approve Amendment 4 to Restore Felon's Voting Rights*, SAN DIEGO UNION TRIBUNE A14 (Mar. 7, 2020).
165 FLA. CONST. art. VI, § 4 (2019); FLA. STAT. §98.0751.
166 Dalia Figueredo, *Affording the Franchise: Amendment 4 & The Senate Bill 7066 Litigation*, 72 FLA. L. REV. 1135, 1137 (2020).
167 *Jones v. DeSantis*, 410 F.Supp.3d 1284, 1291 (N.D. Fla. 2019).
168 *SB 7066: Election Administration*, FLA. SENATE (2019), https://www.flsenate.gov/Session/Bill/2019/07066.
169 Fortes, *supra* note 159.
170 *Jones v. Governor of Florida*, 950 F.3d 795, 804 (11th Cir. 2020).
171 Daniel A. Smith, Second Supplemental Report, *Jones v. DeSantis* 8 (2020).
172 *Jones v. DeSantis*, 462 F.Supp. 3d 1196, 1204 (N. D. Fla. 2019).
173 *Id.* at 1219–20.
174 *Jones v. Governor of Florida*, 975 F.3d 1016 (11th Cir. 2020) (en banc).
175 *Raysor v. DeSantis*, No. 20–12003 (U.S. 2020) (stay denied).
176 Joshua M. Feinzig, *Felon Re-Enfranchisement and the Problem of "Lost" Rights*, 131 YALE L. J. FORUM 689, 690 (2022).
177 Fortes, *supra* note 159.
178 Eliza Sweren-Becker, *Florida Law Throws Voter Rights Restoration into Chaos*, BRENNAN CENTER (July 11, 2019), https://www.brennancenter.org/our-work/analysis-opinion/florida-law-throws-voter-rights-restoration-chaos.
179 Fortes, *supra* note 159.
180 Gabriel J. Chin, *Collateral Consequences and Criminal Justice: Future Policy and Constitutional Directions*, 102 MARQ. L. REV. 233, 254 (2018).
181 American Bar Association, *Ten Guidelines on Court Fines and Fees*, REPORT TO THE HOUSE OF DELEGATES (Aug. 2018), https://finesandfeesjusticecenter.org/content/uploads/2018/12/Ten-Guidelines-on-Court-Fines-and-Fees.pdf.
182 Anthony Izaguirre, *Florida Governor Signs Bill Creating Election Police Unit*, AP (Apr. 25, 2022), https://apnews.com/article/2022-midterm-elections-covid-health-crime-florida-5fad57fac85e0944b6e8eeb423b195b7.
183 Bianca Padró Ocasio & Mary Ellen Klas, *DeSantis Announces 20 Voter Fraud Arrests of Floridians, Calls it an "Opening Salvo,"* TAMPA BAY TIMES (Aug. 18, 2022), https://www.tampabay.com/news/florida-politics/elections/2022/08/18/desantis-announces-20-arrests-of-floridians-for-voter-fraud/.

184 Lawrence Mower, *Police Cameras Show Confusion, Anger over DeSantis' Voter Fraud Arrests*, Tampa Bay Times (Oct. 18, 2022), https://www.tampabay.com/news/florida-politics/2022/10/18/body-camera-video-police-voter-fraud-desantis-arrests/#:~:text=Body%2Dworn%20camera%20footage%20recorded,of%20Election%20Crimes%20and%20Security.

185 Alex Woodward, *They Were Arrested for Voter Fraud in Florida. They Didn't Know They Were Ineligible*, Independent (Aug. 27, 2022), https://www.independent.co.uk/news/world/americas/crime/florida-voter-fraud-arrests-ron-desantis-b2154180.html.

186 Mower, *supra* note 184.

187 *Id.*

188 Maryam Saleh & Ese Olumhense, *DeSantis' Election Police Have Largely Flopped in Florida Voter Prosecutions*, Reveal News (Mar. 9, 2023), https://revealnews.org/article/desantis-election-police-have-largely-flopped-in-florida-voter-prosecutions-a-new-law-aims-to-change-that/.

189 Michaela Mulligan, *Tampa Man Who Was First to Face Trial for Florida Voter Fraud in 2020 Election Gets Probation*, Tampa Bay Times (Feb. 27, 2023), https://www.tampabay.com/news/florida-politics/2023/02/27/tampa-man-who-was-first-face-trial-florida-voter-fraud-2020-election-gets-probation/.

190 *Id.*

191 *Id.*

192 Justin Rohrlich, *DeSantis Conveniently Missed This Case in His Voter Fraud Crusade*, Daily Beast (May 23, 2023), https://www.thedailybeast.com/ron-desantis-conveniently-missed-this-case-in-his-voter-fraud-crusade.

193 *Id.*

194 *Id.*

195 Mike DeForest, *4th Resident of The Villages Admits to Voting Twice in the 2020 Election*, Click Orlando (Jan. 30, 2023), https://www.clickorlando.com/news/local/2023/01/30/4th-resident-of-the-villages-admits-to-voting-twice-in-the-2020-election/.

196 Kevin Krajick, *Why Can't Ex-Felons Vote?*, Wash. Post (Aug. 18, 2004), https://www.washingtonpost.com/archive/opinions/2004/08/18/why-cant-ex-felons-vote/53a30460-1bb1-4cd9-9d05-17016c8fea96/.

197 Michael Morse, *The Future of Felon Disenfranchisement Reform: Evidence from the Campaign to Restore Voting Rights in Florida*, 109 Cal. Law Rev. 1143, 1175 (2021).

198 *Corporate Contributions to Outside Groups 2022*, OpenSecrets, https://www.opensecrets.org/outside-spending/corporate-contributions/2022; *Corporate Contributions to Outside Groups 2020*, OpenSecrets, https://www.opensecrets.org/outside-spending/corporate-contributions/2020; *Corporate Contributions to Outside Groups 2018*, OpenSecrets, https://www.opensecrets.org/outside-spending/corporate-contributions/2018 (last visited June 28, 2023).

199 *Gubernatorial Candidates in Florida 2022*, Follow the Money, https://www.followthemoney.org/show-me?s=FL&y=2022&c-r-ot=G&gro=c-t-id (last visited Dec. 6, 2023).

200 *Gubernatorial Candidates in Florida 2018*, Follow the Money, https://www.followthemoney.org/show-me?s=FL&y=2018&c-r-ot=G&gro=c-t-id (last visited Dec. 6, 2023).

201 *International Payout Systems Inc.*, Follow the Money, https://www.followthemoney.org/entity-details?eid=55111271&default=contributor (last visited Dec. 6, 2023) (listing Crist).

202 *Ghh Inc.*, Follow the Money, https://www.followthemoney.org/entity-details?eid=1620998&default=contributor (last visited Dec. 6, 2023) (listing Crist).
203 *P&T Construction Inc.*, Follow the Money, https://www.followthemoney.org/entity-details?eid=25763016&default=contributor (last visited Dec. 6, 2023) (listing Crist).
204 *Retail Services & Systems*, Follow the Money, https://www.followthemoney.org/entity-details?eid=4593436&default=contributor (last visited Dec. 6, 2023) (listing Crist).
205 *Golden Rule Financial Corp.*, Follow the Money, https://www.followthemoney.org/entity-details?eid=3803&default=contributor (last visited Dec. 6, 2023) (listing Crist).
206 *Legal Consultants Inc.*, Follow the Money, https://www.followthemoney.org/entity-details?eid=16301203&default=contributor (last visited Dec. 6, 2023) (listing Crist).
207 *Printconsultant Inc.*, Follow the Money, https://www.followthemoney.org/entity-details?eid=43898828&default=contributor (last visited Dec. 6, 2023) (listing Crist).
208 *Integrated Data Technology Inc.*, Follow the Money, https://www.followthemoney.org/entity-details?eid=55111270&default=contributor (last visited Dec. 6, 2023) (listing Crist).
209 *S/R Service & Support Corp.*, Follow the Money, https://www.followthemoney.org/entity-details?eid=152046&default=contributor (last visited Dec. 6, 2023) (listing Crist).
210 *City Wise Florida Inc.*, Follow the Money, https://www.followthemoney.org/entity-details?eid=57021888&default=contributor (last visited Dec. 6, 2023) (listing Crist).
211 *Abrikant International Corp.*, Follow the Money, https://www.followthemoney.org/entity-details?eid=55111150&default=contributor (last visited Dec. 6, 2023) (listing Crist).
212 *Liberty Mutual Co.*, Follow the Money, https://www.followthemoney.org/entity-details?eid=1540&default=contributor (last visited Dec. 6, 2023) (listing Gillum).
213 *Brown & Brown of Louisiana*, Follow the Money, https://www.followthemoney.org/entity-details?eid=10600&default=contributor (last visited Dec. 6, 2023) (listing Gillum).
214 *Universal Bond Inc.*, Follow the Money, https://www.followthemoney.org/entity-details?eid=205263&default=contributor (last visited Dec. 6, 2023) (listing Gillum).
215 *American Income Life Insurance Co.*, Follow the Money, https://www.followthemoney.org/entity-details?eid=688365&default=contributor (last visited Dec. 6, 2023) (listing Gillum).
216 *Frontier Communications*, Follow the Money, https://www.followthemoney.org/entity-details?eid=3319315&default=contributor (last visited Dec. 6, 2023) (listing Gillum).
217 *Desoto Beach Development Corp.*, Follow the Money, https://www.followthemoney.org/entity-details?eid=45685416&default=contributor (last visited Dec. 6, 2023) (listing Gillum).
218 *Halifax Injury Physicians*, Follow the Money, https://www.followthemoney.org/entity-details?eid=45882078&default=contributor (last visited Dec. 6, 2023) (listing Gillum).
219 *Johnson Armor Correctional Health Inc.*, Follow the Money, https://www.followthemoney.org/entity-details?eid=46395191&default=contributor (last visited Dec. 6, 2023) (listing Gillum).
220 *Servium Group Inc.*, Follow the Money, https://www.followthemoney.org/entity-details?eid=46603857&default=contributor (last visited Dec. 6, 2023) (listing Gillum).

NOTES

221 *Espmedia Corp.*, FOLLOW THE MONEY, https://www.followthemoney.org/entity-details?eid=19861310&default=contributor (last visited Dec. 6, 2023) (listing Gillum).

222 *Disruptor Inc.*, FOLLOW THE MONEY, https://www.followthemoney.org/entity-details?eid=16661941&default=contributor (last visited Dec. 6, 2023) (listing DeSantis).

223 *Sun Labs USA*, FOLLOW THE MONEY, https://www.followthemoney.org/entity-details?eid=42034241&default=contributor (last visited Dec. 6, 2023) (listing DeSantis).

224 *Hutson Companies*, FOLLOW THE MONEY, https://www.followthemoney.org/entity-details?eid=1286&default=contributor (last visited Dec. 6, 2023) (listing DeSantis).

225 *Florida Care*, FOLLOW THE MONEY, https://www.followthemoney.org/entity-details?eid=55756111&default=contributor (last visited Dec. 6, 2023) (listing DeSantis).

226 *Phillips & Jordan Inc.*, FOLLOW THE MONEY, https://www.followthemoney.org/entity-details?eid=1704342&default=contributor (last visited Dec. 6, 2023) (listing DeSantis).

227 *JM Family Enterprises*, FOLLOW THE MONEY, https://www.followthemoney.org/entity-details?eid=1389&default=contributor (last visited Dec. 6, 2023) (listing DeSantis).

228 *Daytona Toyota*, FOLLOW THE MONEY, https://www.followthemoney.org/entity-details?eid=1967675&default=contributor (last visited Dec. 6, 2023) (listing DeSantis).

229 *Fidelity National Financial*, FOLLOW THE MONEY, https://www.followthemoney.org/entity-details?eid=55439719&default=contributor (last visited Dec. 6, 2023) (listing DeSantis).

230 *Hillcour*, FOLLOW THE MONEY, https://www.followthemoney.org/entity-details?eid=43891544&default=contributor (last visited Dec. 6, 2023) (listing DeSantis).

231 *IGAS USA*, FOLLOW THE MONEY, https://www.followthemoney.org/entity-details?eid=49104831&default=contributor (last visited Dec. 6, 2023) (listing DeSantis).

232 *Anderson Columbia Co.*, FOLLOW THE MONEY, https://www.followthemoney.org/entity-details?eid=201&default=contributor (last visited Dec. 6, 2023) (listing DeSantis).

233 *Testing Matters*, FOLLOW THE MONEY, https://www.followthemoney.org/entity-details?eid=52475299&default=contributor (last visited Dec. 6, 2023) (listing DeSantis).

234 *Dosal Tobacco*, FOLLOW THE MONEY, https://www.followthemoney.org/entity-details?eid=836&default=contributor (last visited Dec. 6, 2023) (listing DeSantis).

235 *Eisenhower Management Inc.*, FOLLOW THE MONEY, https://www.followthemoney.org/entity-details?eid=49104835&default=contributor (last visited Dec. 6, 2023) (listing DeSantis).

236 *United Automobile Insurance Co.*, FOLLOW THE MONEY, https://www.followthemoney.org/entity-details?eid=2680&default=contributor (last visited Dec. 6, 2023) (listing DeSantis).

237 *Southern Wine & Spirits*, FOLLOW THE MONEY, https://www.followthemoney.org/entity-details?eid=2433&default=contributor (last visited Dec. 6, 2023) (listing DeSantis).

238 *CFG Community Bank*, FOLLOW THE MONEY, https://www.followthemoney.org/entity-details?eid=4721064&default=contributor (last visited Dec. 6, 2023) (listing DeSantis).

239 *JL: Holding Corp.*, FOLLOW THE MONEY, https://www.followthemoney.org/entity-details?eid=54980510&default=contributor (last visited Dec. 6, 2023) (listing DeSantis).

240 *South Development Corp.*, FOLLOW THE MONEY, https://www.followthemoney.org/entity-details?eid=54990135&default=contributor (last visited Dec. 6, 2023) (listing DeSantis).

NOTES

241 *Payward Inc.*, Follow the Money, https://www.followthemoney.org/entity-details?eid=57018347&default=contributor (last visited Dec. 6, 2023) (listing DeSantis).
242 *Hudson Capital Group*, Follow the Money, https://www.followthemoney.org/entity-details?eid=39064&default=contributor (last visited Dec. 6, 2023) (listing DeSantis).
243 *JB Coxwell Contracting Inc.*, Follow the Money, https://www.followthemoney.org/entity-details?eid=2214566&default=contributor (last visited Dec. 6, 2023) (listing DeSantis).
244 *ABC Fine Wine & Spirits*, Follow the Money, https://www.followthemoney.org/entity-details?eid=34978&default=contributor (last visited Dec. 6, 2023) (listing DeSantis).
245 *SPF Roofing Systems Inc.*, Follow the Money, https://www.followthemoney.org/entity-details?eid=40803225&default=contributor (last visited Dec. 6, 2023) (listing DeSantis).
246 *Ring Power Corp.*, Follow the Money, https://www.followthemoney.org/entity-details?eid=2230&default=contributor (last visited Dec. 6, 2023) (listing DeSantis).
247 *Middlesex Corp.*, Follow the Money, https://www.followthemoney.org/entity-details?eid=696978&default=contributor (last visited Dec. 6, 2023) (listing DeSantis).
248 *Publix Super Markets*, Follow the Money, https://www.followthemoney.org/entity-details?eid=2131&default=contributor (last visited Dec. 6, 2023) (listing DeSantis).
249 *Nomi Health Inc.*, Follow the Money, https://www.followthemoney.org/entity-details?eid=53408322&default=contributor (last visited Dec. 6, 2023) (listing DeSantis).
250 *Dentaquest*, Follow the Money, https://www.followthemoney.org/entity-details?eid=50474&default=contributor (last visited Dec. 6, 2023) (listing DeSantis).
251 *R & L Transfer Inc.*, Follow the Money, https://www.followthemoney.org/entity-details?eid=58163447&default=contributor (last visited Dec. 6, 2023) (listing DeSantis).
252 *Lewis Bear Co.*, Follow the Money, https://www.followthemoney.org/entity-details?eid=37207&default=contributor (last visited Dec. 6, 2023) (listing DeSantis).
253 *St. Joe co.*, Follow the Money, https://www.followthemoney.org/entity-details?eid=2452&default=contributor (last visited Dec. 6, 2023) (listing DeSantis).
254 *ICI Homes*, Follow the Money, https://www.followthemoney.org/entity-details?eid=26787106&default=contributor (last visited Dec. 6, 2023) (listing DeSantis).
255 *American Property & Casualty Insurance Associates*, Follow the Money, https://www.followthemoney.org/entity-details?eid=1486025&default=contributor (last visited Dec. 6, 2023) (listing DeSantis).
256 *Sunshine Gasoline Distributors*, Follow the Money, https://www.followthemoney.org/entity-details?eid=2516&default=contributor (last visited Dec. 6, 2023) (listing DeSantis).
257 *Jacksonville Kennel Club*, Follow the Money, https://www.followthemoney.org/entity-details?eid=170383&default=contributor (last visited Dec. 6, 2023) (listing DeSantis).
258 *Managed Care of North America*, Follow the Money, https://www.followthemoney.org/entity-details?eid=12611724&default=contributor (last visited Dec. 6, 2023) (listing DeSantis).
259 *Palm Beach Kennel Club*, Follow the Money, https://www.followthemoney.org/entity-details?eid=4233&default=contributor (last visited Dec. 6, 2023) (listing DeSantis).

260 *Vecellio Group*, FOLLOW THE MONEY, https://www.followthemoney.org/entity-details?eid=66329&default=contributor (last visited Dec. 6, 2023) (listing DeSantis).
261 *Cheney Brothers Inc.*, FOLLOW THE MONEY, https://www.followthemoney.org/entity-details?eid=2025249&default=contributor (last visited Dec. 6, 2023) (listing DeSantis).
262 *Launched*, FOLLOW THE MONEY, https://www.followthemoney.org/entity-details?eid=52468386&default=contributor (last visited Dec. 6, 2023) (listing DeSantis).
263 *Teco Energy*, FOLLOW THE MONEY, https://www.followthemoney.org/entity-details?eid=2567&default=contributor (last visited Dec. 6, 2023) (listing DeSantis).
264 *Mastec Inc.*, FOLLOW THE MONEY, https://www.followthemoney.org/entity-details?eid=2005174&default=contributor (last visited Dec. 6, 2023) (listing DeSantis).
265 *Charter Communications LLC*, FOLLOW THE MONEY, https://www.followthemoney.org/entity-details?eid=557&default=contributor (last visited Dec. 6, 2023) (listing DeSantis).
266 *Dream Finders Homes*, FOLLOW THE MONEY, https://www.followthemoney.org/entity-details?eid=16251779&default=contributor (last visited Dec. 6, 2023) (listing DeSantis).
267 *United Health Group*, FOLLOW THE MONEY, https://www.followthemoney.org/entity-details?eid=2692&default=contributor (last visited Dec. 6, 2023) (listing DeSantis).
268 *Centene Corp.*, FOLLOW THE MONEY, https://www.followthemoney.org/entity-details?eid=528&default=contributor (last visited Dec. 6, 2023) (listing DeSantis).
269 *Walt Disney*, FOLLOW THE MONEY, https://www.followthemoney.org/entity-details?eid=2025249&default=contributor (last visited Dec. 6, 2023) (listing DeSantis).
270 *Florida Power & Light*, FOLLOW THE MONEY, https://www.followthemoney.org/entity-details?eid=3741 (last visited Dec. 6, 2023) (listing DeSantis).
271 *Nextera Energy*, FOLLOW THE MONEY, https://www.followthemoney.org/entity-details?eid=1039 (last visited Dec. 6, 2023) (listing DeSantis).
272 *Reynolds American*, FOLLOW THE MONEY, https://www.followthemoney.org/entity-details?eid=2218&default=contributor (last visited Dec. 6, 2023) (listing DeSantis).
273 *Humana*, FOLLOW THE MONEY, https://www.followthemoney.org/entity-details?eid=1277&default=contributor (last visited Dec. 6, 2023) (listing DeSantis).
274 *International Game Technology*, FOLLOW THE MONEY, https://www.followthemoney.org/entity-details?eid=1336&default=contributor (last visited Dec. 6, 2023) (listing DeSantis).
275 *Telecommunications Contributions to DeSantis*, FOLLOW THE MONEY, https://www.followthemoney.org/show-me?dt=1&f-fc=2&c-t-eid=17657831&d-et=3&y=2022&d-ccb=63#[{1|gro=d-id (last visited Dec. 6, 2023) (listing AT&T).
276 *Duke Energy*, FOLLOW THE MONEY, https://www.followthemoney.org/show-me?dt=1&y=2022&f-fc=2&c-t-eid=17657831&d-et=3&d-ccb=84&d-eid=856 (last visited Dec. 6, 2023) (listing DeSantis).
277 *GEO Group*, FOLLOW THE MONEY, https://www.followthemoney.org/entity-details?eid=1096&default=contributor (last visited Dec. 6, 2023) (listing DeSantis); *see also* Steven Donziger, *The Prison-Industrial Complex: What's Really Driving the Rush to Lock 'Em Up*, WASH. POST, Mar. 17, 1996, at C3.
278 Samuel Ludington, Comment, *Publicly Traded Justice*, 29 BUS. L. REV. 93, 107 (Spring 2021) ("One of the lobbyists employed by the GEO Group in 2019 is Pam Biondi, who served as the Florida Attorney General from 2011 to 2019."); Paul Ashton & Amanda Petteruti, *Gaming the System: How the Political Strategies of Private Prison Companies*

Promote Ineffective Incarceration Policies, JUSTICE POLICY INST., 22 & 24 (June 2011), http://www.justicepolicy.org/uploads/justicepolicy/documents/gaming_the_system.pdf (private prison companies have hired lobbyists in Florida and spent millions in elections across the nation).

4. CORPORATE BRIBERY

1 *Oakes Ames*, PBS, https://www.pbs.org/wgbh/americanexperience/features/tcrr-ames/ (last visited June 4, 2023).
2 *Id.*
3 Andrew Glass, *Crédit Mobilier Scandal Exposed, Sept. 4, 1872*, POLITICO (Sept. 4, 2015) https://www.politico.com/story/2015/08/thisday-0904-213171.
4 *Id.*
5 Roger D. Billings, *2012 Legal Heritage of the Civil War Issue: The Homestead Act, Pacific Railroad Act, and Morrill Act*, 39 NORTHERN KY. L. REV. 699, 707 (2012); Rebekah Crowe, *A Madman and a Visionary: George Francis Train, Speculation, and the Territorial Development of the Great Plains*, 34 (1) GREAT PLAINS Q. 35–61 (2014), https://doi.org/10.1353/gpq.2014.0003.
6 *Id.*
7 Paul Kens, *The Crédit Mobilier Scandal and the Supreme Court: Corporate Power, Corporate Person, and Government Control in the Mid-Nineteenth Century*, 34 J. SUP. CT. HIST. 170, 170 (2009).
8 *Id.*
9 Billings, *supra* note 5, at 707.
10 *Id.* at 707–08.
11 Kens, *supra* note 7, at 172.
12 *Id.* at 172.
13 *Id.*
14 Robert Mitchell, *Buying "Friends in this Congress": The Smoking Gun That Triggered a Political Scandal*, WASH. POST (July 18, 2017), https://www.washingtonpost.com/news/retropolis/wp/2017/07/18/buying-friends-in-this-congress-the-smoking-gun-that-triggered-a-political-scandal/ (quoting a letter between Ames and Holcomb).
15 *Oakes Ames*, *supra* note 1.
16 Billings, *supra* note 5, at 708; Abraham Bell & Gideon Parchomovsky, *Givings*, 111 YALE L.J. 547, 576–77 (2001).
17 Glass, *supra* note 3.
18 *The Crédit Mobilier Scandal*, PBS, https://www.pbs.org/wgbh/americanexperience/features/tcrr-credit-mobilier-scandal/ (last visited June 4, 2023).
19 *Id.*
20 Kens, *supra* note 7, at 170.
21 James Surowiecki, *Martin Shkreli and the Temptations of Self-Dealing*, NEW YORKER (Dec. 18, 2015), https://www.newyorker.com/business/currency/martin-shkreli-and-the-temptations-of-self-dealing.
22 Paul Larmer, *Remember, We've Seen This Before*, HIGH COUNTRY NEWS (Mar. 20, 2017), https://www.hcn.org/issues/49.5/remember-weve-seen-this-before.
23 Kens, *supra* note 7, at 172.

NOTES

24 Edward Winslow Martin, *A Complete and Graphic Account of the Crédit Mobilier Investigation from Behind the Scenes in Washington* (1873), http://cprr.org/Museum/Credit_Mobilier_1873.html.
25 Mitchell, *supra* note 14.
26 Glass, *supra* note 3.
27 Benjamin Cassady, *"You've Got Your Crook, I've Got Mine": Why the Disqualification Clause Doesn't (Always) Disqualify*, 32 QUINNIPIAC L. REV. 209, 255 (2014) (quoting H.R. Rep. No. 42-77, at XIV).
28 Billings, *supra* note 5, at 708.
29 Martin, *supra* note 24.
30 *Expulsion Case of James W. Patterson of New Hampshire (1873)*, U.S. SENATE, https://www.senate.gov/about/powers-procedures/expulsion/064JamesPatterson_expulsion.htm (last visited Dec. 11, 2023).
31 SEAN DENNIS CASHMAN, AMERICA IN THE GILDED AGE: FROM THE DEATH OF LINCOLN TO THE RISE OF THEODORE ROOSEVELT 288 (1993); *see also Credit Mobilier Investigation*, HOUSE OF REP., 42nd Cong. 3rd Sess., Rep. No. 77 (Feb. 18, 1873), https://li.proquest.com/elhpdf/histcontext/1577-H.rp.77.pdf.
32 *Oakes Ames*, *supra* note 1 ("Only a last minute resolution of Congress saved Oakes Ames from expulsion.").
33 Robert Longley, *The Credit Mobilier Scandal*, THOUGHT CO. (Feb. 25, 2022), https://www.thoughtco.com/the-credit-mobilier-scandal-5217737.
34 *United States v. Union Pacific Railroad Company*, 98 U.S. 569, 620 (1878) ("[Union Pacific] has fulfilled the purpose of its creation and realized the hopes which were then cherished, and that the government has found it a useful agent, enabling it to save vast sums of money in the transportation of troops, mails, and supplies, and in the use of the telegraph.").
35 *The Crédit Mobilier Scandal*, PBS, *supra* note 18.
36 Ex parte Daugherty, 299 F. 620, 621 (S.D. Ohio 1924).
37 *Id.* at 622; Edgar Bronson Tolman, *Review of Recent Supreme Court Decisions*, 13 A.B.A. J. 79 (1927).
38 Charles W. Shull, *Ten Years of Congressional Inquiry—Contempt for a Decade*, 13 TEMP. L.Q. 322, 323 (1939) ("A subpoena was issued by the committee in charge for the appearance of Mally S. Daugherty, the brother of the Attorney-General.").
39 *Attorney General: Harry Micajah Daugherty*, DOJ (Oct. 24, 2022), https://www.justice.gov/ag/bio/daugherty-harry-micajah.
40 Ex parte Daugherty, 299 F. 620, 622 (S.D. Ohio 1924).
41 *Id.* at 621.
42 Edgar Bronson Tolman, *Review of Recent Supreme Court Decisions*, 13 A.B.A. J. 79 (1927).
43 Ex parte Daugherty, at 640.
44 *McGrain v. Daugherty*, 273 U.S. 135, 150 (1927).
45 Russell Berman, *Warren G. Harding's Terrible Tenure*, ATLANTIC (Aug. 14, 2015), https://www.theatlantic.com/politics/archive/2015/08/warren-g-harding-nan-britton-affair/401288/ (quoting Kruse).
46 Sidney Warren, *Corruption in Politics: IV. The Harding Era*, 22 CURRENT HISTORY 348, 349 (June 1952).

47 Nathan Masters, *The Mysterious Death of a D.C. Power Broker*, CRIME READS (Mar. 21, 2023), https://crimereads.com/the-mysterious-death-of-a-d-c-power-broker/.
48 U.S. CONST. amend. 18 (1919).
49 Carl Sferrazza Anthony, *A President of the Peephole*, WASH. POST (June 7, 1998), https://www.washingtonpost.com/archive/lifestyle/1998/06/07/a-president-of-the-peephole/fef0e4a0-6887-40fe-ad92-478ba2734fb4/.
50 Allison McNearney, *Inside the Little Green House on K Street, D.C.'s Most Scandalous Private Club*, DAILY BEAST (Mar. 3, 2022), https://www.thedailybeast.com/inside-the-little-green-house-on-k-street-dcs-most-scandalous-private-club.
51 Anthony, *supra* note 49.
52 Peter Armenti, *"Wild to be loved": The Poetry of President Warren G. Harding*, LIBRARY OF CONGRESS (Feb. 16, 2015), https://blogs.loc.gov/catbird/2015/02/wild-to-be-loved-the-poetry-of-president-warren-g-harding/.
53 Scott Wilson & Noah Weiland, *Ten Sexy Things President Warren Harding Told His Mistress*, ABC NEWS (July 29, 2014), https://abcnews.go.com/blogs/politics/2014/07/ten-sexy-things-president-warren-harding-told-his-mistress/.
54 Howard Markel, *The "Strange" Death of Warren G. Harding*, PBS (Aug. 2, 2015), https://www.pbs.org/newshour/health/strange-death-warren-harding.
55 Wesley M. Bagby, *The "Smoke Filled Room" and the Nomination of Warren G. Harding*, 41 (4) MISS. VALLEY HIST. REV. 660–64 (Mar. 1955).
56 EDWARD W. KNAPPMAN, 1 GREAT AMERICAN TRIALS 572 (2002).
57 Ronald G. Shafer, *A Century Before Jan. 6, Bombshell Hearings on Another Assault on Democracy*, WASH. POST (Jan. 15, 2022), https://www.washingtonpost.com/history/2022/01/09/teapot-dome-hearings/.
58 KNAPPMAN, *supra* note 56, at 572.
59 Warren, *supra* note 46, at 351.
60 M. R. WERNER, PRIVILEGED CHARACTERS 185 (1935).
61 Katy J. Harriger, *The History of the Independent Counsel Provisions: How the Past Informs the Current Debate*, 49 MERCER L. REV. 489, 491 (1998).
62 KNAPPMAN, *supra* note 56, at 573.
63 Glass, *supra* note 3.
64 Ben Miller, *When the Washington Post Covered Up a Presidential Scandal*, WETA (Dec. 22, 2021), https://boundarystones.weta.org/2021/12/22/when-washington-post-covered-presidential-scandal.
65 *Id.*
66 KNAPPMAN, *supra* note 56, at 574.
67 Bruce Bliven, *Tempest over Teapot*, AMERICAN HERITAGE (Aug. 1965), https://www.americanheritage.com/tempest-over-teapot.
68 *Id.*
69 *$300,000 Protection Paid to Jess Smith, Says "Bootleg King,"* N.Y. TIMES 1 (May 17, 1924).
70 Tim Vollet, *Looking Back: When Jesse Smith Worked Close to the Presidency*, YAHOO (June 5, 2023), https://news.yahoo.com/looking-back-jesse-smith-worked-094418124.html.
71 Bliven, *supra* note 67.
72 Warren, *supra* note 46, at 349.
73 S. JOSEPH KRAUSE, HARDING: HIS PRESIDENCY AND LOVE LIFE REAPPRAISED 54 (2013).
74 Anthony, *supra* note 49.

75 *Looking Back: Remembering Roxy Stinson*, RECORD HERALD (Apr. 3, 2018), https://www.recordherald.com/2018/04/03/looking-back-remembering-roxy-stinson/.
76 *Hearings Before the Select Committee on Investigation of the Attorney General United States Senate Sixty-Eighth Congress First Session Pursuant To S. Res. 157 Directing a Committee to Investigate the Failure of the Attorney General to Prosecute or Defend Certain Criminal and Civil Actions, Wherein the Government Is Interested*, Vol. 1 at 16 (1924) (quoting Stinson).
77 *Id.* at 38 (quoting Stinson).
78 *Id.* at 40 (quoting Stinson).
79 Lauren Eber, *Waiting for Watergate: The Long Road to FEC Reform*, 79 S. CAL. L. REV. 1155, 1161 (2006) (quoting S. Rep. No. 70–1326, pt. 2) (1928).
80 Anthony, *supra* note 49.
81 *Hearings Before the Committee on Public Lands and Surveys United States Senate Pursuant to S. Res. 282, S. Res. 294, And S. Res. 434 Sixty-Seventh Congress Senate Resolutions Providing for an Investigation of the Subject of Leases Upon Naval Oil Reserves and S. Res. 147 Sixty-Eighth Congress Providing for an Investigation of the Subject of Leases Upon Naval Oil Reserves* at 2908–2909 (1924).
82 WERNER, *supra* note 60, at 179.
83 *Id.* at 997–98 (testimony from Doheny).
84 Bliven, *supra* note 67.
85 *Id.*
86 Bryan Craig, *Making the Teapot Dome Scandal Relevant Again!*, MILLER CENTER (Apr. 11, 2017), https://millercenter.org/issues-policy/us-domestic-policy/making-teapot-dome-scandal-relevant-again.
87 *Senate Investigates the "Teapot Dome" Scandal*, U.S. SENATE, https://www.senate.gov/artandhistory/history/minute/Senate_Investigates_the_Teapot_Dome_Scandal.htm (last visited Apr. 12, 2024); Ken Gormley, *An Original Model of the Independent Counsel Statute*, 97 MICH. L. REV. 601, 628 (1998).
88 *Doheny Is Acquitted of Fall Oil Bribe*, N.Y. TIMES 1 (Mar. 23, 1930).
89 *Portraits in Oversight: Thomas Walsh and the Teapot Dome Investigation*, LEVIN CENTER (2023), https://www.levin-center.org/thomas-walsh-and-the-teapot-dome-investigation/.
90 Bliven, *supra* note 67.
91 *Sinclair v. United States*, 279 U.S. 749, 752 (1929).
92 *Portraits in Oversight*, *supra* note 89.
93 William P. Marshall, *The Limits on Congress's Authority to Investigate the President*, 2004 U. ILL. L. REV. 781, 800 (2004).
94 Shull, *supra* note 38, at 324.
95 Marshall, *supra* note 97, at 796 (2004).
96 *Mammoth Oil Co. v. United States*, 275 U.S. 13 (1927); *Pan American Petroleum & Transport. Co. v. United States*, 273 U.S. 456 (1927).
97 WERNER, *supra* note 60, at 167 (quoting Walsh).
98 Sidney Warren, *Corruption In Politics: IV. The Harding Era*, 22 CURRENT HISTORY 348, 349 (June 1952) ("The extent to which Daugherty profited . . . because . . . the records were destroyed.").
99 Shull, *supra* note 38, at 323 ("[Mally] Daugherty . . . destroyed a portion of the subpoenaed records and papers.").

100 Anthony, *supra* note 49.
101 *Id.*
102 *Hearings Before the Committee on Public Lands and Surveys United States Senate Pursuant to S. Res. 282, S. Res. 294, and S. Res. 434 Sixty-Seventh Congress Senate Resolutions Providing for an Investigation of the Subject of Leases upon Naval Oil Reserves Part 5* at 1698 (1924).
103 *Hearings Before the Select Committee on Investigation of the Attorney General, supra* note 76 at 541 (quoting Roxy Stinson).
104 *Id.* at 16 (quoting Roxy Stinson).
105 Ciara Torres-Spelliscy, *What the Teapot Dome Scandal Has to Do with Trump's Tax Returns*, BRENNAN CENTER (Apr. 15, 2019), https://www.brennancenter.org/our-work/analysis-opinion/what-teapot-dome-scandal-has-do-trumps-tax-returns.
106 Amy Howe, *Justices Clear the Way for House Committee to Obtain Trump's Tax Returns*, SCOTUS BLOG (Nov. 22, 2022), https://www.scotusblog.com/2022/11/justices-clear-the-way-for-house-committee-to-obtain-trumps-tax-returns/.
107 Stacey Henson, *Collier County Sheriff's Office Investigating After Bicyclist Finds Body*, NAPLES DAILY NEWS (Mar. 15, 2021), https://www.naplesnews.com/story/news/2021/03/15/body-found-bicyclist-collier-county-sheriff-reports/4703690001/.
108 Jessie Balmert, *Columbus Lobbyist Neil Clark, Accused in HB 6 Scandal, Died by Suicide, Autopsy Confirms*, CINCINNATI ENQUIRER (June 8, 2021), https://www.cincinnati.com/story/news/politics/2021/06/08/prominent-columbus-lobbyist-neil-clark-died-suicide-while-wearing-blue-dewine-governor-t-shirt-accor/7583922002/.
109 Press Release, *Federal Grand Jury Indicts Ohio House Speaker Enterprise in Federal Public Corruption Racketeering Conspiracy Involving $60 Million*, DOJ (July 30, 2020), https://www.justice.gov/usao-sdoh/pr/federal-grand-jury-indicts-ohio-house-speaker-enterprise-federal-public-corruption.
110 Tyler Carey, *Energy Harbor, Former FirstEnergy Subsidiary Tainted by Scandal, Sold to Texas-Based Company*, WKYC (Mar. 6, 2023), https://www.wkyc.com/article/money/business/energy-harbor-firstenergy-subsidiary-scandal-sold-texas-corporation/95-45020ab2-ef80-4fc7-b4bf-49191dfde038.
111 Press Release, *Political Strategist and Lobbyist Each Plead Guilty in Federal Public Corruption Racketeering Conspiracy Involving More than $60 Million*, DOJ (Oct. 29, 2020), https://www.justice.gov/usao-sdoh/pr/political-strategist-lobbyist-each-plead-guilty-federal-public-corruption-racketeering.
112 Jaclyn Diaz, *An Energy Company Behind a Major Bribery Scandal in Ohio Will Pay a $230 Million Fine*, NPR (July 23, 2021), https://www.npr.org/2021/07/23/1019567905/an-energy-company-behind-a-major-bribery-scandal-in-ohio-will-pay-a-230-million-.
113 NEIL CLARK, WHAT DO I KNOW? I'M JUST A LOBBYIST 387 (2020).
114 Press Release, *Ohio House Speaker, Former Chair of Ohio Republican Party, 3 Other Individuals & 501(C)(4) Entity Charged in Fed. Public Corruption Racketeering Conspiracy Involving $60 Million*, DOJ (July 21, 2020), https://www.justice.gov/usao-sdoh/pr/ohio-house-speaker-former-chair-ohio-republican-party-3-other-individuals-501c4-entity.
115 DOJ response to Larry Householder's motion to exclude statements by lobbyist Neil Clark from racketeering trial, *United States v. Householder*, No. 1:20-cr-00077-TSB at 5 (S.D. Ohio Nov. 28, 2022).
116 *Id.* at 4.

NOTES

117 *Id.* at 4–5.
118 Affidavit in Support of a Crim. Complaint at 61–2, *United States v. Householder*, No. 1:20-MJ-00526 at ¶ 185 (S.D. Ohio July 17, 2020).
119 DOJ response to Larry Householder's motion, Diaz, *supra* note 116, at 5–6.
120 Jake Zuckerman, *Judge Will Allow "Pay-to-Play" Recording at Former GOP House Speaker Larry Householder's Trial*, CLEVELAND.COM (Dec. 13, 2022), https://www.cleveland.com/open/2022/12/judge-will-allow-pay-to-play-recording-at-former-gop-house-speaker-larry-householders-trial.html.
121 Affidavit in Support of a Crim. Complaint at 24, *United States v. Householder*, at ¶ 77.
122 *Id.*
123 *Id.* at ¶ 89.
124 *Id.* at ¶ 92.
125 CLARK, *supra* note 117, at 5.
126 *Id.* at 347.
127 *Id.* at 360.
128 John Caniglia, *"The companies drove the bus": Neil Clark's Book Details His Views on House Bill 6, FirstEnergy, and What He Told FBI Agents*, CLEVELAND.COM (July 2, 2021), https://www.cleveland.com/ohio-utilities/2021/07/the-companies-drove-the-bus-neil-clarks-book-details-his-views-on-house-bill-6-firstenergy-and-what-he-told-fbi-agents.html.
129 Jake Zuckerman, *FirstEnergy CEO Chuck Jones Kept Millions in Compensation Despite Firing amid HB6 Scandal, Documents Show*, CLEVELAND.COM (June 23, 2022), https://www.cleveland.com/news/2022/06/firstenergy-ceo-chuck-jones-kept-millions-in-compensation-despite-firing-amid-hb6-scandal-documents-show.html.
130 *FirstEnergy Shareholder Derivative Litigation*, COHEN MILSTEIN (2023), https://www.cohenmilstein.com/case-study/firstenergy-shareholder-derivative-litigation.
131 *Id.*; Anthony Thompson, *FirstEnergy Facing State Organized Crime Investigation, Receives Subpoena*, AKRON BEACON J. (Aug. 2, 2023), https://www.beaconjournal.com/story/news/crime/2023/08/02/firstenergy-facing-organized-crime-investigation-by-ohio-ag-house-bill-6-scandal/70513753007/.
132 Julie Carr Smyth, *What's Next in Ohio Corruption Probe After Guilty Verdicts?*, AP (Mar. 14, 2023), https://apnews.com/article/ohio-firstenergy-larry-householder-corruption-bribery-fb5a5eba0e0addecca2d5f5be300b806.
133 Press Release, *Grand Jury Indicts Former State Public Utilities Chairman for Federal Bribery, Embezzlement Crimes*, DOJ (Dec. 4, 2023), https://www.justice.gov/usao-sdoh/pr/grand-jury-indicts-former-state-public-utilities-chairman-federal-bribery-embezzlement; Julie Carr Smyth, *Two Fired Utility Execs and a Former Top Ohio Regulator Plead Not Guilty in Bribery Scheme*, AP (Feb. 13, 2024), https://apnews.com/article/ohio-bribery-firstenergy-jones-dowling-randazzo-5aea395d6e3e28d-3dc69f61044068e85.
134 Julie Carr Smyth & Samantha Hendrickson, *Former Ohio Utility Regulator, Charged in a Sweeping Bribery Scheme, Has Died*, AP (Apr. 9, 2024), https://apnews.com/article/bribery-investigation-ohio-former-utility-regulator-dies-3059cdbb1508e8b9b1152fdff2b5028f.
135 David Dewitt, *Ohio's Billion-Dollar Bailout Bribery Trial Showcasing Rampant Arrogance, Corruption, and Enabling*, OHIO CAPITAL J. (Feb. 16, 2023), https://ohiocapitaljournal.com/2023/02/16/ohios-billion-dollar-bailout-bribery-trial-showcasing-rampant-arrogance-corruption-and-enabling/.

136 *Id.*
137 Alex Ebert, *Ohio's Historic Corruption Case Tests Limits of Citizens United*, BLOOMBERG LAW (Jan. 20, 2023), https://news.bloomberglaw.com/white-collar-and-criminal-law/ohios-historic-corruption-case-tests-limits-of-citizens-united.
138 Alex Ebert, *"Dark Money" Ohio Bribery Verdict Shows Citizens United Limit*, BLOOMBERG LAW (Mar. 9, 2023), https://news.bloomberglaw.com/white-collar-and-criminal-law/firstenergy-bribery-scheme-nets-landmark-guilty-verdict-in-ohio; CIARA TORRES-SPELLISCY, CORPORATE CITIZEN? AN ARGUMENT FOR THE SEPARATION OF CORPORATION AND STATE (2016) (explaining *Citizens United* and its impact); John Wellington Ennis, *Pay 2 Play* (2014) (documentary explaining *Citizens United* and its impact).
139 *Uncontested, Larry Householder Wins Reelection to Ohio House*, NBC4I (Nov. 3, 2020), https://www.nbc4i.com/news/your-local-election-hq/uncontested-larry-householder-wins-reelection-to-ohio-house/.
140 Kathiann M. Kowalski, *Dark Money Helped Ohio Utilities Subsidize Coal Plants, Delaying Action on Climate Change at Ratepayers' Expense*, ENERGY NEWS (Apr. 18, 2022), https://energynews.us/2022/04/18/dark-money-helped-ohio-utilities-subsidize-coal-plants-delaying-action-on-climate-change-at-ratepayers-expense/.
141 Rachel Treisman, *Ohio House Removes and Replaces Newly Indicted Larry Householder as Speaker*, NPR (July 30, 2020), https://www.npr.org/2020/07/30/897508779/ohio-house-removes-and-replaces-newly-indicted-larry-householder-as-speaker.
142 Andrew Welsh-Huggins, Farnoush Amiri & Julie Carr Smyth, *Ohio House Expels Former Republican Speaker in Historic Vote*, AP (June 16, 2021), https://apnews.com/article/larry-householder-ohio-expel-indictment-bribery-3c0347d54c1669b5243ef2b-5c4f91e0b.
143 Press Release, *FirstEnergy Charged Federally, Agrees to Terms of Deferred Prosecution Settlement*, DOJ (July 22, 2021), https://www.justice.gov/usao-sdoh/pr/firstenergy-charged-federally-agrees-terms-deferred-prosecution-settlement.
144 *Id.*; Deferred Prosecution Agreement at 15, *United States v. FirstEnergy Corp.*, No. 1:21-cr-86 (S.D. Ohio July 22, 2021).
145 *Id.*
146 Press Release, *FirstEnergy Charged Federally*, supra note 142.
147 CLARK, *supra* note 113; Diaz, 112.
148 Press Release, *Jury Convicts Former Ohio House Speaker, Former Chair of Ohio Republican Party of Participating in Racketeering Conspiracy*, DOJ (Mar. 9, 2023), https://www.justice.gov/usao-sdoh/pr/jury-convicts-former-ohio-house-speaker-former-chair-ohio-republican-party.
149 Jeremy Pelzer, *Larry Householder's Corruption Trial Is Nearly Over. Here's How We Got Here*, CLEVELAND.COM (Mar. 3, 2023), https://www.cleveland.com/news/2023/03/larry-householders-corruption-trial-is-nearly-over-heres-how-we-got-here.html.
150 *Id.*
151 Criminal Complaint, *United States v. Householder*, No. 1:20-mj-00526 at ¶ 18 (July 16, 2020), https://www.documentcloud.org/documents/6999280-469930706-Criminal-Complaint#document/p7/a572631.
152 Morgan Trau, *"Unholy alliance"—Chaotic First Day of Larry Householder Corruption Trial*, OHIO CAPITAL J. (Jan. 24, 2023), https://ohiocapitaljournal.com/2023/01/24/unholy-alliance-chaotic-first-day-of-larry-householder-corruption-trial/.

NOTES

153 David A. Graham, *The Dramatic Demise of Aaron Schock*, ATLANTIC (Mar. 17, 2015), https://uk.news.yahoo.com/dramatic-demise-aaron-schock-190110579.html.
154 *Aaron Schock's Downton Abbey Office, Shirtless Magazine Cover, and Other "Image Issues,"* AP (Mar. 17, 2015), https://www.mercurynews.com/2015/03/17/aaron-schocks-downton-abbey-office-shirtless-magazine-cover-and-other-image-issues/.
155 Jack Gillum & Stephen Braun, *AP: Lawmaker with Lavish Decor Billed Private Planes, Concerts*, AP (Feb. 23, 2015), https://www.pbs.org/newshour/politics/lawmaker-lavish-decor-billed-private-planes-concerts.
156 Jake Sherman, Anna Palmer & John Bresnahan, *Schock Resigns*, POLITICO (Mar. 17, 2015), https://www.politico.com/story/2015/03/aaron-schock-resigns-116153.
157 Press Release, *Former U.S. Representative Aaron Schock Indicted for Fraud, Theft of Government Funds, False Statements, and Filing False Income Tax Returns*, DOJ (Nov. 10, 2016), https://www.justice.gov/usao-cdil/pr/former-us-representative-aaron-schock-indicted-fraud-theft-government-funds-false.
158 Katherine Tully-McManus, *Former Rep. Aaron Schock Strikes Deal to Avoid Felony Conviction*, ROLL CALL (Mar. 6, 2019), https://rollcall.com/2019/03/06/former-rep-aaron-schock-strikes-deal-to-avoid-felony-conviction/.
159 Nick Robertson, *Corruption Trial for Former Ohio House Speaker Finishes Closing Arguments*, THE HILL (Mar. 7, 2023), https://thehill.com/regulation/court-battles/3888024-corruption-trial-for-former-ohio-house-speaker-enters-closing-arguments/.
160 *United States v. Householder*, Transcript, Case: 1:20-cr-00077-TSB Doc #: 228 at 138 (Mar. 3, 2023).
161 *Id.* at 45.
162 *Id.* at 46–47.
163 Pelzer, *supra* note 149.
164 Affidavit in Support of a Crim. Complaint at 5, *United States v. Householder*, at ¶ 13.
165 Press Release, *Ohio House Speaker*, *supra* note 114.
166 Press Release, *Jury Convicts*, *supra* note 148.
167 Ebert, *supra* note 138.
168 Jessie Balmert, *Will 2 Supreme Court Rulings Help Former Ohio GOP Chair Matt Borges Appeal His Conviction?*, CINCINNATI ENQUIRER (May 16, 2023), https://sports.yahoo.com/2-supreme-court-rulings-help-142353624.html.
169 *Ciminelli v. United States*, No. 21–1170 (U.S. May 11, 2023); *Percoco v. United States*, No. 21–1158. (U.S. May 11, 2023).
170 Press Release, *Ohio House Speaker*, *supra* note 114.
171 Ebert, *supra* note 148.
172 Press Release, *Political Strategist and Lobbyist*, *supra* note 111.
173 Press Release, *Purported 501(c)(4) Admits to Being Used to Conceal Corrupt Payments Related to Passage Of Legislation*, DOJ (Feb. 19, 2021), https://www.justice.gov/usao-sdoh/pr/purported-501c4-admits-being-used-conceal-corrupt-payments-related-passage-legislation.
174 Marty Schladen, *Guest Commentary: Bribery Scandal Shows How Ohio Politics Is Polluted with Dark Money*, OHIO CAPITAL J. (Mar. 15, 2023), https://www.citybeat.com/news/guest-commentary-bribery-scandal-shows-how-ohio-politics-is-polluted-with-dark-money-14930049.
175 Affidavit in Support of a Crim. Complaint at 65, *United States v. Householder*, at ¶ 200.

176 Deferred Prosecution Agreement at 17, *United States v. FirstEnergy Corp.*, No. 1:21-cr-86 (S.D. Ohio July 22, 2021).
177 Ciara Torres-Spelliscy, *Dark Money as a Political Sovereignty Problem*, 28 (2) KINGS L. J. 239 (2017); Ciara Torres-Spelliscy, *The SEC and Dark Political Money: An Historical Argument for Requiring Disclosure* (2013), https://ssrn.com/abstract=2282576.
178 Ciara Torres-Spelliscy, *How the U.S. Securities and Exchange Commission Could Require Transparency for Corporate Political Expenditures*, SCHOLARS STRATEGY NETWORK (May 2015), https://scholars.org/sites/scholars/files/ssn-key-findings-torres-spelliscy-on-the-sec-and-transparency-for-corporate-political-expenditures_3.pdf.
179 Julie Bykowicz, *Supreme Court's "Dark Money" Rulings Anchor Defense in Ohio Political Corruption Trial*, WALL ST. J. (Mar. 7, 2023), https://www.wsj.com/articles/supreme-courts-dark-money-rulings-anchor-defense-in-ohio-corruption-trial-d0f2f045.
180 Diaz, *supra* note 112.
181 *Repeal HB6*, OHIO CITIZENS ACTION, https://www.ohiocitizen.org/repeal_hb6 (last visited May 26, 2023).

5. SCHEMING IN THE SHADOWS

1 Jennifer Adams, *Ex-Florida Senator Charged for Paying Sham Candidate $45K*, DAILY BEAST (Mar. 18, 2021), https://www.thedailybeast.com/ex-florida-senator-charged-for-paying-sham-candidate-dollar45k.
2 Jerry Lambe, *Authorities Raid Disgraced Former Florida Senator's Home in Connection with Sham Senatorial Candidate Scheme*, LAW & CRIME (Mar. 17, 2021), https://lawandcrime.com/awkward/authorities-raid-disgraced-former-florida-senators-home-in-connection-with-sham-senatorial-candidate-scheme/.
3 Kyle Munzenrieder, *Miami Rep. Frank Artiles Accused of Punching College Kid at Bar*, MIAMI NEW TIMES (Mar. 3, 2015), https://www.miaminewtimes.com/news/miami-rep-frank-artiles-accused-of-punching-college-kid-at-bar-7530945.
4 Arek Sarkissian, *Florida Senator Frank Artiles Resigns After Insults, Racist Remarks in Bar*, NAPLES NEWS (Apr. 22, 2017), https://www.naplesnews.com/story/news/politics/2017/04/21/florida-state-senator-frank-artiles-resigns-over-fury-barroom-insults/100743558/.
5 Ana Ceballos, *Intrigue Grows in Florida's "Ghost" Candidate Case as Prosecutors Seek More Info*, TAMPA BAY TIMES (Aug. 1, 2022), https://www.tampabay.com/news/florida-politics/2022/07/29/prosecutors-seek-info-on-money-transfer-in-ghost-candidate-case/.
6 THOMAS PAINE, THE CRISIS (Dec. 23, 1776).
7 CARL HIAASEN, STRIP TEASE (1993); Andrew Bergman, *Striptease* (1996) (film).
8 Ciara Torres-Spelliscy, *Follow the Money Behind the Capitol Riot*, BRENNAN CENTER (Jan. 25, 2021), https://www.brennancenter.org/our-work/analysis-opinion/follow-money-behind-capitol-riot.
9 Dylan Taylor-Lehman, *Judges Gone Wild*, NARRATIVELY (Jan. 30, 2020), https://narratively.com/the-greatest-political-shtshow-that-ever-was/.
10 Patricia Mazzei, *How a Sham Candidate Helped Flip a Florida Election*, N.Y. TIMES (Mar. 19, 2021), https://www.nytimes.com/2021/03/19/us/florida-senate-race-fraud.html.
11 Jeff Weiner, *Interviews Examine Artiles' Boasts About "Ghost" Candidate Scheme*, ORLANDO SENTINEL (Nov. 17, 2021), https://www.orlandosentinel.com/2021/11/17/

NOTES

interviews-examine-artiles-boasts-about-ghost-candidate-scheme-funding-for-dark-money-group/.

12 Mazzei, *supra* note 10.
13 Jonah Goldman Kay, *Backed by Dark Money, Candidates with No Party Affiliation Appear to Have Changed The Outcome of Several Florida Races*, BUSINESS INSIDER (Dec. 18, 2020), https://www.businessinsider.com/candidates-with-no-party-affiliation-appear-in-several-florida-races-2020-12; Danielle Dietz, *Frank Artiles Charged with Campaign Finance Violation*, FL. POLITICAL REV. (Mar. 31, 2021), http://www.floridapoliticalreview.com/frank-artiles-charged-with-campaign-finance-violations/ ("Republican candidate Sen. Ileana Garcia['s] . . . margin of victory consisted of just 32 votes.").
14 Kay, *supra* note 13.
15 José Javier Rodríguez, *It Has Been an Honor to Serve Senate District 37*, FACEBOOK (Nov. 12, 2020), https://www.facebook.com/JoseJavierJJR/videos/670659936937345/.
16 Katie Shepherd, *Ex-Florida State Senator Paid Bogus Candidate to "Siphon Votes," Police Say, in Race GOP Narrowly Won*, WASH. POST (Mar. 19, 2021), https://www.washingtonpost.com/nation/2021/03/19/florida-fraud-artiles-rodriguez-election/.
17 *Id.*
18 Mazzei, *supra* note 10.
19 Scott Glover et al., *A Dark Money Mystery in Florida Centers on the Campaign of a Spoiler Candidate Who Appeared to Help a Republican Win by 32 Votes*, CNN (Nov. 23, 2020), https://www.cnn.com/2020/11/23/politics/florida-dark-money-mystery-invs/index.html.
20 Jason Garcia & Annie Martin, *Artiles Worked Closely with Top GOP Consulting Firm During "Ghost" Candidate Scheme, Documents Indicate*, ORLANDO SENTINEL (July 27, 2021). https://www.orlandosentinel.com/2021/07/27/artiles-worked-closely-with-top-gop-consulting-firm-during-ghost-candidate-scheme-documents-indicate/.
21 Scott Glover, Curt Devine & Audrey Ash, *Former Florida State Senator Charged in Spoiler Candidate Scheme*, CNN (Mar. 18, 2021), https://www.cnn.com/2021/03/18/politics/frank-artiles-arrested-sham-candidate-invs/index.html.
22 Shepherd, *supra* note 16.
23 Glenna Milberg, *Read the Warrant Alleging Ex-Florida Sen. Frank Artiles Paid Shill Candidate To Dupe Voters*, LOCAL 10 NEWS (Mar. 18, 2021), https://www.local10.com/news/politics/2021/03/18/read-the-warrant-alleging-ex-florida-sen-frank-artiles-paid-shill-candidate-to-dupe-voters/.
24 Garcia & Martin, *supra* note 20.
25 Phil Prazan, *Records Show Defendant in "Ghost" Candidate Case Worked for Powerful GOP Operative*, NBC MIAMI (Aug. 7, 2021), https://www.nbcmiami.com/news/local/records-show-defendant-in-ghost-candidate-case-worked-for-powerful-gop-operative/2523316/.
26 *Id.*
27 Mazzei, *supra* note 10.
28 *Id.*
29 *"Ghost Candidate" Pleads Guilty in Scheme to Siphon Votes in District 37 Race*, NBC 6 SOUTH FLORIDA (Aug. 24, 2021), https://www.nbcmiami.com/news/local/ghost-candidate-pleads-guilty-in-scheme-to-siphon-votes-in-district-37-race/2536139/.
30 Terry Spencer, *Candidate Pleads Guilty in Alleged Florida Vote Scam*, AP (Aug. 24, 2021), https://apnews.com/article/florida-5343b101e96d5c7f42d1ee54da7ccoce; Mark

NOTES

Harper, *Florida Senate "Ghost" Candidate Alex Rodriguez Faces $20,000 Ethics Fine*, DAYTONA BEACH NEWS-JOURNAL A1 (Oct. 27, 2021).

31 Dave Elias, *Some Are Blaming "Ghost Candidates" for Helping Republicans Win in Florida*, NBC 2 (Dec. 3, 2020), https://nbc-2.com/news/politics/2020/12/02/some-are-blaming-ghost-candidates-for-helping-republicans-win-in-florida/.

32 Mazzei, *supra* note 10.

33 Benjamin Fearnow, *Voting Redo Rejected by GOP-Controlled Florida Senate After Election Fraud Charge*, NEWSWEEK (Mar. 20, 2021), https://www.newsweek.com/voting-redo-rejected-gop-controlled-florida-senate-after-election-fraud-charge-1577602.

34 Ben Wilcox, *"Ghost Candidates": How They Manipulate (and Sometimes Steal) Florida Elections*, INTEGRITY FLORIDA, at 3 (Dec. 2022), https://www.integrityflorida.org/wp-content/uploads/2022/12/Report-Ghost-Candidate-final-12.2.2022.pdf.

35 Jason Garcia & Annie Martin, *Florida's Dark Money Playbook: How "Ghost" Candidate Scheme Revealed Secretive Political Tactics*, ORLANDO SENTINEL A1 (Jan. 2, 2022).

36 Glover et al., *supra* note 19; Kay, *supra* note 13.

37 Garcia & Martin, *supra* note 35.

38 Harper, *supra* note 30.

39 Natalie Morera, *"Ghost" Candidate, 2 Operatives Face Charges in Shill Candidate Scheme*, LOCAL 10 (May 24, 2022), https://www.local10.com/news/local/2022/05/24/ghost-candidate-2-operatives-face-charges-in-shill-candidate-scheme/.

40 Sky Palma, *Florida "Ghost Candidate" Who Was Backed by GOP Consultant Is Arrested and Charged*, RAW STORY (May 24, 2022), https://www.rawstory.com/florida-ghost-candidate-is-arrested-and-charged; Greg Fox, *Report Outlines Changes to Florida Election Laws to Cut Down on Ghost Candidates*, WESH2 (Dec. 5 2022), https://www.wesh.com/article/florida-election-law-changes-ghost-candidates/42160145.

41 *Consultant Pleads Not Guilty in "Ghost Candidate" Case*, AP (Aug. 2, 2022), https://apnews.com/article/2022-midterm-elections-florida-campaigns-campaign-contributions-33808ee48213594da171ff0e938a8c70.

42 Press Release, *Three Charged with Campaign Finance Scheme Following FDLE Investigation*, FLORIDA DEPT. OF LAW ENFORCEMENT (May 24, 2022), https://www.fdle.state.fl.us/News/2022/May/Three-charged-with-campaign-finance-scheme-followi.

43 *State of Florida v. Benjamin Richard Paris*, Trial Transcript, Case No. 2022-MM-1796-A, 1, at 668–669 (Sept. 1, 2022) (on file with the author).

44 *Id.* at 713.

45 *Seminole GOP Leader Accused in "Ghost Candidate" Scheme Guilty of Making Illegal Campaign Contribution*, SPECTRUM NEWS 13 (Sept. 1, 2022), https://www.mynews13.com/fl/orlando/news/2022/09/01/jury-deliberating-in--ghost-candidate--trial-of-ben-paris; *see also* Transcript of Motion for a New Trial, *Florida v. Paris,* No. 2022-MM-1796-A (Fla. Cir. Ct. Oct. 10, 2022) (on file with the author).

46 Annie Martin, *New Trial Being Sought in "Ghost" Candidate Case*, ORLANDO SENTINEL A3 (Sept. 16, 2022).

47 Garcia & Martin, *supra* note 35.

48 *Id.*

49 Editorial Board, *Editorial: Follow the Dark Money in Florida's Ghost Candidate Scandal*, SUN-SENTINEL A11 (Aug. 17, 2021).

50 Glover et al., *supra* note 19.

NOTES

51 Mary Ellen Klas, *FPL Parent Company Did Internal Investigation in Response to Dark Money Controversy*, TAMPA BAY TIMES (Jan. 27, 2022), https://www.tampabay.com/news/florida-politics/2022/01/27/fpl-parent-company-investigates-after-dark-money-controversy/.

52 *Id.*

53 *Id.*

54 Mario Alejandro Ariza, Miranda Green& Annie Martin, *Leaked: US Power Companies Secretly Spending Millions to Protect Profits and Fight Clean Energy*, GUARDIAN (July 27, 2022), https://www.theguardian.com/environment/2022/jul/27/leaked-us-leaked-power-companies-spending-profits-stop-clean-energy (quoting Silagy).

55 Mario Ariza & David Folkenflik, *Florida Power CEO Implicated in Scandals Abruptly Steps Down*, NPR (Jan. 25, 2023), https://www.npr.org/2023/01/25/1151453870/fpl-florida-power-ceo-eric-silagy.

56 Jason Garcia & Annie Martin, *Florida Power & Light Execs Worked Closely with Consultants*, ORLANDO SENTINEL (Dec. 2, 2021), https://www.orlandosentinel.com/2021/12/02/florida-power-light-execs-worked-closely-with-consultants-behind-ghost-candidate-scheme-records-reveal-special-report/.

57 Nate Monroe, *EA-Linked Law Firm Also Advised FPL Consultants*, FLORIDA TIMES-UNION A1 (Dec. 19, 2021).

58 Klas, *supra* note 51.

59 Jeff Weiner, *State Board Rebuffs Lawmakers' Call to Audit FPL Ties to "Ghost" Scandal*, ORLANDO SENTINEL A6 (Jan. 11, 2022).

60 Jason Garcia & Annie Martin, *Group Gave $1.15M to Dark-Money Entity*, ORLANDO SENTINEL A1 (Nov. 19, 2021).

61 Wilcox, *supra* note 34, at 8.

62 Glover et al., *supra* note 19.

63 *Id.*

64 *Id.*

65 Kay, *supra* note 13.

66 Matt Dixon, *Donor Name Change Fuels a Florida Dark Money Mystery*, POLITICO (Dec. 14, 2020), https://www.politico.com/states/florida/story/2020/12/14/donor-name-change-fuels-a-florida-dark-money-mystery-1346236.

67 Ceballos, *supra* note 5.

68 Annie Martin, *Ghost" Candidate Probe Unearths Big Business Transfers to Dark Money Groups in '18, '20*, ORLANDO SENTINEL A1 (Feb. 5, 2023).

69 Jason Garcia & Annie Martin, *Big-Business-Linked Group Funded "Ghost" Candidate Ads, Records Show*, ORLANDO SENTINEL (Nov. 18, 2021), https://www.orlandosentinel.com/2021/11/18/big-business-linked-group-gave-over-1-million-to-dark-money-entity-promoting-ghost-candidates/.

70 Jeff Weiner & Annie Martin, *Bank Records Shed Light on Dark-Money Group In Florida "Ghost" Candidate Scandal*, TAMPA BAY TIMES (Apr. 18, 2022), https://www.tampabay.com/news/florida-politics/2022/04/18/bank-records-shed-light-on-dark-money-group-in-florida-ghost-candidate-scandal/.

71 Klas, *supra* note 51.

72 *Id.*

73 *Id.*; *see also* Weiner, *supra* note 59.

74 Weiner, *supra* note 59.
75 Wilcox, *supra* note 34, at 8.
76 Garcia & Martin, *supra* note 35.
77 *Graph: Outside Spending by Nondisclosing Groups, Excluding Party Committees*, OpenSecrets, https://www.opensecrets.org/darkmoney/dark-money-basics.php?range=tot#outside-spending (last visited August 20, 2022).
78 *Id.*
79 Anna Massoglia & Karl Evers-Hillstrom, *"Dark Money"Topped $1 Billion in 2020, Largely Boosting Democrats*, OpenSecrets (Mar. 17, 2021), https://www.opensecrets.org/news/2021/03/one-billion-dark-money-2020-electioncycle/.
80 Sergio Bustos, *Report: FPL Dictated News; Documents Reveal Utility Consultants Controlled Web Publication's Content*, Sarasota Herald Tribune C1 (July 27, 2022).
81 *Id.*
82 Wilcox, *supra* note 34, at 3.
83 @GwenGraham, Twitter (Mar. 18, 2021), https://twitter.com/GwenGraham/status/1372580302292451339.
84 Wilcox, *supra* note 34, at 7.
85 Romy Ellenbogen, *Florida Watchdog Group's Report Raises Questions About Use Of "Ghost Candidates,"* Tampa Bay Times (Dec. 5, 2022), https://www.tampabay.com/news/florida-politics/2022/12/05/integrity-florida-ghost-candidates-elections-funding/.
86 Mary Ellen Klas, Nicholas Nehamas, & Ana Claudia Chacin, *"Nightmare Scenario": How FPL Secretly Manipulated a Florida State Senate Election*, Miami Herald (Aug. 13, 2022), https://www.miamiherald.com/news/politics-government/state-politics/article264196761.html.
87 *Id.* (quoting Ghosh); *see also* Wilcox, *supra* note 34, at 6.
88 Editorial Board, *FPL Wants to Control Solar Power. And State Lawmakers Are Doing Its Bidding*, Miami Herald (Feb. 8, 2022), https://www.theinvadingsea.com/2022/02/08/fpl-solar-power-florida/.
89 Mary Ellen Klas & Alejandro Ariza, *Revealed: The Florida Power Company Pushing Legislation to Slow Rooftop Solar*, Guardian (Dec. 20, 2021), https://www.theguardian.com/environment/2021/dec/20/revealed-the-florida-power-company-pushing-legislation-to-slow-rooftop-solar.
90 *Id.*
91 PIRG Education Fund, *Blocking Rooftop Solar*, U.S. Pirg (June 17, 2021), https://uspirg.org/reports/usp/blocking-rooftop-solar.
92 *Id.*
93 Mary Ellen Klas, *Insider Reveals True Intent of Florida's Proposed Solar Amendment*, Miami Herald (Oct. 18, 2016), https://www.miamiherald.com/news/politics-government/election/article109017387.html.
94 *Sal Nuzzo*, James Madison Institute, https://jamesmadison.org/bio/sal-nuzzo/ (last visited Aug. 12, 2022).
95 Klas, *supra* note 93.
96 *James Madison Institute's Sal Nuzzo Speaking at 2016 State Energy: Environment Leadership Summit*, Soundcloud (Oct. 18, 2016), https://soundcloud.com/cmd-sourcewatch/james-madison-institutes-sal-nuzzo-speaking-at-2016-state-energyenvironment-leadership-summit.

NOTES

97 *Florida Solar Energy Subsidies and Personal Solar Use, Amendment 1 (2016)*, BALLOT-PEDIA, https://ballotpedia.org/Florida_Solar_Energy_Subsidies_and_Personal_Solar_Use,_Amendment_1_(2016) (last visited Aug. 20, 2022) (emphasis added).
98 *Id.*
99 *Florida Property Tax Exemptions for Renewable Energy Equipment, Amendment 4 (August 2016)*, BALLOTPEDIA, https://ballotpedia.org/Florida_Property_Tax_Exemptions_for_Renewable_Energy_Equipment,_Amendment_4_(August_2016) (last visited Aug. 20, 2022).
100 *Nuzzo Speech 2016 State Energy*.
101 *Id.*
102 *Id.*
103 *Id.*
104 *Id.*
105 *Vote no on Crooked Solar Amendment 1 in Florida*, https://www.facebook.com/Vote-NO-on-Crooked-Solar-Amendment-1-in-Florida-289079218097145; *Vote no on Amendment 1 on November 8*, https://www.facebook.com/events/1845929062303606 (last visited Apr. 12, 2024).
106 Florida Solar Energy Industries Association & Floridians for Solar Choice, Petition for Writ of Mandamus Directing Respondent to Remove Constitutional Amendment 1 (Solar Amendment) from General Election Ballot (November 8, 2016) and to Embargo and Not Canvass the Election Results (Nov. 2, 2016); *Florida Solar Energy Industries Ass'n v. Detzner*, SC16-1995, 2016 WL 6584704, at *1 (Fla. Nov. 4, 2016); Mary Ellen Klas, *Court Rejects Suit Over Solar Amendment*, TAMPA BAY TIMES, Local-2 (Nov. 5, 2016).
107 Klas, *supra* note 93.
108 *Id.*
109 *Florida Amendment 1—Solar Energy Subsidies and Personal Solar Use—Results: Rejected*, N.Y. TIMES (Aug. 1, 2017), https://www.nytimes.com/elections/2016/results/florida-ballot-measure-1-solarenergy-equipment-rights.
110 Hiroko Tabuchi, *Rooftop Solar Dims Under Pressure From Utility Lobbyists*, N.Y. TIMES (July 8 2017), https://www.nytimes.com/2017/07/08/climate/rooftop-solar-panels-tax-credits-utility-companies-lobbying.html.
111 *Florida Amendment 4, Require Constitutional Amendments to Be Passed Twice Initiative (2020)*, BALLOTPEDIA, https://ballotpedia.org/Florida_Amendment_4,_Require_Constitutional_Amendments_to_be_Passed_Twice_Initiative_(2020) (last visited Aug. 20, 2022).
112 *Insurers Fail, Schools Stress, Desantis Jets and FPL's Secrets Emerge*, INSURANCE NEWS NET (Aug. 15, 2022), https://insurancenewsnet.com/oarticle/insurers-fail-schools-stress-desantis-jets-and-fpls-secrets-emerge-miami-herald.
113 Antonio Fins, *Palm Beach County Ghost Candidate Exposes "Lies" Behind Florida Election Reform, Voter Groups Say*, PALM BEACH POST (Aug. 31, 2021), https://www.palmbeachpost.com/story/news/politics/2021/08/31/palm-beach-county-ghost-candidate-pleads-guilty-election-case/5593843001/.
114 Marian White, *The 10 Largest States by Population*, MOVING (Jan. 3, 2021), https://www.moving.com/tips/the-10-largest-states-by-population/.
115 Steven Lemongello & Adelaide Chen, *Florida Will Gain 1 Seat In Congress, Not 2, After Trump's Census Moves, covid-19 Pandemic*, ORLANDO SENTINEL (Apr. 26, 2021),

https://www.orlandosentinel.com/2021/04/26/florida-will-gain-1-seat-in-congress-not-2-after-trumps-census-moves-covid-19-pandemic/.
116 Matthew C. Woodruff, *There Was Cheating in 2020 in Florida According to a Report by Watchdog "Integrity Florida,"* NEWSBREAK (Dec. 9, 2022), https://original.newsbreak.com/@matthew-c-woodruff-1599275/2849692394859-there-was-cheating-in-2020-in-florida-according-to-a-report-by-watchdog-integrity-florida (quoting Amandi).
117 Cameron Peters, *Florida Republicans Want to Impose New Voting Restrictions*, VOX (Feb. 21, 2021), https://www.vox.com/2021/2/21/22293921/florida-republicans-new-voting-restrictions-arizona-iowa-georgia.
118 Complaint at 19–20, In the Matter of Grow United Inc. et al., Fed. Election Comm'n (2022), https://www.citizensforethics.org/wp-content/uploads/2022/10/Florida-Dark-Money-FEC-Complaint.pdf.
119 *Id.* at 2.
120 Dan Mangan & Brian Schwartz, *FTX Founder Sam Bankman-Fried Hit with Four New Criminal Charges*, CNBC (Feb. 23, 2023), https://www.cnbc.com/2023/02/23/ftx-founder-sam-bankman-fried-hit-with-new-criminal-charges.html.

6. CRIMINAL ORIGINS

1 Michael Ames, *The Feds Say Pras Is a Foreign Agent*, ROLLING STONE (Mar. 12, 2023), https://www.rollingstone.com/music/music-features/pras-michel-fugees-jho-low-trial-interview-1234694084/.
2 Jude Chan, *Jho Low Splurged Millions on Birthday Party in Las Vegas*, EDGE MARKETS (Aug. 23, 2016), https://www.theedgemarkets.com/article/jho-low-splurged-millions-birthday-party-las-vegas.
3 Sheelah Kolhatkar, *"Billion Dollar Whale," an Absurd Tale of Financial Fraud*, NEW YORKER (Sept. 28, 2018), https://www.newyorker.com/recommends/read/billion-dollar-whale-an-absurd-tale-of-financial-fraud.
4 Chan, *supra* note 2.
5 Alex Ritman, *Malaysian Businessman at Center of "Wolf of Wall Street" Corruption Scandal Threw Himself Outlandish Vegas Birthday Party in 2012*, HOLLYWOOD REPORTER (Aug. 19, 2016), https://www.hollywoodreporter.com/movies/movie-news/malaysian-businessman-at-center-wolf-920867/.
6 Ames, *supra* note 1.
7 Indictment at 109, *United States v.* The Wolf of Wall Street *Motion Picture*, No. CV 16-16-5362 (July 20, 2016), https://www.justice.gov/archives/opa/page/file/877166/download.
8 Nathaniel Ainley, *Um, Leonardo DiCaprio Is Handing a $3.2M Picasso Over to the Feds. Oh, and His Marlon Brando Oscar, Too*, VICE (June 19, 2017), https://www.vice.com/en/article/j5x4kp/leonardo-dicaprio-32m-picasso-fbi-1mdb-jho-low.
9 Travis Clark, *Leonardo DiCaprio Had to Return Marlon Brando's Oscar*, BUSINESS INSIDER (Dec. 12, 2018), https://www.businessinsider.com/why-leonardo-dicaprio-returned-oscar-given-to-him-by-jho-low-2018-12.
10 Callum Burroughs & Yusuf Khan, *The Bizarre Story of 1MDB, the Goldman Sachs-Backed Malaysian Fund That Turned into One of the Biggest Scandals in Financial History*, BUSINESS INSIDER (Feb. 19, 2020), https://www.businessinsider.com/1mdb-timeline-the-goldman-sachs-backed-malaysian-wealth-fund-2018-12 ("An estimated

$4.5 billion was misappropriated from 1MDB by high-level officials and their associates between 2009 and 2014.").

11 Tom Wright & Bradley Hope, *China Offered Bailout for Deals —In Return for Helping Malaysia's Troubled Fund, It Would Get Railroad, Pipeline Stakes*, WALL ST. J. A1 (Jan. 8, 2019) ("Mr. Low . . . is a fugitive, living in China under Beijing's protection, according to Malaysian officials.").

12 Burroughs & Khan, *supra* note 10.

13 *Id.*

14 Marion Maneker, *Jho Low Sells Dustheads for Another Loss*, ART MARKET MONITOR (May 19, 2016), https://www.artmarketmonitor.com/2016/05/19/jho-low-sells-dustheads-for-another-loss/.

15 *Id.*

16 Jonathan Head, *Najib Razak: The Verdict That Sent Malaysia's Untouchable Ex-PM to Prison*, BBC (Aug. 27, 2022), https://www.bbc.com/news/world-asia-62685413.

17 Rozanna Latiff, *Jailed Malaysian Ex-Pm Najib Loses Final Bid to Review Graft Conviction*, REUTERS (Mar. 31, 2023), https://www.reuters.com/world/asia-pacific/jailed-malaysian-ex-pm-najib-loses-bid-review-graft-conviction-2023-03-31/.

18 Heather Chen et al., *1MDB: The Playboys, PMs, and Partygoers Around a Global Financial Scandal*, BBC (Feb. 19, 2020), https://www.bbc.com/news/world-asia-46341603 (quoting Lynch).

19 Shamim Adam et al., *Malaysia's 1MDB Scandal Shook the Financial World*, WASH. POST (Feb. 19, 2020), https://www.washingtonpost.com/business/how-malaysias-1mdb-scandal-shook-the-financial-world/2019/08/09/60e95376-ba73-11e9-8e83-4e6687e99814_story.html.

20 *Id.* ("Of the $8 billion that 1MDB raised via bond sales, the U.S. alleges more than half was siphoned off.").

21 Randeep Ramesh, *1MDB: The Inside Story of the World's Biggest Financial Scandal*, GUARDIAN (July 28, 2016), https://www.theguardian.com/world/2016/jul/28/1mdb-inside-story-worlds-biggest-financial-scandal-malaysia.

22 Burroughs & Khan, Ames, *supra* note 10 ("Between 2012 and 2013, Goldman arranged three bonds worth $6.5 billion for 1MDB with fees totalling $593 million, or 9% of the total, higher than the average fees paid on such deals.").

23 Press Release, *Goldman Sachs Charged in Foreign Bribery Case and Agrees to Pay Over $2.9 Billion*, DOJ (Oct. 22, 2020), https://www.justice.gov/opa/pr/goldman-sachs-charged-foreign-bribery-case-and-agrees-pay-over-29-billion.

24 McKenzie Beard, *Goldman Sachs to Pay Record Fine over 1MDB Scandal*, VOICE OF AMERICA (Oct. 22, 2020), https://www.voanews.com/a/economy-business_goldman-sachs-pay-record-fine-over-1mdb-scandal/6197481.html.

25 Press Release, *Former Goldman Sachs Investment Banker Convicted in Massive Bribery and Money Laundering Scheme*, DOJ (Apr. 8, 2022), https://www.justice.gov/usao-edny/pr/former-goldman-sachs-investment-banker-convicted-massive-bribery-and-money-laundering.

26 Adam et al., *supra* note 19.

27 *Id.*

28 Tommy McArdle, *Leonardo DiCaprio Testifies at Trial of Ex-Fugees Rapper Pras Michel*, PEOPLE (Apr. 3, 2023) ("The Oscar that DiCaprio returned in 2017 is now in a federal warehouse in Texas.").

29 Adam et al., *supra* note 19.
30 Press Release: *United States Reaches Settlement to Recover More than $700 Million in Assets Allegedly Traceable to Corruption Involving Malaysian Sovereign Wealth Fund*, DOJ (Oct. 30, 2019), https://www.justice.gov/opa/pr/united-states-reaches-settlement-recover-more-700-million-assets-allegedly-traceable.
31 Sherisse Pham, *The Malaysian Banker at the Heart of the 1MDB Scandal Says He Was Just an "Intermediary,"* CNN (Feb. 20, 2020), https://www.cnn.com/2020/01/06/business/jho-low-interview-1mdb/index.html.
32 Sridhar Natarajan, *Chris Christie Among Lawyers Making $15 Million in 1MDB Pact*, BLOOMBERG (Oct. 31, 2019), https://www.bloomberg.com/news/articles/2019-10-31/chris-christie-is-among-lawyers-reaping-15-million-in-1mdb-deal#xj4y7vzkg.
33 Becca van Sambeck, *Why Is Jordan Belfort, AKA "The Wolf Of Wall Street," Claiming to Be the Victim of Fraud?*, OXYGEN (July 27, 2020), https://www.oxygen.com/crime-news/wolf-of-wall-street-jordan-belfort-red-granite-lawsuit-1MDB-explained.
34 Sarah N. Lynch & Nathan Layne, *U.S. Charges Ex-Fugees Rapper, Malaysian Businessman Low over Funding in 2012 Election*, REUTERS (May 10, 2019), https://www.reuters.com/article/us-usa-election-fraud/u-s-charges-ex-fugees-rapper-malaysian-businessman-low-over-funding-in-2012-election-idUSKCN1SG2BR.
35 Carrie Johnson, *Actor Leonardo DiCaprio Testifies in Fugees' Pras Michel Conspiracy Trial*, NPR (Apr. 3, 2023), https://www.npr.org/2023/04/03/1167777555/leonardo-dicaprio-pras-michel-fugees-trial.
36 Indictment at 2, *United States v. Michel* (No. 19-148-1), 2019 WL 5790115 (D. D.C. Nov. 6, 2019).
37 Ames, *supra* note 1.
38 Lynch & Layne, *supra* note 34.
39 Michel Indictment, *supra* note 36, at 5.
40 *Id.* ("[Michel] knowingly and willfully make contributions to a candidate for federal office in the names of other persons, aggregating to $25,000 and more in a calendar year, in violation of Title 52, United States Code, Sections 30122 and 30109(a)(1)(A).").
41 Ken Dilanian et al., *Who Is Guo Wengui, the Chinese Billionaire Who Owns the Boat Steve Bannon Was Arrested On?*, NBC NEWS (Aug. 20, 2020), https://www.nbcnews.com/politics/justice-department/who-chinese-mogul-who-owns-boat-steve-bannon-was-busted-n1237511.
42 Press Release: *Ho Wan Kwok, A/K/A "Miles Guo," Arrested for Orchestrating over $1 Billion Dollar Fraud Conspiracy Over $630 Million of Alleged Fraud Proceeds Seized by U.S. Government*, DOJ (Mar. 15, 2023), https://www.justice.gov/usao-sdny/pr/ho-wan-kwok-aka-miles-guo-arrested-orchestrating-over-1-billion-dollar-fraud-conspiracy.
43 Carrie Johnson, *Prosecutors Say Pras Michel Broke the Law "to Get Paid,"* NPR (Mar. 30, 2023), https://www.npr.org/2023/03/30/1167061592/pras-michel-fugees-trial.
44 Press Release, *U.S. Entertainer Convicted of Engaging in Foreign Influence Campaign Rapper, Businessman Found Guilty in Back-Channel Lobbying Campaign to Drop 1MDB Investigation and Remove Chinese National from United States, and Conspiring to Make and Conceal Foreign Contributions During 2012 U.S. Presidential Election*, DOJ (Apr. 26, 2023), https://www.justice.gov/opa/pr/us-entertainer-convicted-engaging-foreign-influence-campaign.

NOTES

45 Alex Isenstadt, *RNC Finance Chair Steve Wynn Resigns After Sexual Harassment Allegations*, POLITICO (Jan. 27, 2018), https://www.politico.com/story/2018/01/27/steve-wynn-resign-rnc-finance-chair-sexual-misconduct-accusations-373768.
46 Press Release, *Justice Department Sues to Compel a U.S. Businessperson to Register Under the Foreign Agents Registration Act*, DOJ (May 17, 2022), https://www.justice.gov/opa/pr/justice-department-sues-compel-us-businessperson-register-under-foreign-agents-registration.
47 Press Release, *Elliott Broidy Pleads Guilty for Back-Channel Lobbying Campaign to Drop 1MDB Investigation and Remove a Chinese Foreign National*, DOJ (Oct. 20, 2020), https://www.justice.gov/opa/pr/elliott-broidy-pleads-guilty-back-channel-lobbying-campaign-drop-1mdb-investigation-and.
48 Isenstadt, *supra* note 45.
49 Yashar Ali, *Ex-Mistress Accuses Longtime RNC Leader Elliott Broidy of Physical, Sexual Abuse*, HUFF. POST (Sept. 7, 2018), https://www.huffpost.com/entry/elliott-broidy-republican-national-committee-leader-mistress-complaint_n_5b9326dbe4b0162f472d2ea3.
50 Lachlan Markay, *Trump Pardons Former GOP Fundraiser Elliott Broidy*, AXIOS (Jan. 20, 2021), https://www.axios.com/2021/01/20/trump-elliott-broidy-pardon.
51 *Id.*
52 Robert Legare, *Fugees Star Pras Michel Testifies in Multimillion-Dollar International Fraud Trial*, CBS NEWS (Apr. 18, 2023), https://www.cbsnews.com/news/pras-michel-testifies-international-fraud-trial-fugees-star/.
53 Michel Indictment, *supra* note 36, at 12 ("Using the money he received from JHO LOW, MICHEL paid approximately $800,000 to multiple straw donors, . . . who in turn made contributions to Political Committee A totaling approximately $755,000.").
54 Legare, *supra* note 52.
55 Holmes Lybrand, *Former Fugees Rapper Pras Michel Testifies in His Own Trial*, CNN (Apr. 18, 2023), https://www.cnn.com/2023/04/18/politics/pras-michel-fugees-trial-testimony/index.html.
56 David Voreacos, *Rapper Michel Says Jho Low Paid $20 Million for Obama Photo*, BLOOMBERG (Apr. 18, 2023), https://www.bloomberg.com/news/articles/2023-04-18/rapper-pras-michel-says-jho-low-was-too-hot-for-obama-campaign#xj4y7vzkg.
57 Ames, *supra* note 1.
58 BRADLEY HOPE & TOM WRIGHT, BILLION DOLLAR WHALE (2016).
59 Michel Indictment, *supra* note 36, at 6.
60 *Id.*
61 *Id.* at 8 ("MICHEL, Company E, and the straw donors made contributions to Political Committees A and B in their own names, rather than the name of JHO LOW, thus concealing the true source of the contributions. As a result, MICHEL caused Political Committees A and B to make false entries in multiple campaign contribution reports submitted to the FEC about the true source of the contributions.").
62 Lynch & Layne, *supra* note 34.
63 Letter from Campaign Legal Center & Democracy 21 to DOJ, re: FEC complaint against Prakazrel "Pras" Michel, SPM Holdings LLC/SPM 2012 Holdings LLC, Black Men Vote, William Kirk Jr., Treasurer, Black Men Vote, Apr. 13, 2015, https://campaignlegal.org/sites/default/files/DOJ%20Letter%20%2B%20FEC%20Complaint%20v.%20Pras%20Michel_4.13.15.pdf.

64 *Donor Detail, spm holdings llc*, OPENSECRETS, https://www.opensecrets.org/outside-spending/donor_detail?cycle=2012&id=SPM%20Holdings&type=O&super=Y (last visited Apr. 26, 2023).
65 Letter from Campaign Legal Center & Democracy 21 to DOJ, *supra* note 63.
66 Carrie Johnson, *Musician Pras Michel Undergoes Withering Cross Examination About Foreign Money*, NPR (Apr. 18, 2023), https://www.npr.org/2023/04/18/1170752495/musician-pras-michel-undergoes-withering-cross-examination-about-foreign-money.
67 *Id.*
68 Legare, *supra* note 52.
69 Marc Griffin, *Pras Speaks on Facing 22 Years in Prison After Declining Plea Deal*, VIBE (Mar. 13, 2023), https://www.vibe.com/news/national/pras-prison-plea-deal-22-years-1234742145/.
70 Johnson, *supra* note 43.
71 *U.S. Entertainer Convicted, supra* note 44.
72 Tassanee Vejpongsa, *Disbanded Thai Party Says Gov't Colluded in 1MDB Scandal*, AP (Feb. 20, 2020), https://apnews.com/dedc56f5d455cfeb62387a27134b56d4 ("Low had freely visited Thailand five times in 2016–2018 even though an Interpol 'Red Notice' requested by Singapore seeking his arrest.").
73 Bart Jansen, Kevin McCoy & Kevin Johnson, *Two Giuliani Associates Involved in Trump-Ukraine Controversy Arrested on Campaign Finance Charges*, USA TODAY (Oct. 10, 2019), https://www.usatoday.com/story/news/politics/2019/10/10/impeachment-inquiry-lev-parnas-igor-fruman-witness-list/3866159002/.
74 Lachlan Markay & Betsy Swan, *Five Cellphones, Trump Straws, a Lot of Cash—What This Giuliani Crony Was Carrying When the FBI Arrested Him*, DAILY BEAST (Nov. 14, 2019), https://www.thedailybeast.com/five-cellphones-trump-straws-a-lot-of-cash-what-this-giuliani-crony-was-carrying-when-the-fbi-arrested-him.
75 Press Release, *Lev Parnas and Igor Fruman Charged with Conspiring to Violate Straw and Foreign Donor Bans*, DOJ (Oct. 10, 2019), https://www.justice.gov/usao-sdny/pr/lev-parnas-and-igor-fruman-charged-conspiring-violate-straw-and-foreign-donor-bans.
76 *Donor Profile: Lev Parnas & Igor Fruman*, OPENSECRETS, https://www.opensecrets.org/featured-datasets/25 (last visited August 12, 2022).
77 Dan Friedman, *Prosecutors Say a Company Named "Fraud Guarantee" Was a Scam*, MOTHER JONES (Sept. 18, 2020), https://www.motherjones.com/politics/2020/09/rudy-giuliani-lev-parnas-fraud-guarantee/.
78 Dan Mangan, *Russian Oligarch Andrey Muraviev Indicted in Political Contribution Scheme Linked to Illegal Donors to Trump PAC*, CNBC (Mar. 14, 2022), https://www.cnbc.com/2022/03/14/russian-oligarch-andrey-muraviev-indicted-linked-to-trump-donors.html ("Giuliani, who has not been charged with any of the men, received $500,000 in 2018 for work for Fraud Guarantee.").
79 FEC Complaint, *Campaign Legal Center v. Global Energy Producers LLC et al.* (July 25, 2018), https://campaignlegal.org/sites/default/files/2018-07/SIGNED%2007-25-18%20GEP%20LLC%20Straw%20Donor%20Complaint.pdf.
80 *Id.* at 2.
81 Ilya Marritz, *An Intimate Dinner with President Trump*, WNYC'S TRUMP INC. (Feb. 5, 2020), https://www.wnycstudios.org/podcasts/trumpinc/episodes/trump-inc-parnas-money.

NOTES

82 *Citizens United v. FEC*, 558 U.S. 310 (2010); Speechnow.org v. FEC, No. 08–5223 (D.C. Cir. 2010).
83 Josh Gerstein, *Giuliani Ally Lev Parnas Pleads Guilty to Fraud Fundraising for "Fraud Guarantee,"* POLITICO (Mar. 25, 2022), https://www.politico.com/news/2022/03/25/giuliani-lev-parnas-guilty-fraud-fundraising-00020477.
84 *Dinesh D'Souza Sentenced in Manhattan Federal Court to Five Years of Probation for Campaign Finance Fraud*, FBI (Sept. 23, 2014), https://www.fbi.gov/contact-us/field-offices/newyork/news/press-releases/dinesh-dsouza-sentenced-in-manhattan-federal-court-to-five-years-of-probation-for-campaign-finance-fraud.
85 Kaitlan Collins, Maegan Vazquez & Laura Jarrett, *Trump Pardons Dinesh D'Souza— and Hints at More Celebrity Pardons*, CNN (May 31, 2018), https://www.cnn.com/2018/05/31/politics/trump-dinesh-dsouza-pardon/index.html.
86 Press Release, *Russian Oligarch Charged with Making Illegal Political Contributions Andrey Muraviev Charged with Conspiring to Fund One Million Dollars in Illegal Donations*, DOJ (Mar. 14, 2022), https://www.justice.gov/usao-sdny/pr/russian-oligarch-charged-making-illegal-political-contributions.
87 Sealed Indictment, *United States v. Lev Parnas, Igor Fruman, David Correia & Andrey Kukushin*, 19CR725 (2019).
88 *Ron DeSantis Met Indicted Giuliani Associates at a Pro Israel Event*, TAMPA BAY TIMES (Nov. 4, 2019), https://www.tampabay.com/florida-politics/buzz/2019/11/04/ron-desantis-met-indicted-giuliani-associates-at-a-pro-israel-event/.
89 David Smiley & Steve Contorno, *DeSantis Muted on Meetup*, TAMPA BAY TIMES Metro-1 (Nov. 5, 2019).
90 Steve Contorno, *Gov. Can't Shake This Duo*, TAMPA BAY TIMES A1 (Oct. 26, 2019).
91 *United States v. Kukushkin*, 61 F.4th 327, 330–31 (2d Cir. 2023).
92 Press Release, *Russian Oligarch Charged*, supra note 86.
93 Indictment at 11, *United States v. Parnas et al.*, 19CR725 (Mar. 14, 2022),
94 *United States v. Parnas et al.*, No. 19CR725, 2022 WL 669869 (S.D.N.Y. Mar. 7, 2022).
95 *Id.* at 12.
96 *Id.* at 14.
97 *The Trump-Ukraine Impeachment Inquiry Report*, HOUSE INTELLIGENCE COMMITTEE (Dec. 2019), https://intelligence.house.gov/uploadedfiles/the_trump-ukraine_impeachment_inquiry_report.pdf.
98 Impeachment of Donald J. Trump President of the United States Report to accompany H. Res 755, House Judiciary Committee (Dec. 13, 2019), https://d3i6fh83elv35t.cloudfront.net/static/2019/12/Judicarycommitteeimpeachmentreport.pdf.
99 Ellen Cranley, *A New Collection of Personal Photos Show Giuliani's "Fixer" Lev Parnas with Trump's Inner Circle*, BUSINESS INSIDER (Jan. 18, 2020), https://www.businessinsider.com/giuliani-fixer-lev-parnas-photos-trump-family-2020-1?amp.
100 Erica Orden, *Parnas Recording Shows Trump Talking with Indicted Businessmen the President Has Said He Doesn't Know*, CNN (Jan. 26, 2020), https://www.cnn.com/2020/01/25/politics/recording-trump-lev-parnas-igor-fruman-ukraine-ambassador/index.html.
101 Ben Protess & William K. Rashbaum, *Giuliani Ally Expected to Plead Guilty in Case on Campaign Finances*, N.Y. TIMES A16 (Aug. 25, 2021).
102 Lauren del Valle, *Lev Parnas Found Guilty on Campaign Finance Charges*, CNN (Oct. 22, 2021), https://www.cnn.com/2021/10/22/politics/lev-parnas-verdict/index.html/.

103 Press Release, *Russian Oligarch Charged*, supra note 86; Press Release, *U.S. Entertainer Convicted*, supra note 44 ("Low ... is a fugitive.").

7. CREATING A MONSTER

1 Jeremy Diamond, *Donald Trump Jumps In: The Donald's Latest White House Run Is Officially On*, CNN (June 17, 2015), https://www.cnn.com/2015/06/16/politics/donald-trump-2016-announcement-elections/index.html.
2 Luciana Lopez, *At Trump's Presidential Rallies, a Combustible Mix of Glee, Fear*, REUTERS (Nov. 26, 2015), https://www.reuters.com/article/us-usa-election-trump/at-trumps-presidential-rallies-a-combustible-mix-of-glee-fear-idUSKBN-0TE2NV20151126.
3 *Id.*
4 Yoni Appelbaum, *Trump's Promise to Jail Clinton Is a Threat to American Democracy*, ATLANTIC (Oct. 10, 2016), https://www.theatlantic.com/politics/archive/2016/10/trumps-promise-to-jail-clinton-is-a-threat-to-american-democracy/503516/.
5 *Id.*
6 Hadas Gold, *Donald Trump: We're Going to "Open Up" Libel Laws*, POLITICO (Feb. 26, 2016), http://www.politico.com/blogs/on-media/2016/02/donald-trump-libel-laws-219866.
7 Terrance Smith, *Trump Has Longstanding History of Calling Elections "Rigged" If He Doesn't Like The Results*, ABC NEWS (Nov. 11, 2020), https://abcnews.go.com/Politics/trump-longstanding-history-calling-elections-rigged-doesnt-results/story?id=74126926.
8 Jeet Heer, *In Tonight's Most Exciting Reality Show Plot Twist, Trump Says He Won't Necessarily Support the GOP Nominee*, NEW REPUBLIC (Mar. 29, 2016), https://newrepublic.com/article/132231/tonights-exciting-reality-show-plot-twist-trump-says-wont-necessarily-support-gop-nominee.
9 Patricia Zengerle & Emily Stephenson, *Trump Says He Will Accept Election Result—If He Wins*, REUTERS (Oct. 19, 2016), https://www.reuters.com/article/us-usa-election/trump-says-he-will-accept-election-result-if-he-wins-idUSKCN12J0ZM.
10 Ari Berman, *The Trump Administration's Lies About Voter Fraud Will Lead to Massive Voter Suppression*, NATION (Feb. 13, 2017), https://drwho.virtadpt.net/files/2017-02/lies-about-voter-fraud.pdf.
11 Ciara Torres-Spelliscy, *How Trump's Tax Records Could Point to Campaign Finance Violations*, BRENNAN CENTER (Oct. 16, 2020), https://www.brennancenter.org/our-work/analysis-opinion/how-trumps-tax-records-could-point-campaign-finance-violations.
12 *Super PACs*, OPENSECRETS, https://www.opensecrets.org/PACS/superpacs.php?cycle=2020 (last visited Dec. 12, 2023); Isaac Stanley-Becker, *New Trump-Backed Super PAC Formed Ahead of Midterms*, WASH. POST (Sept. 23, 2022), https://www.washingtonpost.com/politics/2022/09/23/trump-super-pac-midterms/.
13 *Rebuilding American Now Receipts*, FEC (2016), https://www.fec.gov/data/receipts/?cycle=2016&data_type=processed&committee_id=C00618876&line_number=F3X-11AI (listing GEO).
14 *Id.* (listing Hamilton).
15 *Id.* (listing Columbia).

NOTES

16 *Id.* (listing Calandra).
17 *Id.* (listing Murray Energy).
18 *Id.* (listing Southeast QSR).
19 *Id.* (listing $25,000 donors).
20 *Id.*
21 *Id.*
22 *Id.*
23 *Id.*
24 *Id.*
25 *Id.*
26 *Id.*
27 *Id.*
28 *Id.*
29 Robert Mitchell, *The Democrat Who Cried (Maybe) in New Hampshire and Lost the Presidential Nomination*, WASH. POST (Feb. 9, 2020), https://www.washingtonpost.com/history/2020/02/09/new-hampshire-ed-muskie-tears-primary/.
30 *Id.*
31 *Read Trump's Phone Conversation with Volodymyr Zelensky*, CNN (Sept. 26, 2019), https://www.cnn.com/2019/09/25/politics/donald-trump-ukraine-transcript-call/index.html.
32 *Giuliani Contradicts Himself over Ukraine Probe of Biden*, CNN (Sept. 20, 2019), https://www.cnn.com/videos/politics/2019/09/20/cuomo-rudy-giuliani-ukraine-biden-sot-cpt-vpx.cnn.
33 Ari Shapiro & Dave Blanchard, *How a Complicated Web Connects 2 Soviet-Born Businessmen with the Impeachment Inquiry*, NPR (Oct. 23, 2019), https://www.npr.org/2019/10/23/771849041/how-a-complicated-web-connects-2-soviet-born-businessmen-with-the-impeachment-in.
34 *read: Articles of Impeachment Against President Trump*, NPR (Dec. 10, 2019), https://www.npr.org/2019/12/10/786579846/read-articles-of-impeachment-against-president-trump.
35 *How Senators Voted on Trump's Impeachment*, POLITICO (Feb. 5, 2020), https://www.politico.com/interactives/2021/trump-second-impeachment-senate-vote/.
36 *Impeachment*, U.S. SENATE, https://www.senate.gov/about/powers-procedures/impeachment/senate-impeachment-role.htm (last visited Dec. 13, 2023).
37 Campbell Robertson et al., *U.S. Sets Coronavirus Case Record amid New Surge*, N.Y. TIMES (Oct. 23, 2020), https://www.nytimes.com/2020/10/23/us/covid-worst-day.html.
38 *1918 Pandemic Influenza Historic Timeline*, CENTERS FOR DISEASE CONTROL (Mar. 20, 2018), https://www.cdc.gov/flu/pandemic-resources/1918-commemoration/pandemic-timeline-1918.htm.
39 *Naming the Coronavirus Disease (covid-19)*, WORLD HEALTH ORGANIZATION (Feb. 11, 2020), https://www.who.int/emergencies/diseases/novel-coronavirus-2019/technical-guidance/naming-the-coronavirus-disease-(covid-2019)-and-the-virus-that-causes-it.
40 *Deaths Involving Coronavirus Disease 2019 (covid-19), Pneumonia, and Influenza Reported to NCHS by Week Ending Date, United States. Week Ending 2/1/2020 to 11/7/2020*,

CDC (Nov. 7, 2020), https://www.cdc.gov/nchs/nvss/vsrr/covid19/index.htm (listing over 225,000 deaths from COVID as of Nov.7, 2020).

41 Rob Stein, *U.S. Confirmed Coronavirus Infections Hit 10 Million*, NPR (Nov. 9, 2020), https://www.npr.org/sections/coronavirus-live-updates/2020/11/09/933023659/u-s-confirmed-coronavirus-infections-hit-10-million.

42 Quinn Scanlan, *Here's How States Have Changed the Rules Around Voting amid the Coronavirus Pandemic*, ABC NEWS (Sept. 22, 2020), https://abcnews.go.com/Politics/states-changed-rules-voting-amid-coronavirus-pandemic/story?id=72309089.

43 Joanna Walters, *Pennsylvania Politicians Go Topless to Warn Voters: Don't Mail in "Naked Ballots,"* GUARDIAN (Sept. 29, 2020), https://www.theguardian.com/us-news/2020/sep/29/pennsylvania-politicians-naked-ballots-election-secrecy-envelope.

44 Brittany Martin, *Celebrities Get Naked to Remind Voters of the Importance of Following Ballot Instructions*, L.A. MAGAZINE (Oct. 7, 2020), https://lamag.com/news/naked-ballot-celebrities-psa.

45 Madasyn Lee, *"Naked Celebs" Star in Political PSA About "Naked Ballots," Following Example of Allegheny County Pols*, TRIB LIVE (Oct. 7, 2020), https://triblive.com/news/pennsylvania/naked-celebs-star-in-political-psa-about-naked-ballots-following-example-of-allegheny-county-pols/.

46 Julia Hatmaker, *Bradley Cooper and Phillies' Star Andrew McCutchen Want You to Vote*, PENN LIVE (Oct. 5, 2020), https://www.pennlive.com/news/2020/10/bradley-cooper-wants-you-to-vote.html (showing the PSA).

47 Orion Rummler, *Pennsylvania's "Naked Ballots" Are 2020's Hanging Chads*, AXIOS (Sept. 25. 2020), https://www.axios.com/pennsylvania-naked-ballots-mail-in-voting-biden-9bbcf26f-c9d1-49bf-8939-0422242ed36e.html.

48 Daniel J. Hopkins, Marc Meredith, & Kira Wang, *How Many Naked Ballots Were Cast in Pennsylvania's 2020 General Election?*, MEDIUM (Aug. 26, 2021), https://medium.com/mit-election-lab/how-many-naked-ballots-were-cast-in-pennsylvanias-2020-general-election-91a277a1c19d.

49 Nicholas Riccardi & Marc Levy, *Democrats in Pa. Scramble to Limit Number of "Naked Ballots,"* AP NEWS (Sept. 24, 2020), https://apnews.com/article/election-2020-pennsylvania-joe-biden-voting-2020-voting-c7ef583c7b7981513830cae8fc1f0174.

50 Kadia Goba, *Pennsylvania's "Naked Ballot" Problem Is Spooking Elections Officials*, BUZZFEED (Sept. 25, 2020), https://www.buzzfeednews.com/article/kadiagoba/pennsylvania-naked-ballots-court-mail-in-vote.

51 Grace Panetta, *Pennsylvania's Election Is in Uncharted Territory with a New Rule That Rejects "Naked" Ballots*, BUSINESS INSIDER (Sept. 25, 2020), https://www.businessinsider.com/pennsylvania-ballots-will-be-rejected-if-not-sealed-in-two-envelopes-2020-9.

52 Holly Otterbein, *Pennsylvania Election Officials Warn of 2000 Florida Redux*, POLITICO (Sept. 22, 2020), https://www.politico.com/news/2020/09/22/pennsylvania-officials-warn-2000-florida-redux-420275.

53 Goba, *supra* note 50.

54 Hopkins et al., *supra* note 48.

55 *Philly's Final Vote Tally: Highest Turnout Since 1984*, NBC PHILADELPHIA (Nov. 18, 2020), https://www.nbcphiladelphia.com/news/politics/decision-2020/philadelphia-to-announce-final-election-vote-tally-certification-next-week/2601041/.

NOTES

56 Juana Summers, *Stripper Polls: The Racy Voting PSA That's Actually All About the Issues*, NPR (Oct. 5, 2020), https://www.npr.org/2020/10/05/918711192/stripper-polls-the-racy-voting-psa-thats-actually-all-about-the-issues.

57 Kerry Justich, *Exotic Dancers' PSA Targeting Black Male Voters Praised by Activist: "It Speaks Volumes,"* YAHOO (Sept. 25, 2020), https://www.yahoo.com/lifestyle/exotic-dancers-psa-targeting-black-male-voters-praised-by-activist-171718817.html.

58 Portia Bruner, *The Story Behind the Viral "Get Your Booty to the Poll" PSA*, FOX 5 ATLANTA (Oct. 7, 2020), https://www.fox5atlanta.com/news/the-story-behind-the-viral-get-your-booty-to-the-poll-psam.

59 Lisa Respers France, *Atlanta Exotic Dancers' "Get Your Booty to the Poll" PSA Grabs Attention*, CNN (Sept. 30, 2020), https://www.cnn.com/2020/09/30/entertainment/exotic-dancer-booty-to-poll/index.html.

60 Bruner, *supra* note 58.

61 *Id.* (quoting Paul Fox).

62 France, *supra* note 59.

63 Summers, *supra* note 56.

64 Justich, *supra* note 57.

65 Abby Budiman & Luis Noe-Bustamante, *Black Eligible Voters Have Accounted for Nearly Half of Georgia Electorate's Growth Since 2000*, PEW (Dec. 15, 2020), https://www.pewresearch.org/fact-tank/2020/12/15/black-eligible-voters-have-accounted-for-nearly-half-of-georgia-electorates-growth-since-2000/.

66 *Id.*

67 Ruth Igielnik, *Men and Women in the U.S. Continue to Differ in Voter Turnout Rate, Party Identification*, PEW (Aug. 18, 2020), https://www.pewresearch.org/fact-tank/2020/08/18/men-and-women-in-the-u-s-continue-to-differ-in-voter-turnout-rate-party-identification/.

68 Juana Summers, *Trump Push to Invalidate Votes in Heavily Black Cities Alarms Civil Rights Groups*, NPR (Nov. 24, 2020), https://www.npr.org/2020/11/24/938187233/trump-push-to-invalidate-votes-in-heavily-black-cities-alarms-civil-rights-group.

69 Bruner, *supra* note 58.

70 Luis Noe-Bustamante & Abby Budiman, Black, *Latino and Asian Americans Have Been Key to Georgia's Registered Voter Growth Since 2016*, PEW (Dec. 21, 2020), https://www.pewresearch.org/fact-tank/2020/12/21/black-latino-and-asian-americans-have-been-key-to-georgias-registered-voter-growth-since-2016/.

71 Emma Hurt, *How Democrats Found Thousands of New Voters and Flipped Georgia's Senate Seats*, NPR (Feb. 6, 2021), https://www.npr.org/2021/02/06/964614820/how-democrats-found-thousands-of-new-voters-and-flipped-georgias-senate-seats.

72 Deena Zaru, *Kanye West Declares 2020 Presidential Bid at VMAs*, CNN (Sept. 5, 2015), https://www.cnn.com/2015/08/31/politics/kanye-west-2020-running-for-president-vma/index.html.

73 David Smith, *Kanye West Declares He Will Run for US President in 2020*, GUARDIAN (July 4, 2020), https://www.theguardian.com/music/2020/jul/05/kanye-west-declares-he-will-run-for-us-president-in-2020.

74 Daniel Kreps, *A "Kanye 2020" Committee Just Filed with the FEC*, ROLLING STONE (July 15, 2020), https://www.rollingstone.com/music/music-news/kanye-2020-fec-1029361/.

75 Emily Jacobs, *Kanye West Submits over 9,000 Extra Signatures for Ohio Presidential Ballot*, N.Y. POST (Aug. 6, 2020), https://nypost.com/2020/08/06/kanye-west-submits-over-9000-extra-signatures-for-ohio-ballot/.
76 Ben Jacobs, *Kanye West Is Trying to Get on the Ballot in Wisconsin, a Crucial Swing State*, N.Y. INTELLIGENCER (Aug. 3, 2020), https://nymag.com/intelligencer/2020/08/kanye-west-is-still-trying-to-get-on-the-ballot.html.
77 Alia Slisco, *Kanye West Ballot Petition Gets Challenged in Illinois over Signatures*, NEWSWEEK (July 28, 2020), https://www.newsweek.com/kanye-west-ballot-petition-gets-challenged-illinois-over-signatures-1521170.
78 Shia Kapos, *"When you're late, you're late": Kanye Falls Short in Wisconsin*, POLITICO (Aug. 20, 2020), https://www.politico.com/news/2020/08/20/kanye-west-campaign-wisconsin-399672.
79 Sara Murray & Scott Glover, *Kanye West's Campaign Has Hired GOP Operative with History of Controversial Work*, CNN (Sept. 22, 2020), https://www.cnn.com/2020/09/22/politics/kanye-west-gop-operative/index.html.
80 Peter Jamison & Laura Vozzella, *Kayne West Campaign in Virginia Is Accused of Deceptive Signature Gathering*, WASH. POST (Aug. 29, 2020), https://www.washingtonpost.com/local/kanye-west-campaign-in-virginia-is-accused-of-deceptive-signature-gathering/2020/08/29/b0a2fa56-ea07-11ea-bc79-834454439a44_story.html.
81 *Id.*
82 Murray & Glover, *supra* note 79.
83 *Official 2020 Presidential General Election Results General Election Date: 11/03/2020*, FEC, at 8, https://www.fec.gov/resources/cms-content/documents/2020presgeresults.pdf (last visited Aug. 9, 2022).
84 Charles Trepany, *Kanye West Skips "Kimmel" After Receiving Just 60,000 Votes*, USA TODAY (Nov. 4, 2020), https://www.usatoday.com/story/entertainment/celebrities/2020/11/03/kanye-west-votes-first-time-ever-writes-himself-president/6151882002/.
85 *Official 2020 Presidential General Election Results*, *supra* note 83.
86 Wyo. Stat. 22-16-106, write-in candidates, https://wyoleg.gov/statutes/compress/title22.pdf.
87 Danny Hakim & Maggie Haberman, *Republicans Aid Kayne West's Bid to Get on the 2020 Ballot*, N.Y. TIMES (Aug. 4, 2020), https://www.nytimes.com/2020/08/04/us/politics/kanye-west-president-republicans.html.
88 Barbara Sprunt, *Here's How Republicans Are Boosting Kanye West's Presidential Campaign*, NPR (Aug. 13, 2020), https://www.npr.org/2020/08/13/901534846/heres-how-republicans-are-boosting-kanye-west-s-presidential-campaign.
89 Katie Couric, Chris Krebs & Rashad Robinson, *Commission on Information Disorder Final Report*, ASPEN INSTITUTE 12 (Nov. 15, 2021), https://www.aspeninstitute.org/publications/commission-on-information-disorder-final-report/ ("Research shows that economic, social, and racial disparities have created an environment ripe for targeted disinformation that can cause significant harm to communities of color.").
90 Jacobs, *supra* note 75; Slisco, *supra* note 77.
91 Murray & Glover, *supra* note 79.
92 Tommy Beer, *Here's Everything Trump Has Said About Refusing to Give Up Power*, FORBES (Sept. 24, 2020), https://www.forbes.com/sites/tommybeer/2020/09/24/heres-everything-trump-has-said-about-refusing-to-give-up-power/.

93 William Cummings, *Fact Check: 5 Falsehoods Trump Repeated at CPAC, from Election Fraud to Texas' Wind Power*, USA TODAY A3 (Mar. 2, 2021).
94 *Id.*
95 Penny M. Venetis, *Opposition to Voting by Mail Is a Form of Voter Suppression That Disproportionately Impacts Communities of Color*, 72 RUTGERS U. L. REV. 1387, 1396 (2020).
96 Nicholas Riccardi, *ap fact check: Trump's Big Distortions on Mail-In Voting*, AP (Sept. 17, 2020), https://apnews.com/article/virus-outbreak-election-2020-ap-fact-check-elections-voting-fraud-and-irregularities-8c5db90960815f91f39fe115579570b4.
97 Miles Parks, *Ignoring FBI and Fellow Republicans, Trump Continues Assault on Mail-In Voting*, NPR (Aug. 28, 2020), https://www.npr.org/2020/08/28/906676695/ignoring-fbi-and-fellow-republicans-trump-continues-assault-on-mail-in-voting.
98 Sarah Niebler, *Vote-by-Mail: covid-19 and the 2020 Presidential Primaries*, 57 SOC'Y 547, 547 (2020): Nicholas Riccardi, Jonathan Drew & Scott Bauer, *In Big States, Tiny Counties, Trump Attacking Voting Rules*, AP (Oct. 1, 2020), https://apnews.com/article/virus-outbreak-election-2020-donald-trump-local-elections-lawsuits-4298a514550323d39931f3e5fff2ccae.
99 Yochai Benkler & Casey Tilton, *Mail-In Voter Fraud: Anatomy of a Disinformation Campaign*, BERKMAN KLEIN CENTER 5 (Oct. 2, 2020), https://papers.ssrn.com/sol3/papers.cfm?abstract_id=3703701.
100 *Id.* at 5 & 9.
101 Joey Garrison, *"He's Scaring Our Own Voters": Republicans Run into a Donald Trump Problem as They Push Mail Voting*, USA TODAY (July 25, 2020), https://www.usatoday.com/story/news/politics/elections/2020/07/25/republicans-have-donald-trump-problem-they-push-mail-voting-base/5452373002/.
102 Ledyard King, *Trump Backtracks on His Condemnation of Mail-In Voting, Says Florida Is An exception*, USA TODAY (Aug. 4, 2020), https://www.usatoday.com/story/news/politics/elections/2020/08/04/trump-backtracks-mail-vote-criticism-says-florida-exception/3291012001/.
103 *Id.*
104 Niebler, *supra* note 98, at 549; Kadia Goba, *Trump's False Rhetoric About Mail-In Voting Is Spooking Voters in a Vital State*, BUZZFEED (Aug. 20, 2020), https://www.buzzfeednews.com/article/kadiagoba/trump-usps-mail-in-vote-fear.
105 Niebler, *supra* note 98, at 551.
106 Vera Bergengruen & Lissandra Villa, *How Donald Trump's Misinformation Campaign Against Mail-In Voting Is Undermining Faith in Democracy*, TIME (Sept. 10, 2020), https://time.com/5887438/trump-mail-in-voting/.
107 Alison Durkee, *Poll: Voters Saying They'll Vote by Mail Plunges amid Trump Attacks*, FORBES (Oct. 1, 2020), https://www.forbes.com/sites/alisondurkee/2020/10/01/poll-voters-saying-vote-by-mail-plunges-amid-trump-attacks-usps-issues/?sh=75195be133b1.
108 Press Release, *Joint Statement from Elections Infrastructure Government Coordinating Council & the Election Infrastructure Sector Coordinating Executive Committees*, CISA (Nov. 12, 2020), https://www.cisa.gov/news-events/news/joint-statement-elections-infrastructure-government-coordinating-council-election ("The [2020] November 3rd election was the most secure in American history.").
109 Scanlan, *supra* note 42 ("The states are: Alabama, Arkansas, California, Connecticut, Delaware, District of Columbia, Georgia, Illinois, Iowa, Kentucky, Maryland, Massachusetts, Michigan, Minnesota, Missouri, Montana, Nebraska, Nevada, New Hamp-

shire, New Jersey, New York, North Carolina, Ohio, Oklahoma, Pennsylvania, Rhode Island, South Carolina, Texas, Vermont, West Virginia and Wisconsin.").
110 Id.
111 Katie Meyer, *"Bad Things Happen In Philadelphia," and Other Takeaways from the Trump-Biden Debate*, NPR (Sept. 30, 2020), https://whyy.org/articles/bad-things-happen-in-philadelphia-and-other-takeaways-from-the-debate/.
112 Chris Brennan, Sean Collins Walsh & Cynthia Fernandez, *Trump Has Put Philly on the Front Lines of His Attack on Voting*, PHILA. INQUIRER (Oct. 3, 2020), https://www.inquirer.com/politics/election/trump-philadelphia-pennsylvania-voting-20201003.html.
113 Id.
114 Id.
115 Amy Sherman, *Trump's Falsehoods About Mail Voting in Nevada, Fact-Checked*, POLITIFACT (Sept. 13, 2020), https://www.politifact.com/article/2020/sep/13/trumps-falsehoods-about-mail-voting-nevada-fact-ch/.
116 Id.
117 Gary D. Robertson, *North Carolina Board Agrees to More Absentee Ballot Changes*, AP (Sept. 22, 2020), https://apnews.com/article/election-2020-virus-outbreak-north-carolina-elections-raleigh-6798f202bccc5070c1649b24c77b0bd1.
118 Igor Derysh, *"Openly Trying to Cheat": Trump Campaign Tells Election Officials to Ignore Voting Rules*, SALON (Oct. 5, 2020), https://www.salon.com/2020/10/05/openly-trying-to-cheat-trump-campaign-local-election-officials-to-ignore-voting-rules/.
119 Riccardi et al., *supra* note 98; N.C. Gen. Stat. Ann. §163–275.
120 James Oliphant, *Trump Encourages Supporters to Try to Vote Twice, Sparking Uproar*, REUTERS (Sept. 3, 2020), https://www.reuters.com/article/uk-usa-election-trump-vote-idUKKBN25U2FY.
121 William Cummings, *North Carolina Elections Chief Says "It is illegal to vote twice in an election" After Trump Comment on Double Voting*, USA TODAY (Sept. 3, 2020), https://www.usatoday.com/story/news/politics/elections/2020/09/03/nc-elections-illegal-vote-twice-after-trump-comment/5702513002/.
122 Lynn Bonner, *Fewer People Voted Illegally in 2020, but Voting Rights Groups Want the State to Stop Punishing People Who Say They Voted by Mistake*, NC POLICY WATCH (Jan. 21, 2021), https://ncpolicywatch.com/2021/01/21/fewer-people-voted-illegally-in-2020-but-voting-rights-groups-want-the-state-to-stop-punishing-people-who-say-they-voted-by-mistake/.
123 Karl Evers-Hillstrom, *Most Expensive Ever: 2020 Election Cost $14.4 Billion*, OPENSECRETS (Feb. 11, 2021), https://www.opensecrets.org/news/2021/02/2020-cycle-cost-14p4-billion-doubling-16/.
124 Id.
125 *Presidential Election Campaign Finance, 2020, Fundraising Chart*, BALLOTPEDIA, https://ballotpedia.org/Presidential_election_campaign_finance,_2020 (last visited Aug. 12, 2022).
126 Karl Evers-Hillstrom, *Biden Campaign Becomes First to Raise $1 Billion from Donors*, OPENSECRETS (Dec. 7, 2020), https://www.opensecrets.org/news/2020/12/biden-campaign-1billion-from-donors/.
127 Evers-Hillstrom, *supra* note 123.
128 Chase Peterson-Withorn, *Trump Is Set to Become Only Billionaire to Spend $0 on White House Run*, FORBES (Nov. 1, 2020), https://www.forbes.com/sites/chasewith-

orn/2020/11/01/trump-is-set-to-become-only-billionaire-to-spend-0-on-white-house-run/?sh=531f4d142f82.
129 Greta Kaul, *What the Hell Is ActBlue?*, MINN. POST (Aug. 17, 2018), https://www.minnpost.com/politics-policy/2018/08/what-hell-actblue-and-why-it-showing-so-many-democratic-candidates-campaign/.
130 Ally Mutnick, *WinRed Collects Record $275M for Republicans in Second Quarter*, POLITICO (July 6, 2020), https://www.politico.com/news/2020/07/06/winred-republican-fundraising-349490.
131 Sarah K. Burris, *WinRed Loses Attempt to Dismiss Massive Case from Four AGs over Their Auto-Checked Donations*, RAW STORY (Jan. 26, 2022), https://www.rawstory.com/winred-scandal-lawsuit-moves-forward/.
132 Daniel N. Jellins, *The First Amendment Can Help Stop Dark Patterns in Campaign Fundraising*, BROOKINGS (Feb. 17, 2022), https://www.brookings.edu/blog/techtank/2022/02/17/the-first-amendment-can-help-stop-dark-patterns-in-campaign-fundraising/.
133 Shane Goldmacher, *How Trump Steered Supporters into Unwitting Donations*, N.Y. TIMES (Apr. 5, 2021), https://www.nytimes.com/2021/04/03/us/politics/trump-donations.html.
134 *Id.*
135 Burris, *supra* note 131.
136 *Super PACs Hammer Trump*, OPENSECRETS (Oct. 2020), https://www.opensecrets.org/news/2020/10/super-pacs-hammer-trump/.
137 *Top Organizations Disclosing Donations to America First Action, 2020*, OPENSECRETS, https://www.opensecrets.org/outside-spending/detail/2020?cmte=C00637512&tab=donors (last visited Mar. 27, 2023).
138 *Id.*
139 *Preserve America PAC, Receipts*, FEC (2020), https://www.fec.gov/data/receipts/?committee_id=C00756882&two_year_transaction_period=2020&cycle=2020&line_number=F3X-11AI&data_type=processed.
140 Chris Edelson, *Democracy Won't Survive Another Trump Presidency*, BALTIMORE SUN A9 (Dec. 18, 2023).
141 *Make America Great Again Inc., Receipts*, FEC (Oct. 5, 2022), https://www.fec.gov/data/receipts/?committee_id=C00825851&two_year_transaction_period=2022&cycle=2022&line_number=F3X-11AI&data_type=processed.
142 *Id.*
143 *Probity International Corporation*, DUN & BRADSTREET, https://www.dnb.com/business-directory/company-profiles.probity_international_corporation.4c60dff9ff57cbf3901d80c569a8b9aa.html (last visited Feb. 6, 2022).
144 Brian Schwartz, *Meet the Megadonors Backing the Trump Super PAC as Some Top Donors Opt Out of Supporting 2024 Candidacy*, CNBC (Dec. 11, 2022), https://www.cnbc.com/2022/12/11/some-megadonors-support-trump-super-pac-as-it-backs-him-for-president.html.
145 *Id.*
146 *Make America Great Again Inc., Receipts*, FEC (last visited Dec. 6, 2023), https://www.fec.gov/data/receipts/?cycle=2024&data_type=processed&committee_id=C00825851&contributor_name=churchill&two_year_transaction_period=2024&line_number=F3X-11AI; Jaxon White, *Lancaster County Gives Big to*

[259]

Trump Campaign, Biden Raises More than Other Republicans, LANCASTER ONLINE (Dec. 3, 2023), https://lancasteronline.com/news/politics/lancaster-county-gives-big-to-trump-campaign-biden-raises-more-than-other-republicans/article_700717e2-8fd2-11ee-b347-db274b078de3.html.

147 *Make America Great Again, Again! Inc., Receipts*, FEC (last visited Dec. 6, 2023), https://www.fec.gov/data/receipts/?committee_id=C00790477&two_year_transaction_period=2022&cycle=2022&line_number=F3X-11AI&data_type=processed (listing donations from Fanjul and Florida Crystals).

148 *Id.*

149 *Make America Great Again Inc., Receipts*, FEC (last visited Dec. 6, 2023), https://www.fec.gov/data/receipts/?cycle=2024&data_type=processed&committee_id=C00825851&contributor_name=duggan&two_year_transaction_period=2024&line_number=F3X-11AI (listing Duggan); Matt Dixon, *Florida Scientologist Becomes Huge Trump Donor*, POLITICO (Sept. 21, 2020), https://www.politico.com/states/florida/story/2020/09/21/florida-scientologist-becomes-huge-trump-donor-1317635.

150 *Make America Great Again Inc., Receipts*, FEC (last visited Dec. 6, 2023), https://www.fec.gov/data/receipts/?cycle=2024&data_type=processed&committee_id=C00825851&contributor_name=duggan&two_year_transaction_period=2024&line_number=F3X-11AI (listing Ruffin); *Phil Ruffin*, FORBES (Dec. 6, 2023), https://www.forbes.com/profile/phil-ruffin/?sh=306151407ec4.

151 *Make America Great Again Inc., Receipts*, FEC (last visited Dec. 6, 2023), https://www.fec.gov/data/receipts/?cycle=2024&data_type=processed&committee_id=C00825851&contributor_name=johnson&two_year_transaction_period=2024&line_number=F3X-11AI; *Chairman Woody Johnson*, N.Y. JETS, https://www.newyorkjets.com/team/front-office-roster/woody-johnson (last visited Dec. 6, 2023).

152 *Make America Great Again Inc., Receipts*, FEC (last visited Dec. 6, 2023), https://www.fec.gov/data/receipts/?cycle=2024&data_type=processed&committee_id=C00825851&contributor_name=kushner&two_year_transaction_period=2024&line_number=F3X-11AI.

153 *Id.*

154 Amy Bracken, *A Sweet Deal: The Royal Family of Cane Benefits from Political Giving*, AL-JAZEERA (July 23, 2015), http://america.aljazeera.com/multimedia/2015/7/fanjul-family-benefits-political-donations.html.

155 *Id.*

156 Bloomberg *Report Sheds Light on Political Influence of Top Sugar Producers*, NATIONAL CONFECTIONERS ASSOC. (Aug. 10, 2017), https://candyusa.com/cst/bloomberg-report-sheds-light-on-political-influence-of-top-sugar-producers/.

157 Bracken, *supra* note 154.

158 Virginia Chamlee, *How Big Sugar Gets What It Wants*, COLO. INDEPENDENT (Sept. 20, 2011), https://www.coloradoindependent.com/2011/09/20/how-big-sugar-gets-what-it-wants-from-congress/.

159 Guy Rolnik, *Meet the Sugar Barons Who Used Both Sides of American Politics to Get Billions in Subsidies*, PROMARKET (Sept. 19, 2016), https://www.promarket.org/2016/09/19/sugar-industry-buys-academia-politicians/ ("The Fanjuls . . . com-

pany's American brands include Domino's, Florida Crystals, Redpath, Tate & Lyle, and C&H.").

8. THE BIG LIE

1 Donald Trump (@realDonaldTrump), TWITTER (Dec. 19, 2020, 1:42 a.m.) ("Statistically impossible to have lost the 2020 Election.").
2 Interview of Carolyn Bourdeaux with the author (Apr. 25, 2023).
3 *From Inside the Capitol Rep. Carolyn Bourdeaux Describes the Insurrection*, 11 ALIVE (Jan. 6, 2021), https://www.youtube.com/watch?v=WoVaqyRF9rQ.
4 Michael German, *Written Testimony Submitted to the Select Committee to Investigate the January 6th Attack*, BRENNAN CENTER (Oct. 17, 2022), https://www.brennancenter.org/our-work/research-reports/written-testimony-submitted-select-committee-investigate-january-6th.
5 Sheila Blackford, *Disputed Election of 1876: The Death Knell of the Republican Dream*, UVA MILLER CENTER (2022), httds://millercenter.org/the-presidency/educational-resources/disputed-election-1876.
6 Sushovan Sircar, *What Are "Blue Shift," "Red Mirage," and Why They Give Biden the Edge*, QUINT (Nov. 5, 2020), https://www.thequint.com/news/world/us-presidential-elections-2020-red-mirage-blue-shift-pennsylvania-georgia-trump-biden#read-more.
7 Marshall Cohen, *Deciphering the "Red Mirage," the "Blue Shift," and the Uncertainty Surrounding Election Results This November*, CNN (Sept. 1, 2020), https://www.cnn.com/2020/09/01/politics/2020-election-count-red-mirage-blue-shift/index.html.
8 Nicholas Riccardi, *ap fact check: Trump's Big Distortions on Mail-In Voting*, AP (Sept. 17, 2020), https://apnews.com/article/virus-outbreak-election-2020-ap-fact-check-elections-voting-fraud-and-irregularities-8c5db90960815f91f39fe115579570b4.
9 Edward B. Foley, *A Big Blue Shift: Measuring an Asymmetrically Increasing Margin of Litigation*, 28 J. OF L. & POLITICS 501 (2013).
10 Ellen Konar & Joe Wlos, *How Red Mirage Shaped the 2020 Election Narrative*, MEDIUM (Jan. 14, 2021), https://hwkfsh.medium.com/how-red-mirage-shaped-the-2020-election-narrative-81e404d2a58b.
11 Cohen, *supra* note 7.
12 AD HOC COMMITTEE FOR 2020 ELECTION FAIRNESS AND LEGITIMACY, FAIR ELECTIONS DURING A CRISIS: URGENT RECOMMENDATIONS IN LAW, MEDIA, POLITICS, AND TECH TO ADVANCE THE LEGITIMACY OF, AND THE PUBLIC'S CONFIDENCE IN, THE NOVEMBER 2020 U.S. ELECTIONS (2020), https://www.law.uci.edu/faculty/full-time/hasen/2020ElectionReport.pdf.
13 Cohen, *supra* note 7.
14 David A. Graham, *The "Blue Shift" Will Decide the Election*, ATLANTIC (Nov. 3, 2020), https://www.theatlantic.com/ideas/archive/2020/08/brace-blue-shift/615097/.
15 Paul Blumenthal, *The Nightmare Scenario That Keeps Election Lawyers Up at Night—And Could Hand Trump a Second Term*, HUFF. POST (Sept. 20, 2020), https://www.huffpost.com/entry/election-2020-nightmare_n_5f65163fc5b6de79b674a9d5.
16 AD HOC COMMITTEE, *supra* note 12, at 6.
17 Graham, *supra* note 14.
18 Sircar, *supra* note 6.

NOTES

19 Quint Forgey, *Trump's Premature Victory Claim Prompts Quick Rebukes*, POLITICO (Nov. 4, 2020), https://www.politico.com/news/2020/11/04/trump-premature-victory-claim-434024.
20 *Donald Trump 2020 Election Night Speech Transcript*, REV (Nov. 4, 2020), https://www.rev.com/blog/transcripts/donald-trump-2020-election-night-speech-transcript; *see also* Alana Wise, *fact check: Trump Falsely Claims Widespread Election Fraud in Latest Election Speech*, NPR (Nov. 5, 2020), https://www.npr.org/2020/11/05/931930379/fact-check-trump-falsely-claims-widespread-fraud-in-latest-election-speech.
21 *Id.*
22 Matthew Brown, *Trump Is Heard on Audiotape Pressuring Georgia Secretary of State to "Find" Votes to Overturn Biden's Win*, USA TODAY (Jan. 4, 2021), https://www.usatoday.com/story/news/politics/elections/2021/01/03/trump-pressured-georgia-election-official-call-washington-post-report-says/4119948001/.
23 *Id.*
24 Jeff Amy, Darlene Superville & Jonathan Lemire, *GA Election Officials Reject Trump Call to "Find" More Votes*, AP (Jan. 4, 2021), https://apnews.com/article/trump-raffensperger-phone-call-georgia-d503c8b4e58f7cd648fbf9a746131ec9.
25 Kate Brumback, *Georgia Official Says Sen. Lindsey Graham Asked Him About Tossing Ballots*, STAR TRIBUNE (Nov. 17, 2020), https://www.startribune.com/hand-tally-of-georgia-presidential-race-continues/573092151/.
26 Indictment, *Georgia v. Trump*, No. 23SC188947EJ15 McAffee (Aug. 14, 2023).
27 Molly Ball, *The Secret History of the Shadow Campaign That Saved the 2020 Election*, TIME (Feb. 4, 2021), https://time.com/5936036/secret-2020-election-campaign/.
28 Eric Lutz, *Lindsey Graham Takes His Trump Fealty to a New Level*, VANITY FAIR (Nov. 17, 2020), https://www.vanityfair.com/news/2020/11/lindsey-graham-throw-out-ballots-georgia.
29 *Official 2020 Presidential General Election Results*, FEC, https://www.fec.gov/resources/cms-content/documents/2020presgeresults.pdf (last visited Mar. 14, 2022).
30 *Id.* at 1.
31 *Id.* at 2, 8.
32 Press Release, *Joint Statement from Elections Infrastructure Government Coordinating Council & the Election Infrastructure Sector Coordinating Executive Committees*, CISA (Nov. 12, 2020), https://www.cisa.gov/news-events/news/joint-statement-elections-infrastructure-government-coordinating-council-election ("The [2020] November 3rd election was the most secure in American history . . . There is no evidence that any voting system deleted or lost votes, changed votes, or was in any way compromised.").
33 *January 6 Committee Final Report* at 196–97.
34 *Here's Every Word of the First Jan. 6 Committee Hearing on Its Investigation*, NPR (June 10, 2022), https://www.npr.org/2022/06/10/1104156949/jan-6-committee-hearing-transcript (quoting Cheney).
35 *Id.* (quoting Thompson).
36 Norman L. Eisen et al., *Trump on Trial: A Model Prosecution Memo for Federal Election Interference Crimes Second Edition*, JUST SECURITY (July 13, 2023), https://www.justsecurity.org/87236/trump-on-trial-a-model-prosecution-memo-for-federal-election-interference-crimes/.
37 *January 6 Committee Final Report* at 300 (internal citation omitted).

38 *Id.* at 300–301 (internal citation omitted).
39 *Big Lie "Big Rip-Off,"* MARKETPLACE (June 13, 2022), https://www.marketplace.org/shows/make-me-smart/big-lie-big-rip-off/.
40 Ciara Torres-Spelliscy, *The Perils of Fundraising Using the Disinformation of the Big Lie* in DISINFORMATION, MISINFORMATION, AND DEMOCRACY (forthcoming 2024), https://ssrn.com/abstract=4541489.
41 Einer Elhauge, Brandenburg v. Ohio *Doesn't Protect Trump's Incitement,* WASH. POST (Jan. 14, 2021), https://www.washingtonpost.com/outlook/2021/01/14/trump-brandenburg-impeachment-first-amendment/.
42 Katelyn Polantz, *Giuliani, Who Urged Trump Supporters to Have "Trial By Combat," Says He Wasn't Literally Calling for Insurrection,* CNN (May 18, 2021), https://www.cnn.com/2021/05/18/politics/rudy-giuliani-january-6-insurrection-lawsuit/index.html (quoting Giuliani); Ryan Bort, *Rep. Mo Brooks on Incendiary Jan. 6th Speech: Trump Made Me Do It,* ROLLING STONE (July 6, 2021), https://www.rollingstone.com/politics/politics-news/mo-brooks-insurrection-speech-lawsuit-1193229/ (quoting Brooks).
43 Donald J. Trump, *Rally on Electoral College Vote Certification* at 3:33:05–3:33:10, 3:33:32–3:33:54, 3:37:19–3:37:29, C-SPAN (Jan. 6, 2021), https://www.c-span.org/video/?507744-1/rally-electoral-college-vote-certification.
44 Ron Fournier, *The Art of Deception,* ATLANTIC (July 21, 2016), https://www.theatlantic.com/politics/archive/2016/07/the-art-of-deception/492554/.
45 *Id.*
46 *Id.*
47 Catherine J. Ross, *What the First Amendment Really Says About Whether Trump Incited the Capitol Riot,* SLATE (Jan. 19, 2021), https://slate.com/technology/2021/01/trump-incitement-violence-brandenburg-first-amendment.html.
48 Statement of Offense, *United States v. Dresch,* Document 36 at 3, No. 21-CR-71 (ABJ) (Aug. 4, 2021), https://www.justice.gov/usao-dc/case-multi-defendant/file/1421976/download; Statement of Offense, *United States v. Fitchett,* Document 82 at 3, No. 1:21-CR-41 (CJN) (Aug. 10, 2021), https://www.justice.gov/usao-dc/case-multi-defendant/file/1423411/download; Statement of Offense, *United States v. Griffith,* Document 63 at 4, No. 21-cr-00204-04 (BAH) (July 29, 2021), https://www.justice.gov/usao-dc/case-multi-defendant/file/1419011/download; Statement of Offense, *United States v. Young,* Document 250 at 5, No. 1:21-cr-00028-APM (June 23, 2021), https://www.justice.gov/usao-dc/case-multi-defendant/file/1405771/download.
49 Statement of Offense, *United States v. Vinson,* Document 31, 1, 4, No. 1:21-cr-00355-RBW (July 27, 2021), https://www.justice.gov/usao-dc/case-multi-defendant/file/1418031/download.
50 Statement of Offense, *United States v. Rosa,* Document 60, 1, 6, No. 1:21-cr-00068-TNM (July 29, 2021), https://www.justice.gov/usao-dc/case-multi-defendant/file/1419001/download.
51 *January 6 Committee Final Report* at 110–11.
52 *Trump v. Thompson,* 20 F.4th 10, 18 (D.C. Cir. 2021) (internal citations omitted).
53 *US Dominion Inc. v. Fox News Network LLC.* at 27.
54 Memorandum Opinion at 13, *United States v. Chrestman,* Case 1:21-cr-00160-TJK (Feb. 26, 2021), https://s3.documentcloud.org/documents/20698736/2-26-21-william-chrestman-detention-opinion.pdf.

55 *Trump v. Thompson*, 20 F.4th at 18.
56 Press Release, *Leader of Oath Keepers and 10 Other Individuals Indicted in Federal Court for Seditious Conspiracy and Other Offenses Related to U.S. Capitol Breach*, DOJ (Jan. 13, 2022), https://www.justice.gov/opa/pr/leader-oath-keepers-and-10-other-individuals-indicted-federal-court-seditious-conspiracy-and.
57 18 U.S. Code § 2384.
58 Freddy Brewster, *The Jan. 6 Committee's Focus on Sedition, Explained*, L.A. TIMES (July 12, 2022), https://www.latimes.com/politics/story/2022-07-12/jan-6-committee-hearing-sedition.
59 *Id.*
60 *Id.*
61 Kyle Cheney, Josh Gerstein & Nicholas Wu, *DOJ Charges Proud Boys Leaders with Seditious Conspiracy over Jan. 6 attack*, POLITICO (June 6, 2022), https://www.politico.com/news/2022/06/06/doj-charges-proud-boys-leaders-with-seditious-conspiracy-over-jan-6-attack-00037518.
62 Indictment, Nordean et al. at 8, 21-cr-175TJK (D.D.C. June 6, 2022).
63 *Id.*
64 Cheney, Gerstein & Wu, *supra* note 61.
65 Jacob Schulz, *The Last Time the Justice Department Prosecuted a Seditious Conspiracy Case*, LAWFARE (Feb. 24, 2021), https://www.lawfareblog.com/last-time-justice-department-prosecuted-seditious-conspiracy-case.
66 Brewster, *supra* note 58.
67 *Id.*
68 Statement of Offense at 4, *United States v. Berry*, No. 21-cr-460 (D.D.C. Aug. 6, 2021).
69 Press Release, *Leader of Oath Keepers and 10 Other Individuals Indicted in Federal Court for Seditious Conspiracy and Other Offenses Related to U.S. Capitol Breach*, DOJ (Jan. 13, 2022), https://www.justice.gov/opa/pr/leader-oath-keepers-and-10-other-individuals-indicted-federal-court-seditious-conspiracy-and.
70 Press Release, *Four Oath Keepers Found Guilty of Seditious Conspiracy Related to U.S. Capitol Breach Defendants Also Convicted of Related Felony Charges*, DOJ (Jan. 23, 2023), https://www.justice.gov/opa/pr/four-oath-keepers-found-guilty-seditious-conspiracy-related-us-capitol-breach.
71 Carrie Johnson, *Jury Convicts Enrique Tarrio of the Proud Boys on Seditious Conspiracy Charge*, NPR (May 4, 2023), https://www.npr.org/2023/05/04/1172530436/proud-boys-jan-6-sedition-trial-verdict.
72 Press Release, *Court Sentences Two Oath Keepers Leaders to 18 Years in Prison on Seditious Conspiracy and Other Charges Related to U.S. Capitol Breach*, DOJ (May 25, 2023), https://www.justice.gov/usao-dc/pr/court-sentences-two-oath-keepers-leaders-18-years-prison-seditious-conspiracy-and-other.
73 Press Release, *Proud Boys Leader Sentenced to 22 Years in Prison on Seditious Conspiracy and Other Charges Related to U.S. Capitol Breach*, DOJ (Sept. 5, 2023), https://www.justice.gov/usao-dc/pr/proud-boys-leader-sentenced-22-years-prison-seditious-conspiracy-and-other-charges.
74 *United States v. Sandlin*, No. 21-cr-88, at *2–3 (D.D.C. Dec. 10, 2021).
75 Press Release, *Tennessee Man Sentenced to 63 Months in Prison for Felony Charges Related to Jan. 6 Capitol Breach*, DOJ (Dec. 9, 2022), https://www.justice.gov/usao-dc/pr/tennessee-man-sentenced-63-months-prison-felony-charges-related-jan-6-capitol-breach.

76 *DeGrave, Nathaniel J. (aka, Nathan DeGrave) Case Number: 1:21-cr-90*, DOJ, https://www.justice.gov/usao-dc/defendants/degrave-nathaniel-j-aka-nathan-degrave (last visited Feb. 13, 2023).
77 Michael Kunzelman, *Jan. 6 Rioters Are Raking in Thousands in Donations. Now the US Is Coming After Their Haul*, AP (May 28, 2023), https://abcnews.go.com/US/wireStory/government-claw-back-money-jan-6-rioters-profit-99660355.
78 Mark Sherman, *Supreme Court to Hear a Case That Could Erase 2020 Capitol Riot Charge Against Hundreds, Including Trump*, PBS (Dec. 13, 2023), https://www.pbs.org/newshour/politics/supreme-court-to-hear-a-case-that-could-erase-2020-capitol-riot-charge-against-hundreds-including-trump.
79 Indictment, *United States v. Trump*, Case No. 1:23-cr-00257-TSC (Aug. 1, 2023); Indictment, *Georgia v. Trump*, No. 23SC188947EJ15 McAffee (Aug. 14, 2023).
80 Brewster, *supra* note 58; Statement of Offense at 3, *United States v. Bennett*, Doc. 22, No. 21-CR-227JEB (D.D.C. July 22, 2021), https://www.justice.gov/usao-dc/case-multi-defendant/file/1414711/download; Statement of Offense at 3, *United States v. Berry*, No. 21-cr-__ (D.D.C. Aug. 6, 2021).
81 January 6 Committee, *Transcribed Interviews and Depositions of Virginia L. Thomas* at 126 (Sept. 29, 2022), https://www.govinfo.gov/content/pkg/GPO-J6-TRANSCRIPT-CTRL0000923619/pdf/GPO-J6-TRANSCRIPT-CTRL0000923619.pdf.
82 Alia Shoaib, *Trump Supporter Who Took Private Jet to Jan. 6 Riot and Called Capitol Police "Traitors" Pleads Guilty to Federal Misdemeanor*, BUSINESS INSIDER (Aug. 20, 2022), https://www.businessinsider.com/trump-supporter-private-jet-capitol-riot-pleads-guilty-police-traitors-2022-8.
83 *Schwab, Katherine Staveley (aka Katie), Case Number: 1:21-cr-50*, DOJ, https://www.justice.gov/usao-dc/defendants/schwab-katherine-staveley-aka-katie (last visited Dec. 28, 2022).
84 *hyland, Jason Lee Case Number: 1:21-cr-50*, DOJ, https://www.justice.gov/usao-dc/defendants/hyland-jason-lee (last visited Dec. 28, 2022).
85 *ryan, Jennifer Leigh Case Number: 1:21-cr-50*, DOJ, https://www.justice.gov/usao-dc/defendants/ryan-jennifer-leigh (last visited Dec. 28, 2022).
86 Simone Carter, *"I Did Nothing Wrong": Jenna Ryan Says She Won't Face Jail for Capitol Riot*, DALLAS OBSERVER (Mar. 31, 2021), https://www.dallasobserver.com/news/jenna-ryan-convinced-she-wont-go-to-jail-apologizes-for-having-white-skin-blond-hair-12000445.
87 January 6 Committee, *Deposition of Roger Stone* at 18–19 (Dec. 17, 2021), https://www.govinfo.gov/content/pkg/GPO-J6-TRANSCRIPT-CTRL0000034613/pdf/GPO-J6-TRANSCRIPT-CTRL0000034613.pdf.
88 *January 6 Committee Final Report* at 531.
89 *Id.* at 531.
90 *Id.* at 501–502 (internal citations omitted).
91 Anna Massoglia, *Details of the Money Behind Jan. 6 Protests Continue to Emerge*, OPENSECRETS (Oct. 25, 2021), https://www.opensecrets.org/news/2021/10/details-of-the-money-behind-jan-6-protests-continue-to-emerge/.
92 *January 6 Committee Final Report* at 531.
93 *Id.* at 532.
94 *Id.* at 532 (internal citations omitted).
95 *Id.* at 502.

96 *Id.* at 532.
97 Massoglia, *supra* note 91.
98 Deposition of Julia Fancelli, January 6 Committee at 128 (Feb. 18, 2022), https://january6th.house.gov/sites/democrats.january6th.house.gov/files/20220218_Julia%20Fancelli.pdf.
99 *Id.* at 60–61 & 65.
100 *January 6 Committee Final Report* at 294 ("Senator Mastriano, who would later charter and pay for buses to Washington for the President's 'Stop the Steal' rally on January 6th and was near the Capitol during the attack.").
101 Jon Delano, *Democrats Say Doug Mastriano Breached Police Lines During Jan. 6 Insurrection and Should Release Video to Prove Otherwise*, CBS PITTSBURGH (July 21, 2022), https://www.cbsnews.com/pittsburgh/news/democrats-say-doug-mastriano-breached-police-lines-jan-6-insurrection/.
102 *US Dominion Inc. v. Powell*, 554 F. Supp. 3d 42, 54 (D.D.C. 2021) ("Lindell leveraged MyPillow as a sponsor of several rallies in support of President Trump.").
103 Brian Schwartz, *MyPillow CEO Mike Lindell Says He Spent $25 Million to Push False Pro-Trump Election Claims: "I will spend whatever it takes,"* CNBC (Dec. 16, 2021), https://www.cnbc.com/2021/12/16/;mypillow-ceo-mike-lindell-spent-25-million-to-push-false-pro-trump-election-claims.html ("Lindell . . . confirmed that MyPillow paid $100,000 to the organization for a sponsorship ad on the group's bus, which traveled to various pro-Trump rallies across the country.").
104 *January 6 Committee Final Report* at 644.
105 First Superseding Indictment at 9, *United States v. Nordean et al.*, No. 1:21-cr-175 (D.D.C. Mar. 10, 2021).
106 *January 6 Committee Final Report* at 514–15 (internal citations omitted).
107 Massoglia, *supra* note 91.
108 *Id.*
109 Fancelli Deposition, *supra* note 98.
110 PRACTICAL STAKE: CORPORATIONS, POLITICAL SPENDING & DEMOCRACY, CENTER FOR POLITICAL ACCOUNTABILITY, 10 (2022).
111 *Id.*
112 *Id.*
113 *Id.*
114 *Id.*
115 Massoglia, *supra* note 91.
116 *January 6 Committee Final Report* at 519 ("Nick Fuentes is an online provocateur who leads a white nationalist movement known as 'America First,' or the 'Groypers.'").
117 *Id.* at 520.
118 *Id.* at 558 n. 527 ("Fuentes personally earned $50,000 from his livestreams between November 3, 2020, and January 19, 2021.")
119 Fancelli Deposition, *supra* note 99 at 77.
120 Anna Massoglia, *Trump's Political Operation Paid More than $4.3 Million to Jan. 6 Organizers But Questions Remain About the Full Extent of Its Involvement*, OPENSECRETS (Aug. 30, 2021), https://www.opensecrets.org/news/2021/08/trumps-political-operation-paid-more-than-4-3-million-to-jan-6-organizers-questions-remain-about-full-involvement/.
121 Kunzelman, *supra* note 77.

122 Ben Werschkul, *Even More Companies That Pledged Not to Give to "Sedition Caucus" Have Reversed Course*, YAHOO (Oct. 4, 2022), https://news.yahoo.com/even-more-companies-give-to-sedition-caucus-170717866.html.
123 Anna Massoglia & Keith Newell, *Election Objectors in Congress Received More than $61 Million from Corporate PACs and Industry Trade Groups in the 2022 Cycle*, OPENSECRETS (Nov. 14, 2022), https://www.opensecrets.org/news/2022/11/election-objectors-in-congress-received-more-than-61-million-from-corporate-pacs-and-industry-trade-groups-in-the-2022-cycle/.
124 Andy Kroll, *What Insurrection? Corporate America Can't Stop Bankrolling the Jan. 6 Sedition Caucus*, ROLLING STONE (Oct. 25, 2021), https://www.rollingstone.com/politics/politics-features/corporate-donors-sedition-caucus-insurrection-1247707/.
125 *In Bad Company*, ACCOUNTABLE.US (Jan. 3, 2022), https://accountable.us/projects/in-bad-company/.
126 *Id.*
127 Massoglia & Newell, *supra* note 123.
128 *Id.*
129 *Id.*
130 *Id.*
131 Srijita Datta & Anna Massoglia, *Corporate PACs Have Given More than $22.2 Million to Election Objectors Since Jan. 6 Capitol Attack*, OPENSECRETS (Aug. 25, 2022), https://www.opensecrets.org/news/2022/08/corporate-pacs-have-given-more-than-22-2-million-to-election-objectors-since-jan-6-capitol-attack/.
132 Massoglia & Newell, *supra* note 123.
133 *Id.*
134 Datta & Massoglia, *supra* note 131.
135 *Id.*
136 Angela Li & Caitlin Moniz, *Corporations Have Given Over $50 Million to the Sedition Caucus*, CREW (Jan. 6, 2023), https://www.citizensforethics.org/reports-investigations/crew-reports/corporations-have-given-over-50-million-to-the-sedition-caucus/.
137 *Id.*
138 *Id.*
139 *Id.* ("Incoming members who made election denialism central to their campaigns include Representatives-elect Derrick Van Orden, Anna Paulina Luna, Harriet Hageman, and Senator J. D. Vance.").
140 *Id.*
141 *Id.*
142 Datta & Massoglia, *supra* note 131.
143 *Id.*
144 *Id.*
145 Massoglia & Newell, *supra* note 123.
146 *Id.*
147 *Id.*
148 *Total Corporate and Industry Spending on Sedition Caucus Members*, CITIZENS FOR RESPONSIBILITY & ETHICS IN WASHINGTON, https://www.citizensforethics.org/reports-investigations/crew-reports/this-sedition-is-brought-to-you-by/ (last visited Dec. 11, 2023) (listing $91 million from corporate PACs to members of the Sedition Caucus).

9. DUSTING OFF THE DISQUALIFICATION CLAUSE

1 State of New Mexico, ex. rel., *White v. Griffin*, Findings of Fact, Conclusions of Law, and Judgment, 32–33 (Sept. 6, 2022), https://www.citizensforethics.org/wp-content/uploads/2022/09/D101CV202200473-griffin.pdf; Complaint at 29, Challenge to the Constitutional Qualifications of Rep. Madison Cawthorn, N.C. State Bd. of Elections (2022) ("On the evening of January 6, . . . Senator Mitch McConnell of Kentucky, the Senate Majority Leader, described the assault as a 'failed insurrection.'"); *id.* ("Bipartisan majorities of the House and Senate voted for articles of impeachment describing the attack as an 'insurrection.'"); *id.* ("In the impeachment trial, President Trump's own defense lawyer stated that 'the question before us is not whether there was a violent insurrection of [sic] the Capitol. On that point, everyone agrees.'") (quoting 167 Cong. Rec. H191) (daily ed. Jan. 13, 2021).
2 U.S. CONST. amend. XIV, § 3 (1868).
3 Danielle Campoamor, *Did Madison Cawthorn Lie About the Accident That Left Him Paralyzed?*, REFINERY 29 (Mar. 1, 2021), https://www.refinery29.com/en-us/2021/03/10336858/madison-cawthorn-wheelchair-accident-lie-washington-post; Peter Slevin, *Madison Cawthorn's Icarus Moment*, NEW YORKER (May 27, 2022), https://www.newyorker.com/news/daily-comment/madison-cawthorns-icarus-moment.
4 Complaint at 13–14, Challenge to the Constitutional Qualifications of Rep. Madison Cawthorn, *supra* note 1 (quoting Turning Point, *Live! SAS 2020 Day 3! Madison Cawthorn, Allie Stuckey, and More!*, FACEBOOK, Dec. 21, 2021, at 3:44:00, https://bit.ly/DecemberTurningPointVideo).
5 Charles Bethea, *Speed Demons*, NEW YORKER 16 (May 9, 2022).
6 Daniel Villarreal, *Madison Cawthorn's Bail Fund for Anti-Mask Republicans Seemingly Funds His Own Campaign*, NEWSWEEK (July 29, 2021), https://www.newsweek.com/madison-cawthorns-bail-fund-anti-mask-republicans-seemingly-funds-his-own-campaign-1614506.
7 @TheHill, TWITTER (June 25, 2021, 8:37 p.m.), https://twitter.com/thehill/status/1401337529484382211?s=20&t=q-qRK7Yoyt7THjvqPlwNOw.
8 Addy Baird & Brianna Sacks, *"Danger Warning": Women Say Madison Cawthorn Harassed Them in College*, BUZZFEED (Feb. 26, 2021), https://www.buzzfeednews.com/article/addybaird/madison-cawthorn-sexual-misconduct-allegations-patrick.
9 Michael Kruse, *"He's Not OK": The Entirely Predicable Unraveling of Madison Cawthorn*, POLITICO (May 13, 2022), https://www.politico.com/news/magazine/2022/05/13/madison-cawthorn-injury-profile-00032002.
10 Jonathan Weisman & Annie Karni, *Cawthorn Under Pressure to End Career in Congress as His Scandals Multiply*, N.Y. TIMES A14 (Apr. 30, 2022).
11 Emma Bowman, *Rep. Madison Cawthorn Is Under Mounting Pressure from Scandals Ahead of Midterms*, NPR (May 2, 2022), https://www.npr.org/2022/05/02/1095770735/madison-cawthorn-allegations; Amber Phillips, *The Many Controversies Surrounding Madison Cawthorn*, WASH. POST (May 23, 2022), https://www.washingtonpost.com/politics/2022/05/02/madison-cawthorn-controversies-explained/; Kruse, *supra* note 9.
12 Slevin, *supra* note 3.
13 Andrew Kerr, *Madison Cawthorn Implicated in Potential Insider Trading Scheme, Experts Say*, WASH. EXAMINER (Apr. 26, 2022), https://www.washingtonexaminer.com/

news/1915788/madison-cawthorn-implicated-in-potential-insider-trading-scheme-experts-say/; Phillips, *supra* note 11.
14. Virginia Chamlee, *Outgoing Rep. Madison Cawthorn Ordered to Pay $15,000 After House Ethics Investigation*, PEOPLE (Dec. 7, 2022), https://people.com/politics/madison-cawthorn-must-pay-15k-house-ethics-investigation/.
15. Kerr, *supra* note 13.
16. Roger Sollenberger, *Mark Meadows Performed Life-Changing Favors for Madison Cawthorn, Then Turned on Him*, SALON (Jan. 28, 2021), https://www.salon.com/2021/01/28/mark-meadows-performed-life-changing-favors-for-madison-cawthorn-then-turned-on-him-why/.
17. *Oath of Office*, HOUSE OF REPRESENTATIVES, https://history.house.gov/Institution/Origins-Development/Oath-of-Office/ (last visited July 26, 2022).
18. D. G. Martin, *Who Is Our Best-Known NC Native?*, RICHMOND COUNTY DAILY J. (Apr. 4, 2022), https://www.yourdailyjournal.com/opinion/op-ed/105959/d-g-martin-who-is-our-best-known-nc-native (quoting Madison's tweet).
19. Matthew Choi, *Trump Is on Trial for Inciting an Insurrection. What About the 12 People Who Spoke Before Him?*, POLITICO (Feb. 10, 2021), https://www.politico.com/news/2021/02/10/trump-impeachement-stop-the-steal-speakers-467554.
20. Weisman & Karni, *supra* note 10 ("In rapid succession, Mr. Cawthorn, who entered Congress as a rising star of the party's far right.").
21. Madison Cawthorn, *Biography*, U.S. HOUSE OF REP., https://cawthorn.house.gov/about (last visited July 28, 2022).
22. Charles Duncan, *"This Crowd Has Some Fight in It": N.C. Rep Spoke at Rally Before Attack at Capitol*, SPECTRUM NEWS (Jan. 7, 2021), https://spectrumlocalnews.com/nc/charlotte/politics/2021/01/07/nc-rep--madison-cawthorn-spoke-at-rally-before-capitol-attacked.
23. *Id.*
24. *Id.*
25. Li Zhou, *147 Republican Lawmakers Still Objected to the Election Results After the Capitol Attack*, VOX (Jan. 7, 2021), https://www.vox.com/2021/1/6/22218058/republicans-objections-election-results.
26. Daniel Villarreal, *GOP Lawmaker Madison Cawthorn Claimed "Democratic Machine" Paid Capitol Rioters to Make Trump Look Bad*, NEWSWEEK (Jan. 18, 2021), https://www.newsweek.com/gop-lawmaker-claimed-democratic-machine-paid-capitol-rioters-make-trump-look-bad-1562458.
27. Bryan Metzger, *Rep. Madison Cawthorn Calls Jan. 6 Rioters "Political Prisoners," Suggests He Wants to 'Try and Bust Them Out" of Jail*, BUSINESS INSIDER (Aug. 30, 2021), https://www.businessinsider.com/rep-cawthorn-bust-jan-6th-rioters-out-jail-political-prisoners-2021-8 (emphasis added); *see also Madison Cawthorn Macon County Republican Party Appearance 8-29-2021*, YOUTUBE (Aug. 31, 2021, 1:28:33), https://youtu.be/2RtsGikgAqA; Rachel Janfaza et al., *Who Is Madison Cawthorn, the Freshman Congressman Causing Headline Chaos for the GOP?*, CNN (Apr. 1, 2022), https://www.cnn.com/2022/03/31/politics/madison-cawthorn-background-controversy/index.html.
28. *Id.*
29. Hunter Walker, *exclusive: Jan. 6 Protest Organizers Say They Participated in "Dozens" of Planning Meetings with Members of Congress and White House Staff*, ROLLING STONE (Oct. 24, 2021) ("Along with Greene, the conspiratorial pro-Trump Republican

from Georgia who took office earlier this year, the pair both say the members who participated in these conversations or had top staffers join in included Rep. Paul Gosar [R-Ariz.], Rep. Lauren Boebert [R-Colo.], Rep. Mo Brooks [R-Ala.], Rep. Madison Cawthorn [R-N.C.], Rep. Andy Biggs [R-Ariz.], and Rep. Louie Gohmert [R-Texas]. 'We would talk to Boebert's team, Cawthorn's team, Gosar's team like back to back to back to back,' says the [January 6 rally] organizer.").

30 Barack Obama, Stanford University, *Keynote Address at the Challenges to Democracy in the Digital Information Realm Symposium: Disinformation Is a Threat to Our Democracy* (Apr. 21, 2022).

31 14th Amendment, *Statutes at Large*, 39th Congress, 1st Session, 358–59, https://goo.gl/TraZUU.

32 *Powell v. McCormack*, 395 U.S. 486, 1158 (1944).

33 *14th Amendment Drafting Table*, NATIONAL CONSTITUTION CENTER (2019), https://draftingtable.constitutioncenter.org/item/14th-amendment (last visited May 26, 2022) (quoting the May 9, 1866 Joint Committee on Reconstruction from the 39th Congress).

34 Id.

35 Jennifer K. Elsea, *The Insurrection Bar to Office: Section 3 of the Fourteenth Amendment*, CONGRESSIONAL RESEARCH SERVICE 2 (Jan. 29, 2021), https://crsreports.congress.gov/product/pdf/LSB/LSB10569#.

36 Id.

37 Id. ("Section 3 of the Fourteenth Amendment was last used in 1919 to refuse to seat a socialist congressman accused of having given aid and comfort to Germany during the First World War, irrespective of the Amnesty Act.").

38 Jonathan Weisman, *Effort Expands to Disqualify Republicans Over Jan. 6*, N.Y. TIMES A19 (Apr. 8, 2022) ("In all three suits, the plaintiffs claim that the politicians are disqualified from seeking office because their support for rioters who attacked the Capitol made them 'insurrectionists' under the Constitution."); Jan Wolfe, *U.S. court Revives "Insurrection" Challenge to Congressman Cawthorn*, REUTERS (May 24, 2022), https://www.reuters.com/world/us/us-court-revives-insurrection-challenge-congressman-cawthorn-2022-05-24/ ("The North Carolina voters are represented by Free Speech For People.").

39 Complaint at 1, Challenge to the Constitutional Qualifications of Rep. Madison Cawthorn, *supra* note 1.

40 Id. at 1–2 (quoting U.S. CONST. amend. XIV, § 3).

41 Id. at 30.

42 Id. at 2.

43 Id. at 23 (quoting *Hassan v. Colorado*, 495 F. App'x 947, 948) (10th Cir. 2012).

44 Id. at 2.

45 Mackenzie Wilkes, *Rep. Madison Cawthorn Sues N.C. Election Board over Candidacy Challenge*, POLITICO (Feb. 1, 2022), https://www.politico.com/news/2022/02/01/cawthorn-north-carolina-reelection-lawsuit-00004111.

46 Id.

47 14th Amendment, Section 3, U.S. Const. (1868).

48 Laurence H. Tribe & Elizabeth B. Wydra, *Confederate Amnesty Act Mustn't Shield Insurrectionists*, BOSTON GLOBE A9 (Mar. 14, 2022).

49 Act of May 22, 1872, ch. 193, 17 Stat. 142.

NOTES

50 *Cawthorn v. Amalfi*, 2022 WL 1635116, at *8 (4th Cir. 2022) (quoting 17 Stat. 142 (1872)).
51 Gerard Magliocca, *The 14th Amendment's Disqualification Provision and the Events of Jan. 6th*, LAWFARE (Jan. 19, 2021), https://www.lawfareblog.com/14th-amendments-disqualification-provision-and-events-jan-6.
52 *Id.*
53 *Powell v. McCormack*, 395 U.S. 486, 1158 (1944); Will Doran, *NC Delays Challenge to Madison Cawthorn's Eligibility for Congress*, NEWS & OBSERVER (Jan. 16, 2022), https://www.newsobserver.com/news/politics-government/article257290357.html.
54 *Cawthorn v. Circosta*, 2022 WL 738073, at *11 (E.D.N.C. 2022).
55 Amnesty Act of 1872, Pub. L. No. 42–193, 17 Stat. 142 (emphasis added).
56 *Cawthorn v. Circosta*, at *11.
57 *Id.*
58 Joe Schneider, *Insurrectionists May Be Barred from Office, Court Rules*, BLOOMBERG (May 24, 2022), https://news.bloomberglaw.com/us-law-week/insurrectionists-may-be-barred-from-office-appeals-court-rules; Wolfe, *supra* note 38.
59 *Cawthorn v. Amalfi*, at *1 (emphasis).
60 *Id.* at *8 (emphasis in the original).
61 Nicholas Reimann, *Madison Cawthorn Calls for Rise of "Dark MAGA" in Wild Rant After Loss*, FORBES (May 19, 2022), https://www.forbes.com/sites/nicholasreimann/2022/05/19/madison-cawthorn-calls-for-rise-of-dark-maga-in-wild-rant-after-loss/?sh=7210adf0ac1f.
62 Slevin, *supra* note 3.
63 Weisman, *supra* note 38 ("A cluster of voters and a progressive group filed suit against three elected officials in Arizona to bar them under the 14th Amendment from running again."); Sam Gringlas, *Marjorie Taylor Greene Testifies as Part of a Legal Challenge to Her Candidacy*, GEORGIA PUBLIC BROADCASTING (Apr. 22, 2022), https://www.gpb.org/news/2022/04/22/marjorie-taylor-greene-testifies-part-of-legal-challenge-her-candidacy.
64 Hannah Demissie, *Judge Rules GOP Rep. Marjorie Taylor Greene Can Stay on Ballot*, ABC NEWS (May 6, 2022), https://abcnews.go.com/Politics/judge-rules-gop-rep-marjorie-taylor-greene-stay/story?id=84314532 ("Judge Charles Beaudrot said . . . that the evidence in the case was insufficient to establish that Greene 'engaged in insurrection or rebellion against the same, or [gave] aid or comfort to the enemies thereof under the 14th Amendment to the Constitution.'").
65 Complaint at 27, Challenge to the Constitutional Qualifications of Rep. Madison Cawthorn, *supra* note 1.
66 *Oliver v. Otero County Commission*, No. S-1-SC-39426 (N.M. June 15, 2022).
67 *New Mexico v. Griffin*, Findings of Fact, Conclusions of Law, and Judgment at 34 (Sept. 6, 2022), https://www.citizensforethics.org/wp-content/uploads/2022/09/D101CV202200473-griffin.pdf (internal quotation marks omitted); *see also Rowan v. Greene*, Initial Decision, 1, 13–14 (May 6, 2022), https://www.scribd.com/document/573096054/Greene-Decision#download&from_embed ("It appears that it is not necessary that an individual personally commit an act of violence to have "engaged" in insurrection. See . . . Gerard N. Magliocca, *Amnesty and Section Three of the Fourteenth Amendment*, 36 CONST. COMMENT. 87, 1498–99 [2021] [in special congressional action in 1868 to enforce Section Three and remove Georgia legislators, none of the legislators had been charged criminally].").

68 *New Mexico v. Griffin* at 36.
69 *Id.* at 35.
70 *Id.* at 27.
71 Dean Obeidallah, *Let's Hope This Ruling Against "Cowboys for Trump" Founder Has Ripple Effect*, MSNBC (Sept. 11, 2022), https://www.msnbc.com/opinion/msnbc-opinion/cowboys-trump-ruling-might-be-key-preserving-our-democracy-n1298820.
72 Marilyn Upchurch, *New Mexico Supreme Court Maintains Couy Griffin Office Removal*, KRQE (Feb. 19, 2023), https://www.krqe.com/news/politics-government/new-mexico-supreme-court-maintains-couy-griffin-office-removal/.
73 Petition for Writ of Certiorari, *Griffin v. New Mexico*, No. 23–279 at 13–15 & 16–20 (Sept. 22, 2023), https://www.supremecourt.gov/DocketPDF/23/23-279/280152/20230921142348810_230504a%20Petition%20for%20efiling.pdf.
74 Indictment, *United States of America v. Trump*, Case No. 1:23-cr-00257-TSC (D.D.C. Aug. 1, 2023); Indictment, *The State of Georgia v. Trump and Others*, No. 23SC188947EJ15 McAffee (Fulton Sup. Ct. Aug. 14, 2023).
75 Petition Pursuant to Minn. Stat. § 204b.44 to Challenge Placement of Donald J. Trump on the 2024 Primary and General Election Ballots, *Growe v. Simon*, No. A23–1354 (Sept. 12, 2023).
76 Order at 3, *Growe et al. v. Simon*, A23–1354 (Minn. Sept. 20, 2023), https://assets.bwbx.io/documents/users/iqjWHBFdfxIU/r7QLwhbTYAjA/v0.
77 *Id.* at 4.
78 Verified Petition, *Anderson v. Griswold*, No. 2023CV32577 (Sept. 6, 2023).
79 *Id.*
80 Final Order at 90–95 & 102, *Anderson v. Griswold*, Case No. 2023CV32577 (Denver D. Ct. Nov. 17, 2023).
81 *Id.* at 95–102.
82 Application for Review Under § 1-1-113(3) C.R.S., *Anderson v. Griswold*, Case No. 2023SA300 (Colo. Nov. 20, 2023) (from plaintiff voters).
83 Application for Review and Adjudication, *Anderson v. Griswold*, Case No. 2023SA300 (Colo. Nov. 20, 2023) (from Trump).
84 *Watch Live: Colorado Supreme Court Hears Challenge to Remove Trump from Ballot Under 14th Amendment*, PBS NEWSHOUR (Dec. 6, 2023), https://www.youtube.com/watch?v=Cz4ZqwrsipA.
85 *Id.*
86 *Anderson v. Griswold*, 2023 WL 8770111 at *3 (Colo. 2023).
87 *Id.* at *12 (citing *Hassan v. Colorado*, 495 F.App'x 947, 948, 10th Cir. 2012).
88 *Id.* at *31.
89 *Id.* at *19 (citing the Civil Rights Cases 109 U.S. 3, 20, 3 S.Ct. 18, 27 L.Ed. 835) (1883).
90 *Id.* at *50.
91 *Id.* at *41 (internal citations omitted).
92 *Id.* at *47.
93 *Id.* at *13.
94 *Id.* at *15.
95 *Id.* at *38.
96 *Id.* at *44.
97 Order, *LaBrant v. Secretary of State*, No. 166470 (Mich. Dec. 27, 2023) (refusing to reconsider a lower court's ruling keeping Trump on the Michigan primary ballot).

NOTES

98 Ruling of the Secretary of State, In re: Challenges of Kimberley Rosen, Thomas Saviello, and Ethan Strimling; Paul Gordon; and Mary Anne Royal to Primary Petition of Donald J. Trump, Republican Candidate for the President of the United States, State of Maine, Secretary of State (Dec. 28, 2023).
99 *Id.* at 1.
100 *Id.* at 11.
101 *Id.* at 12 (citing 21-A M.R.S. Section 336).
102 *Id.* at 16.
103 *Id.* at 33.
104 *Id.* at 19.
105 *Id.* at 20.
106 *Id.* at 23.
107 *Id.* at 32–33.
108 *Id.* at 14.
109 *Id.* at 33.
110 Hyemin Han & Caleb Benjamin, *Tracking Section 3 Trump Disqualification Challenges*, LAWFARE (Nov. 29, 2023), https://www.lawfaremedia.org/current-projects/the-trump-trials/section-3-litigation-tracker.
111 J. Michael Luttig & Laurence H. Tribe, *The Constitution Prohibits Trump from Ever Being President Again*, ATLANTIC (Aug. 19, 2023), https://www.theatlantic.com/ideas/archive/2023/08/donald-trump-constitutionally-prohibited-presidency/675048/.
112 David Frum, *The Fourteenth Amendment Fantasy: The Constitution Won't Disqualify Trump from Running*, ATLANTIC (Aug. 29, 2023), https://www.theatlantic.com/ideas/archive/2023/08/trump-disqualified-president-14th-amendment/675163/.
113 Lawrence Lessig, *A Terrible Plan to Neutralize Trump Has Entranced the Legal World*, SLATE (Sept. 19, 2023), https://slate.com/news-and-politics/2023/09/trump-disqualification-colorado-ballot-hail-mary.html.
114 Jordan Rubin, *Enforcing the 14th Amendment Isn't Antidemocratic. It Can't Be*, MSNBC (Dec. 20, 2023), https://www.msnbc.com/deadline-white-house/deadline-legal-blog/14th-amendment-isnt-antidemocratic-rcna130607.
115 *Trump v. Anderson*, 144 S.Ct. 539 (U.S. Jan. 4, 2024) (cert. granted).
116 *Id.*
117 *Trump v. Anderson*, 2024 WL 899207 at *1 (U.S. 2024) ("Because the Constitution makes Congress, rather than the States, responsible for enforcing Section 3 against federal officeholders and candidates, we reverse.").
118 *Id.* at *3 ("We conclude that States may disqualify persons holding or attempting to hold state office. But States have no power under the Constitution to enforce Section 3 with respect to federal offices, especially the Presidency.").
119 *Id.* at *8 ("In a case involving no federal action whatsoever, the Court opines on how federal enforcement of Section 3 must proceed. Congress, the majority says, must enact legislation under Section 5 prescribing the procedures to ascertain[ ] what particular individuals should be disqualified. . . . These musings . . . are gratuitous.") (internal quotation marks omitted) (Sotomayor, Kagan & Jackson concurring in the judgment).
120 Summer Concepcion, *"QAnon Shaman" Who Stormed the Capitol on Jan. 6 Files Paperwork to Run for Congress*, NBC NEWS (Nov. 13, 2023), https://www.nbcnews.com/politics/2024-election/qanon-shaman-stormed-capitol-jan-6-files-paperwork-run-congress-rcna124858.

NOTES

10. DON'T BE FOOLED

1 Michael Gehlken @GehlkenNFL, TWITTER (Sept. 27, 2021, 7:20 p.m.), https://twitter.com/GehlkenNFL/status/1442630316288626690.
2 *Id.*
3 Tanya Dua & Angela Wang, *AT&T has Bankrolled Politicians Behind Anti-Abortion "Trigger Laws" in 13 States*, BUSINESS INSIDER (June 24, 2022), https://www.businessinsider.com/att-biggest-corporate-benefactor-to-anti-abortion-lawmakers-in-trigger-states-2022-5#.
4 *Recent History of Restrictive Abortion Laws in Texas*, TEXAS ACLU (2023), https://www.aclutx.org/en/recent-history-restrictive-abortion-laws-texas.
5 *Abortion Policy Tracker*, KAISER FAMILY FOUNDATION (June 6, 2023), https://www.kff.org/other/state-indicator/abortion-policy-tracker/.
6 Tracking *Abortion Bans Across the Country*, N.Y. TIMES (April 9, 2024), https://www.nytimes.com/interactive/2022/us/abortion-laws-roe-v-wade.html.
7 Joe Biden, *Message to the House of Representatives—President's Veto of H.J. Res 30*, WHITE HOUSE (Mar. 20, 2023), https://www.whitehouse.gov/briefing-room/presidential-actions/2023/03/20/message-to-the-house-of-representatives-presidents-veto-of-h-j-res-30/.
8 *Final Rule on Prudence and Loyalty in Selecting Plan Investments and Exercising Shareholder Rights*, DEPARTMENT OF LABOR (Nov. 22, 2022), https://www.dol.gov/agencies/ebsa/about-ebsa/our-activities/resource-center/fact-sheets/final-rule-on-prudence-and-loyalty-in-selecting-plan-investments-and-exercising-shareholder-rights.
9 Victor Nava, *Senate Kills Biden's "Woke" ESG Investment Rule in Bipartisan Vote*, N.Y. POST (Mar. 1, 2023), https://nypost.com/2023/03/01/senate-kills-bidens-woke-esg-investment-rule-veto-awaits/.
10 Biden, *supra* note 7.
11 Zoë Richards, *House Fails to Override Biden's First Veto*, NBC NEWS (Mar. 23, 2023), https://www.nbcnews.com/politics/congress/house-fails-override-bidens-first-veto-rcna76002.
12 Chuck Schumer, *Republicans Ought to Be All for ESG*, WALL ST. J. A17 (Mar. 1, 2023).
13 *Report on US Sustainable Investing Trends*, US SIF (2022), https://www.ussif.org//Files/Trends/2022/Trends%202022%20Executive%20Summary.pdf.
14 Matt Egan, *Exclusive: A $5 Billion Foundation Literally Founded on Oil Money Is Saying Goodbye to Fossil Fuels*, CNN BUSINESS (Dec. 18, 2020), https://www.cnn.com/2020/12/18/investing/rockefeller-foundation-divest-fossil-fuels-oil/index.html.
15 Haleluya Hadero, *Fossil Fuel Divestment Gains Momentum in Philanthropy*, AP (Nov. 1, 2021), https://apnews.com/article/climate-science-business-environment-and-nature-philanthropy-83a2713d184ce0a983f4f1eb89f088f8.
16 Rachel Treisman, *Harvard University Will Stop Investing in Fossil Fuels After Years of Public Pressure*, NPR (Sept. 10, 2021), https://www.npr.org/2021/09/10/1035901596/harvard-university-end-investment-fossil-fuel-industry-climate-change-activism.
17 Evan Castillo, *These Colleges Have Divested from Fossil Fuels*, BEST COLLEGES (Sept. 19, 2023), https://www.bestcolleges.com/news/list-of-colleges-divested-from-fossil-fuels/.
18 *Aspirational Requests Become Accountability Requirements*, TIAA at 1 (2019), https://www.tiaa.org/public/pdf/2019_proxy_season_preview.pdf ("Approximately 450 ESG

shareholder proposals were voted in 2018. The overall average vote result on these proposals resumed a long-term upward trend with over 35% of proposals receiving at least 30% support.").

19 Caroline Flammer, Michael W. Toffel, & Kala Viswanathan, *Shareholders Are Pressing for Climate Risk Disclosures. That's Good for Everyone*, HARVARD BUSINESS REV. (Apr. 22, 2021), https://hbr.org/2021/04/shareholders-are-pressing-for-climate-risk-disclosures-thats-good-for-everyone ("Our analysis shows that shareholder activism . . . does induce firms to voluntarily disclose climate change risks. . . . We also found that environmental shareholder activism is more effective when initiated by institutional shareholders with a long-term holding horizon: The effect rises from 4.6% to 6.8%.").

20 *Id.*

21 Quinn Curtis, Jill E. Fisch, & Adriana Robertson, *Do ESG Mutual Funds Deliver on Their Promises*, 120 MICH. L. REV. 393, 396 (2021).

22 Heidi Welsh, *Proxy Season Mid-Year Review: Social, Environmental & Sustainable Governance Shareholder Proposals in 2020*, S12 at 4 (2020), *available at* https://siinstitute.org/reports.html (showing charts of ESG shareholder proposals from 2011–2020).

23 *Id.* at 3.

24 *2022 CPA-Zicklin Index of Corporate Political Disclosure and Accountability*, CENTER FOR POLITICAL ACCOUNTABILITY (Oct. 2022), https://www.politicalaccountability.net/wp-content/uploads/2022/10/2022-CPA-Zicklin-Index.pdf.

25 Lucian A. Bebchuk, Robert J. Jackson Jr., James D. Nelson & Roberto Tallarita, *The Untenable Case for Keeping Investors in the Dark*, 10 HARV. BUS. L. REV. 1, 2 (2020).

26 *Id.* at 27.

27 Leo E. Strine Jr., *Fiduciary Blind Spot: The Failure of Institutional Investors to Prevent the Illegitimate Use of Working Americans' Savings for Corporate Political Spending*, 97 WASH. U. L. REV. 1007, 1033 (2020).

28 *Id.* at 1036.

29 David Rosenberg, *Goodwill and the Excesses of Corporate Political Spending*, 11 HASTINGS BUS. L.J. 29, 38 (2015).

30 Miguel Alzola, *Corporate Dystopia: The Ethics of Corporate Political Spending*, 52 BUSINESS & SOCIETY 388, 412 (Feb. 24, 2013) ("The principle of consent . . . simply holds that corporate members must have a role in determining how their contributions will be used for activities in which their political standing is at stake."); *see also* CIARA TORRES-SPELLISCY, CORPORATE CITIZEN? AN ARGUMENT FOR SEPARATION OF CORPORATION AND STATE (2016) (arguing for shareholder consent to corporate political spending).

31 Bebchuk et al., *supra* note 25.

32 *Id.* at 26.

33 Larry Fink, *Larry Fink's 2020 Letter to CEOs A Fundamental Reshaping of Finance*, BLACKROCK (2020), https://www.blackrock.com/americas-offshore/en/larry-fink-ceo-letter.

34 Marco Quiroz-Gutierrez, *American Companies Pledged $50 Billion to Black Communities, Most of It Hasn't Materialized*, FORTUNE (May 6, 2021), https://fortune.com/2021/05/06/us-companies-black-communities-money-50-billion/.

35 Mark Brnovich, *ESG May Be an Anti-Trust Violation*, WALL ST. J. A15 (Mar. 7, 2022).

36 *Id.*

37 Lydia Moynihan, *BlackRock Faces Scrutiny from 19 State AGs over ESG Investments*, N.Y. Post (Aug. 16, 2022), https://nypost.com/2022/08/16/blackrock-faces-scrutiny-from-19-state-ags-over-esg-investments/.

38 *Mark Brnovich*, BALLOTPEDIA (2023), https://ballotpedia.org/Mark_Brnovich.

39 Press Release, *Arizona Attorney General Kris Mayes Announces Exit from Investigation into ESG Investment Practices*, AZ A.G. (Feb. 13, 2023), https://www.azag.gov/press-release/arizona-attorney-general-kris-mayes-announces-exit-investigation-esg-investment; *ESG Battles Continue with Republican AG Info Requests to Major Asset Managers*, STATE AG REPORT (June 8, 2023), https://www.stateagreport.com/news/esg-battles-continue-with-republican-ag-info-requests-to-major-asset-managers/.

40 John Nichols, *ALEC's Corporate Funders Are Complicit in State-Based Assaults on Voting Rights and Democracy*, NATION (June 17, 2021), https://www.thenation.com/article/politics/alec-corporations-democracy/.

41 Yvonne Wingett Sanchez & Rob O'Dell, *What Is ALEC? "The Most Effective Organization" for Conservatives, Says Newt Gingrich*, USA TODAY (Apr. 3, 2019) ("At a kickoff luncheon, . . . the blue ALEC logo flashed across a giant screen along with the sponsors' logos: UPS, CenturyLink, Anheuser-Busch, Farmers Insurance, Chevron, AT&T, and pharmaceutical giant Eli Lilly and Co.").

42 *Id.* ("Joining an ALEC task force, where model legislation is drafted and debated behind closed doors, costs an additional $5,000.").

43 Elliot Negin, *How the American Legislative Exchange Council Turns Disinformation into Law*, UNION OF CONCERNED SCIENTISTS (June 29, 2022), https://blog.ucsusa.org/elliott-negin/how-the-american-legislative-exchange-council-turns-disinformation-into-law/.

44 Karin Rives, *Texas Bans 10 Banks, 348 Investment Funds over Fossil Fuel Policies*, S&P GLOBAL: MARKET INTELLIGENCE (Aug. 24, 2022), https://www.spglobal.com/marketintelligence/en/news-insights/latest-news-headlines/texas-bans-10-banks-348-investment-funds-over-fossil-fuel-policies-71842914.

45 David Garrett & Ivan Ivano, *Gas Guns and Governments: Financial Costs of Anti-ESG Policies*, BROOKINGS (Apr. 2022), https://www.brookings.edu/wp-content/uploads/2023/03/WP85-Ivanov-Garrett_formatted.pdf.

46 Ross Kerber, *Business Fights Back as Republican State Lawmakers Push Anti-ESG Agenda*, REUTERS (Apr. 24, 2023), https://www.reuters.com/business/sustainable-business/business-fights-back-republican-state-lawmakers-push-anti-esg-agenda-2023-04-22/.

47 North Dakota, S.B. 2291 (2022).

48 Montana H.B. 228 (2023).

49 Idaho H.B. 190 (2023).

50 Indiana H.B. 1008 (2023).

51 Arkansas H.B. 1307 (2023).

52 Alabama S.B. 261 (2023); Gov. Ivey, *Signing Statement for S.B. 261*, https://governor.alabama.gov/newsroom/2023/06/governor-ivey-further-defends-alabama-values-signs-senate-bill-261/.

53 Kelsey Snell & Greg Allen, *What a DeSantis Presidential Run Means for the 2024 Election*, NPR (May 24, 2023), https://www.npr.org/2023/05/24/1178021268/what-a-desantis-presidential-run-means-for-the-2024-election.

54 *Florida Governor Ron DeSantis Announces 2024 Presidential Run on Twitter Spaces with Elon Musk Transcript,* REV (May 24, 2023), https://www.rev.com/blog/transcripts/florida-governor-ron-desantis-announces-2024-presidential-run-on-twitter-spaces-with-elon-musk-transcript.

55 Go Woke, Go Broke Act, 169 Congressional Record at H1889 (Apr. 20, 2023), https://www.congress.gov/congressional-record/volume-169/issue-66/house-section/article/H1889-7.

56 Robert G. Eccles & Svetlana Klimenko, *The Investor Revolution,* HARVARD BUSINESS REV. (May–June 2019), https://hbr.org/2019/05/the-investor-revolution.

57 Cynthia A. Williams & Jill E. Fisch, *SEC Petition 4–730 on ESG Rulemaking,* SEC (Oct. 1, 2018), https://www.sec.gov/rules/petitions/2018/petn4-730.pdf.

58 Press Release, *SEC Proposes to Enhance Disclosures by Certain Investment Advisers and Investment Companies About ESG Investment Practices 2022–92,* SEC (May 25, 2022), https://www.sec.gov/news/press-release/2022-92.

59 Soyoung Ho, *SEC Once Again Delays Action on Final Climate Disclosure Rule,* THOMSON REUTERS (Dec. 12, 2023), https://tax.thomsonreuters.com/news/sec-once-again-delays-action-on-final-climate-disclosure-rule/.

60 The Enhancement and Standardization of Climate-Related Disclosures for Investors, Release No. 33-11275, SEC (2024), https://www.sec.gov/files/rules/final/2024/33-11275.pdf; see also Soyoung Ho, *SEC Scales Back Requirements in Final Climate Disclosure Rule,* THOMSON REUTERS (Mar. 7, 2024), https://tax.thomsonreuters.com/news/sec-scales-back-requirements-in-final-climate-disclosure-rule/.

61 Jacob H. Hupart, *That Didn't Take Long ... Fifth Circuit Temporarily Blocks New SEC Climate Disclosure Rule,* NATIONAL LAW REVIEW (Mar. 16, 2024), https://www.natlawreview.com/article/didnt-take-long-fifth-circuit-temporarily-blocks-new-sec-climate-disclosure-rule.

62 Curtis, Fisch, & Robertson, *supra* note 21, at 407.

63 James Mackintosh, *ESG Is All the Rage. Big Investors Can't Agree on Why,* WALL ST. J. (Mar. 4, 2021), https://www.wsj.com/articles/everyone-sees-esg-investing-differently-but-they-all-want-to-buy-11614866558.

64 Virginia Harper Ho, *Modernizing ESG Disclosure,* U. OF ILLINOIS L. REV. 277, 292 (2022).

65 Ruth Jebe, *The Convergence of Financial and ESG Materiality: Taking Sustainability Mainstream,* 56 AMERICAN BUSINESS L.J. 645, 651 (2019).

66 Paul Hodgson, *Corporate Lobbying: How an Energy Giant Is Hindering Climate Action,* CAPITAL MONITOR (Dec. 7, 2021), https://capitalmonitor.ai/factor/environmental/corporate-lobbying-how-an-energy-giant-is-hindering-climate-action/.

67 Rochelle Toplensky, *Time To Take the "E" Out of ESG Investing,* WALL ST. J. (June 1, 2022), https://www.wsj.com/articles/time-to-take-the-e-out-of-esg-investing-11654088792?mod=markets_major_pos3.

68 Ed Silverman, *Amid Concerns over U.S. Democracy, Pharma Helped Finance Committees That Support Election Deniers,* STAT NEWS (Nov. 7, 2022), https://www.statnews.com/pharmalot/2022/11/07/democracy-pharmaceuticals-donations-contributions-trump-election/.

69 David Armiak, *ALEC Lied About Its Work on Election Suppression Bills New Insights into Its Model Bills on Voting Restrictions,* AMERICAN PROSPECT (Sept. 3, 2021),

https://prospect.org/civil-rights/alec-lied-about-its-work-on-election-suppression-bills/ (quoting Nelson).
70 Nichols, *supra* note 40 ("In 2019, ALEC created a secret working group on redistricting, ballot measures, and election law, known as the 'ALEC Political Process Working Group.'").
71 *The League Condemns the American Legislative Exchange Council*, League of Women Voters (June 14, 2021), https://www.lwv.org/expanding-voter-access/league-condemns-american-legislative-exchange-council.
72 *January 6 Committee Final Report* at 204 ("Other attorneys who collaborated with Giuliani's legal team included Sidney Powell, Cleta Mitchell, and John Eastman.").
73 Peter Stone, *Alarm After Lawyer Who Aided Trump's 2020 Election Lie Attacks Campus Voting*, Guardian (May 8, 2023), https://www.theguardian.com/us-news/2023/may/08/lawyer-trump-2020-election-attacks-college-student-voting.
74 *Id.*
75 Josh Dawsey & Amy Gardner, *Top GOP Lawyer Cleta Mitchell Decries Ease of Campus Voting in Private Pitch to RNC*, Wash. Post (Apr. 20, 2023), https://www.washingtonpost.com/nation/2023/04/20/cleta-mitchell-voting-college-students/.
76 Elliot Negin, *How the American Legislative Exchange Council Turns Disinformation into Law*, Union of Concerned Scientists (June 29, 2022), https://blog.ucsusa.org/elliott-negin/how-the-american-legislative-exchange-council-turns-disinformation-into-law/.
77 *The League Condemns the American Legislative Exchange Council*, supra note 71.
78 Nicholas Reimann, *Hundreds of Companies Pressured to Cut Ties with Group Behind Restrictive Voting Legislation Push Across U.S.*, Forbes (June 14, 2021), https://www.forbes.com/sites/nicholasreimann/2021/06/14/hundreds-of-companies-pressured-to-cut-ties-with-group-behind-restrictive-voting-legislation-push-across-us/?sh=31e5fe5a5b89.
79 *Id.*
80 David Daley, *How to Get Away with Gerrymandering*, Slate (Oct. 2, 2019), https://slate.com/news-and-politics/2019/10/alec-meeting-gerrymandering-audio-recording.html.
81 *Id.*
82 *Id.*
83 *Id.*
84 *Id.*
85 *Id.*
86 *Berger v. North Carolina State Conference of the NAACP*, 597 U.S. 179 (2022); Ciara Torres-Spelliscy, *Legislators as Defendants but Not as Plaintiffs*, Regulatory Rev. (July 21, 2022), https://www.theregreview.org/2022/07/21/torres-spelliscy-berger/.
87 Karen Yourish, Larry Buchanan & Denise Lu, *Those Who Objected: The 147 Republicans Who Voted to Overturn Election Results*, N.Y. Times A10 (Jan. 8, 2021).
88 Elliot Negin, *How the American Legislative Exchange Council Turns Disinformation into Law*, Union of Concerned Scientists (June 29, 2022), https://blog.ucsusa.org/elliott-negin/how-the-american-legislative-exchange-council-turns-disinformation-into-law/.

89 Nichols, *supra* note 40.
90 *The League Condemns the American Legislative Exchange Council*, *supra* note 71.
91 Nichols, *supra* note 40.
92 *Id.*
93 David Armiak, *Pfizer Dumps ALEC*, CENTER FOR MEDIA & DEMOCRACY (June 16, 2021), https://www.exposedbycmd.org/2021/06/16/pfizer-dumps-alec/.
94 *Corporations That Have Cut Ties to ALEC*, SOURCE WATCH (2023), https://www.sourcewatch.org/index.php/Corporations_that_Have_Cut_Ties_to_ALEC.
95 SUSTAINABLE INVESTMENTS INSTITUTE, CORPORATE SUPPORT FOR POLITICAL CANDIDATES IN STATES WITH POST–*Roe v. Wade* TRIGGER BANS 1 (June 2022).
96 *Id.*
97 *Id.*
98 *Abortion in New York State: Know Your Rights*, N.Y.S. (Apr. 7, 2023), https://www.ny.gov/programs/abortion-new-york-state-know-your-rights; Press Release, *Historic California Constitutional Amendment Reinforcing Protections for Reproductive Freedom Goes Into Effect*, GOV. OF CALIFORNIA (Dec. 21, 2022), https://www.gov.ca.gov/2022/12/21/historic-california-constitutional-amendment-reinforcing-protections-for-reproductive-freedom-goes-into-effect.
99 Liam Denning, *The Tricky Politics of Anti-ESG Investing*, BLOOMBERG (May 19, 2022), https://www.bloomberg.com/opinion/articles/2022-05-19/the-tricky-politics-of-a-new-asset-firm-backed-by-peter-thiel (referencing "corporate hypocrisy").
100 Stephanie Kirchgaessner & Lauren Aratani, *These Companies Claim to Support Abortion Rights. They Are Backing Anti-Abortion Republicans*, GUARDIAN (Nov. 6, 2022), https://www.theguardian.com/world/2022/nov/06/us-companies-abortion-rights-donation-anti-abortion-republicans.
101 Kimberly Leonard, Andrea Michelson, & Angela Wang, *Healthcare Corporations Pfizer and UnitedHealthcare Are Among the Biggest Financial Backers Of Lawmakers Behind State Abortion Bans*, BUSINESS INSIDER (June 24, 2022), https://www.businessinsider.com/healthcare-corporations-and-pharma-give-big-to-anti-abortion-movement-2022-5.
102 *Id.*
103 58th Presidential Inaugural Committee, FEC Form 13 at 163 (Apr. 18, 2017), https://docquery.fec.gov/pdf/286/201704180300150286/201704180300150286.pdf (listing Pfizer).
104 *Repro Receipts*, ULTRAVIOLET (2022), https://reproreceipts.com/.
105 *Id.*
106 *Florida Repro Receipts*, ULTRAVIOLET, https://reproreceipts.com/state/florida/.
107 Judd Legum & Rebecca Crosby, *These 13 Corporations Have Spent $15 Million Supporting Anti-Abortion Politicians Since 2016*, POPULAR INFORMATION (May 4, 2022), https://popular.info/p/these-13-corporations-have-spent.
108 *Id.*
109 *Id.*
110 Andrew Ross Sorkin et al., *Abortion Is a Business Issue*, N.Y. TIMES (May 4, 2022), https://www.nytimes.com/2022/05/04/business/dealbook/us-businesses-roe-wade-abortion.html; Todd C. Frankel, Taylor Telford & Danielle Abril, *After State Abortion Fights, Corporate America Braces for End of* Roe, WASH. POST (May 4, 2022), https://www.washingtonpost.com/business/2022/05/04/companies-abortion-decision/.

NOTES

111 David Goldman, *Citi's Response to Abortion Bans: We'll Pay for Workers to Travel*, CNN (Mar. 16, 2022), https://www.cnn.com/2022/03/16/investing/citi-abortion-travel-expenses/index.html.

112 Ike Swetlitz & Spencer Soper, *Amazon, Disney, AT&T Gave to Abortion Foes Like DeSantis While Vowing to Help Employees*, BLOOMBERG (June 30, 2022), https://www.bloomberg.com/news/articles/2022-06-30/amazon-disney-at-t-donated-to-desantis-and-other-abortion-opponents.

113 Srijita Datta, *Corporate PACs Contributed over a Million Dollars to Lawmakers Who Opposed Abortion Rights Bill*, OPENSECRETS (July 14, 2022), https://www.opensecrets.org/news/2022/07/corporate-pacs-contributed-over-a-million-dollars-to-lawmakers-who-opposed-abortion-rights-bill/ ("41 companies that publicly committed to covering travel expenses of their employees as of when the Supreme Court announced its decision.").

114 Legum & Crosby, *supra* note 107.

115 Swetlitz & Soper, *supra* note 112.

116 *Id.*

117 Judd Legum & Tesnim Zekeria, *Corporations Send Large Donations to GOP Group Behind Abortion Bans and Voter Suppression*, POPULAR INFORMATION (Feb. 2, 2022), https://popular.info/p/corporations-send-large-donations ("Numerous corporations that publicly declare their commitment to women's equality and voting rights donated large sums to the RSLC in 2021. The information was buried in a 10,055 page PDF that the RSLC filed with the IRS.").

118 *Id.*

119 Legum & Crosby, *supra* note 107 ("Since 2016, Google has donated $525,702 to anti-abortion political committees, including $195,000 to the RSLC, $225,702 to the RGA, and $105,000 to the NRSC.").

120 Legum & Zekeria, *supra* note 117.

121 Legum & Crosby, *supra* note 107.

122 Tracy Jan, Jena McGregor & Meghan Hoyer, *Corporate America's $50 Billion Promise*, WASH. POST (Aug. 23, 2021), https://www.washingtonpost.com/business/interactive/2021/george-floyd-corporate-america-racial-justice/.

123 Richard Feloni & Yusuf George, *These Are the Corporate Responses to the George Floyd Protests That Stand Out*, JUST CAPITAL (June 30, 2020), https://justcapital.com/news/notable-corporate-responses-to-the-george-floyd-protests/ ("A subsidiary of PepsiCo . . . announced it was ending its Aunt Jemima breakfast foods brand. Mars Inc. told JUST Capital that 'now is the right time to evolve the Uncle Ben's brand.'").

124 Nat Ives, *Consumers Are More Likely to Use or Drop Brands Based on Racial Justice Response, Survey Finds*, WALL ST. J. (May. 6, 2021), https://www.wsj.com/articles/consumers-are-more-likely-to-use-or-drop-brands-based-on-racial-justice-response-survey-finds-11620333257; Liza Walworth, *What Consumers Agree on Brands Participating in Racial Justice Issues*, IPSOS (July 7, 2020), https://www.ipsos.com/en-us/knowledge/new-services/What-consumers-agree-on-brands-participating-in-racial-justice-issues.

125 Geeta Menon & Tina Kiesler, *When a Brand Stands up for Racial Justice, Do People Buy It?*, HARVARD BUSINESS REV. (July 31, 2020), https://hbr.org/2020/07/when-a-brand-stands-up-for-racial-justice-do-people-buy-it.

126 Danni White, *What Are Diversity, Equity and Inclusion, and Why Do Marketers Need Them?*, MARTECH (July 18, 2022), https://martech.org/what-are-diversity-equity-and-inclusion-and-why-marketers-need-them/.

NOTES

127 *Id.*
128 Jason Wiese, *How Diversity and Inclusion Campaigns Drive Brand Outcomes*, Assoc. of Nat. Advertisers (Sept. 15, 2020), https://www.ana.net/blogs/show/id/mm-blog-2020-09-vab-diversity-drives-brand-outcomes
129 Practical Stake: Corporations, Political Spending & Democracy, Center for Political Accountability, 25 (2022).
130 *Id.*
131 Reimann, *supra* note 78.
132 Rashad Robinson, *Corporations Profit from Racism. It's Time for Us to Stand Up to Them*, Guardian (May 16, 2019), https://www.theguardian.com/commentisfree/2019/may/16/racial-justice-corporations.
133 Julie N. W. Goodridge & Christine Jantz, *Corporate Political Spending: Why Shareholders Must Weigh In*, 5 J. of Values-Based Leadership 1, 2 (July 2012).
134 *Id.* at 6.
135 Quiroz-Gutierrez, *supra* note 34.
136 *Id.*
137 *Id.*
138 Isabel Togoh, *Corporate Donations Tracker: Here Are the Companies Giving Millions to Anti-Racism Efforts*, Forbes (June 3, 2020), https://www.forbes.com/sites/isabeltogoh/2020/06/01/corporate-donations-tracker-here-are-the-companies-giving-millions-to-anti-racism-efforts/?sh=b6952e37dc78.
139 Leslie Albrecht, *Facebook, Amazon, Google and Others Pledged Billions for Racial Justice in 2020. Tracking Where All the Money Went Is "Almost Impossible,"* MarketWatch (Nov. 3, 2021), https://www.marketwatch.com/story/companies-pledged-billions-toward-racial-justice-in-2020-tracking-where-all-the-money-went-is-almost-impossible-11635201572 ("A year after Floyd's death, most of the money [92%] had gone to either 'unknown' or 'multiple' recipients.").
140 Quiroz-Gutierrez, *supra* note 34 ("Only $250 million has actually been spent or committed to a specific initiative.").
141 Menon & Kiesler, *supra* note 125.
142 Jan, McGregor & Hoyer, *supra* note 122.
143 *Id.* ("About $70 million—went to organizations focused specifically on criminal justice reform.").
144 Center for Political Accountability, *supra* note 129.
145 Rhett Buttle, *Strengthening Our Democracy Is Critical For Maintaining America's Economic Competitiveness*, Forbes (Oct 19, 2022), https://www.forbes.com/sites/rhettbuttle/2022/10/19/strengthening-our-democracy-is-critical-for-maintaining-americas-economic-competitiveness/?sh=4d8f855f3a7c (quoting Bonk).

11. GO DIRECTLY TO JAIL, DO NOT PASS GO

1 Final Order, *Anderson v. Griswold*, Case No. 2023CV32577 at 90–95 & 102 (Denver D. Ct. Nov. 17, 2023).
2 *Public Events*, State Bar of California (June 2023), https://www.statebarcourt.ca.gov/Portals/2/documents/notices/State-Bar-Court-Public-Events.pdf.
3 Indictment, *Georgia v. Trump*, No. 23SC188947EJ15 McAffee (Fulton Sup. Ct. Aug. 14, 2023).

NOTES

4 Gregory Korte & Zoe Tillman, *Here Are the Unindicted Trump Co-Conspirators Mentioned in the Case*, BLOOMBERG (Aug. 1, 2023), https://www.bloomberg.com/news/articles/2023-08-02/all-the-president-s-co-conspirators-trump-indictment-ids-allies (concluding Eastman is Unindicted Co-Conspirator No. 2).

5 *Pardons Granted by President Donald J. Trump (2017–2021)*, DOJ (Jan. 20, 2021), https://www.justice.gov/pardon/pardons-granted-president-donald-j-trump-2017-2021.

6 *Commutations Granted by President Donald J. Trump (2017–2021)*, DOJ (Jan. 20, 2021), https://www.justice.gov/pardon/commutations-granted-president-donald-j-trump-2017-2021.

7 Amanda Terkel, *Trump Says He Would Pardon a "Large Portion" of Jan. 6 Rioters*, NBC NEWS (May 10, 2023), https://www.nbcnews.com/politics/donald-trump/trump-says-pardon-large-portion-jan-6-rioters-rcna83873.

8 Press Release, *Florida Man Found Guilty of Felony Charges Related to Jan. 6 Capitol Breach*, DOJ (Nov. 22, 2023), https://www.justice.gov/usao-dc/pr/florida-man-found-guilty-felony-charges-related-jan-6-capitol-breach-0.

9 Karl Baker, *Delaware Dissolves LLCs Created to Pay Off Women*, DELAWARE NEWS J. (Oct. 5, 2020), https://www.delawareonline.com/story/news/2020/10/05/delaware-dissolves-llcs-created-pay-off-women-trump-fixer-michael-cohen/3623443001/.

10 Press Release, *Michael Cohen Pleads Guilty in Manhattan Federal Court to Eight Counts, Including Criminal Tax Evasion and Campaign Finance Violations*, DOJ (Aug. 21, 2018), https://www.justice.gov/usao-sdny/pr/michael-cohen-pleads-guilty-manhattan-federal-court-eight-counts-including-criminal-tax.

11 Lucien Bruggeman, *Inside the 3 So-Called "Catch and Kill" Payments in Trump's Indictment*, ABC NEWS (Apr. 6, 2023), https://abcnews.go.com/US/inside-3-called-catch-kill-payments-trumps-indictment/story?id=98385606.

12 *DA Alvin Bragg Press Conference Transcript*, REV (Apr. 5, 2023), https://www.rev.com/blog/transcripts/da-alvin-bragg-press-conference-transcript.

13 *New York v. Trump*, IND-71543-23, Statement of Facts at 8 (Apr. 5, 2023), https://manhattanda.org/wp-content/uploads/2023/04/2023-04-04-SOF.pdf.

14 Indictment, *United States v. Trump*, Case No. 9:23-cr-80101-AMC (D.S.Fl. June 8, 2023).

15 Presidential Records Act (PRA) of 1978, 44 U.S.C. 2201–2209.

16 Superseding Indictment, *United States v. Trump* at 11–12 (D.S.Fl. July 27, 2023).

17 *Id.* at 16–17.

18 *Id.* at 17.

19 *Id.* at 24.

20 *Id.* at 4.

21 Tatyana Tandanpolie, *Mar-a-Lago Judge Blasted for Late Trial Date: "Cannon is slow-walking this case to benefit Trump,"* SALON (Sept. 26, 2023), https://www.salon.com/2023/09/26/mar-a-lago-blasted-for-late-trial-date-cannon-is-slow-walking-this-case-to-benefit-trump/.

22 Meg Anderson & Nick McMillan, *1,000 People Have Been Charged for the Capitol Riot*, NPR (Mar, 25, 2023), https://www.npr.org/2023/03/25/1165022885/1000-defendants-january-6-capitol-riot.

23 Indictment, *United States v. Trump*, Case No. 1:23-cr-00257-TSC (D.D.C. Aug. 1, 2023); Indictment, *Georgia v. Trump*, No. 23SC188947EJ15 McAffee (Fulton Sup. Ct. Aug. 14, 2023).

NOTES

24 Guilty Plea, *Georgia v. Chesebro* (Fulton Co. Oct. 20, 2023), https://s3.documentcloud.org/documents/24074001/plea-of-guilty-statement.pdf; Guilty Plea, *Georgia v. Powell* (Fulton Co. Oct. 19, 2023), https://s3.documentcloud.org/documents/24042671/powell-plea-of-guilty-statement.pdf; Guilty Plea, *Georgia v. Hall* (Fulton Co. Oct. 3, 2023), https://s3.documentcloud.org/documents/24004834/scott-hall-plea-of-guilty-statement.pdf; Anna Hickey, *Transcript of Jenna Ellis's Plea Hearing in Georgia*, LAWFARE (Oct. 24, 2023), https://www.lawfaremedia.org/article/transcript-of-jenna-ellis%27s-plea-hearing-in-georgia.

25 Chris Kenning, *Can Trump Be Pardoned in a State Conviction? It's Possible. But in Georgia, It's Complicated*, USA TODAY (Aug. 16, 2023), https://www.usatoday.com/story/news/politics/2023/08/16/trump-indictments-pardon-parole-georgia/70594725007/.

26 Meredith Deliso, *How the Georgia Pardon Process Works in Light of Trump's Latest Indictment*, ABC NEWS (Aug. 15, 2023), https://abcnews.go.com/Politics/georgia-pardon-process-works-light-trumps-latest-indictment/story?id=102289957.

27 Linton Weeks, *The 5 Most Unusual Nominees For President. Ever*, NPR (June 5, 2011), https://www.npr.org/2011/06/06/136865262/the-5-most-unusual-nominees-for-president-ever/.

28 Memorandum Order at 29–30, *United States v. Trump*, Criminal Action No. 23–257 (TSC) (D.D.C. Dec. 1, 2023).

29 Marcia Coyle, *Analysis: Trump's Legal Thicket Ensnares the Supreme Court*, PBS (Dec. 21, 2023), https://www.pbs.org/newshour/politics/analysis-trumps-legal-thicket-ensnares-the-supreme-court.

30 Ciara Torres-Spelliscy, *The Political Branding of the Big Lie*, 2022 (5) U. OF ILLINOIS L. REV. 1711 (2022).

31 Luke Broadwater, *Jan 6. Panel Subpoenas Lawyers Who Worked to Overturn Trump's Loss*, N.Y. TIMES (Mar. 1, 2022), https://www.nytimes.com/2022/03/01/us/politics/jan-6-subpoenas-trump.html.

32 Helen Coster, *Special Report: Voting-System Forms Battle Right-Wing Rage Against the Machines*, REUTERS (Nov. 7, 2022), https://www.reuters.com/world/us/voting-system-firms-battle-right-wing-rage-against-machines-2022-11-06/ ("[Trump] tweeted on Nov. 12, days after the election, that Dominion 'deleted' votes or 'switched' them to his Democratic rival, Joe Biden. As Trump's misinformation went viral, Denver-based Dominion faced an onslaught of Republican voter rage.").

33 Erin B. Logan, *As the For the People Act Voting Bill Is Debated, Republicans in Dozens of States Push Restrictions*, L.A. TIMES (Mar. 24, 2021) ("About 70% of Republicans believ[e] the presidential election was invalid."); Eli Stokols, *Republicans' Belief in Trump's "Big Lie" Holds Steady as Confidence in U.S. Elections Dips*, L.A. TIMES (Dec. 16, 2021), https://www.latimes.com/politics/story/2021-12-16/republicans-belief-in-trumps-big-lie-holds-steady-as-eroding-confidence-in-u-s-elections-wanes ("There was a hope there would see growing acceptance of Biden's victory over time, as people moved away from the 'Stop the Steal' movement after Jan. 6. Instead, we saw the numbers stay in place,' said Brendan Nyhan, a Dartmouth political scientist.").

34 Coster, *supra* note 32.

35 William Cummings, *Dominion Voting Sues Fox for $1.6 Billion over False 2020 Election Fraud Claims*, USA TODAY (Mar. 26, 2021), https://www.usatoday.com/story/

news/politics/2021/03/26/dominion-voting-sues-fox-news-1-6-b-over-2020-election-claims/7010134002/.
36 Jeremy W. Peters, *Defamation Suit About Election Falsehoods Puts Fox on Its Heels*, N.Y. TIMES (Apr. 13, 2022), https://www.nytimes.com/2022/08/13/business/media/fox-dominion-lawsuit-first-amendment.html.
37 Alison Durkee, *After Lawsuits Against Newsmax and OANN, Here's Who Dominion and Smartmatic Have Sued So Far—And Who Could Be Next*, FORBES (Nov. 3, 2021), https://www.forbes.com/sites/alisondurkee/2023/04/19/fox-news-defamation-settlement-here-are-where-dominion-and-smartmatics-other-lawsuits-stand-now/?sh=725aa0d24a24.
38 Erik Larson, *Dominion Voting Sues Fox, Seeking Election Evidence From Murdochs*, BLOOMBERG (Nov. 10, 2021), https://www.bloomberg.com/news/articles/2021-11-10/fox-sued-as-dominion-seeks-election-evidence-from-rupert-murdoch.
39 Merrit Kennedy & Bill Chappell, *Dominion Voting Systems Files $1.6 Billion Defamation Lawsuit Against Fox News*, NPR (Mar. 26, 2021), https://www.npr.org/2021/03/26/981515184/dominion-voting-systems-files-1-6-billion-defamation-lawsuit-against-fox-news.
40 Complaint and Demand for Jury Trial at 2, *US Dominion v. Herring Networks Inc.*, Doc. 1, No. 1:21-cv-02130 (Aug. 10, 2021), https://www.documentcloud.org/documents/21039565-dominion-oan-complaint.
41 Dominion's Brief in Support of Its Motion for Summary Judgment on Liability of Fox News Network LLC and Fox Corp. at 2, *US Dominion Inc. v. Fox News Network LLC*, No. N21C-03–257 EMD (Del. Super. Ct. Feb. 16, 2023), https://www.washingtonpost.com/documents/59b93674-ba03-4bc1-94da-5e15f776fc43.pdf?itid=lk_inline_manual_10.
42 *US Dominion Inc. v. Fox News Network LLC*, C.A. No.: N21C-03–257 EMD at 69 (Del. Super. Ct. Mar. 31, 2023).
43 Shweta Sharma, *Fox Dominion Payout Becomes Largest Media Settlement in History*, INDEPENDENT (Apr. 19, 2023), https://www.independent.co.uk/news/world/americas/us-politics/fox-news-dominion-largest-media-settlement-history-b2322336.html.
44 David Folkenflik, *Fox News Stands in Legal Peril*, NPR (Mar. 6, 2023), https://www.npr.org/2023/03/06/1161221798/if-fox-news-loses-defamation-dominion-media.
45 *US Dominion Inc. v. Fox News Network LLC*, 2023 WL 2730567 at 8 (Mar. 31, 2023 Del. Super.) (internal citation omitted).
46 *Id.* at 23 (quoting Dominion MSJ).
47 *Id.* at 38.
48 *Id.* at 72.
49 *Id.*
50 *Id.* at 49 (quoting *Celle v. Filipino Rep. Enterprises Inc.*, 209 F. 3d 163, 183 [2d Cir. 2000], *Solano v. Playgirl*, 292 F. 3d. 1078, 1085–86 [9th Cir. 2002], and *Sweeney v. Prisoners' Legal Servs. of New York Inc.*, 84 N.Y.2d 786, 792 [N.Y. 1995] [quoting *Sullivan v. N.Y. Times*, 376 U.S. 254, 280 (U.S. 1964)]).
51 *Id.* at 43 (emphasis in the original).
52 *Id.* at 80.
53 David Bauder, Randall Chase & Geoff Mulvihill, *Fox, Dominion Reach $787M Settlement over Election Claims*, AP (Apr. 18, 2023), https://apnews.com/article/fox-news-dominion-lawsuit-trial-trump-2020-0ac71f75acfacc52ea80b3e747fb0afe.

NOTES

54 Helen Coster, *Fox News Says Little on Air About $787.5 Million Dominion Settlement*, REUTERS (Apr. 19, 2023), https://www.reuters.com/business/media-telecom/fox-news-says-little-air-about-its-7875-million-settlement-with-dominion-2023-04-19/.
55 Sam Levine, *Dominion Is Not Done Fighting 2020 Election Lies*, GUARDIAN (May 4, 2023), https://www.theguardian.com/us-news/2023/may/04/dominion-fox-lawsuit-newsmax-oan-news.
56 Complaint & Demand for Jury Trial, at 205, *US Dominion Inc. v. Herring Networks Inc.*, Doc. 1, No. 1:21-cv-02130 (Aug. 10, 2021), https://www.documentcloud.org/documents/21039565-dominion-oan-complaint.
57 *Here's Every Word of the First Jan. 6 Committee Hearing on Its Investigation*, NPR (June 10, 2022), https://www.npr.org/2022/06/10/1104156949/jan-6-committee-hearing-transcript (quoting Liz Cheney).
58 Matter of Giuliani, No. 2021–00506, at *2 (N.Y. App. Div. May 3, 2021).
59 *United States v. Alvarez*, 567 U.S. 709 (2012) (allowing biographical lying about nonexistent military service); *Gentile v. State Bar of Nevada*, 501 US at 1056.
60 *Id.* at *6.
61 *Id.* at *9–10 (emphasis added).
62 *Id.* at *14.
63 *Id.* at *18 ("Respondent claimed that . . . 165,00 underage voters illegally voted in the Georgia 2020 election. The Georgia Office of the Secretary of State . . . audit revealed that there were zero [0] underage voters in the 2020 election"); *id.* at *23 ("Respondent made false and misleading statements that 'illegal aliens' had voted in Arizona during the 2020 presidential election.").
64 *Id.* at *30–31.
65 *Id.* at *31.
66 Zoe Tillman, *Rudy Giuliani Faces Disbarment Push in DC Legal Ethics Case*, BLOOMBERG LAW (Dec. 15, 2022), https://news.bloomberglaw.com/business-and-practice/giuliani-likely-committed-misconduct-washington-bar-panel-finds.
67 *King v. Whitmer*, No. 20–13134, 2021 WL 3771875, at *1 (E.D. Mich. Aug. 25, 2021).
68 *Id.* ("And this case was never about fraud—it was about undermining the People's faith in our democracy and debasing the judicial process to do so.").
69 *Id.* at *15.
70 *Id.* at *38.
71 *Id.* at *38.
72 *Id.* at *35.
73 David Eggert, *Lawyers Allied with Trump Ordered to Pay $175K in Sanctions*, AP (Dec. 2, 2021), https://apnews.com/article/donald-trump-joe-biden-michigan-detroit-election-2020-4fd2ba9b84e9d9a6bcddd51872ba3f97.
74 *King*, at *56.
75 Nicholas Riccardi, *Former Trump Lawyer Censured for Falsehoods About Election*, AP (Mar. 9, 2023), https://apnews.com/article/donald-trump-jenna-ellis-lawyer-censure-2020-election-falsehoods-fd6d72667a1f3bd01cd2249747bbbd85.
76 *Colorado v. Ellis*, #44026, No. 23PDJ004, Opinion Approving Stipulation to Discipline Under C.R.C.P. 242.19© at 5–6 (Mar. 8, 2023), https://stateuniteddemocracy.org/wp-content/uploads/2023/03/2304-OPINION-APPROVING-STIPULATION-TO-DISCIPLINE-UNDER-C.R.C.P.-242.19c.pdf.
77 *Id.* at 6.

78 Anna Hickey, *Transcript of Jenna Ellis's Plea Hearing in Georgia*, LAWFARE (Oct. 24, 2023), https://www.lawfaremedia.org/article/transcript-of-jenna-ellis's-plea-hearing-in-georgia.
79 Sarah N. Lynch, *Ex-Trump Justice Official Clark Faces Legal Disciplinary Charges*, REUTERS (July 22, 2022), https://www.reuters.com/legal/legalindustry/ex-trump-justice-official-clark-faces-legal-disciplinary-charges-2022-07-22/.
80 *January 6 Committee Final Report* at 382–401.
81 Indictment, *Georgia v. Trump*, No. 23SC188947EJ15 McAffee (Fulton Sup. Ct. Aug. 14, 2023).
82 Order, *Georgia v. Clark*, No. 1:23-CV-03721-SCJ Re: Notice of Removal of Fulton County Superior Court Indictment No. 23SC188947 (N.D. Ga. Aug. 23, 2023).
83 Rebecca Falconer & Jacob Knutson, *Trump DOJ Official Likely Broke Ethics Rules, D.C. Bar Panel Finds*, AXIOS (Apr. 4, 2024), https://www.axios.com/2024/04/05/jeffrey-clark-bar-trump-review-ethics-rules.
84 Aaron Keller, *Here's What We Learned from Lin Wood's 1,677-Page 'Confidential' Georgia State Bar Disciplinary Grievance*, LAW & CRIME (Feb. 18, 2021), https://lawandcrime.com/2020-election/heres-what-we-learned-from-lin-woods-1677-page-confidential-georgia-state-bar-discipline-grievance/.
85 *Wood v. Frederick*, No. 1:2021-cv-01169 (N. D. Ga 2021).
86 *Wood v. Frederick*, No. 21–12238 (11th Cir. May. 31, 2022).
87 Ryan Bort, *Trump Election Lawyer Facing Disbarment Decides to Go Ahead and Just Retire*, ROLLING STONE (July 5, 2023), https://www.rollingstone.com/politics/politics-news/lin-wood-asks-retire-disbarment-election-lies-1234783125/.
88 Final Summary Judgment, *Commission for Lawyer Discipline v. Sidney Powell*, No. DC-22-02562 (116th Judicial Feb. 22, 2023), https://abovethelaw.com/uploads/2023/02/Powell.pdf.
89 Zoe Tillman, *Sidney Powell's Tossed Ethics Case Appealed by Texas Bar Panel*, BLOOMBERG (May 22, 2023), https://www.bloomberg.com/news/articles/2023-05-22/sidney-powell-s-tossed-ethics-case-appealed-by-texas-bar-panel.
90 Powell Guilty Plea, *supra* note 24.
91 Adolfo Pesquera, *17 Lawyers Want Sidney Powell Punished: Letter Sent to Bar About Trump Attorney*, TEXAS LAWYER (Nov. 7, 2023), https://www.law.com/texaslawyer/2023/11/07/17-lawyers-want-sidney-powell-punished-letter-sent-to-bar-about-trump-attorney/.
92 Carol D. Leonnig & Aaron C. Davis, *FBI Resisted Opening Probe into Trump's Role in Jan. 6 for More than a Year*, WASH. POST (June 19, 2023), https://www.washingtonpost.com/investigations/2023/06/19/fbi-resisted-opening-probe-into-trumps-role-jan-6-more-than-year/.
93 Auburn K. Daily & S. Britta Thornquist, *Has the Exception Outgrown the Privilege? Exploring the Application of the Crime-Fraud Exception to the Attorney-Client Privilege*, 16 GEO. J. LEGAL ETHICS 583, 584 (2003); *see also Nix v. Whiteside*, 475 U.S. 157, 166 (1986).
94 Cameron Joseph, *Meet the Obscure Think Tank Powering Trump's Biggest Lies*, VICE (Nov. 4, 2021), https://www.vice.com/en/article/qjb4y3/john-eastman-claremont-institute-supporting-jan-6-trumpism.
95 *Id.*

NOTES

96 *Id.*
97 George Thomas, *John Eastman's Big Lie*, CONSTITUTIONALIST (Oct. 13, 2021), https://theconstitutionalist.org/2021/10/13/john-eastmans-big-lie/.
98 Elie Honig, *Pro-Trump lawyer's Memo Begins with a Lie, Then Descends into Madness*, CNN (Sept. 21, 2021), https://www.cnn.com/2021/09/21/opinions/trump-lawyer-memo-begins-with-lie-honig/index.html.
99 Ed Pilkington, *"A roadmap for a coup": Inside Trump's Plot to Steal the Presidency*, GUARDIAN (Oct. 30, 2021), https://www.theguardian.com/us-news/2021/oct/30/trump-2020-election-steal-presidency-coup-inside-story.
100 Steve Benen, *Lawyers Seek Investigation into Author of Pro-Trump Eastman Memo*, MSNBC (Oct. 6, 2021), https://www.msnbc.com/rachel-maddow-show/lawyers-seek-investigation-author-pro-trump-eastman-memo-n1280892 ("Eastman filed the brief . . . on Trump's behalf that asked the U.S. Supreme Court to overturn the 2020 presidential election. [It was filled with factual errors—including an obvious one literally on the first page.]").
101 *Eastman v. Thompson*, 2022 WL 894256 at *20–21 (C.D.Cal. 2022) (internal citations omitted).
102 *Id.* at *21 (emphasis added).
103 *Id.* at *22.
104 *Id.* at *21.
105 *Id.* at *27 (emphasis added).
106 *Id.* at *27.
107 Liz Dye, *Conservative Superlawyer John Eastman Knows Who Is to Blame for the Capitol Riot and It Is Mike Pence*, ABOVE THE LAW (Nov. 1, 2021), https://abovethelaw.com/2021/11/conservative-superlawyer-john-eastman-knows-who-is-to-blame-for-the-capitol-riot-and-it-is-mike-pence/.
108 Jonathan Alter, *The Final Triumph of the January 6th Committee—Day 10 from Day One Through Day Ten, These Hearings Set a New Standard for Congressional Oversight*, WASH. MONTHLY (Dec. 24, 2022), https://washingtonmonthly.com/2022/12/24/the-final-triumph-of-the-january-6th-committee-day-ten/.
109 Cheryl Miller, *Chemerinsky Urges State Bar to Investigate Lawyer Who Wrote Electoral Challenge Blueprint*, RECORDER (Sept. 30, 2021), https://www.law.com/therecorder/2021/09/30/chemerinsky-urges-state-bar-to-investigate-lawyer-who-wrote-electoral-challenge-blueprint/ ("Chemerinsky also urged the state bar to consider disciplining Eastman.").
110 Kyle Cheney & Josh Gerstein, *Jack Smith Is Still Scrutinizing John Eastman*, POLITICO (Dec. 14, 2023), https://www.politico.com/news/2023/12/14/jack-smith-john-eastman-trump-records-00131823.
111 Defendant Eastman's Opposition to the State's Motion to Schedule Trial Date for August 5, 2024, *Georgia v. Eastman*, Case No.: 23SC188947 (Fulton Co. Nov. 27, 2023), https://s3.documentcloud.org/documents/24175692/112723-defendant-eastmans-opposition-to-the-states-motion-to-schedule-trial-date-for-august-5-2024-response-4.pdf.
112 Leila Fadel & Tom Dreisbach, *Judge in California Recommends Disbarment of Pro-Trump Attorney John Eastman*, NPR (Mar. 28, 2024), https://www.npr.org/2024/03/28/1241357592/judge-in-california-recommends-disbarment-of-pro-trump-attorney-john-eastman.

113 Moira Warburton, *Two U.S. House Democrats File Ethics Complaint Against Republican George Santos*, REUTERS (Jan. 10, 2023), https://www.reuters.com/world/us/two-us-house-democrats-file-ethics-complaint-against-republican-george-santos-2023-01-10/.

114 Alia Shoaib, *Video Shows George Santos Calling Himself Anthony Devolder at a 2019 Event, Raising Questions About His Name*, YAHOO (Jan. 14, 2023), https://news.yahoo.com/video-shows-george-santos-calling-124511851.html.

115 Jacqueline Sweet, *Santos Was Charged with Theft in 2017 Case Tied to Amish Dog Breeders*, POLITICO (Feb. 9, 2023), https://www.politico.com/news/2023/02/09/santos-charged-theft-2017-dog-breeders-00082091.

116 Rachel Scott et al., *Alleged George Santos Scam Victims Speak Out*, ABC NEWS (Mar. 10, 2023), https://abcnews.go.com/US/alleged-george-santos-scam-victims-speak/story?id=97710377.

117 Warburton, *supra* note 113.

118 Michael Gold & Grace Ashford, *House Ethics Committee Opens Inquiry into George Santos*, N.Y. TIMES A17 (Mar. 3, 2023).

119 Jason Lange, *U.S. Watchdog Accuses Rep. George Santos of Breaking Campaign Finance Laws*, REUTERS (Jan. 9, 2023), https://www.reuters.com/world/us/us-watchdog-accuses-rep-george-santos-breaking-campaign-finance-laws-2023-01-09/.

120 Gold & Ashford, *supra* note 118.

121 *Id.*

122 *Id.*

123 *Devolder-Santos for Congress, Disbursements Between $199 and $200, 2019–2020*, FEC https://www.fec.gov/data/disbursements/?data_type=processed&committee_id=C00721365&two_year_transaction_period=2022&min_date=01%2F01%2F2021&max_date=12%2F31%2F2022&min_amount=199&max_amount=200.

124 *Recording Disbursements*, FEC, https://www.fec.gov/help-candidates-and-committees/keeping-records/records-disbursements/ (last visited Jan. 1, 2024).

125 Lange, *supra* note 119 ("The Campaign Legal Center, a non-partisan government watchdog, made the complaint in a filing with the Federal Election Commission.").

126 *Id.*

127 *Id.*

128 Press Release, *Congressman George Santos Charged with Fraud, Money Laundering, Theft of Public Funds, and False Statements*, DOJ (May 10, 2023), https://www.justice.gov/usao-edny/pr/congressman-george-santos-charged-fraud-money-laundering-theft-public-funds-and-false.

129 Indictment at 5, *United States v. George Anthony Devolder Santos*, No. CR-23-197 (E.D.N.Y. May 9, 2023).

130 *Id.* at 7 ("Shortly after the contributions . . . were received by Company #1 . . . , they were transferred into bank accounts controlled by the defendant GEORGE ANTHONY DEVOLDER SANTOS.").

131 *Id.* ("The funds . . . were spent by DEVOLDER SANTOS for his personal benefit.").

132 Press Release, *Congressman George Santos*, *supra* note 128.

133 Benjamin S. Weiss, *House Ethics report: Santos Spent Campaign Funds on OnlyFans, Botox*, COURTHOUSE NEWS (Nov. 16, 2023), https://www.courthousenews.com/house-ethics-report-santos-spent-campaign-funds-on-onlyfans-botox/.

NOTES

134 Kyle Stewart, *George Santos Was Expelled from the House—What Happens Next?*, NBC News (Dec. 1, 2023), https://www.nbcnews.com/politics/congress/george-santos-expelled-house-what-happens-how-rcna127518.

135 Soo Rin Kim, *Santos Lists New Treasurer—Who Says He Doesn't Work for the Congressman*, ABC News (Jan. 25, 2023), https://abcnews.go.com/US/santos-lists-new-treasurer-claims-doesnt-work-congressman/story?id=96675494.

136 Gregory Korte, *George Santos Appoints Himself as His Own Campaign Treasurer*, Bloomberg (May 19, 2023), https://www.bloomberg.com/news/articles/2023-05-19/george-santos-names-himself-as-campaign-treasurer-after-fraud-indictment?embedded-checkout=true.

137 Clare Hymes & Robert Legare, *What Does George Santos' Ex-Campaign Treasurer Nancy Marks' Guilty Plea Mean for His Criminal Defense?*, CBS News (Oct. 6, 2023), https://www.cbsnews.com/news/george-santos-defense-ex-campaign-treasurer-nancy-marks-guilty-plea/.

138 Press Release, *Congressional Campaign Staffer Pleads Guilty to Wire Fraud*, DOJ (Nov. 14, 2023), https://www.justice.gov/usao-edny/pr/congressional-campaign-staffer-pleads-guilty-wire-fraud.

139 Press Release, *Congressman George Santos Charged With Conspiracy, Wire Fraud, False Statements, Falsification of Records, Aggravated Identity Theft, and Credit Card Fraud*, DOJ (Oct. 10, 2023), https://www.justice.gov/usao-edny/pr/congressman-george-santos-charged-conspiracy-wire-fraud-false-statements-0.

12. DEMOCRACY ON THE BALLOT

1 *Two Churches Burned by Suspected Arsonist in Mississippi as Manhunt Continues*, PBS (Nov. 8, 2022), https://www.pbs.org/newshour/nation/two-churches-burned-by-suspected-arsonist-in-mississippi-as-manhunt-continues.

2 Francesca Chambers, *Biden Rejects Criticisms He Is Dividing Americans by Calling Trump Supporters a Threat to Democracy*, USA Today (Sept. 5, 2022), https://www.usatoday.com/story/news/politics/2022/09/05/biden-maga-republican-criticism-speech/7941978001/.

3 Jonathan Lemire, *Biden Closes the Election with a Big Roll of the Dice*, Politico (Nov. 7, 2022), https://www.politico.com/news/2022/11/07/joe-biden-midterm-elections-00065355.

4 Monica Potts, *Turnout Was High Again. Is This the New Normal?*, FiveThirtyEight (Nov. 15, 2022), https://fivethirtyeight.com/features/turnout-was-high-again-is-this-the-new-normal/.

5 Nicholas Riccardi, *Explainer: What's in the Texas GOP's Voting Bills?*, AP (July 14, 2021), https://apnews.com/article/health-government-and-politics-texas-voting-coronavirus-pandemic-9bc36a6e8c967757340ab25f49b8ddbf.

6 *Voter Turnout, 2018–2022*, Pew (July 12, 2023), https://www.pewresearch.org/politics/2023/07/12/voter-turnout-2018-2022/ ("About two-thirds [66%] of the voting-eligible population turned out for the 2020 presidential election—the highest rate for any national election since 1900.").

7 *Voting Laws Roundup: October 2022*, Brennan Center (Oct. 6, 2022), https://www.brennancenter.org/our-work/research-reports/voting-laws-roundup-october-2022.

NOTES

8 Emily Czachor, *Arizona State Rep Says "Quality" of Votes Should Matter, Only Informed Should Cast Ballots*, NEWSWEEK (Mar. 11, 2021), https://www.newsweek.com/arizona-state-rep-says-quality-votes-should-matter-only-informed-should-cast-ballots-1575573.
9 *Voting Laws Roundup: December 2021*, BRENNAN CENTER (Jan. 12, 2022), https://www.brennancenter.org/our-work/research-reports/voting-laws-roundup-december-2021.
10 Jane C. Timm, *19 States Enacted Voting Restrictions in 2021. What's Next?*, NBC NEWS (Dec. 21, 2021), https://www.nbcnews.com/politics/elections/19-states-enacted-voting-restrictions-2021-rcna8342.
11 *Voting Laws Roundup: December 2022*, BRENNAN CENTER (Feb. 1, 2023), https://www.brennancenter.org/our-work/research-reports/voting-laws-roundup-december-2022.
12 Erin B. Logan, *As the For the People Act Voting Bill Is Debated, Republicans in Dozens of States Push Restrictions*, L.A. TIMES (Mar. 24 2021), https://www.latimes.com/politics/story/2021-03-24/voting-rights-bill-state-restrictions-for-the-people-georgia.
13 *The Global State of Democracy 2021: Building Resilience in a Pandemic Era*, INT'L INST. FOR DEMOCRACY & ELECTORAL ASSISTANCE, at 15 (2021), https://www.idea.int/gsod/sites/default/files/2021-11/the-global-state-of-democracy-2021_1.pdf; *US Added to List of "backsliding" Democracies for First Time*, GUARDIAN (Nov. 22, 2021), https://www.theguardian.com/us-news/2021/nov/22/us-list-backsliding-democracies-civil-liberties-international.
14 GLOBAL STATE OF DEMOCRACY, *supra* note 13, at 27.
15 Stephen Fowler et al., *After Record 2020 Turnout, State Republicans Weigh Making it Harder to Vote*, NPR (Feb. 7, 2021), https://www.npr.org/2021/02/07/964598941/after-record-2020-turnout-state-republicans-weigh-making-it-harder-to-vote.
16 Stephen Gruber-Miller, *Republicans Seek to Shorten Iowa's Early Voting, Tighten Absentee Ballot Rules*, DES MOINES REGISTER (Feb. 17, 2021), https://www.desmoinesregister.com/story/news/politics/2021/02/17/legislature-republicans-advance-bills-shorten-early-voting-iowa-restrict-absentee-ballots/6780255002/.
17 Penny M. Venetis, *Opposition to Voting by Mail Is a Form of Voter Suppression That Disproportionately Impacts Communities of Color*, 72 RUTGERS U. L. REV. 1387, 1401 (2019–20).
18 David Wickert, Patricia Murphy & Mark Niesse, *Georgia Recount Confirms Biden Win, Again, but Trump Still Battling*, ATLANTA J. CONSTITUTION (Dec. 7, 2020).
19 Julia Anzari, *"The pattern . . . [is to] drive a wedge through the GOP coalition,"* POLITICO (Aug. 2, 2023), https://www.politico.com/news/magazine/2023/08/02/trump-indictment-roundup-00109391.
20 Veronica Stracqualursi, *Arizona GOP Representative Struggles to Justify State Bill That Would Purge Early Voting List*, CNN (Apr. 27, 2021), https://www.cnn.com/2021/04/23/politics/arizona-lawmaker-early-voting-list-legislation-cnntv/index.html; Jonathan J. Cooper, *Republican-Backed Arizona Voting Bill Explained*, AP (May 11, 2021), https://apnews.com/article/donald-trump-arizona-race-and-ethnicity-bills-voting-rights-a06a005420048eb04e8e71cc99f106f0.
21 Czachor, *supra* note 8.
22 Logan, *supra* note 12.
23 Roberto Foa & Yascha Mounk, *Are Americans Losing Faith in Democracy?*, Vox (Dec. 18, 2015), https://www.vox.com/polyarchy/2015/12/18/9360663/is-democracy-in-trouble.

24 Nathaniel Persily & Jon Cohen, *Americans are losing faith in democracy—and in each other*, WASH. POST (Oct. 14, 2016), https://www.washingtonpost.com/opinions/americans-are-losing-faith-in-democracy--and-in-each-other/2016/10/14/b35234ea-90c6-11e6-9c52-0b10449e33c4_story.html.
25 *Americans Feel Divided on Core Values*, MONMOUTH UNIVERSITY (Oct. 14, 2019), https://www.monmouth.edu/polling-institute/reports/monmouthpoll_us_101419/.
26 Vera Bergengruen, *The United States of Political Violence*, TIME (Nov. 4, 2022), https://time.com/6227754/political-violence-us-states-midterms-2022/.
27 Affidavit in Support of Application for Complaint and Arrest Warrant at 5, *United States v. Depape* (Oct. 31, 2022), https://www.justice.gov/opa/press-release/file/1548106/download.
28 Joe Biden, *Remarks by President Biden on Standing Up for Democracy at Columbus Club, Union Station Washington, D.C.*, WHITE HOUSE (Nov. 2, 2022), https://www.whitehouse.gov/briefing-room/speeches-remarks/2022/11/03/remarks-by-president-biden-on-standing-up-for-democracy/.
29 *Id.*
30 *Id.*
31 Press Release, *David DePape Convicted of Assault and Attempted Kidnapping Charges*, DOJ (Nov. 17, 2023), https://www.justice.gov/usao-ndca/pr/david-depape-convicted-assault-and-attempted-kidnapping-charges.
32 William Vaillancourt, *Gunman Who Tried to Break into Cincinnati FBI Office Was at Capitol on Jan. 6*, ROLLING STONE (Aug. 11, 2022), https://www.rollingstone.com/politics/politics-news/cincinnati-fbi-shooting-1395818/.
33 Cat Zakrzewski, *Election Workers Brace for a Torrent of Threats: "I KNOW WHERE YOU SLEEP,"* WASH. POST (Nov. 8, 2022), https://www.washingtonpost.com/technology/2022/11/08/election-workers-online-threats/.
34 Linda So, Peter Eisler & Jason Szep, *"Kill Them": Arizona Election Workers Face Midterm Threats*, REUTERS (Nov. 6, 2022), https://www.reuters.com/world/us/kill-them-arizona-election-workers-face-midterm-threats-2022-11-06/ ("Since the 2020 election, Reuters has documented more than 1,000 intimidating messages to election officials across the country, including more than 120 that could warrant prosecution.").
35 Press Release, *Justice Department Launches Task Force to Combat Threats Against Election Workers*, DOJ (July 29, 2021), https://www.justice.gov/opa/blog/justice-department-launches-task-force-combat-threats-against-election-workers-0.
36 Press Release, *Readout of Election Threats Task Force Briefing with Election Officials and Workers*, DOJ (Aug. 1, 2022), https://www.justice.gov/opa/pr/readout-election-threats-task-force-briefing-election-officials-and-workers.
37 Tom Hamburger & Yvonne Wingett Sanchez, *One Charged, Another Sentenced for Threatening Election Officials*, WASH. POST (Oct. 6, 2022), https://www.washingtonpost.com/national-security/2022/10/06/election-threats-hickman-ford-rissi/.
38 Ruby Edlin & Turquoise Baker, *Poll of Local Election Officials Finds Safety Fears for Colleagues—and Themselves*, BRENNAN CENTER (Mar. 10, 2020), https://www.brennancenter.org/our-work/analysis-opinion/poll-local-election-officials-finds-safety-fears-colleagues-and.
39 Press Release, *Justice Department's Election Threats Task Force Secures Ninth Conviction*, DOJ (Aug. 31, 2023), https://www.justice.gov/opa/pr/justice-departments-election-threats-task-force-secures-ninth-conviction.

40 Stephanie Sy & Geoffrey Lou Guray, *Expert fears Partisan Actors May Replace Election Workers Who Quit over Threats*, PBS (Nov. 2, 2021), https://www.pbs.org/newshour/show/expert-fears-partisan-actors-may-replace-election-workers-who-quit-over-threats.

41 Ines Kagubare, *US Faces Election Worker Shortage Ahead of Midterms Due to Rise in Threats*, THE HILL (Oct. 2, 2022), https://thehill.com/policy/cybersecurity/3669329-us-faces-election-worker-shortage-ahead-of-midterms-due-to-rise-in-threats/.

42 *John Lewis and Others React to the Supreme Court's Voting Rights Act ruling*, WASH. POST (June 25, 2013), https://www.washingtonpost.com/opinions/john-lewis-and-others-react-to-the-supreme-courts-voting-rights-act-ruling/2013/06/25/acb96650-ddda-11e2-b797-cbd4cb13f9c6_story.html.

43 Press Release, *Joint Statement from Chairman Bill Gates and Recorder Stephen Richer on Drop Box Watchers*, MARICOPA COUNTY 2022 ELECTION COMMAND CENTER (Oct. 22, 2022), https://content.govdelivery.com/accounts/AZMARIC/bulletins/333cdba.

44 Complaint, *League of Women Voters of Arizona v. Lions of Liberty LLC* (Oct. 25, 2022), https://www.documentcloud.org/documents/23189851-league-of-women-voters-election-intimidation-complaint.

45 Complaint, Arizona Alliance for Retired Americans; *Voto Latino v. Clean Elections USA et al.* (Oct. 24, 2022), https://www.democracydocket.com/wp-content/uploads/2022/10/12022-10-24-Complaint-.pdf.

46 Temporary Restraining Order at 1–2, *Arizona Alliance for Retired Americans et al. v. Clean Elections USA et al.*, No. CV-22-01823-PHX-MTL (D. Az Nov. 1, 2022), https://www.democracydocket.com/wp-content/uploads/2022/10/D.-Ariz.-22-cv-01823-dckt-000051_000-filed-2022-11-01.pdf.

47 *Id.* at 2.

48 Katie Friel & Jasleen Singh, *Voter Intimidation and Election Worker Intimidation Resource Guide*, BRENNAN CENTER (Oct. 28, 2022), https://www.brennancenter.org/our-work/research-reports/voter-intimidation-and-election-worker-intimidation-resource-guide.

49 Ali Swenson, *2022 Early Voting Levels Haven't Surpassed 2020, Don't Indicate Fraud*, AP (Nov. 7, 2022), https://apnews.com/article/fact-check-early-voting-numbers-2018-2020-2022-333179317067.

50 Biden, *supra* note 28.

51 Joe Biden, *Remarks by President Biden on the Continued Battle for the Soul of the Nation*, WHITE HOUSE (Sept. 1, 2022), https://www.whitehouse.gov/briefing-room/speeches-remarks/2022/09/01/remarks-by-president-bidenon-the-continued-battle-for-the-soul-of-the-nation/.

52 *Id.*

53 *Id.*

54 Joe Biden, *Statement by President Joseph R. Biden, Jr. on the International Day of Democracy*, WHITE HOUSE (Sept. 15, 2022), https://www.whitehouse.gov/briefing-room/statements-releases/2022/09/15/statement-by-president-joseph-r-biden-jr-on-the-international-day-of-democracy-2/.

55 Joe Biden, *Remarks by President Biden Before the 77th Session of the United Nations General Assembly*, WHITE HOUSE (Sept. 21, 2022), https://www.whitehouse.gov/

briefing-room/speeches-remarks/2022/09/21/remarks-by-president-biden-before-the-77th-session-of-the-united-nations-general-assembly/.
56 Biden, *supra* note 28.
57 *Id.*
58 Miles Parks, *Here's Where Election-Denying Candidates Are Running to Control Voting*, NPR (Feb. 3, 2022), https://www.npr.org/2022/01/04/1069232219/heres-where-election-deniers-and-doubters-are-running-to-control-voting.
59 Adam Edelman, *Election Deniers Who Say Trump Won in 2020 Are Running to Be Top Cop in 4 Battleground States*, NBC NEWS (May 22, 2022), https://www.nbcnews.com/politics/2022-election/election-deniers-say-trump-won-2020-are-running-top-cop-4-battleground-rcna29705 ("At least 15 men and women who have denied the results of the 2020 election are running to be their states' attorneys general in 14 states.").
60 *Id.*
61 Amy B. Wang, *Greitens Slammed for "RINO Hunting" Campaign Ad*, WASH. POST (June 20, 2022), https://www.washingtonpost.com/politics/2022/06/20/greitens-rino-hunting-ad/.
62 Becky Sullivan, *A Missouri Senate Candidate Holds a Shotgun and Calls for "RINO Hunting" in a New Ad*, NPR (June 20, 2022), https://www.npr.org/2022/06/20/1106228594/a-missouri-senate-candidate-holds-a-shotgun-and-calls-for-rino-hunting-in-a-new-.
63 Kevin Breuninger, *Eric Schmitt Beats Former Gov. Eric Greitens in Missouri GOP Senate Primary, NBC Projects*, CNBC (Aug. 2, 2022), https://www.cnbc.com/2022/08/02/eric-greitens-loses-missouri-gop-senate-primary-nbc-projects.html.
64 Tim Murphy, *Eric Defeats Eric in a Battle of GOP Election Deniers*, MOTHER JONES (Aug. 2, 2022), https://www.motherjones.com/politics/2022/08/eric-schmitt-eric-greitens-missouri-senate-trump/.
65 *United States Senate Eection in Missouri, 2022*, BALLOTPEDIA (last visited Nov. 21, 2022), https://ballotpedia.org/United_States_Senate_election_in_Missouri,_2022.
66 Rob Beschizza, *Watch the Creepy Blake Masters Campaign Ad Where He Quietly Plays with a Silenced Handgun*, BOING BOING (Nov. 12, 2022), https://boingboing.net/2022/11/12/watch-the-creepy-blake-masters-campaign-ad-where-he-plays-with-a-silenced-handgun.html.
67 *Id.*
68 Nikki Mccann Ramirez, *Blake Masters Joins the Ranks of MAGA Wipeouts*, ROLLING STONE (Nov. 11, 2022), https://www.rollingstone.com/politics/politics-news/blake-masters-loses-mark-kelly-arizona-senate-1234627047/.
69 Parks, *supra* note 58.
70 Adrian Blanco & Amy Gardner, *Where Republican Election Deniers Are on the Ballot near You*, WASH. POST (Nov. 8, 2022), https://www.washingtonpost.com/elections/interactive/2022/election-deniers-running-for-office-elections-2022/.
71 Scott MacFarlane et al., *More than Half of GOP Midterm Candidates Are "Election Deniers,"* CBS MORNINGS (Nov. 3, 2022), https://www.cbsnews.com/news/midterm-elections-gop-candidates-more-than-half-election-deniers-cbs-news-review/.
72 *Sixty Percent of Americans Will Have an Election Denier on the Ballot This Fall*, FIVETHIRTYEIGHT (Nov. 8, 2022), https://projects.fivethirtyeight.com/republicans-trump-election-fraud/; Nathaniel Rakich & Kaleigh Rogers, *At Least 120 Republican Nominees Deny the Results of the 2020 Election*, FIVETHIRTYEIGHT (July 18, 2022),

https://fivethirtyeight.com/features/at-least-120-republicans-who-deny-the-2020-election-results-will-be-on-the-ballot-in-november/ ("Thirty percent [346 out of 1,148] of all Republican candidates for those offices [winners *and* losers] explicitly denied the election's legitimacy, and another 16 percent [185 out of 1,148] questioned it.").

73 Fredreka Schouten, *Election Deniers Are Winning Political Nominations Across the Country*, CNN (June 15, 2022), https://www.cnn.com/2022/06/15/politics/nevada-new-mexico-election-deniers/index.html; Amy Gardner, *A Majority of GOP Nominees Deny or Question the 2020 Election Results*, WASH. POST (Oct. 12, 2022), https://www.washingtonpost.com/nation/2022/10/06/elections-deniers-midterm-elections-2022/.

74 Ellen Ioanes, *How a Surprising Democratic Strategy May Have Staved Off the Midterm Red Wave*, VOX (Nov. 12, 2022), https://www.vox.com/2022/11/12/23454725/democrat-republican-maga-strategy-midterm-red-wave ("Democratic groups and political action committees [PACs] spent tens of millions of dollars in at least seven states to elevate Republicans.").

75 Stephanie Santostasi, *Operation Chaos 2020: Movement Encourages Republicans to Strategically Vote in SC Primary*, WLOS (Feb. 25, 2020), https://wlos.com/news/election/operation-chaos-2020-movement-encourages-republicans-to-strategically-vote-in-sc-primary; *but see* John Opdycke, *Lessons to Be Learned from the "Real" Operation Chaos in South Carolina*, BILL TRACK 50 (Mar. 18, 2020), https://www.billtrack50.com/blog/random-awesomeness/soapbox/lessons-to-be-learned-from-the-real-operation-chaos-in-south-carolina-guest-post-from-john-opdycke/ ("5 percent of the people who voted in the South Carolina primary were Republicans.").

76 Ioanes, *supra* note 74.

77 Parks, *supra* note 58; Christina A. Cassidy, *GOP Election-Deniers Elevate Races for Secretary Of State*, PBS (Apr. 30, 2022), https://www.pbs.org/newshour/politics/gop-election-deniers-elevate-races-for-secretary-of-state.

78 Reid J. Epstein, *Midterm Stakes Grow Clearer: Election Deniers Will Be on Many Ballots*, N.Y. TIMES (May 18, 2022), https://www.nytimes.com/2022/05/18/us/politics/midterms-trump-2020-election-deniers.html.

79 Rakich & Rogers, *supra* note 72.

80 Brittany Shammas, *A Jan. 6 Defendant Is Running for Office in Florida—from Jail*, WASH. POST (July 28, 2022), https://www.washingtonpost.com/politics/2022/07/28/january-6-candidate-florida/.

81 Nick Corasaniti, *Voters Reject Election Deniers Running to Take Over Elections*, N.Y. TIMES (Nov. 12, 2022), https://www.nytimes.com/2022/11/12/us/politics/jim-marchant-nevada.html; *General Election for Florida House of Representatives District 62*, BALLOTPEDIA, https://ballotpedia.org/Florida_House_of_Representatives_District_62_candidate_surveys,_2022 (last visited Dec. 6, 2022).

82 Matt Vasilogambros, *Voters Push Back Against Election Deniers in Key States*, PEW (Nov. 9, 2022), https://www.pewtrusts.org/en/research-and-analysis/blogs/stateline/2022/11/09/voters-push-back-against-election-deniers-in-key-states.

83 Lee Rainie & Andrew Perrin, *Key Findings About Americans' Declining Trust in Government and Each Other*, PEW (July 22, 2019), https://www.pewresearch.org/fact-tank/2019/07/22/key-findings-about-americans-declining-trust-in-government-and-each-other/.

84 Larry Diamond, *Are People Losing Faith in Democracy?*, AMERICAN INTEREST (Mar. 16, 2018), https://www.the-american-interest.com/2018/03/16/people-losing-faith-de-

mocracy/; *see also* Amy Walter, *Where Americans Agree—and Disagree—on Civics and Democracy*, COOK POLITICAL REPORT (July 12, 2017), https://cookpolitical.com/analysis/national/national-politics/where-americans-agree-and-disagree-civics-and-democracy.

85 Alan Greenblatt, *What Are the Dangers of Putting Election Deniers in Charge of Elections?*, GOVERNING (Nov. 2, 2022), https://www.governing.com/now/what-are-the-dangers-of-putting-election-deniers-in-charge-of-elections.

86 Kim Chandler, *Election Skeptics Seek Alabama Secretary Of State's Office*, AP (June 17, 2022), https://apnews.com/article/2022-midterm-elections-covid-health-campaigns-government-and-politics-bed7f04b10d5ecd9186f37de656c2c13.

87 Kaitlin Lange, Alexandria Burris & Binghui Huang, *Republican Diego Morales Wins Indiana Secretary Of State Race*, INDIANAPOLIS STAR (Nov. 9, 2022), https://www.indystar.com/story/news/politics/2022/11/08/diego-morales-destiny-wells-indiana-secretary-of-state-election-results/69541301007/.

88 Eric Mayer & Dan Santella, *Secretary of State Candidate on Biden 2020 Win: "I'm not going to acknowledge that,"* KELOLAND (Oct. 19, 2022), https://www.keloland.com/keloland-com-original/secretary-of-state-candidate-on-biden-2020-win-im-not-going-to-acknowledge-that/.

89 *Live Results: GOP Candidates Who Will Have Influence or Control over Elections*, PBS (last visited Nov. 13, 2022), https://www.pbs.org/newshour/elections-2022/gop-election-deniers.

90 Kayleen Devlin & Jack Goodman, *Boebart to Lake: How Election Deniers Have Fared in US Midterms*, BBC MONITORING & BBC WORLD DISINFORMATION UNIT (Nov. 10, 2022), https://www.bbc.com/news/world-us-canada-63568003.

91 Rakich & Rogers, *supra* note 71; Jacob Rosen, Robert Legare & Aaron Navarro, *2022 Midterm Elections: Election Deniers Who Won and Lost*, CBS NEWS (Nov. 15, 2022), https://www.cbsnews.com/news/election-deniers-2022-midterm-elections/.

92 Rucho v. Common Cause, 139 S. Ct. 2484 (2019).

93 Epstein, *supra* note 78.

94 Rakich & Rogers, *supra* note 72 ("We found that nominees for the U.S. House were the likeliest to embrace Trump's lies about the election. Full-blown election deniers constitute 40 percent (105 out of 263) of Republican nominees for the House thus far.").

95 Anna Massoglia & Keith Newell, *Election Objectors in Congress Received More than $61 Million from Corporate PACs and Industry Trade Groups in the 2022 Cycle*, OPENSECRETS (Nov. 14, 2022), https://www.opensecrets.org/news/2022/11/election-objectors-in-congress-received-more-than-61-million-from-corporate-pacs-and-industry-trade-groups-in-the-2022-cycle/.

96 Alexi McCammond & Stef W. Kight, *Democrats Make Quiet History with State-Level Gains*, AXIOS (Nov. 10, 2022), https://www.axios.com/2022/11/11/state-legislatures-governors-democrats.

97 *Flipped State Legislative Chambers, 2022 Elections*, BALLOTPEDIA (last visited Nov. 13, 2022), https://ballotpedia.org/Election_results,_2022.

98 *The Leadership Conference September Poll Confirmed by Election Results: The Majority of the Country Rejects Anti-Democratic Extremism*, LEADERSHIP CONFERENCE ON CIVIL & HUMAN RIGHTS (Nov. 17, 2022), https://civilrights.org/2022/11/17/the-leadership-conference-september-poll-confirmed-by-election-results-the-majority-of-the-country-rejects-anti-democratic-extremism/.

99 Harry Enten, *Analysis: Democrats Would Have Gotten Crushed This Election Without Young Voters*, CNN (Nov. 12, 2022), https://www.cnn.com/2022/11/12/politics/young-voters-democrats-midterm-elections/index.html.
100 Isabella Murray, *Young Voters "Canceled Out" Midterm Voters over 65, Blocking GOP Gains: Experts*, ABC News (Nov. 16, 2022), https://abcnews.go.com/Politics/gen-millennials-voters-2022-midterms-favored-democrats-stopping/story?id=93338313.
101 Matt Vasilogambros, *College Students Push to Ease Voting Access After Midterm Barriers*, Pew (Nov. 18, 2022), https://www.pewtrusts.org/en/research-and-analysis/blogs/stateline/2022/11/18/college-students-push-to-ease-voting-access-after-midterm-barriers.
102 William Bunch, *The Day Young Voters Lined Up to Keep the American Republic for 2 More Years*, Phil. Inquirer (Nov. 9, 2022), https://www.inquirer.com/opinion/2022-midterms-young-voters-abortion-20221109.html.
103 Erika Ryan, Justine Kenin & Elissa Nadworny, *How Young Voters Became the Wall for the "Red Wave,"* NPR (Nov. 9, 2022), https://www.npr.org/2022/11/09/1135619172/how-young-voters-became-the-wall-for-the-red-wave.
104 Liz Scheltens, *Why So Many "Election Deniers" Lost in 2022: The Everyday People Who Beat Back the Assault on Democracy (for Now)*, Vox (Nov. 18, 2022), https://www.vox.com/videos/2022/11/18/23466119/why-election-deniers-lost-in-2022.
105 Chris Taylor, *Gen Z Takes Control of Its Future*, Mashable (Nov. 10, 2022), https://mashable.com/article/gen-z-election.
106 William A. Galston, *What Do the 2022 Midterms Mean for 2024?*, Brookings (Nov. 9, 2022), https://www.brookings.edu/blog/fixgov/2022/11/09/what-do-the-2022-midterms-mean-for-2024/.
107 Ryan Teague Beckwith, *Election Deniers Who Campaigned on "Stop the Steal" Lost*, Bloomberg (Nov. 9, 2022), https://www.bloomberg.com/news/articles/2022-11-09/election-deniers-who-campaigned-on-stop-the-steal-lost-across-the-us#xj4y7vzkg.
108 William Brangham, Ali Schmitz & Alexa Gold, *What to Expect When Trump's 1st Criminal Trial Begins Monday*, PBS News Hour (Apr 12, 2024), https://www.pbs.org/newshour/show/what-to-expect-when-trumps-1st-criminal-trial-begins-monday.

CONCLUSION

1 Ciara Torres-Spelliscy, *Transparent Elections After* Citizens United, Brennan Center (2011), https://papers.ssrn.com/sol3/papers.cfm?abstract_id=1776482.
2 *Seattle, Washington: Democracy Vouchers Renewal*, Represent US (2024), https://represent.us/2024-campaigns/seattle-democracy-vouchers/.
3 *Transparency Is a Fundamental Feature of a Healthy Democracy: Voters Have A Right to Know Who Is Trying to Influence Their Vote*, Campaign Legal Center (2024), https://campaignlegal.org/democracyu/transparency/digital-ad-disclosure.
4 Press Release, *Whitehouse Joins Senators In Calling on SEC to Demand Disclosure Of Corporate Political Spending*, Senator Sheldon Whiitehouse (Jan. 20, 2012), https://www.whitehouse.senate.gov/news/release/whitehouse-joins-senators-in-calling-on-sec-to-demand-disclosure-of-corporate-political-spending/.
5 Press Release, *Warren, Banking Committee Colleagues Call on SEC to Require Disclosure of Corporate Lobbying Expenditures to Increase Transparency and Fight Dark Money*, Senator Elizabeth Warren (Nov. 15, 2023), https://www.warren.senate.

gov/newsroom/press-releases/warren-banking-committee-colleagues-call-on-sec-to-require-disclosure-of-corporate-lobbying-expenditures-to-increase-transparency--and-fight-dark-money.

6 Ciara Torres-Spelliscy, *Corporate Democracy from Say on Pay to Say on Politics*, 30 (2) CONSTITUTIONAL COMMENTARY 431 (Summer 2015); *Shareholder Protection Act*, CORPORATE REFORM COALITION (2022), https://corporatereformcoalition.org/policy-solutions.

7 *Expand Early Voting*, BRENNAN CENTER (Feb.4, 2016), https://www.brennancenter.org/our-work/research-reports/expand-early-voting.

8 Press Release, *Raskin and Wasserman Schultz Working on Legislation to Adjudicate and Bar Officeholding Insurrectionists from Returning to Office*, CONGRESSMAN JAMIE RASKIN (Mar. 5, 2024), https://raskin.house.gov/press-releases?ContentRecord_id=DF7AF1C7-4849-4F67-BE67-2E1E2D7859BA.

9 *Automatic Voter Registration*, MIT ELECTION LAB (Feb. 16, 2023), https://electionlab.mit.edu/research/automatic-voter-registration.

10 Kristen M. Budd & Niki Monazzam, *Increasing Public Safety by Restoring Voting Rights*, SENTENCING PROTECT (Apr. 25, 2023), https://www.sentencingproject.org/policy-brief/increasing-public-safety-by-restoring-voting-rights/.

11 *For Our Freedom Amendment*, AMERICAN PROMISE (2024), https://americanpromise.net/for-our-freedom-amendment/.

12 Ellen L. Weintraub, *Overturn* Buckley v. Valeo, POLITICO (2019), https://www.politico.com/interactives/2019/how-to-fix-politics-in-america/corruption/overturn-buckley-valeo/.

13 *End Partisan Gerrymandering*, REPRESENT US (2024), https://represent.us/policy-platform/ending-partisan-gerrymandering/.

14 Judge Jeremy Fogel & Noah Bookbinder, *Building Public Confidence: How the Supreme Court Can Demonstrate Its Commitment to the Highest Ethical Standards*, CITIZENS FOR RESPONSIBILITY & ETHICS IN WASHINGTON (Aug. 9, 2023), https://www.citizensforethics.org/reports-investigations/crew-reports/building-public-confidence-how-the-supreme-court-can-demonstrate-its-commitment-to-the-highest-ethical-standards/.

15 Alicia Bannon & Michael Milov-Cordoba, *Supreme Court Term Limits*, BRENNAN CENTER (June 20, 2023), https://www.brennancenter.org/our-work/policy-solutions/supreme-court-term-limits.

16 Glenn Fine, *The Supreme Court Needs Real Oversight*, ATLANTIC (Dec. 5, 2022), https://www.theatlantic.com/ideas/archive/2022/12/supreme-court-ginni-thomas-january-6-ethics-oversight/672357/.

17 Adriane Fugh-Berman, *The Supreme Court Justices Are Just Like Anyone Else*, ATLANTIC (Sept. 1, 2023), https://www.theatlantic.com/ideas/archive/2023/09/gifts-supreme-court-marketing-to-doctors/675160/.

INDEX

1MDB, 68, 86, 87, 88, 89, 91, 95, 167
3M, 41
45 SRL Inc., 110

Abbott Laboratories, 40
abortion, 5, 148, 159–62, 166
ActBlue, 108
Adidas, 17–18
ads: political, 9, 68, 101–3, 116, 191; computer-generated, 84
AEG. *See* Anschutz Entertainment Group
Aqua Waterfront LLC, 110
AT&T, 40, 51, 124, 126, 148, 160, 161
Alabama Republican Party, 48
Alameda, 7, 10–14
Alexander, Ali, 121–22
Alexander, Michelle, 31–32
Allstate Insurance, 41
Altria (formerly Philip Morris), 8, 9, 124, 160
Amazon, 3, 5, 125, 161, 165
Amendment 1 (2016 Florida), 81–83
Amendment 4 (2016 Florida), 82
Amendment 4 (2018 Florida), 46
American Apparel, 41
American Bankers Association, 126
Americans for Prosperity Foundation v. Bonta, xii
American Legislative Exchange Council (ALEC), 81, 153, 156, 157, 158, 163, 164
American Fuel and Petrochemical Manufacturers, 124
America First Action, 92–94, 97, 109
American Petroleum Institute, 124
Ames, Oakes, 52–55, 68
Anderson Columbia Co, 49, 98
Anderson v. Griswold, 142–47, 272nn72, 78, 80, 83, 86; 281n1
Anheuser-Busch, 124, 159; InBev, 124

Anschutz Entertainment Group (AEG), 4, 124, 159; Philip Anschutz, 4, 5
Anthem, 124, 160
Apache Corp, 127
Apple, 41, 161, 164
Apollo Global Management, 126
Aramark, 42
Arby's, 41
Artificial Intelligence (AI), 84
Artiles, Frank, 71–74, 76–77
Associated Industries of Florida, 76
Association of Dental Support Organizations, 124
AstroTurf campaign, 7–9
Athena PAC, 15
audits, 78, 183, 186
AutoZone, 40
Axne PAC, 15

Bayer, 23, 29, 40
Bellows, Shenna, 144–46
Biden, Joseph R., ix, xi, xv, xvi, 6, 13, 88, 92, 99, 103–4, 108, 112, 114–15, 118–19, 125, 133, 149, 155, 158, 171–72, 177, 180
ballot measure, 7, 46, 83, 151
Bank of America, 92, 165
Bankman-Fried, Sam, 7, 9–15
Bannon, Steve, 88, 168
Berkshire Hathaway, 153
Beatty, Joyce, 15
the "Big Lie," xiv, 114–15, 117, 122, 127, 131, 133, 166, 171–73, 175, 176, 178, 186, 192, 195
Bingham, John, 53
Black Codes, 35, 45
Black Men Vote PAC, 90, 102
Black Male Voter Project, 102
Blue Cross Blue Shield, 127, 159

[299]

Bluman v. FEC, 91
BMW, 25, 29
Boeing, 125, 126, 127
Boozman, John, 14
Borden (brand), 41
Borges, Mathew, 63, 65, 66, 67
Bourdeaux, Carolyn, 112
Bourdeaux, Margaret, 112
BPH Properties Inc, 110
Brady, Tom, 9, 10
Bragg, Alvin, 169
bribe, xiv, 38, 39, 53–68, 72, 195
Breakstone, 41
Brennan Center for Justice at NYU, 47, 181, 189, 201, 301
Brodeur, Jason, 72, 74
Broidy, Elliot, 89
Brownstein Hyatt et al, 127
Budd, Ted, 127, 194
Bucshon, Larry, 14
Bündchen, Gisele, 9, 10

campaign finance, ix, xi, xii, 10, 11, 12, 38, 54, 68, 73–75, 84, 87, 88, 91–93, 97, 160, 168, 183, 184
Campaign Legal Center (CLC), 80, 90, 92, 93, 183, 193
Carbajal, Salud, 14
Cargill, 40
Carter, Buddy, 15
Carter, David, 180, 181
Casar, Greg, 14
Casten, Sean, 15
Castor, Kathy, 15
Caterpillar, 40
Cawthorn, Madison, 131–40, 141
Centene Corp, 51, 160
Center for Political Accountability, 124, 151, 163, 166
CenturyLink, 159
Cespedes, Juan, 66
chain gangs, 31–35, 42
Chavez-DeRemer, Lori, 15
Charter Communications, 51, 160
Cheney, Liz, 176
Chesebro, Kenneth, 114, 170
Chevron, 40, 160
Chipotle, 42

Christie, Chris, 87
Churchill Business Consultants, 110
Church's Chicken, 41
Citigroup, 161, 162
Citizens for Responsibility and Ethics in Washington, 13, 84, 126, 142, 301
Citizens United v. Federal Election Commission, 64, 65, 91, 93, 137, 199
"civil death," meaning and extent of, 31–32, 34, 42, 199. *See also* chain gangs
Clark, Jeffrey, 179
Clark, Neil, 62–65
Coachella, 4
Coca-Cola, 19, 161
Colfax, Schuyler, 53, 54, 55
Colorado Supreme Court, 142, 143, 144, 146, 147
Color of Change, 164
Comcast, 124, 127, 160, 161
Community Bancshares of Mississippi, 127
Concerned American Voters Super PAC, 3
Concord Fund, 124
Conners, Marty, 48
Continental Trading Company, 58, 61
convict leasing, 32, 34–40, 41, 43, 45, 67
CoreCivic, 40
corporation(s), ix–xv, 3–5, 7, 12, 17–19, 25, 26, 28, 30, 34, 40–42, 48–51, 58, 61, 71, 79, 84, 92, 93, 95, 98, 108–10, 124–25, 128, 147, 149–50, 152–53, 156, 158, 160–66, 169, 183, 185, 199
corruption, xiv, 38, 57, 65, 66, 86, 92, 168
Costco, 40, 42
Crane, Eli, 14
Credit Mobilier America, 52, 53, 54, 55, 58, 68, 167
Crenshaw, Dan, 14
crime, ix–xi, 11, 14, 23, 27–32, 34, 36, 37, 38, 42– 45, 47, 54, 60–61, 64, 68, 87, 89, 91, 93, 95, 112, 119, 121, 125, 141, 168, 169, 180
crime/fraud exception (to attorney-client privilege), 180, 181, 184, 190
Cruz, Ted, 127
crypto currency, 7, 9, 10, 11, 13, 16
CVS, 124

dark money, xii, 6, 12, 13, 16, 24, 64, 67, 68, 72, 76–80, 84, 90, 92, 95, 108, 109, 124, 152
Data Targeting (firm), 73, 76

INDEX

Daugherty, Harry, 55, 56, 58, 59, 61, 62
Daugherty, Mally, 55, 60, 61
Davis, Nickie Lum, 88
deepfakes, 84
Defending America Together, 11
democracy, ix–xvi, 3, 17, 18–19, 20, 21, 22, 24, 25, 30, 31, 69, 83, 96, 100, 101, 103, 108, 116, 147, 159, 162, 166, 171, 177, 182, 185, 185, 187, 189, 190, 191, 193, 194, 195
Democracy 21, FEC complaint filed by, 90
Democratic Congressional Campaign Committee, 15
Democratic Governors Association, 3, 192
Democratic Party, 60
Democratic Senatorial Campaign Committee, 14
DePape, David, 188
Department of Labor, 149, 150, 155
DePerno, Matthew, 191
DeSantis, Ron, 5, 6, 47–51, 83, 94, 154, 161
DeWine, Michael "Mike," 62
Diaz-Balart, Mario, 15
DiCaprio, Leonardo, 85–87; *The Wolf of Wall Street*, 85, 87
Disqualification Clause, application of, 131, 139–47, 198. *See also* Dominion Voting Systems Inc.
Doheny, Edward, 55, 57, 60
Domino Sugar, 111
Domino's Pizza, 41
Dominion Voting Systems Inc., 171–75, 180
Don McGill Toyota, 110
DoorDash, 7, 8
Dowling, Michael "Mike," 64, 66, 67
Dream Finders Homes, 51
D'Souza, Dinesh, 93, 168
Dubois, Josiah E. Jr., 28
DuBois, W. E. B., 38
Duggan, Patricia "Trish," 111
Duke Energy, 51, 80, 159, 160
Duncan, Jeff, 14
Du Pont, 19
Durant, Thomas, 52, 54

Eastman, John, 114, 133, 167, 180, 181, 182
Eastman Kodak, 19
Eddie Bauer, 40
Edwards, Chuck, 14

Election (2012), 85–89, 90, 96
Election (2016), ix, 3, 4, 81, 96, 97, 98, 101, 102, 109, 168
Election (2020), x–xv, 4, 6, 8, 10–12, 46–48, 71, 72–74, 76, 79, 80, 83, 84, 91, 92, 95, 98–109, 113–19, 123–24, 127, 131–33, 141, 143–44, 150–52, 156–58, 160–63, 167, 170–80, 182, 185–86, 188, 191–93, 195
Election (2022), xiv, 4–6, 10–13, 15, 47–51, 80, 126–27, 132, 134, 139–40, 151, 156, 160, 182, 183, 185, 187–95
Election (2024), ix–xi, xiv, 14, 42, 109–10, 128, 141–42, 146–48, 154, 161, 167–68, 170, 175, 194, 195
Eli Lilly, 40, 156, 159, 160
Ellipse speech (Trump), 121, 125, 143, 167, 180
Ellis, Jenna, 170, 178
Ellison, Caroline, 11, 13
Energy Harbor, 62. *See also* First Energy
Enron, 10
Entertainment Software Association, 124
ESG (Environmental, Social Governmental), 149, 150–56, 165
Ex parte Quirin, 18. *See also* Supreme Court
ExxonMobil, 40, 125

Fall, Albert, 55–58, 60, 61, 68
Fancelli, Julie 122–25
Fanjul Corp, 98, 109, 110, 111
FedEx, 41, 127
Federal Bureau of Investigations (FBI), 18, 48, 63, 64, 66, 87, 112, 188
Federal Election Commission, 13, 15, 64, 84, 90, 91, 93, 103, 110, 183, 199
Federalist Society, xiii, 4, 6, 157
felony disenfranchisement laws, 43–45, 47–48
Fertitta Entertainment, 110
Flick, Friedrich, 23, 24, 26–30
First Amendment, 45, 96, 141, 176, 178
FirstEnergy, 62–68, 198
Fitzpatrick, Brian, 14
Florida Chamber of Commerce, 78
Florida Crystals, 72, 109, 110
Florida Power & Light (FP&L), 51, 71, 72, 75–80, 83, 84, 126
Floyd, George, 102, 162, 164, 165, 166
Foglesong, James 'Eric,' 74, 75

[301]

Ford Motor Company, 19, 21
Ford, Henry, 19–21
Foundations: Americans for Prosperity, xii, 4; Anschutz, 5, 6; Ford, 150; MacArthur, 150; Rockefeller, 150; Uihlein, 6
Fox, xiii, 105, 118, 139, 171–75
Foxx, Jamie, 85
Frank Calandra Inc., 98
Frecka, David, 110
Free Speech for People, 141
Fresnius, 124
Frito Lay, 41
Frost, Maxwell Alejandro, 15
Fruit of the Loom, 40
Fruman, Igor, 92–95, 99
FTX, 7, 9–12, 14, 15
Fujifilm, 41

Gallego, Ruben, 14
Garfield, James, 53
GEICO, 40
General Electric, 19
General Motors (GM), 19, 125, 161
Generation Now, 63, 64, 65, 67, 68
Generation Z/Gen Z, 194
GEO Group, 40, 97
German Constitution (post-World War II), 30
"ghost" candidates, 71–80, 83, 84, 126, 161
Gillette, 19
Giuliani, Rudolph "Rudy," 92, 94, 99, 114, 117, 133, 171, 174–77
Gilded Age, 7, 54, 55
GlaxoSmithKline, 40
Glaxo Wellcome, 40
Global Energy Producers, 92, 93
Goodrich, 19
Goldman Sachs, 86, 125, 182
Google, 161, 162, 163
Granger, Kay, 15
Grau, Elizabeth, 111
Greitens, Eric, 191
Griffin, Couy, xiv, 140–46
Griffith, Morgan, 15

Hamilton Co, 97
Harding, Warren G., 56, 59, 61
Harvard, 105, 150, 154

Hassan, Maggie, 14
Hayes, William, 60
H.B. 6 (Ohio), 62, 64, 65
Hewlett-Packard, 41
Hickory Farms, 41
Hill, Jonah, 85
Hitler, Adolph, xi, 17–27, 30
Hobbs, Katie, 187
Hoffmann-La Roche, 40–41
Home Depot, 98, 109, 124, 126, 164
House Ethics Committee, 132, 183–184
Householder, Larry, 62–68
Hubbard Construction Company, 98
Husky Hogs, 41
Humana, 51

Iannotti, Jestine, 72, 74, 75
IBM, 19
I. G. Farben, 23, 25–30; as worst of worst, 28
impeachment, x, 94, 95, 99, 100, 105, 108, 109, 110, 111, 180
InBev. *See* Anheuser-Busch
indictment, x, 12, 13, 14, 28, 58, 60, 63, 65, 66, 85, 88, 90, 94, 141, 168, 169, 170, 183, 184
Infiniti, 41
Instacart, 7, 8
Insurrection, 109, 111, 112, 113, 116, 117, 119, 121, 125, 131, 135, 136, 140, 142, 144, 145, 146, 147, 166, 167, 177, 193
International Game Technology, 51
International IDEA, 186
International Paper, 41
ITT, 19

JanSport, 41
January 6, 2001, x–xvi, 4, 6, 30, 111, 112, 113, 116, 118–28, 131, 133, 134, 136–47, 158, 166–68, 170, 171, 176–82, 185, 187, 188, 193, 194
January 6th Select Committee, 115–17, 122, 123, 179, 180, 182
John Deere, 40
Johnson & Johnson, 41
Johnson, Bill, 15
Johnson, Robert Wood "Woody," 111
Jones, Chuck, 64, 66
Judicial Crisis Network, 15, 124
Juul, 7–9, 12

INDEX

KFC, 42
Klaffky, Bob, 66
Kleptocracy Asset Recovery Initiative, 87
Kmart, 41
Koch, David, xii
Koch, Charles, xii
Koch Industries, 41, 126, 159
Kroger, 42
Krupp, 22–30
Kushner, Charles, 111
Kushner, Jared, 111, 117

LaCivita, Chris, x
Lake, Kari, 187
LA Lakers, 4
Latta, Bob, 14
League of Women Voters, 158, 189
Legum, Judd, 161–62
Leprino Foods, 41
Leo, Leonard, xiii, xv, 124, 157
Leissner, Tim, 86
Let's Preserve the American Dream, 77, 78
Letlow, Julia, 14
Liberty Bonds, 57, 58, 60, 61
Lindell, Michael, 123, 175
Little Caesars, 41–42
Little Green House, 56, 58, 59
Low, Jho, 85–91, 95
Lowe's, 42
Lyft, 7, 8

MA Carr Enterprises LLC, 110
Make America Great Again PAC, 97, 110, 111
Make America Great Again, Again!, 97, 110
Mammoth Oil, 57, 58
Mar-a-Lago, x, 169, 170
Marathon Petroleum, 160
Mary Kay, 41
MasTec Inc, 50
Masters, Blake, 127, 192
Matrix LLC, 77–79, 84
McCarthy, Kevin, xv, xvi, 4, 127
McConnell, Mitch, xv, 5, 11, 15
McDonald's, 41, 42, 162
McGrain, John, 55
McLean, Ned, 57, 61, 62
Menendez, Robert, xiv

Merck, 41, 156
Michel, Pras, 85, 87–91, 102
Michigan Supreme Court, 144
Microsoft, 41
Middleton Oil Co., 110
Mitchell, Cleta, 157, 158
Minnesota Supreme Court, 142, 144
ML Organization LLC, 110
Molinaro, Marc, 14
Moolenaar, John, 15
Mooney, Alex, 14
money in politics, xi, xiv, xv, 7, 10, 38, 62, 76, 79, 88, 90, 92–95, 111, 126, 151, 152, 184, 197, 198, 199
Motorola, 41
Mug shot, ix, x
Murray Energy Corporation, 98
MyPillow, 123

National Association of Realtors, 126
National Beer Wholesalers Association, 126
National Republican Senatorial Committee (NRSC), 15, 127, 161, 162
Nazi, xi, 17, 19–30, 34
Nessel, Dana, 191
NewsMax, 171, 175
NextEra Energy, 51, 76, 83, 84, 126, 160, 161
Nintendo, 41
NJoy, 9
North Point Mergers and Acquisitions, 110
Nuremberg (Nurenberg), 23, 25, 27–30
NYU, 150, 201

OAN (One America News), 171, 172, 175
Oath Keepers, 119, 120, 121, 143
Obama, Barack, 8, 68, 85, 86, 88–91, 96, 134, 142, 168
Occidental Petroleum, 160
OfficeMax, 42
Ohio Gang, 56, 58, 60
Ohio Republican Party 63
1MDB, 68, 86, 87, 88, 89, 91, 95, 167
One Nation, 11
OpenSecrets, 4, 11, 79, 124, 126, 127
Operation Pastorius, 18, 19
Oracle, 159

[303]

INDEX

Palmer, Gary, 15
Paris, Benjamin 'Ben,' 74, 75, 155, 156
Parnas, Lev, 92–95, 99
Papa John's, 41
Pelosi, Nancy, 173, 188
Pepsi-Co, 42
Pfizer, 41, 124, 156, 159, 160
PhRMA, 124
Priorities USA Action, 15
Pizza Hut, 41
Plugrá, 41
Popeyes, 41
Postmates, 7, 8
Powell, Sidney, 114, 170, 175, 179
Probity International Corporation, 110
Procter & Gamble, 41
Proud Boys 119–21, 143
PSAs (Public Service Announcements), 100–102
Psy (singer), 85
Public Citizen, 158
Publix, 50, 122
Pulte, Diana, 110

Quaker Oats, 41

Raffensperger, Brad, 114
Randazzo, Samuel, 64
Raytheon, 159
Razak, Najib, 86
Rebuilding America Now, 97, 98
recount, 73, 186
RepresentUS, 101
Republican Attorneys General Association (RAGA), xv, 3, 4, 124
Republican Governors Association (RGA), xv, 3, 161
Republican National Committee (Republican Party), 4, 14, 59, 60, 61, 88, 89, 133, 142
Republican State Leadership Committee (RSLC), xv, 3 161, 162, 163
reproductive rights, 5, 6, 12, 148, 159, 160, 161, 162, 166, 194
Reynolds American, 51
Rhodes, Stewart,119, 120, 123
"penitentiary rings," 38, 52

Rock, Chris, 100
Rodriguez, Alex, 72–74
Rodríguez, José Javier, 72, 74, 77
Roe v. Wade, 4, 148
Romney, Mitt, 96, 99
Rucho v. Common Cause, 194, 199
Ruffalo, Mark, 100
Ruffin, Phil, 111
Rule of Law Defense Fund, xv, 124
Rustin, Bayard, 31, 32, 33, 34, 36
Ryan, Jenna, 122

Salame, Ryan, 11, 12, 15
Salesforce, 159
Sara Lee, 41, 42
Sasse, Ben, 14
S.B. 7066 (Florida), 46, 48, 51
Schmitt, Eric, 191
Schumer, Amy, 100
Schumer, Chuck, 12, 150
Schlitz, 5
Scott, Tim, 15
Senate Leadership Fund, xv, 5, 84
Sears, 41
Securities and Exchange Commission, 151, 154, 198
Sedition Caucus, 12, 15, 125–28, 158, 193, 194
Shell, 41
Si2 (data tracker), 151, 159
Silagy, Eric, 76, 77, 84
Silverman, Sarah, 100
Simpson, Mike, 14
Simpson, Wilton, 76
Sinclair, Harry, 55, 57–61
Singh, Nishad, 11, 12, 15
Singer, 19
slavery: convict, 34, 40, 42; ending of, 134–35. *See also* "penitentiary rings"
Southeast QSR LLC, 98
Southern Co, 126
Southern Poverty Law Center, 6
Spears, Britney, 85
Splitco Holdings LLC, 110
SPM Holdings LLC, 90, 91
Sprint, 41
Standard Oil, 26, 30, 58, 150
Starbucks, 41, 42

[304]

INDEX

State Farm Insurance, 41
Stefanik, Elise, 14
Sterling Medical Group, 110
Stinson, Roxy, 59, 62
Stone, Roger, 115, 122, 168
Subway, 42
Super PAC, 3, 5, 6, 11, 13, 15, 31, 72, 77, 84, 90, 92, 93, 97, 98, 109, 110
Supreme Court (state and US), xii, xiii, 4, 13, 42, 44, 55, 56, 61, 64, 67, 91, 112, 122, 135, 137, 141, 146–48, 158–59, 166–67, 171, 176, 181, 194, 199, 200
Swift, Taylor, 9

Target, 42
Tarrio, Enrique, 119, 120
Taylor, Telford, 23
Taylor Farms, 42
TC Energy, 127
Tea Party Patriots, 6, 124
Teapot Dome scandal, 55–62, 158, 167; Jess Smith and, 60–62
TECO Energy, 50
T. G. Lee Dairy, 41
Thirteenth Amendment, 34, 35, 42, 135
Thompson, Bernie, 116
Three Percenters, 143
T-Mobile, 42, 161
Torch Technologies, 126
Train, George, 52
Tranquil Path Investments, 110
Troutt, Kenny, 110
Trump, Donald J., ix–xiv, 8, 14, 62, 67, 72, 74, 88–123, 125, 127, 128, 131–34, 139, 141, 142, 143, 144, 145, 146, 147, 156, 157, 160, 167–82, 184, 186, 187, 190–95
Turning Point Action, 124
tweeting, 79, 148, 156; Trump and, 112, 133, 143, 173, 181
Tyson Foods, 41

Uber, 7, 8
Uihlein, Richard, 5, 6. *See also* Uline
Uline, 5, 6
UltraViolet, 148, 160, 161
Union Carbide, 19
Union Pacific, 52

United Airlines, 41
United Health Group, 51
United Parcel Service (UPS), 41, 126
U.S. Chamber of Commerce, 8, 124

Valero Energy, 160
Vance, J. D., 127, 267n139
vaping, 7–9
Vecellio Group Inc, 50, 98
Verizon, 41
Victoria's Secret, 41
violence, xi, 24, 33, 36, 96, 112, 116, 121, 132, 134, 140, 141, 142, 143, 146, 165, 178, 180, 182, 185, 187, 188, 190
Vistra, 62
voting, ix, xiii, xiv, 12, 30, 42–48, 51, 83, 84, 92, 100, 102, 103, 105–7, 113, 114, 115, 157, 158, 159, 163, 165, 171–75, 177, 180, 185, 186, 190, 194, 195, 198, 199
Voting Fraud Squad (Florida), 47, 48, 51

Waldman, Michael, 181
Walgreens, 161
Walmart, 41, 43, 124, 161
Walsh, Thomas, 61, 235n89
Walt Disney, 51, 160
Wells Fargo, 127, 161
Wendy's, 41
West, Kanye, 17, 85, 103, 104
Westinghouse, 19
Whole Foods, 3, 42
Willis, Fani, 141, 170
Wilson, Henry, 53, 555
WinRed, 108
The Wolf of Wall Street. *See* DiCaprio, Leonard
Women for America First, 4, 121, 122, 123
Wren, Caroline, 122, 124, 125
Wynn, Steve, 88, 89

Xerox, 42
XLR-8 LLC (investment company), 98

Yeezy, 17
Yelp, 161

Z & A Infotek Corp., 110
Zeldin, Lee, 14

[305]

ABOUT THE AUTHOR

CIARA TORRES-SPELLISCY is Professor of Law at Stetson University College of Law and the author of *Political Brands* (2019) and *Corporate Citizen? An Argument for the Separation of Corporation and State* (2016). She is also a Brennan Center Fellow, Vice Chair of the board of directors of the Mertz Gilmore Foundation, a member of the board of directors for Citizens for Responsibility and Ethics in Washington (CREW), a member of the Executive Committee of the Constitutional Law Section of the Association of American Law Schools (AALS). Torres-Spelliscy received her Juris Doctor from Columbia Law School and her bachelor's degree from Harvard University.